econoguide '97

Disneyland®, Universal Studios Hollywood®,

and other major Southern California attractions

Corey Sandler

CB

CONTEMPORARY BOOKS

A TRIBUNE COMPANY

Library of Congress Cataloging-in-Publication Data

Sandler, Corey, 1950–
    Econoguide '97—Disneyland, Universal Studios Hollywood, and other major southern California attractions / Corey Sandler. — Newly rev. and updated for 1997.
        p.   cm.
    Includes index.
    ISBN 0-8092-3317-7 (pbk.)
        1. California, Southern—Guidebooks.   2. Disneyland (Calif.)—Guidebooks.   3. Universal Pictures (Firm)—Guidebooks.   I. Title.
    F867.S217   1996
    917.94'90453—dc20   96-32305
                                                                                                     CIP

To Willie and Tessa
May their lives always be a magic theme park

Cover design by Kim Bartko

Copyright © 1996 by Word Association, Inc.
All rights reserved
Published by Contemporary Books
An imprint of NTC/Contemporary Publishing Company
Two Prudential Plaza, Chicago, Illinois 60601-6790
Manufactured in the United States of America
International Standard Book Number: 0-8092-3317-7
10   9   8   7   6   5   4   3   2   1

Contents

I Southern California–Bound

II Disneyland

Stunt Show / Beetlejuice's Graveyard Revue / Fievel's Playland

IV Knott's Berry Farm

V Six Flags California

VIII Sporting Activities

XI Sea World of California

Acknowledgments

Dozens of hard-working and creative people helped move my words from the keyboard to the place where you read this book now.

Among the many to thank are Linda Gray and Christine Albritton of Contemporary Books for working with me as we expand the series and Dan Bial for his capable agentry. Thanks, too, to Eugene Brissie, our original champion, and to Bill Gladstone of Waterside Productions.

Dawn Barker of Contemporary Books gave the text a professional polish, and Kathy Willhoite managed the editorial and production processes.

Many talented hands helped shape the production of the book. Thanks to Kim Bartko, Monica Baziuk, Dana Draxten, Gigi Grajdura, Pamela Juárez, Todd Petersen, Audrey Sails, and Terry Stone.

Our appreciation extends to Susan Berglund, Lori Miller, Palmer Moody, Dana Hammontree, Bob Ochsner, Mark Mitchell, and other representatives of attractions including Universal Studios Hollywood, Knott's Berry Farm, Six Flags California, Sea World California, the *Queen Mary*, and others. Thanks to the hotels, restaurants, and attractions who offered discount coupons to our readers. Special thanks go to Janice Keefe who worked long and hard to collect and process the discount coupons.

And, finally, thanks to you for buying this book. We all hope you find it of value; please let us know how we can improve the book in future editions. (Please enclose a stamped envelope if you'd like a reply; no phone calls, please.)

To send us electronic mail, use the following address:
econoguide@pobox.com *or* sandler@pobox.com

You can also consult our Web page at:
http://www.pobox.com/~econoguide *or*
http://www.netcom.com/~econogd/travel.html

Corey Sandler
Econoguide Travel Books
P.O. Box 2779
Nantucket, MA 02584

Introduction to the 1997 Edition

Welcome to the 1997 edition of the *Econoguide to Disneyland, Universal Studios Hollywood, and Other Major Southern California Attractions.*

We love LA . . . and Hollywood and Anaheim. From the make-believe world of movieland and the theme parks to the very real world of the mountains and canyons of Southern California, from the spectacular museums of Los Angeles to the pounding surf. We don't know of many other places with so much to do, so many interesting places to visit . . . and so many ways to spend your hard-earned dollars.

Our goal in the Econoguide series is to help you get the most for your money and make the best use of your time.

This edition combines Disneyland and other major theme parks (Knott's Berry Farm, Universal Studios, and Six Flags California) with the appeals of the big city of Los Angeles and the magic of Hollywood. You'll also learn about many of the myriad attractions of Southern California, from Santa Barbara and Malibu down to San Juan Capistrano and Sea World in San Diego.

We've gone back once again and walked every mile of every park and attraction and looked for changes and new features everywhere.

And we've got a selection of money-saving coupons to many of the attractions you're going to want to visit, including Universal Studios, Knott's Berry Farm, Six Flags California, Paramount Studios, Warner Bros. Studios, and more.

Pardon us for saying so, but we think buying this book is a no-brainer: you'll save many times the cover price by using just a few of the coupons.

The Econoguide to the Best of Los Angeles and Southern California

WOW Disneyland

WOW Universal Studios Hollywood

WOW CityWalk at Universal Studios

WOW Knott's Berry Farm

WOW Six Flags California

WOW Sea World California

WOW Paramount Studios Tour

WOW Warner Bros. Studios Tour

WOW The *Queen Mary*

WOW Downtown Los Angeles Museums

About Independence

That other book about Disneyland, the one with "The Official Guide" stamped on its cover, is an interesting collection of material. But, in our humble opinion, it suffers from a fatal closeness to its subject: it is prepared with the Walt Disney Company (and published by a Disney company). We suspect that explains why it finds very little that is anything less than wonderful within the boundaries of Disneyland, and why it almost ignores the world outside.

So, let us state again our independence: the author and publisher of this book have no connection with Disneyland, Universal Studios Hollywood, Knott's Berry Farm, Six Flags California, or any of the other attractions written about here. Similarly, there is no financial interest in any of the discount coupons published within the book.

Our profit comes from you, the readers of this book, and it is you we hope to serve as best we can.

About the Author

Corey Sandler is a former newsman and editor for the Associated Press, Gannett Newspapers, IDG, and Ziff-Davis Publishing. He has written more than 90 books on travel, video game, and computer topics; his titles have been translated into French, Spanish, German, Italian, Portuguese, Polish, and Chinese. When he's not traveling, he lives with his wife and two children on Nantucket island, 30 miles off the coast of Massachusetts.

I
Southern California–Bound

Chapter 1
Planes, Trains, Monorails, and Automobiles

I'm flying to Los Angeles on a new jumbo jet. The ticket I handed in at the counter in Boston cost $349 for a round-trip.

The businessman across the aisle will suffer through the same mystery meal, watch the same crummy movie, and arrive at LAX a millisecond before I do—and pay $804 for his ticket.

But I'm not even going to claim to be the winner in the airline ticket sweepstakes. Somewhere else on this plane there is a couple who were happily bumped off a previous flight because of overbooking and are discussing where to use the two free round-trip tickets they received in compensation.

Up front in first class, where the food is ever so slightly better, a family of four is traveling on free tickets earned through Mom's frequent flyer plan.

Me, I've got that cut-rate ticket and I'm due for a 5 percent rebate on airfare, hotel, and car rental arranged through my travel agent.

And on my trip back home, I will get on the flight I really wanted to take instead of the less-convenient reservation I was forced to sign up for when I bought that cut-rate ticket.

Alice in Airlineland

In today's strange world of air travel, there is a lot of room for maneuvering for the dollarwise and clever traveler. You can pay an inflated full price, you can take advantage of the lowest fares, or you can play the ultimate game and parlay tickets into free travel. In this chapter, I'll show you how to do each.

There are three golden rules to saving hundreds of dollars on travel: be flexible, be flexible, and be flexible.

• Be flexible about when you choose to travel. Go to the theme parks during the off-season or low-season when airfares, hotel rooms, and other attractions offer substantial discounts.

• Be flexible about the day of the week you travel. In many cases, you can save hundreds of dollars by changing your departure date one or two

1

days in either direction. Ask your travel agent or airline reservationist for current fare rules and restrictions.

The days of lightest air travel are generally midweek, Saturday afternoons, and Sunday mornings. The busiest days are Sunday evenings, Monday mornings, and Friday afternoons and evenings.

In general, you will receive the lowest possible fare if you include a Saturday in your trip, buying what is called an excursion fare. Airlines use this as a way to exclude business travelers from the cheapest fares, assuming that business people will want to be home by Friday night.

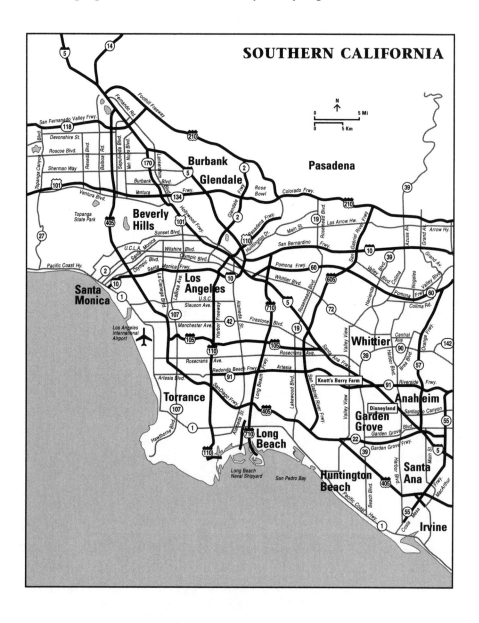

- Be flexible on the hour of your departure. There is generally lower demand—and, therefore, lower prices—for flights that leave in the middle of the day or very late at night.

- Be flexible on the route you will take, or your willingness to put up with a change of plane or stopover. Once again, you are putting the law of supply and demand in your favor. A direct flight from Boston to California for a family of four may cost hundreds more than a flight from Boston that includes a change of planes in Dallas (an American Airlines hub) or Minneapolis (a Northwest hub) before proceeding to Anaheim or Los Angeles.

Don't overlook the possibility of flying out of a different airport, either. For example, metropolitan New Yorkers can find domestic flights from La Guardia, Newark, or White Plains. Suburbanites of Boston might want to consider flights from Worcester or Providence as possibly cheaper alternatives to Logan Airport.

You may even be able to save money, time, or both by flying into a Los Angeles–area airport other than LAX; consider Orange County (nearest to Disneyland), or Burbank—they're each a bit of a drive from Los Angeles, but if you save a

Checking in again. Having a boarding pass issued by a travel agent is not the same as checking in at the airport; you'll still need to show your ticket at the counter so that the agent knows you're there.

Double indemnity. Your homeowner's or renter's insurance policy may include coverage for theft of your possessions while you travel, making it unnecessary to purchase a special policy. Check with your insurance agent.

Olympiad 1984 *sculpture, Stuart Ketchum YMCA, Los Angeles*

Finding a bucket shop. Look for ads for ticket brokers and bucket shops in places like the classified ads in *USA Today*, the "Mart" section of the *Wall Street Journal*, or specialty magazines like *Frequent Flyer*.

few hundred dollars it may be worthwhile to use them.

• Plan way ahead of time and purchase the most deeply discounted advance tickets, which usually are noncancelable. Most carriers limit the number of discount tickets on any particular flight; although there may be plenty of seats left on the day you want to travel, they may be offered at higher rates.

In a significant change over the past few years, most airlines have modified "nonrefundable" fares to become "noncancelable." What this means is that if your plans change or you are forced to cancel your trip, your tickets retain their value and can be applied against another trip, usually for a fee of about $35 or $50 per ticket.

• Conversely, you can take a big chance and wait for the last possible moment, keeping in contact with charter tour operators and accepting a bargain price on a "leftover" seat and hotel reservation. You may also find that some airlines will reduce the prices on leftover seats within a few weeks of departure date; don't be afraid to check regularly with the airline, or ask your travel agent to do it for you. In fact, some travel agencies have automated computer programs that keep a constant electronic eagle eye on available seats and fares.

• Take advantage of special discount programs like senior citizens' clubs, military discounts, or offerings from organizations to which you may belong. If you are in the over-60 category, you may not even have to belong to a group like AARP; simply ask the airline reservationist if there is a discount available. You may have to prove your age when you pick up your ticket or boarding pass.

Air Wars

Airlines are forever weeping and gnashing their teeth about huge losses due to cutthroat competition. And then they regularly turn around and drop their prices radically with major sales.

We, of course, won't waste time worrying about the bottom line of the airlines; it's our own wallets we want to keep full. Therefore, the savvy traveler keeps an eye out for airline fare wars all the time. Read the ads in daily newspapers and keep an ear open to news broadcasts that often cover the outbreak of price drops. If you have a good relationship with a travel agent, you can ask to be notified of any fare sales.

The most common times for airfare wars are in the weeks leading up to the quietest seasons for carriers, including the period between Labor Day and Thanksgiving and again in the winter with the exception of Christmas, New Year's, and Presidents' Day holiday periods.

There are three important strategies to employ here:

1) If you can, hold off on vacation travel plans as long as you can in

hopes of snaring a discount fare. Don't wait too long, though—the deepest standard discounts are for tickets purchased at least 21 days before the date of travel. And remember that the chances for a fare sale for Memorial Day weekend or Thanksgiving are very slim, and tickets may be hard to obtain at any price.

2) Consider grabbing a discount fare ticket even if your travel dates are not firm. In most cases (be sure to check with the airline) you will be able to adjust dates for a small penalty; the final price of the ticket should still be less than a regular fare.

3) Ask for a refund on previously purchased tickets if fares go down for the period of your travel. The airline may refund the difference, or you may be able to reticket your itinerary at the new fare, paying a $35 to $50 penalty for cashing in the old tickets. Be persistent—if the difference in fare is significant, it may be worthwhile making a visit to the airport to meet with a supervisor at the ticket counter.

Another money-saving strategy involves the use of discount coupons distributed directly by the airlines, or through third parties such as supermarkets, catalog companies, and direct marketers. A typical coupon offers $50 or $100 off full fare or certain types of discount fare. It has been our experience that these coupons are often less valuable than they seem—they are certainly better than paying full fare, but often result in a price that is higher than readily available discounts. Read the fine print carefully and be sure to ask reservationists if the price they quote you with the coupon is higher than another fare you qualify for.

Convention Fares

If you are traveling to a convention that happens to take place in Los Angeles or Anaheim, you may be able to get in on a discount negotiated by the group with a particular airline.

In fact, you may not have to have any affiliation at all with a convention group in order to take advantage of special rates, if offered. All the airline will ask is the name or number of the discount plan for the convention; the reservationist is almost certainly not going to ask to see your union card or funny hat.

Check with conventions and visitors bureaus at your destination to see if any large groups are traveling when you plan to fly. Is this sneaky and underhanded? Yes. But we think it is sneaky and underhanded for an airline to charge hundreds of dollars more for the seat to the left and right of the one we're sitting in.

• Consider doing business with a discounter, known in the industry as consolidators or, less flatteringly, as "bucket shops." Look for their ads in the classified sections of many Sunday newspaper travel sections. These companies buy the airlines' slow-to-sell tickets in volume and resell them to consumers at rock-bottom prices. Be sure to study and understand the restrictions; if they fit your needs and wants, this is a good way to fly.

• A bit more in the shadows are ticket brokers who specialize in the resale of frequent flyer coupons and other free or almost-free tickets. Are you willing to take a small financial risk with the hope of saving hundreds or even thousands of dollars on a long trip?

Although most airlines attempt to prohibit the resale or transfer of free tickets from the original "owner" to a second or third party, the fact is that very rarely are they successful in preventing such reuse.

We're not going to make a recommendation about using such brokers, but we will note that many flyers use them with success. If you join them, be sure to read and understand the terms of your contract with the broker, and pay for your ticket with a credit card, if possible.

Playing the Ticket Game

In my opinion, the airlines deserve all the headaches we travelers can give them because of the illogical and costly pricing schemes they throw at us—things like a fare of $350 to fly 90 miles between two cities where they hold a monopoly, and $198 bargain fares to travel 3,000 miles across the nation. Or even more annoying are round-trip fares of $300 if you leave on a Thursday and return on a Monday, and $1,200 if you leave on a Monday and return on the next Thursday.

But a creative traveler can find ways to work around most of these roadblocks. Here are a few strategies:

Nested tickets. This scheme generally works in either of two situations—where regular fares are more than twice as high as excursion fares that include a Saturday night stayover, or in situations where you plan to fly between two locations twice within less than a year.

Let's say you want to fly from Boston to Los Angeles; here's how a nested purchase works: Buy two sets of tickets in your name, one from Boston to Los Angeles and back to Boston with the return date for when you want to come back from your *second* trip, and the other ticket from Los Angeles to Boston to Los Angeles, this time making the first leg of the ticket for the date you want to come back from the first trip, and the second leg of the trip the date you want to depart for the second trip.

If this sounds complicated, that's because it is. But it is perfectly legal, and any capable travel agent should be able to help you construct the nested pair of tickets. It will be up to you to keep your tickets straight when you travel.

Split Tickets. Fare wars sometimes result in super-cheap fares through a connecting city. For example, an airline seeking to boost traffic at a hub in Salt Lake City might set up a situation in which a pair of round-trip tickets from Boston to Salt Lake City, and then from Salt Lake City to Los Angeles work out to be considerably less expensive than a single nonstop from Boston to Salt Lake City and back.

Once again, this is perfectly legal and an area in which a good travel agent should be able to help you. The possible fly in the ointment involves missed connections; be sure to book a schedule that allows enough time between flights and offers backups.

Hidden City Fares. Here's an area that is a bit chancy and may not be worthwhile unless there is a lot of money to be saved. In certain competitive situations, an airline might offer a long-distance fare with a stopover en route that is cheaper than a direct ticket to the stopover city. Confused? Here's an example: You might find a flight from Atlanta to Los Angeles with a stopover in Dallas priced at $300, while a ticket from Atlanta to Dallas is set at $400. If Dallas is your goal, all you have to do is get off the plane when it lands there.

The problem with this scheme is that airlines have learned how to use their computers to track this sort of practice, and some will cancel a return ticket if they find a passenger has deplaned somewhere other than the agreed-upon destination. That's no problem at all if your trip is one-way, or if the special fare is less than half of the regular fare—in that case, just buy two cheap round-trip fares and throw away the tickets you don't use.

Once again, a good travel agent should be able to help you here, although some may be squeamish about violating airline regulations. You might have to construct this sneaky itinerary yourself.

A Loophole Closes a Bit

The biggest change to hit the airline industry in 1995 had nothing to do with fancy new jetliners, improved service, or (heaven forbid) a decent meal at 30,000 feet: it was the near-universal end to transferable tickets.

It used to be that for any domestic airline flight, all you needed to get on board the plane was your ticket. Just like showing your ticket at the theater, all that mattered was that you had an admission pass.

Travelers were often able to resell or give away unneeded "nested" ticket pairs, sell off promotional free tickets, or sell tickets issued under a frequent flyer program.

But in the fall of 1995, the federal government called a security alert at the nation's airports because of perceived threats from the Middle East and elsewhere. As part of a

Six Flags Magic Mountain

Second chance. Tour cancellations are rare. Most tour operators, if forced to cancel, will offer another package or other incentives as a goodwill gesture. If a charter flight or charter tour is canceled, the tour operator must refund your money within 14 days.

Lug-it-yourself. If you are using a scheduled airline to connect with a charter flight, or the other way around, your baggage will not be automatically transferred. You must make the transfer yourself.

Charter and tour flights operate independently of other flights. If you are on a trip that combines scheduled and nonscheduled flights, or two unrelated charter flights, you may end up losing your money and flight because of delays.

It may make sense to avoid such combinations for that reason, or to leave extra hours or even days between connections. Some tour operators offer travel delay insurance that pays for accommodations or alternative travel arrangements necessitated by certain types of delays.

package that included elimination of some parking spaces directly in front of terminals, increased scrutiny of carry-on and checked baggage, and other measures, airline check-in agents began asking for a photo ID for each ticketholder and comparing that name against the ticket. The airlines took to this practice with particular relish, and news reports said that some of the major carriers found they were earning a significant increase in profits by blocking the use of tickets issued under another name.

Although the security alert was reduced later in the year (subject to future reinstatement), many airlines have continued the practice of asking for identification.

Standing Up for Standing By

One of the little-known secrets of air travel on most airlines and most types of tickets is the fact that travelers with valid tickets are allowed to stand by for flights other than the ones for which they have reservations; if there are empty seats on the flight, standby ticketholders are permitted to board.

Some airlines are very liberal in their acceptance of standbys within a few days of the reserved flight, while others will charge a small fee (usually $35 to $50) for changes in itinerary. And some airline personnel are stricter about the regulation than others.

Here's what I do know: if I cannot get the exact flight I want for a trip, I make the closest acceptable reservations available and then show up early at the airport and head for the check-in counter for the flight I really want to take. Unless you are seeking to travel during an impossibly overbooked holiday period or arrive on a bad weather day when flights have been canceled, your chances of successfully standing by for a flight are usually pretty good.

One trick is to call the airline the day before the flight and check on the availability of seats for the flight you want to try for. Some reservation clerks are very forthcoming with information; many times I have been told something like, "There are 70 seats open on that flight."

Be careful with standby maneuvers if your itinerary requires a change of plane en route; you'll need to check availability of seats on all of the legs of your journey.

And a final note: be especially careful about standing by for the very last flight of the night. If you somehow are unable to get on that flight, you're stuck for the night.

My personal strategy usually involves making a reservation for that last flight and standing by for one or more earlier flights on the same day.

About Travel Agencies

Here's my advice about travel agents, in a nutshell: get a good one, or go it alone.

A good travel agent is someone who remembers who he or she works for: You.

> **Don't wait to drop a card.** Keep in touch with your travel agent or tour operator. In many cases they can anticipate major changes before departure time and will let you know. And many operators will try hard to keep you from demanding a refund if you find a major change unacceptable. They may offer a discount or upgrade on a substitute trip or adjust the price of the changed tour.

Of course, there is a built-in conflict of interest here, since the agent is in most cases paid by someone else. Agents receive a commission on airline tickets, hotel reservations, car rentals, and many other services they sell you. The more they sell (or the higher the price) the more they earn.

I would recommend you start the planning for any trip by calling the airlines and a few hotels and finding the best package you can put together for yourself. Then call your travel agent and ask them to do better.

If your agent contributes knowledge or experience, comes up with dollar-saving alternatives to your own package, or offers some other kind of convenience, then go ahead and book through the agency. If, as I often find, you know a lot more about your destination and are willing to spend a lot more time to save money than will the agent, do it yourself.

There is one special type of travel agency worth considering. A number of large agencies offer rebates of part of their commissions to travelers. Some of these companies cater only to frequent flyers who will bring in a lot of business; other rebate agencies offer only limited services to clients.

I use an agency that sends me a check after each trip equal to 5 percent of all reservations booked through them. I have never set foot in their offices, and I conduct all of my business over the phone; tickets arrive by mail or by overnight courier when necessary.

You can find discount travel agencies through many major credit card companies (Citibank and American Express among them) or through various associations and clubs. Some warehouse shopping clubs have rebate travel agencies.

And if you establish a regular relationship with your local travel agency and bring them enough business to make them glad to see you walk through

The best policy. Consider buying trip cancellation insurance from a travel agency or tour operator or directly from an insurance company (ask your insurance agent for advice). The policies are intended to reimburse you for any lost deposits or prepayments if you must cancel a trip because you or certain specified members of your family become ill. Read the policy carefully to understand the circumstances under which the company will pay.

Take care not to purchase more coverage than you need; if your tour package costs $5,000 but you would lose only $1,000 in the event of a cancellation, then the amount of insurance required is just $1,000. Some policies will cover you for health and accident benefits while on vacation, excluding any preexisting conditions.

And be sure you understand your contract with your airline. You may be able to reschedule a flight or even receive a refund after payment of a service charge; some airlines will give full refunds or free rescheduling if you can prove a medical reason for the change.

their door, don't be afraid to ask them for a discount equal to a few percentage points.

Overbooking

Overbooking is a polite industry term that refers to the legal business practice of selling more than an airline can deliver. It all stems, alas, from the unfortunate habit of many travelers of neglecting to cancel flight reservations that will not be used. Airlines study the patterns on various flights and city pairs and apply a formula that allows them to sell more tickets than there are seats on the plane in the expectation that a certain percentage will not show up at the airport.

But what happens if all passengers holding a reservation do show up? Obviously, the result will be more passengers than seats, and some will have to be left behind.

The involuntary bump list will begin with the names of passengers who are late to check in. Airlines must ask for volunteers before bumping any passengers who have followed the rules on check-in.

Now, assuming that no one is willing to give up his or her seat just for the fun of it, the airline will offer some sort of compensation—either a free ticket or cash, or both. It is up to the passenger and the airline to negotiate an acceptable deal.

The U.S. Department of Transportation's consumer protection regulations set some minimum levels of compensation for passengers who are bumped from a flight due to overbooking.

If a passenger is bumped involuntarily, the airline must provide a ticket on its next available flight. Unfortunately, there is no guarantee that there will be a seat on that plane, or that it will arrive at your destination at a convenient time.

If a passenger is bumped involuntarily and is booked on a flight which arrives within one hour of the original arrival time, no compensation need be paid; if the airline gets the bumpee to his or her destination more than one hour but less than two hours after the scheduled arrival, the traveler is entitled to receive an amount equal to the one-way fare of the oversold flight, up to $200; if the delay is more than two hours, the bumpee will receive an amount equal to twice the one-way fare of the original flight, up to $400.

It is not considered "bumping" if a flight is canceled because of weather, equipment problems, or the lack of a flight crew. You are also not eligible for compensation if the airline substitutes a smaller aircraft for operational or safety reasons, or if the flight involves an aircraft with 60 seats or less.

How to Get Bumped

Why in the world would you want to be bumped? Well, perhaps you'd like to look at missing your plane as an opportunity to earn a little money for your time instead of an annoyance. Is a two-hour delay worth $100 an hour to you? How about $800 for a family of four to wait a few hours on the way home—that will pay for a week's hotel plus a meal at the airport.

If you're not in a tremendous rush to get to California—or to get back home—you might want to volunteer to be bumped. We wouldn't recommend doing this on the busiest travel days of the year, or if you are booked on the last flight of the day, unless you are also looking forward to a free night in an airport motel.

Tour Packages and Charter Flights

Tour packages and flights sold by tour operators or travel agents may look similar, but the consumer may end up with significantly different rights.

It all depends whether the flight is a scheduled or nonscheduled flight. A scheduled flight is one that is listed in the *Official Airline Guide* and is available to the general public through a travel agent or from the airline.

AIRPORTS NEAR LOS ANGELES

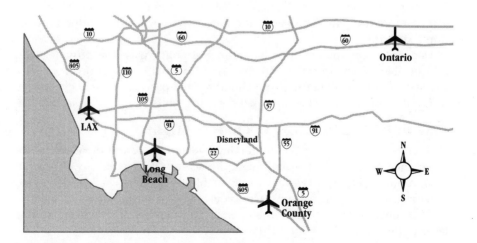

This doesn't mean that a scheduled flight will necessarily be on a major carrier or that you will be flying on a 747 jumbo jet; your plane could just as easily be the propeller-driven pride of Hayseed Airlines. In any case, though, a scheduled flight does have to meet stringent federal government certification requirements.

In the event of delays, cancellations, or other problems with a scheduled flight, your recourse is with the airline.

A nonscheduled flight is also known as a charter flight. The term charter is sometimes also applied to a complete package that includes a nonscheduled flight, hotel accommodations, ground transportation, and other elements.

Charter flights are generally a creation of a tour operator who will purchase all of the seats on a specific flight to a specific destination or who will rent an airplane and crew from an air carrier.

Charter flights and charter tours are regulated by the federal government, but your rights as a consumer are much more limited than those afforded to scheduled flight customers.

Written Contracts

You wouldn't buy a hamburger without knowing the price and specifications (two all-beef patties on a sesame seed bun, etc.). Why, then, would you spend hundreds or even thousands of dollars on a tour and not understand the contract that underlies the transaction?

When you purchase a charter flight or a tour package, you should review and sign a contract that spells out your rights. This contract is sometimes referred to as the "Operator Participant Contract" or the "Terms and Conditions." Look for this contract in the booklet or brochure that describes the packages; ask for it if one is not offered. The proper procedure for a travel agent or tour operator to follow requires that they wait until the customer has read and signed the contract before any money is accepted.

Remember that the contract is designed mostly to benefit the tour operator, and each contract may be different from others you may have agreed to in the past. The basic rule here is: **if you don't understand it, don't sign it**.

Depending on your relative bargaining strength with the provider, you may be able to amend the contract so that it is more in your favor; be sure to obtain a countersignature from an authorized party if you make a change in the document, and keep a signed copy for yourself.

How to Book a Package or Charter Flight

If possible, use a travel agent—preferably one you know and trust from prior experience. In general, the tour operator pays the travel agent's commission. Some tour packages, however, are available only from the operator who organized the tour; in certain cases, you may be able to negotiate a better price by dealing directly with the operator, although you are giving up one layer of protection for your rights.

Flight Information and Reservations

Aero California	(800) 237-6225	Korean Airlines	(310) 484-1900
Aerolineas Argentinas	(800) 333-0276	LACSA	(310) 646-1210
Aeromexico	(800) 237-6639	LTU	(800) 888-0200
Aeroquetzal	(213) 623-9999	Lufthansa	(800) 645-3880
Air Canada	(800) 776-3000	Malaysian	(310) 642-0849
Air France	(800) 321-4538	Mexicana	(310) 646-9500
Air New Zealand	(310) 615-1111	MGM Grand Air	(800) 933-2646
	or (800) 262-1234	Midwest Express	(800) 452-2022
Alaska	(800) 426-0333	Northwest	(800) 225-2525
Alitalia	(800) 223-5730	Philippine	(800) 435-9725
America West	(800) 235-9292	Qantas	(800) 227-4500
American Airlines	(800) 223-5436	Reno Air	(800) 736-6247
ANA (All Nippon)	(310) 646-1480	Sabena	(800) 873-3900
Asiana	(415) 877-3010	SAS	(310) 646-5187
Avianca	(800) 284-2622	Singapore	(800) 742-3333
British Airways	(800) 247-9297	Skywest	(800) 453-9417
Canadian International	(800) 426-7000	Southwest	(800) 435-9792
Cathay Pacific	(800) 233-2742	Swissair	(800) 221-4750
China Air	(213) 776-4740	TACA	(213) 629-1159
China Eastern	(310) 649-3994	Thai	(800) 426-5204
Continental Airlines	(800) 525-0280	TWA	(213) 484-2244
Delta	(800) 221-1212		or (800) 892-4141
	or (310) 386-5510	United	(800) 241-6522
El Al	(800) 223-6700		or (310) 772-2121
Finnair	(800) 950-5000	United Express	(310) 550-1400
Garuda	(213) 387-3323	USAir	(310) 646-6897
Great American	(702) 786-7373		or (800) 428-4322
Hawaiian Airlines	(800) 367-5320	Varig	(800) 468-2744
Iberia	(213) 623-6228	VASP Brazilian Airlines	(310) 364-0160
Japan Airlines	(800) 525-3663	Virgin Atlantic	(800) 862-8621
KLM	(800) 374-7747		

Pay for your ticket with a credit card; this is a cardinal rule for almost any situation in which you are prepaying for a service or product.

Realize that charter airlines don't have large fleets of planes available to substitute in the event of a mechanical problem or an extensive weather delay. They may or may not be able to arrange for a substitute piece of equipment from another carrier.

If you are still willing to try a charter after all of these warnings, make one more check of the bottom line before you sign the contract. First of all, is the air travel significantly less expensive than the lowest nonrefundable fare from a scheduled carrier? (Remember that you are, in effect, buying a nonrefundable fare with most charter flight contracts.)

Have you included taxes, service charges, baggage transfer fees, or other charges the tour operator may put into the contract?

Are the savings significantly more than the 10 percent the charter operator may boost the price without your permission? Do any savings come at a cost of time? Put a value on your time.

Finally, don't buy a complete package until you have compared it to the a la carte cost of such a trip. Call the hotels offered by the tour operator, or similar ones in the same area, and ask them a simple question: "What is your best price for a room?" Be sure to mention any discount programs that are applicable, including AAA or other organizations. Do the same for car rental agencies, and place a call to Disneyland and any other attractions you plan to visit to get current prices.

And, of course, don't overlook the discount coupons for hotels, motels, restaurants, and attractions that are included in this book—that's why they're there.

Kids in Mid-Air

If you are flying with children, discuss with your airline or travel agent any special needs you might have. These might include a request for a bulkhead seat to give children a little extra room for fidgeting (although you will lose the storage space underneath the seat in front of you) or special meals (most airlines offer a child's meal of a hot dog or hamburger on request, which may be more appealing to a youngster than standard airline fare).

Be sure to pack a special bag for young children and carry it on board the plane. Extra diapers in the baggage compartment won't help you at all in an emergency at 25,000 feet. Include formula, food, and snacks as well as a few toys and books to occupy young ones.

Changes in altitude at takeoff and landing may cause some children discomfort in their ears. Try to teach them to clear their ears with an exaggerated yawn. Bubble gum or candy, or a bottle for babies, can help, too.

Accident and Sickness Insurance

The idea of falling ill or suffering an injury while hundreds or thousands of miles away from home and your family doctor can be a terrifying thought.

But before you sign on the bottom line for an Accident and Sickness insurance policy, be sure to consult with your own insurance agent or your company's personnel office to see how far your personal medical insurance policy will reach. Does the policy cover vacation trips and exclude business travel? Are all international locations excluded? Can you purchase a "rider" or extension to your personal policy to cover travel?

The only reason to purchase an Accident and Sickness policy is to fill in any gaps in the coverage you already have. If you don't have health insurance of any kind, a travel policy is certainly valuable, but you might want to consider whether you should spend the money on a year-round policy instead of taking a vacation in the first place.

Also be aware that nearly every kind of health insurance has an exclusionary period for preexisting conditions. If you are sick before you set out on a trip, you may find the policy will not pay for treating the problem.

Inside Los Angeles International Airport (LAX)

Information: (310) 646-5252.

LAX is located in Westchester, at the intersections of Century and Sepulveda boulevards. The airport is near the Inglewood/Century Boulevard exit of Interstate 405.

An MTA bus stop is located between the passenger terminals. Call (213) 626-4455 for schedules.

Terminal 1: America West, Southwest, USAir, USAir Express

Terminal 2: Air Canada, Avianca, Great American, Hawaiian Airlines, Northwest, VASP Brazilian Airlines

Terminal 3: Alaska, Midwest Express, TWA

Tom Bradley International-West Terminal: Aero California, Aeroquetzal, Aerolineas Argentinas, Aeromexico, Air France, Air New Zealand, Alitalia, ANA (All Nippon), Asiana, British Airways, Canadian International, Cathay Pacific, China Air, China Eastern, El Al, Garuda, Iberia, Japan Airlines, KLM, Korean Airlines, LACSA, LTU, Lufthansa, Malaysian, Mexicana, Philippine, Qantas, SAS, Singapore, TACA, Thai, Varig

Terminal 4: American, American Eagle

Terminal 5: Delta

Terminal 6: Continental, Delta, Morris Air, Skywest

Terminal 7: United, United Express, Virgin Atlantic

Imperial Terminal—6661 West Imperial Highway: Air LA, Alpha Grand Airways, MGM Grand Air, Pacific Coast

Airport Bus Services

Here is a list of a few of the larger transportation services that connect LAX and other airports to the Greater Los Angeles area. Be aware that you may have to share your ride and take some side trips en route if you share a van with others. For direct service, use a taxi or limousine service.

AAA Shuttle. Door-to-door service to LAX and area airports. (800) 400-8060.

Airport Coach and Airport Cruiser. Bus service between LAX and Disneyland-area hotels (adult round-trip about $22), between John Wayne/Orange County Airport and Disneyland-area hotels (adult round-trip about $16), and between LAX and John Wayne/Orange County (adult round-trip $32). (800) 772-5299 or (715) 938-8900.

Best Shuttle. Shuttle from hotels in Orange County to LAX and Orange County airports. (800) 606-7433.

FlyAway. Bus service between LAX and Van Nuys Airport Bus Terminal. (818) 994-5554.

Metropolitan Express. Vans to airports, Amtrak, harbors. (310) 417-5050.

Prime Time Airport Shuttle. Van service in Los Angeles and Orange County. (800) 262-7433.

Southern California Rapid Transit District. LAX to surrounding communities. (213) 626-4455.

Super Shuttle. Door-to-door service to LAX and area airports. (800) 258-3826, (213) 777-8000, or (310) 775-6600.

Los Angeles Region Bus and Train Service

Los Angeles County
Metropolitan Transportation Authority (MTA)

Information: (213) 626-4455.

Disabled Riders Emergency Hotline: (800) 621-7828.

The MTA serves the Greater Los Angeles area from the San Fernando Val-

Fast food. One advantage to bringing a car to a theme park is the chance to save a bit of money and get a more relaxed, better meal by ducking out at lunch or dinner and visiting a decent buffet or menu restaurant; come back to the park for some evening rides and the fireworks. (Be sure to get your hand stamped when you leave the park *and* hold onto your ticket stub—both are needed for readmission on the same day. Your parking receipt is also valid for reentry to any of the parking lots.)

ley to northern Orange County with bus, rail, and light-rail service on more than 200 routes. MTA buses connect to all Metro Blue Line and Red Line stations, Union Station, and Metrolink stations in Los Angeles County.

Buses run 24 hours a day, with limited service during late-night hours and on weekends and holidays.

Los Angeles' local rail system is in its infancy, with about 25 miles of a planned 400-mile system now in service.

The Blue Line runs 22 miles from Los Angeles to Long Beach, from 5 A.M. to 11 P.M. daily.

The Red Line serves as a connector in downtown, with five stops:

Union Station. Connections to Metrolink commuter rail trains and Amtrak terminal. Nearby to Chinatown, Olvera Street, and Little Tokyo

Tom Bradley Civic Center Station (First and Hill Streets). Nearby to the Music Center, City Hall, Times Mirror Square, and several city, county, and government buildings

Pershing Square Station (Fifth and Hill Streets). Transfer point to the Metro Blue Line

Westlake/MacArthur Park Station
7th Street/Metro Center Station

Fares vary by distance traveled, and exact change is required. All buses and trains are wheelchair-accessible. Special family and tourist passes are available, usually limited to off-peak times.

For a timetable and route map, call MTA Information or write to: MTA Customer Relations, 425 South Main Street, Los Angeles, CA 90013-1393.

Metrolink

Information: (800) 371-5465.

Metrolink is a long-distance commuter train system that serves Los Angeles and area communities including Burbank, Glendale, Riverside, and San Bernardino. Trains run from about 4 A.M. to 9 P.M. weekdays. Fares are based on distance traveled; free transfers to MTA lines are available.

Amtrak

Information: (800) 872-7245.

Amtrak connects Union Station (800 North Alameda Street) in downtown Los Angeles to points in California including Orange County and San Diego, as well as cross-country service. California stops include Fullerton, Anaheim, Santa Ana, San Juan Capistrano, Oceanside, Del Mar, and San Diego.

Mileage to/from Disneyland				Mileage to/from Los Angeles			
San Juan Capistrano	27 miles	:31 hour		Hollywood	6 miles	:11 hour	
Los Angeles	28	:42		Disneyland	28	:42	
Hollywood	34	:53		San Juan Capistrano	54	1:13	
San Diego	93	1:49		Santa Barbara	102	1:57	
Palm Springs	96	1:47		Palm Springs	105	2:06	
Santa Barbara	129	2:39		San Diego	121	2:31	
Las Vegas, NV	271	4:56		Las Vegas, NV	271	5:04	
San Francisco	407	7:54		San Francisco	380	7:14	
South Lake Tahoe	498	9:48		South Lake Tahoe	471	9:08	
Disney World, FL	2,512	46:14		Disney World, FL	2,521	46:33	

Intercity Buses

Greyhound Bus Lines. Information: (800) 231-2222.

   Orange County Transportation Authority (OCTA). (714) 636-7433.

   Southern California Rapid Transit District (RTD). Greater Los Angeles area, downtown, and airport service. Information: (213) 626-4455 or (800) 252-9040.

Typical Cab Fares from Los Angeles International Airport	
To Downtown	$24 flat rate
To Hollywood	$24
To Beverly Hills	$22
To Santa Monica	$20
To Pasadena	$44

Taxis in Los Angeles

Up to four passengers can use a Los Angeles taxi within the "One-Fare Zone" for a $4 flat fare. You'll find One-Fare Zone signs at taxi stands downtown; the zone includes the Convention Center, California Plaza, the Museum of Contemporary Art, and Olvera Street.

   Cab stands also include Union Station, bus terminals, and major hotels. Most taxis will not respond to street hails. In 1995, taxi rates were $1.90 at the start of a ride plus $1.60 per mile.

Taxi Companies

Bell Cab Cooperative. (213) 221-1112 or 250-4199
   Beverly Hills Cab Company. (310) 273-6611 or 837-0260
   Checker Cab Co. (800) 300-5007, (213) 482-3456 or (310) 330-3720
   City Cab Company. (818) 848-1000
   Independent Cab Co. (213) 666-0050
   L.A. Taxi. (310) 715-1968
   United Independent Taxi. (310) 642-8294 or (213) 462-1088

Orange County and Outlying Areas

Burbank-Glendale-Pasadena Airport

Information: (818) 840-8847.

Mass Transit and Parking Information: (818) 840-8837.

The airport is located in Burbank, one mile south of the Golden State Freeway (Interstate 5). The main entrance is at Thornton Avenue and Hollywood Way. An MTA bus stop is located at the airport entrance and a Cal-Train station is just outside the gates.

Airlines serving Burbank include Alaska, American, America West, Reno Air, Skywest, Southwest, and United.

Long Beach Municipal Airport

Information: (310) 570-2600.

The airport is located at 4100 Donald Douglas Boulevard, near the intersection of Lakewood Boulevard and Spring Street in Long Beach. From Interstate 405, take the Lakewood Boulevard exit.

Airlines serving Long Beach include Alaska and America West.

Ontario International Airport

Information: (909) 988-8644.

The airport is located two miles east of Ontario, on Airport Drive at Vineyard Avenue, near the Vineyard Avenue exit of Interstate 10.

Airlines serving Ontario include American, America West, Delta, Northwest, TWA, United, United Express, and USAir.

John Wayne Airport/Orange County Airport

Information: (714) 252-5200.

The airport is located at Interstate 405 and MacArthur Boulevard in Santa Ana. Bus service is available from points in Orange County by OCTA; call (714) 636-7433 for information.

Airlines serving John Wayne Airport include America West, American, Continental, Delta, Northwest, TWA, United, and USAir.

Drive?, He Said

Everyone's conception of the perfect vacation is different, but for me, I draw a distinction between getting there and being there. I want the getting part to be as quick and simple as possible, and the being there part to be as long as I can manage and afford. Therefore, I fly to most any destination more than a few hundred miles from my home. The cost of driving, hotels, meals en route, and general physical and mental wear and tear rarely equals a deeply discounted excursion fare.

If you do drive, though, you can save a few dollars by using the services of the AAA or another major automobile club. Spend a bit of time and money before you head out to make certain your vehicle is in traveling shape: a tuneup and fully inflated, fully inspected tires will certainly save gas, money, and headaches.

L.A. Freeways
Directions refer to the path of the freeway through the Los Angeles area.

North–South

5	Golden State/Santa Ana
101	Hollywood
110	Harbor/Pasadena
170	Hollywood
405	San Diego
605	San Gabriel River
710	Long Beach

East–West

2	Glendale
10	Santa Monica/San Bernardino
60	Pomona
91	Artesia/Redondo
134	Ventura
210	Foothill

If you plan to travel by bus or train, be aware that the national carriers generally have the same sort of peak and off-peak pricing as the airlines. The cheapest time to buy tickets is when the fewest people want them.

> **Extra miles.** Don't let it force you to pay too much for a rental car, but all things being equal, use a rental agency that awards frequent flyer mileage in a program you use.

Renting a Car

Southern California is a very popular business and vacation destination. Millions of visitors fly to one of the area airports and then rent a car for use during their stay. There is a good supply of rental cars, and highly competitive rates.

You should have little problem with renting a car at one airport in California and dropping it off at another without paying exorbitant dropoff rates; many agencies do not levy a charge at all within the state. Be sure you understand your contract on this matter.

Car rental companies will try—with varying levels of pressure—to convince you to purchase special insurance coverage. They'll tell you it's "only" $7 or $9 per day. What a deal! That works out to about $2,500 or $3,330 per year for a set of rental wheels. The coverage is intended primarily to protect the rental company, not you.

Check with your insurance agent before you travel to determine how well your personal automobile policy will cover a rental car and its contents. We strongly recommend you use a credit card that offers rental car insurance; such insurance usually covers the deductible below your personal policy. The extra auto insurance by itself is usually worth an upgrade to a "gold card" or other extra-service credit card.

The only sticky area comes for those visitors with a driver's license but no car, and therefore no insurance. Again, consult your credit card company and your insurance agent to see what kind of coverage you have, or need.

Your travel agent may be of assistance in finding the best rates; you can make a few phone calls by yourself, too. Rental rates generally follow the same low-shoulder–high-season structure. We have obtained rates as low as $59 a week for a tiny subcompact (a convertible, no less) in low-season.

Although it is theoretically possible to rent a car without a credit card, you will find it to be a rather inconvenient process. If they cannot hold your credit card account hostage, most agencies will require a large cash deposit— perhaps as much as several thousand dollars—before they will give you the keys.

Be aware that the least expensive car rental agencies usually do not have their stations at the airport itself. You will have to wait for a shuttle bus to take you from the terminal to their lot, and you must return the car to the outlying area at the end of your trip. This may add about 20 to 30 minutes to your arrival and departure schedule.

Pay attention, too, when the rental agent explains the gas tank policy. The most common plan says that you must return the car with a full tank; if the agency must refill the tank, you will be billed a service charge plus what is usually a very high per-gallon rate.

Other optional plans include one where the rental agency sells you a full tank when you first drive away and takes no note of how much gas remains when you return the car. Unless you somehow manage to return the car with the engine running on fumes, you are in effect making a gift to the agency with every gallon you bring back.

We prefer the first option, making a point to refill the tank on the way to the airport on getaway day.

Should You Rent a Car?

Do you need to rent a car? In a word, probably.

If you can arrange to stay at a hotel that offers shuttle bus service to and from one of the Los Angeles area airports (Los Angeles International, Orange County, or Ontario) and a shuttle to and from Disneyland, you may be able to do without a car. You'll be limited, though, in your ability to visit other attractions such as Knott's Berry Farm, Universal Studios, or Six Flags Magic Mountain.

An alternative is to hire a car service from your hotel to attractions and back; expect hourly rates of $40 to $80.

From Here to There in Los Angeles and Orange County

Getting from here to there in Los Angeles and Orange County mostly involves driving, and mostly on one of the famed California freeways. These free expressways are among the wonders of the world—broad four- or even six-lane ribbons of concrete winding through valleys or arching over canyons.

The most important freeways for readers of this book are the north-south roads, including Interstates 5 and 405, which run between Los Angeles and

Orange County, and Highway 101, which connects Pasadena to Hollywood. I-5 also serves visitors traveling between Disneyland, Knott's Berry Farm, Universal Studios, and Six Flags.

There are two idiosyncrasies about California driving that may be confusing to out-of-towners. First is the fact that most of the highways have names as well as numbers, and some have more than one name for different sections. Second, many of the exit signs do not emphasize north or south but instead indicate a major destination point of the road.

Your rental car will come with a small map which probably should be relegated to the glove compartment; pick up a decent Los Angeles map from AAA or a bookstore and give it a few minutes of study before you set out on a trip.

There are some times when you can drive at or near the speed limit, but from early morning through early evening, the roads coagulate with traffic. The drive from Disneyland to Six Flags California, for example, is about 63 miles, which should take just a bit more than an hour, which is probably possible at midnight. At 8 A.M. or 5 P.M., you will be in and among commuters, and the drive could easily take two hours. At midday, the drive should be somewhere between one and two hours.

Keep your radio on as you drive. Nearly every Los Angeles area station offers regular traffic reports, and you may be able to avoid unusual traffic jams by taking detours.

Triptiks

Here are driving plans for some of the attractions in this book.

Los Angeles International Airport to Disneyland

Freeway route: From the airport, take Interstate 105 east to its end where it meets Interstate 605. Head south on I-605 about five miles to Highway 91 east to Buena Park where it meets Interstate 5. Take I-5 south about five miles to the Harbor Boulevard exit which leads into Disneyland. About 45 miles, 1:20.

Fastest route: From the airport, take State Route 46 (Manchester Avenue) about 24 miles east through Inglewood, Huntington Park, Bell Gardens, and Downey to Interstate 5. Head south on I-5, 11 miles to the Harbor Boulevard exit which leads into Disneyland. About 35 miles, 1:06.

Disneyland to Knott's Berry Farm

Take Interstate 5 north three miles to the Lincoln Avenue exit. Go four miles west to Knott's Berry Farm. About seven miles, 10 minutes.

Disneyland to Los Angeles

Take Interstate 5 north 23 miles through Buena Park, Norwalk, Santa Fe Springs, and Pico Rivera. At East Los Angeles, turn off onto Highway 101 north into Los Angeles. About 27 miles, 42 minutes.

Disneyland to Universal Studios

Take Interstate 5 north 23 miles through Buena Park, Norwalk, Santa Fe Springs, and Pico Rivera. At East Los Angeles, turn off onto Highway 101 north into Los Angeles. Continue on Highway 101 about 12 miles to Universal Studios exit. About 40 miles, 60 minutes.

Disneyland to Six Flags California

Take Interstate 5 north 60 miles through Buena Park, Norwalk, Santa Fe Springs, Pico Rivera, East Los Angeles, and Newhall. Exit at Magic Mountain Parkway in Valencia. About 63 miles, 1:30.

Disneyland to Long Beach and Queen Mary

Take Interstate 5 south three miles toward Santa Ana. At Orange, turn off onto Highway 22 west toward Garden Grove and drive eight miles. Turn right onto Interstate 405 north toward Long Beach. About 25 miles, 40 minutes.

The Anaheim Area

Bus Service

Airport Coach. From LAX, $14 adults one-way, $22 round-trip; $8 children (3 to 11), $14 round-trip. (714) 938-8900 or (800) 772-5299.

Best Shuttle. On-call, $12 to and from LAX, $10 Orange County. (800) 606-7433 within Orange County.

L.A.Xpress Airport Shuttle. (714) 522-2224 or (800) 427-7483.

Prime Time Shuttle International. LAX, Orange County, Ontario, Burbank Airport, San Pedro Harbor. (800) 262-7533.

SuperShuttle. To Anaheim from LAX, $13; from Orange County, $10. (714) 517-6600.

Taxi

Yellow Cab of Orange County. Fixed rate service to and from Anaheim for up to five passengers per cab: Orange County, $22; LAX, $60; Ontario Airport, $60; Long Beach Airport, $22. (714) 535-2211.

Beach, Attraction, and Shopping Buses

Beach Express Shuttle. Connecting hotels, Disneyland, beaches, shopping, and other points in Orange County. One-way, daily, and three-day passes available. (800) 468-2322 or (714) 434-1140.

Fashion Island Shopper. Connects to Fashion Island from various locations in Orange County. Call Beach Express Shuttle for information.

MainPlace/Santa Ana Shopper Shuttle. From Disneyland-area hotels to the shopping mall every half hour. Call (714) 547-7000 for information.

II
Disneyland

Chapter 2
From Your Land to Disneyland

When and How—We Already Know Where and Why

Here are two hypothetical days spent at Disneyland:

July 4. It wasn't exactly the flight you wanted. However, you're grateful for the privilege of forking over $840 for a coach seat in the jammed cabin of the wide-body jet. All of the rooms at the official park hotel—at $230 per night—are sold out, but you were lucky enough to pay just $100 for a very ordinary hotel room and a 20-minute bumper-to-bumper drive from the parking lots.

According to the tram driver in the parking lot, you are in the same county as the Matterhorn, although you're not really sure. When you get to the entrance, there's a 30-minute wait just to buy your ticket.

Once inside, you sprint to Tomorrowland to find that the line for the Indiana Jones Adventure includes what seems like the entire population of Boston. And you'd better plan on showing up for lunch at 10:45 A.M. and dinner at 4:30 P.M. if you hope to find a table at the lowliest overpriced burger stop.

March 20. It seems like it's just your family and a crew of flight attendants, stretched out across the empty seats in the warm sun at 30,000 feet. Even nicer, you were able to grab a deep-discount excursion-fare ticket for $298. Your hotel room cost you $29.95 (you could have rented one next to the park for just a bit more), and the highway to the park is empty.

Your leisurely walk to the Indiana Jones Adventure puts you into a 10-minute queue; later in the day you skate onto a rocket car at Space Mountain without breaking stride.

Take your pick of restaurants, and feel free to take a break in the afternoon and run over to the hotel pool.

Do we have to point out which trip is likely to be more enjoyable?

Our Guiding Rule

The basic *Econoguide* strategy to getting the most out of your trip to Disneyland and Los Angeles is this:

Go when most people don't; stay home when everyone else is standing in line.

Specifically, we suggest you try to come to California when school is in session and in the weeks between holidays.

Come between Labor Day and Thanksgiving, between Thanksgiving and Christmas, between New Year's Day and Presidents' Week, between Presidents' Week and Spring Break/Easter, and after Spring Break until Memorial Day.

We're not just talking about the crowds at Disneyland, Universal Studios, Knott's Berry Farm, Six Flags California, and elsewhere in Southern California. We're also talking about the availability of discount airline tickets, off-season motel rates, and restaurant specials.

You'll find the lower prices when your business is needed, not when the "No Vacancy" lamp is lit. The best deals can be found in low-season or the shoulder-season, midway between the least crowded and busiest periods.

This doesn't mean you can't have a good time if your schedule (or your children's) requires you to visit at high-season. We'll show you ways to save money and time any time of the year.

DISNEYLAND AND SURROUNDING AREA

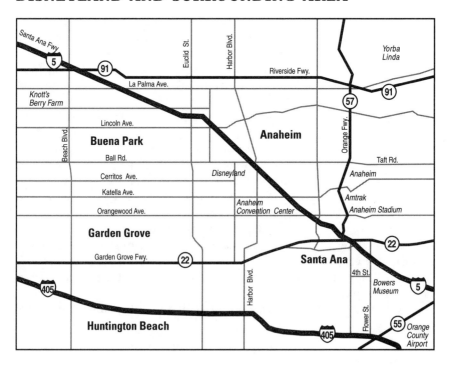

A Disneyland Vacation Calendar
January–March

🕴 🕴 🕴 🕴 *New Year's Day, 40–50,000 visitors*

🕴 *Second week of January through mid-March, 10–20,000 weekdays,*
20–40,000 weekends

🕴 🕴 🕴 🕴 *Presidents' Weekend in February and days surrounding,*
35–50,000 visitors

Headaches on New Year's Day and too much company for the week-
end of Presidents' Day.
January through mid-March is a semiprivate experience.
Room rates at low-season level.
New Year's Day and a day or two afterward present the crowded aftermath
of the Christmas rush. But after the Christmas–New Year's holiday the kids
go back to school and most of the adults go back to work, and attendance
drops off sharply.

From the beginning of January through mid-March is usually among the
least crowded periods of the year, with attendance of about 10,000–20,000
daily; on weekends the crowds double to a moderate to heavy level of
20,000–40,000 per day.

The park closes early and does not offer nighttime parades or fireworks
except during holiday periods.

Mid-March to Pre-Easter

🕴 🕴 *Moderate crowds on weekdays, 15–25,000*

🕴 🕴 🕴 *Lots of company on weekends, 20–50,000*

From mid-March until the first week of April attendance begins to
grow slowly.
The park generally closes early and there are no nighttime parades or fireworks in the first half of the month; during Spring Break the parks are open
later.

Easter

🕴 🕴 🕴 🕴 *Week before Easter Sunday, 40–60,000*

🕴 🕴 🕴 *Week after Easter Sunday, 20–30,000 weekdays, 30–40,000 weekends*

The Easter Parade can get pretty thick. Room rates at high-season.
The second and third weeks of April are among the most crowded times
of the year, with Easter visitors and Spring Break students clogging the turn-

stiles at rates of up to 60,000 per day. The park is open late, with nighttime parades and fireworks.

End of April to Pre-Memorial Day

🚶 🚶 *Weekdays, 10–25,000*

🚶 🚶 🚶 🚶 *Weekends, 30–60,000*

A lovely time, with moderate attendance during the week and growing crowds on the weekends. Room rates at shoulder- or creeping into high-season rates.

As the summer approaches, the park is open late on weekends.

Memorial Day Holiday Period

🚶 🚶 🚶 *Weekdays leading up to Memorial Day, 20–25,000*

🚶 🚶 🚶 🚶 *Memorial Day weekend, 40–50,000*

🚶 🚶 🚶 🚶 *Memorial Day, 45–65,000*

Lots of company. High-season rates.

June, July, and August to Pre-Labor Day

🚶 🚶 🚶 🚶 *Weekdays, 40–60,000*

🚶 🚶 🚶 🚶 *Weekends, 45–65,000*

The crazy days of summer.

Just after Memorial Day the throngs come. They stick around from the first week of June through the third week of August. Room rates are at high-season for the entire summer. The park is open late, with nighttime parades and fireworks scheduled.

September to Mid-October

🚶 🚶 🚶 *Labor Day Week, Weekdays, 25–35,000*

🚶 🚶 🚶 *Labor Day Weekend, 45–50,000*

Postsummer doldrums.

🚶 *Weekdays, 10–20,000*

🚶 🚶 *Weekends, 20–40,000*

Where have all the tourists gone?

On the day after Labor Day, the turnstiles slow to a crawl, averaging about

20,000 visitors per day. The locals return on the weekends. The park generally closes early; there are some late hours on weekends, with parades or fireworks.

Columbus Day to Pre-Thanksgiving

🚶 🚶　*Weekdays, 10–15,000*

🚶 🚶 🚶　*Weekends, 20–35,000*

A great time to explore.

Thanksgiving Weekend

🚶 🚶 🚶 🚶　*25,000–60,000*

No thanks.
Merchants give thanks for the huge crowds at Thanksgiving. Rates at
high-season level.

Post-Thanksgiving to Pre-Christmas

🚶　*Weekdays, 7–20,000*

🚶 🚶　*Weekends, 15–45,000*

Mickey can get lonely at times like these, especially during the week.
This is it: the secret season. From after Thanksgiving until the day Christmas vacation starts is *the* quietest time of the year for a visit. Room rates
are rock-bottom during the week, too. The park generally closes early, and
there are no nighttime parades or fireworks, except for weekends.

December *Christmas Holidays*

🚶 🚶　*Weekdays, 15–20,000*

🚶 🚶 🚶　*Weekends, 40–45,000*

'Twas the Week before Christmas.

Christmas Through New Year's Day

🚶 🚶 🚶 🚶　*Weekdays, 40–65,000*

🚶 🚶 🚶 🚶　*Weekends, 50–65,000*

Your sisters and cousins and aunts will all be in line, in front of
you. You may need a loan for the high-season room rates.
The Christmas–New Year's holiday is the most crowded, least time-effi-
cient time to visit Disneyland. The park is open late, with nighttime parades
and fireworks.

If you must go, be sure to arrive at the park early and follow the Power
Trip plan for your best chance.

The Best Day to Go to the Park

Disneyland draws much of its audience from day-trippers in the surrounding area; the only time when a large proportion of visitors comes from out of the area is during school vacation periods.

Overall, Saturdays are usually the busiest day of the week; Tuesdays through Thursdays are usually the least crowded days to visit. Here are the days of the week, from least crowded to most crowded.

Tuesday, Wednesday, Thursday	**Least crowded**
Monday, Friday	
Sunday	↓
Saturdays and Holidays	**Most crowded**

Christmastime

Christmas is a special place at Disneyland, with holiday decorations, celebrity appearances, and a Christmas parade usually scheduled to run from just before Thanksgiving until New Year's Day. You may even get a chance to be a part of the nationally televised festivities on Christmas Day—West Coast activities are usually taped a day or two ahead of time.

The bad news is that if you visit Disneyland at this time of year, you will not be alone.

Weather or Not

Temperatures can go through a fairly broad range from cool mornings to hot afternoons and back to chilly evenings. And you can get wet on Splash Mountain or from the spray from Fantasmic! Think about bringing along sweatshirts and jackets and stowing them in a locker in the park; some visitors bring backpacks for the family. If there is a hint of rain in the forecast, you may want to bring along a lightweight raincoat. At the first drop of rain, Disney stores will uncrate cases of throwaway plastic covers which may or may not match your ensemble or please your pocketbook.

You've Got to Have a Ticket

Ticket prices were in effect in the summer of 1996 and are subject to change.

	1-Day	2-Day	3-Day	Guided Tour
Adults	$34	$59	$82	$12
Children (3 to 11)	$26	$45	$63	$10
Seniors (60+)	$30			

Annual Passes	Regular	Deluxe	Premium
	$99	$129	$199

Parking	Car: $6
	Vans, campers, RVs: $7
	Preferred Parking: $12

Two- and three-day passports do not have to be used on consecutive days, but they expire 7 days or 14 days after they are first used.

Disneyland will be perfectly happy to accept just about any form of payment for tickets, including cash, checks, and most credit cards.

There are four automatic teller machines at the park. One is located outside the main gate at the left side near the Group Sales window. In the park you will find ATMs at the Main Street Bank, at the Frontierland fort entrance marked "Paymaster," and at Tomorrowland, in the Premiere Shop near the Circlevision theater. The ATMs work with Cirrus, Interlink, Exchange, and Plus systems, and Visa, MasterCard, and American Express. A fifth ATM can be found at the Disneyland Hotel Travelport.

Y'all come back. If you want to leave the park during the day and return, be sure to have your hand stamped at the exit and hold onto your passport; you'll need to show both to get back in.

You can cash a check for up to $20 at the Penny Arcade on Main Street or in the Starcade in Tomorrowland.

Checks are accepted for amount of purchase in any of the shops within Disneyland, with appropriate identification.

Special Ticket Plans

Flexrise Passport. This pass (sometimes called the Signature Flex Passport or something similar) is available from time to time through hotels near Disneyland; you cannot buy them at the park. Priced at the same level as the two-day pass, the ticket allows you to come and go at Disneyland on any of five consecutive days. On one of those days you will be allowed to enter one section of the park one hour ahead of the time Disneyland opens to the general public.

Annual Pass. Valid 305 days of the year, except for Saturdays from March through August, all Fridays in May, June, and July, and holiday periods. Unlimited free parking can be added for $30 more. If you absolutely must go to Disneyland on the Fourth of July or New Year's Eve, you can always buy a regular ticket and keep your pass in your pocket—you'll still probably save money.

Deluxe Pass. Valid 335 days of the year, except Saturdays from March to June and some holiday periods including Thanksgiving and Christmas. Unlimited free parking can be added for $30 more.

Premium Pass. Valid every day of the year, and includes parking. Also includes a subscription to *Disney Magazine* and a 10 percent discount at selected restaurants in the park and on rooms and restaurants at the Disneyland Hotel.

Lines at the ticket booths can grow to unhappy lengths at the start of the day and continue on very busy days. Arrive early to buy the tickets, or get them ahead of time to save aggravation. Tickets can be purchased by mail (with a check or money order, including $2.50 for processing) from Disneyland Ticket Mail Order, P.O. Box 61061, Anaheim, CA 92803-6161. Call (714) 781-4043 to confirm current prices and handling charge; the same number can also be used to purchase by credit card.

Disney Stores around the country also sell daily tickets as well as a special version of the "Flex" pass that offers three days of admission for the price of a two-day ticket.

Discounts for Southern California Residents. In past years, Disneyland has offered substantial discounts to local residents—as much as one third off daily admission tickets. Visitors must show a driver's license or utility bill; in 1996, the documentation had to show permanent residence in California zip codes 90000–93599. These tickets are available only at Disneyland ticket booths and only for the day of purchase. Californians can, though, bring along a few friends; maybe you can meet one on line.

Guided Tours. Half-day guided tours are available daily; guides will take you on a tour of the park and onto a few of the attractions. They won't, alas, allow you to cut the lines. For information, call (714) 999-4573.

Joining the Club

Think of the Magic Kingdom Club as the Mickey Mouse Club for adults and seniors.

The **Magic Kingdom Club Gold Card** offers a small discount on admission tickets to Disneyland, Walt Disney World, Disneyland Paris, and Tokyo Disneyland. In recent years, the club was worth a $2 per day discount, or $10 off an annual pass at Disneyland.

In addition to Disneyland and Walt Disney World discounts, the card is also worth money at Walt Disney World attractions including Pleasure Island, River Country, Typhoon Lagoon, Blizzard Beach, and Discovery Island. The card can also deliver a discount from regular prices at the more expensive restaurants in the Magic Kingdom, Epcot, and Disney-MGM Studios resorts.

In 1996, a two-year membership sold for $65 for a family. We'd estimate the card makes sense if you spend $500 or more over a two-year period on flights, rooms, and meals that are covered by the card. Note that you may end up spending more money on a Disney room than you would outside one of the parks.

To join the Magic Kingdom Club, call (800) 413-4763.

As with any "deal," be sure to compare prices you could obtain by yourself. For example, the airfare discount generally applies to full ticket price, and excursion fares may be cheaper; the hotel discounts may still be more costly than a direct booking at a lower-priced hotel, even another Disney property.

Character Breakfasts

Here's your chance to break bread with one of the Disney characters for breakfast at the Plaza Inn, year-round on days when the park opens at 9 a.m. or earlier. Adult tickets for special meals are $7.95; children from 2 to 11 are admitted for $5.25. Visitors can also order from the menu. Note that Mickey and Minnie do not attend the character breakfasts.

A Disneyland Phone and Address Directory

Disneyland recorded information line: (714) 999-4565. You'll hear a menu of options. Press 1 for ticket prices, 2 for annual pass information, 3 for hours of operation, 4 for entertainment schedules, 5 for special events, 6 for attraction closures, 7 for information about promotions, and 8 for directions to the park.

Disneyland operator: (714) 999-4560. Available Mondays through Fridays 7 A.M. to 7 P.M., Saturdays and Sundays 7 A.M. to 10 P.M.

Disneyland Hotel: (714) 956-6425.

Character Meal reservations at hotel restaurants: (714) 956-6406.

Disneyland Guest Relations, City Hall, Disneyland: (714) 999-4565.

The Walt Disney Travel Company: For information on travel packages including "Magic Mornings" (early admission to Toontown and hotel packages): (714) 520-5050.

Information is also available via mail by writing to Walt Disney Travel Company Inc., Travel Port Boulevard, 1441 South West Street, Anaheim, CA 92803.

You may also write for information on the park (at least three weeks in advance): Disneyland Guest Relations, 1313 Harbor Boulevard, P.O. Box 3232, Anaheim, CA 92803-6161.

Disneyland with Children

Doesn't the title of this section sound ridiculously obvious? Well, yes and no: the fact is that for many kids a visit to Disneyland is the biggest thing that has ever happened to them—and although it almost always will be the most wonderful vacation they've ever had, there are also special concerns for youngsters and their parents.

Here are 10 suggestions to make a trip with young children go well.

1. Involve the children in the planning of the trip. Obtain maps and brochures and study them at the dinner table; read sections of this book together. Work together on a schedule for the places you want to go on each day of the trip.

2. Draw up the "rules" for the visit and make sure each child understands them and agrees with them. The basic rule in our family is that our young children always have to be within an arm's length of mom or dad.

3. Study and understand the height and age minimums for some of the more active rides at the parks. Don't build up expectations of your 41-inch-tall child for a ride that requires you to be 42 inches in height. (Did we hear someone say something about lift pads in shoes? Just remember that the rules are there to protect children from injury.)

Autopia (alone): 52 inches minimum
Autopia (with adult): One year old minimum
Big Thunder Mountain Railroad: 40 inches minimum
Chip 'N Dale's Treehouse and Acorn Crawl: 49 inches *maximum*
Gadget's Go-Coaster: Three years old minimum
Goofy Bounce House: 52 inches *maximum*
Indiana Jones Adventure: 48 inches minimum
Matterhorn Bobsleds (alone): Seven years old minimum
Matterhorn Bobsleds (with adult): Three years old minimum
Space Mountain: 40 inches minimum
Splash Mountain: Three years old and 40 inches minimum

Star Tours (alone): Seven years old minimum
Star Tours (with adult): Three years old minimum

4. Come to a family agreement on financial matters. Few parents can afford to buy everything a child demands; even if you could, you probably would not want to. Consider giving your children a special allowance they can spend at the park. Encourage them to wait a day or two into the trip so that they don't hit bottom before they find the souvenir they really want to take home.

5. When you arrive at the park, and as you move through various areas, always pick a place to meet if you become separated. You should also have a backup plan—instruct your children to find a uniformed park attendant if they are lost, and plan on checking with attendants yourself if you have misplaced a child.

You might want to attach a name tag to youngsters (available at Guest Services in the parks if you don't have your own) or put a piece of paper with your name and hotel in your child's pockets. Some parents even issue their kids walkie-talkie radios and keep one in their own pockets!

6. In summer and most any other time keep your kids (and yourself) under hats and behind sunscreens, especially at midday. You may want to bring bottles of water for the entire family—it's a lot cheaper than soda at the snack bars, and better, too.

7. You are not supposed to bring food into the park. Then again, we've never seen a paying guest being searched for hidden sandwiches inside the park.

8. A good strategy with youngsters, especially if you are staying inside the park or nearby, is to arrive early and then leave at lunchtime for a quick nap or a swim in the pool; return at dusk to enjoy the evening at the park. You'll miss the hottest and most crowded part of the day and probably enjoy yourself much more. Be sure to have your hands stamped when you leave the park and hold onto your tickets (including your parking pass) if you intend to return.

9. Although you can bring your own stroller, it is also easy to rent one for the day at the park. Park the stroller near the *exit* to the attraction so that it is waiting for you when you come out. Don't leave any valuables with the stroller.

10. Most restrooms (male and female) in the park include changing tables. You can also purchase diapers and even formula at Baby Services or City Hall. There are also places set aside for nursing mothers.

Dad, I Promise . . .

One of the best things about going to Disneyland with kids is that a resourceful parent should be able to milk the upcoming trip for at least three weeks of "If you don't behave right now, I'm not taking you to Disneyland" threats.

My even-more-resourceful 12-year-old son Willie went even further and came up with his own contract. Call it:

The Ten Commandments of Disneyland for Kids

I. Thou shalt not leave thy parents' sight.

II. Thou shalt not go on twister rides after a meal.

III. Thou shalt not complain about the lines.

IV. Thou shalt not fight with thy sister or brother.

V. Thou shalt not ask to buy something at the shops
that costs more than the admission ticket.

VI. Thou shall enjoy any of the boring things
that Mom and Dad want to see.

VII. Thou shall stand still so Dad can take
at least one picture.

VIII. Thou shalt not pester the characters to talk.

IX. Thou shalt not sing "It's a Small World After All"
more than 16 times in a row.

X. Thou shall go on at least one educational ride
even if it has a long line.

A Kid's-Eye View of the Best of Disneyland

What are the best attractions for youngsters (3 to 10 years old)? Some youngsters find Haunted Mansion to be a real hoot, while others will have nightmares for weeks. My daughter has been a roller coaster fanatic since she was old enough to stand in line. You know your particular child's interests and fears better than anyone else, but here are some of the more common favorites and a few warnings.

Disneyland for Youngest Visitors

Autopia (Tomorrowland) ***

Country Bear Playhouse (Critter Country)

Dumbo, the Flying Elephant (Fantasyland)

Enchanted Tiki Room (Adventureland)

Gadget's Go-Coaster (Mickey's Toontown)**

It's a Small World (Fantasyland)

Jungle Cruise (Adventureland)*

King Arthur Carrousel (Fantasyland)

Mad Tea Party (Fantasyland)**

Mickey's House, Minnie's House (Mickey's Toontown)

Peter Pan's Flight (Fantasyland)

Pirates of the Caribbean (New Orleans Square)*

Roger Rabbit's Car Toon Spin (Mickey's Toontown)

Snow White's Scary Adventures (Fantasyland)*

Storybook Land Canal Boats (Fantasyland)

Submarine Voyage (Tomorrowland)

Tom Sawyer's Island (Frontierland)

Notes:

* Loud noises and special effects (pirates, skeletons, beasts) may startle unprepared children.

** Can make some children dizzy.

*** Adult must accompany small children.

Bathroom Break

Someday you're going to thank me. Here is a list of some of the larger rest rooms within Disneyland.

Ticket Gates. Left of the entrance gates

Main Street, U.S.A. Near the Bank of Main Street, just past the right arch under the train; between City Hall and the Fire Station, just past the left arch under the train; and between the Carnation Restaurant and the Watch Shop

Adventureland. Behind the gray rocks at the entrance to Adventureland; and Enchanted Tiki Room waiting area

New Orleans Square. Behind the French Market, near the train station

Critter Country. Under the Hungry Bear restaurant

Frontierland. In Big Thunder Ranch, on the right side; and on Tom Sawyer Island, follow path to the right as you exit the raft

Fantasyland. Right of the Village Haus restaurant, near the Big Thunder Trail to Frontierland; and between the Matterhorn Bobsleds and Alice in Wonderland

Mickey's Toontown. Near the gas station

Tomorrowland. Right of Star Tours; near the entrance to Starcade; and behind the Hatmosphere.

Chapter 3
The World of Disneyland

Once upon a mouse, back in 1928, Walter Elias Disney created the character of Mickey Mouse for a short cartoon called *Steamboat Willie*.

Everything else has been built upon the slender shoulders of the cute little rodent, along with his gal, Minnie, buddies Donald, Daisy, Snow White, and a cast of thousands of other cartoon and movie favorites.

Disney, who set up a little park alongside his first movie studios to entertain visitors, expanded his world considerably with the opening of Disneyland in California in 1955. Although much has changed in the more than 40 years since Disneyland was first planned, the basic structure of that park, and all that have followed, is the same.

Today, breathes there a man, woman, girl, boy, or mouse who has not dreamed of visiting Disneyland? The entertainment vision of Walt Disney—along with the incredible marketing skills of the company he left behind—has made Disney's parks and symbols probably the world's best-known popular icons. You can see Mickey Mouse T-shirts on the streets of Moscow, Epcot towels on the beaches of the Caribbean, Minnie dresses on the boulevards of Paris, and Roger Rabbit hats in the alleys of Tokyo.

Power Trip 1

The Indy Rush for Adults and Thrill-Seeking Kids

Get to the park before opening. On weekends and holidays you will be allowed to go through the gates and up Main Street to a rope barrier. When the park is officially opened, walk briskly into Adventureland (along with hundreds of others) to **Indiana Jones Adventure, Temple of the Forbidden Eye**. With a bit of luck you'll be on the ride and off in less than an hour and ready to ride the Disneyland Mountain Range. In fact, if you are there really early you may be able to catch two rides before the lines become unacceptably long.

Move on over to Frontierland and join up with the queue for **Splash**

MUST-SEES

Indiana Jones Adventure, Temple of the Forbidden Eye
(Adventureland)

Jungle Cruise
(Adventureland)

Splash Mountain
(Critter Country)

Pirates of the Caribbean
(New Orleans Square)

The Haunted Mansion
(New Orleans Square)

Big Thunder Mountain Railroad
(Frontierland)

Fantasmic!
(Frontierland)

Tom Sawyer Island
(Frontierland)

It's a Small World
(Fantasyland)

Matterhorn Bobsleds
(Fantasyland)

Roger Rabbit's Car Toon Spin
(Mickey's Toontown; adults excused)

Space Mountain
(Tomorrowland)

Star Tours
(Tomorrowland)

Mountain. If the lines are still reasonable, head for **Big Thunder Mountain**.

Now take a break from action rides and bop on over to New Orleans Square and visit the ghouls at **Haunted Mansion**. Catch an early lunch and backtrack to **Pirates of the Caribbean**, which usually has reasonable lines at midday.

Move to the center of the park toward Toontown. Your goal is **Roger Rabbit's Car Toon Spin**, but if the line is not too long at the **Matterhorn** this is a good time to go bobsledding.

The middle of the afternoon is a good time to visit the less-popular attractions, catch an afternoon parade, do some shopping, and eat an early dinner.

As suppertime and the evening **Fantasmic!** show (in season only) approach, head for Tomorrowland. The lines for **Space Mountain** and especially **Star Tours** thin out considerably after dark. When **"Honey, I Shrunk the Audience"** is open, you can avoid the lines and visit late in the day, too.

By this time you have completed your tour of the major attractions of Disneyland. Depending on how crowded the park is, you may want to repeat a few of the rides in the dark. I especially like after-dark rides on the Matterhorn and Big Thunder Mountain. You can also catch some of the story rides at Fantasyland including **Peter Pan, Mr. Toad's Wild Ride,** and (for the hopelessly romantic or the hopelessly child-directed) **It's a Small World**.

In peak season and holidays, you will still be able to catch the late performance of the Fantasmic! show to end your day with a bang.

Power Trip 2

A Contrarian Approach for Adults and Adventuresome Kids

The Indiana Jones ride will be the top draw at Disneyland for some time to come. Therefore, all of the folks heading directly for that ride will take some of the pressure off the other major attractions. Here is a contrarian approach that should work well on busy days. Once again, it depends on an early arrival at the park.

When the park opens, head to the right to Tomorrowland and ride **Space Mountain.** When "**Honey, I Shrunk the Audience**" is open, shrink into a seat early, before the lines build. Then move on over to the nearby **Star Tours.** At this point you should still be going against the general flow. Move to the center of the park and ride the **Matterhorn Bobsleds** and **Roger Rabbit's Car Toon Spin.**

You should begin to meet the crowds moving away from Indiana Jones somewhere around New Orleans Square. Jump onto a Doom Buggy at **Haunted Mansion** and move to **Pirates of the Caribbean** for its midday lull.

Break for the afternoon and take in a show or visit the shops and less-popular rides including Fantasyland. Move on over to Frontierland and join up with the queue for **Splash Mountain** and then head for **Big Thunder Mountain.**

The **Fantasmic!** show draws huge crowds to the west side of the park, making it difficult to get around. Some visitors find it easier to hop on the Disneyland Railroad to make a grand circle to Frontierland.

By evening, and especially during parades or Fantasmic! performances, the lines for **Indiana Jones Adventure, Temple of the Forbidden Eye** should lessen. After you've completed your ride, you may want to double up on a few of your favorites, with nighttime spins on Matterhorn and Big Thunder Mountain.

A Typical Day at the Park

Opening Hour: Most visitors make a rush to the most popular rides, including Indiana Jones, Space Mountain, and Splash Mountain. The rest of the park has small or moderate crowds. On busy days, weekends, and holidays the gates open about 30 minutes before the park itself is open; you will be able to stroll to a rope barrier at the top of Main Street. On extremely busy days, the park may open earlier than officially announced. Our advice: get to the park at least 45 minutes before the "official" opening time any time you visit, and especially during busy periods.

11 A.M.–1 P.M.: The midday crush. A good time to stay away from the most popular rides. Have an early lunch before lines grow.

4 P.M.–7 P.M.: The afternoon slump. Some of the youngest visitors head back home, and older guests spend time at dinner. Many rides have reduced lines. Have your dinner early.

Waiting times for the major rides are listed on a board near the Plaza Restaurant, just outside the entrance to Frontierland and Adventureland. Cast a quick eye on the waiting times as you enter to help adjust your Power Trip, and check it out any time you're in the neighborhood. Your goal: go where the crowds are not.

Suspend all disbelief. As you are about to pass through the tunnels under the railroad and enter Main Street, glance up to read the words on the plaques: "Here you leave today and enter the world of yesterday, tomorrow, and fantasy."

The dedication plaque on a flag pole on Main Street, dated July 17, 1955, reads, "To all that come to this happy place, welcome. Disneyland is your land. Here, age relives fond memories of the past, and here youth may savor the challenge and promise of the future. Disneyland is dedicated to the ideals, the dreams, and the hard facts that have created America . . . with the hope that it will be a source of joy and inspiration to all the world."

Private digs. Proprietor Walt Disney built a private apartment over the Fire House on Main Street for special occasions when he stayed overnight at Disneyland. The lamp in the window is kept burning in his memory.

Parade and Fantasmic!: On weekends and holidays, huge crowds gather to watch the nighttime parades. This is a good time to visit the most popular rides. Watch out for the huge release of visitors after a parade or Fantasmic! show; many visitors will try to jump on nearby rides including Indiana Jones, Splash Mountain, Big Thunder Mountain, and Pirates of the Caribbean; it's a good time to be all the way over on the other side of the park. If you want to see Fantasmic!, wait for the late show and visit attractions during the early performance.

The much-loved Main Street Electrical Parade was due to come to an end in 1996 after a year of celebrations.

An exciting addition to the Disney nighttime entertainment is **"Light Fantastic,"** a computer-controlled light show using 25 computer-controlled searchlights around the park; it is included within the nightly fireworks show and also presented in little snippets at other times during the night.

Main Street, U.S.A.

Somewhere, someplace, at some time, there was an America like this. It's a place of small stores with friendly proprietors, where the streets are clean and the landscape neat, and where a scrap of paper never lingers on the ground.

At the start of your visit to the Magic Kingdom, think of Main Street, U.S.A. as an interesting place to walk through on the way to somewhere else. Come back later to browse, shop, or eat; if you are following our advice, you will have arrived early at the park with a specific destination in mind.

But when you do come back, marvel at the attention to detail of the storefronts and interior decorations of the shops. Most of the names on the second-story windows are those of former and present Disney employees responsible for creation or maintenance of the park.

Main Street is the place to be if you are a serious parade fan. The entertainment moves toward or begins at the railroad station just inside the gates— that may be the best seat in the house to watch the parade. You can, though, also see the parades near Sleeping Beauty Castle and on the streets of Frontierland, both of which are nearer the major attractions of the park.

Disneyland Railroad. A pleasant way to tour the park (our favorite way to end a day), these real steam engines take passengers on a 1½-mile, 20-minute circuit of the park.

Walt Disney was a railroad nut, even running a small-scale system in his own backyard. The Disneyland line includes four engines, each one of them named for former executives of the Santa Fe Railroad.

The oldest is the *Fred G. Gurley,* originally built in 1894 and used to haul sugarcane from plantations to the docks in New Orleans; it was rebuilt for Disney using original parts. The *Ernest S. Marsh* dates to 1925 and was built for a New England lumber mill.

The two original locomotives, the *C. K. Holiday* and the *E. P. Riley,* were designed and assembled by the Walt Disney Studios. Each of the engines has a slightly different design. Notice the number of wheels on each side of the engines and whether there are wheels beneath the tender (coal car). The locomotives no longer burn coal, by the way; each has been converted to oil-fired boilers.

Closing time. Closing time varies according to the season and is sometimes adjusted from day to day based on attendance patterns; it can be as early as 6 P.M. or as late as midnight. Check at the park for details. The announced closing time is actually a relative thing, usually meaning the time when the last person is allowed to join a ride line. The parks themselves are cleared out about an hour or so after then, and the final bus or other transportation to parking lots or hotels leaves about 90 minutes after closing time.

The trains run in a clockwise circle from Main Street to Adventureland, New Orleans Square, Frontierland, Fantasyland, Tomorrowland, and back to Main Street. If you ask nicely, you may be permitted to ride on the seat directly behind the engineer at the front of the train.

The railroad passes through the Zip-a-Dee Lady scene from Splash Mountain, alongside Big Thunder Ranch, and through the loading area for It's a Small World.

Just past Small World on the right side you'll also pass something called The Disneyland Oceanographic Research Station. Not open to the public, this is a maintenance area for the Submarine Voyage and other watery attractions in the park.

In addition to transport around the park and interesting views of many areas that can only be seen from the train, the railroad also passes through two of Disneyland's less well-known attractions: the **Grand Canyon Diorama** and the **Primeval World.**

The Grand Canyon display re-creates the South Rim of the canyon with a football-field-long painting, stuffed animals of all sorts, and trees and plants from the real thing. Primeval World, originally created for the Ford Motor Pavilion at the New York World's Fair in 1964–65, draws some of its inspiration from the Disney animated classic *Fantasia* and in turn helped set the tone

Disney subway. The fabulous theme-park empire that bears Walt Disney's name can trace its roots back to Disney's private miniature train set which he ran in the backyard of his home.

Train fanciers and Disneyphiles will want to visit the waiting room of the Main Street Train Station. There is an interesting display of photographs of Disney's private line, the Carolwood-Pacific Railroad, which he operated in the backyard of his Holmby Hills home. Disney was fond of taking his daughters, employees, family, and friends for a ride on the miniature line which later served as a ⅛-scale model for the full-sized *C. K. Holiday* that has circled Disneyland since 1955. You will also see old pictures of Disney with his railroad system in his backyard seated on the little steam train.

A wooden display case exhibits a caboose from the Carolwood-Pacific Railroad built by Walt Disney himself. He handcrafted all of its interior appointments including bunk beds, clothes lockers, a magazine rack with miniature newspapers, a desk, washstands, and a potbellied stove.

for the considerably more detailed and realistic world of the dinosaurs at the Universe of Energy at Epcot.

The Walt Disney Story and Great Moments with Mr. Lincoln. An interesting mix of heroes: Walt, Mickey, and Abe. You can mix and match any or all of the three.

As you enter the Disneyland Opera House you'll find a small museum dedicated to presenting the life of Walter Elias Disney, without whom none of the rest of Disneyland would have been necessary.

Among the remembrances of Uncle Walt is his original office from Burbank, as Disney used it for 26 years. On one side is his working office, and the other his formal office where he held appointments with important visiting guests. At the grand piano Disney often sat with songwriters who stopped by to play their newly composed tunes, or with famous singers trying out for parts in Disney films.

You'll see some old pictures of Disney announcing Disneyland, and a speeded-up film of construction of the park, which opened on July 17, 1955, in fairy-tale fashion exactly a year and a day after work began.

Not particularly related to anything else, but still interesting, is a large and intricate model of the U.S. Capitol. It was carved out of caenstone in 1932 by George Lloyd of Belleville, New Jersey, and was based on photographs and blueprints of the actual building.

Finally, there is a section of the museum that salutes Disney as a pioneer of animation. There are some drawings showing the combination of animation and live action pioneered by Disney and a description of how a multiplane camera works. You'll also see some drawings created in 1967 for the sculptures used in the Pirates of the Caribbean ride, including the familiar drunken pirate hanging onto a post.

After a short film about Disney, guests are ushered into a larger theater where they are greeted by Audio-Animatronic Abe, who presents a speech drawn from Lincoln's own statements. The Disney film takes about 7 minutes; Abe, about 15 minutes.

Lincoln's speech is made up of excerpts from addresses delivered by the Great Emancipator including his famous speech at the Cooper Institute in New York in 1860.

Here is part of Lincoln's speech:

The world has never had a good definition of the word liberty, and the American people, just now, are much in want of one. We all declare for liberty; but in using the same word we do not all mean the same thing.

What constitutes the bulwark of our liberty and independence? It is not our frowning battlements, our bristling sea coasts. These are not our reliance against tyranny. Our reliance is in the love of liberty which God has planted in our bosoms. Our defense is in the preservation of the spirit which prizes liberty as the heritage of all men, in all lands, everywhere. Destroy this spirit, and you have planted the seeds of despotism around your own doors.

At what point shall we expect the approach of danger? By what means shall we fortify against it? Shall we expect some trans-Atlantic military giant to step the ocean and crush us in a blow? Never! All the armies of Europe, Asia, and Africa combined could not by force take a drink from the Ohio or make a track on the Blue Ridge in a trial of a thousand years. At what point then is the approach of danger to be expected? I answer, if it ever reaches us, it must spring up from amongst us. It cannot come from abroad. If destruction be our lot, we ourselves must be its author and finisher. As a nation of free men, we must live through all times, or die by suicide.

Neither let us be slandered from our duty by false accusations against us, nor frightened from it by the menaces of destruction to the Government nor of dungeons to ourselves. Let us have faith that right makes might, and in that faith, let us, to the end, dare to do our duty as we understand it.

Lockers. The main bank of coin-operated lockers is on the right side of Main Street about midway between the Main Street Train Station and the Hub. The available storage spaces often fill up on busy days.

Another group of lockers can be found deeper within the park at Videopolis in Tomorrowland, between the bathrooms and the Yumz refreshment stand. The third set is outside the park next to the group sales window; these lockers have the largest capacity.

Going to the dogs. You can't bring the family pet into the park—it might scare the mice, you know. And please don't be so cruel as to leave Bowser or Kitty in the car; temperatures in a glass and metal box in the sun can kill. Disney offers a day kennel to the right of the main gate. The exercise area for dogs offers canines their own private fire hydrant.

Main Street Cinema. What else would you expect to be playing in the moviehouse on Disneyland's main drag but continuous Disney cartoons? Among the biggest treats are those that reach back to the dawn of Disney,

The unhappy kingdom.
Look up at the store
windows on Main Street
for some neat surprises.
Above the Cone Shop
you'll see a dentist's
office; listen carefully and
you can hear some poor
soul having a tooth
extracted. And speaking
of pain, listen beneath
the piano teacher's
window for the sounds
of a not-particularly-
talented child receiving a
piano lesson.

Sounds like. More
sounds on Main Street:
there are some strange
goings-on at the Hotel
Marceline. (The hotel
gets its name from Walt
Disney's childhood home
in Marceline, Missouri.)
Listen in at the Detec-
tive's Office for the
sounds of a snoring
sergeant.

Peanuts. A recent
addition to the Penny
Arcade on Main Street is
Penny, a 1,000-pound
green elephant. All right,
she's only a statue . . .
but she's sort of French.
Penny was designed to
stand in front of the
Boardwalk Candy Palace
on Main Street at
Disneyland Paris but a
change in plans kept her
in sunny California
instead.

like *Steamboat Willie,* the first Mickey Mouse cartoon, released in 1928.

The small theater has six small screens and no
seats; it's rarely busy and is a great place to cool
off on a hot day or dry off on a rare wet day. It's
also a great meeting place if you and your party
are separated.

Penny Arcade. Disney has brought together
a marvelous collection of antique games and
amusements, including penny hand-crank
movies and some coin-swallowing modern video
games. The old nickelodeons in the front work
on a penny, probably the only thing in all of
Orange County available at that price; the new
machines eat quarters and dollars.

Antiques include the Love Tester, a hand-
squeeze meter that claims to measure your sex
appeal. Nickelodeon movies include Snitz
Edwards in *Small Town Sheik*, and Ben Turpin in
Home Sweet Home. Esmeralda, the Card Reading
Gypsy, stands in the position of honor right on
Main Street.

Main Street Vehicles. Old-fashioned cars, a
horse-drawn trolley, and fire engines move
slowly down one end of Main Street to the other.
(Following not far behind the horses are uniformed sanitation engineers with shovels.)

Unless you can jump right on a vehicle, it will
usually be faster to walk the length of Main
Street; then again, a seated ride at the end of a
long day looks mighty appealing.

Adventureland

One of the sleepiest corners of Disneyland—the
home of the quirky charm of the Enchanted Tiki
Birds, the robotic alligators and the awful puns
of the Jungle Cruise, and the cement branches of
the Swiss Family Treehouse—became the busiest
part of the park at the start of 1995 with the
opening of the Indiana Jones Adventure, one of
the most impressive theme-park rides anywhere.

WOW **Indiana Jones Adventure, Temple of
the Forbidden Eye.** Whatever you do, don't
look at the Forbidden Eye. You know, the one
that's right ahead of you, the one that's pulsing
brightly in front of your car full of explorers, the

one that will make the walls of the temple crash down all around you if you sneak a peek. Oh no!

Disneyland's newest thrill ride is a spectacular combination of a (slow) roller coaster and a simulator with more special effects than anywhere else in Disneyland or anywhere we know of, based on the famous (and always exciting) explorations of Indiana Jones. There are about 2,200 feet of track for the cars, including a segment that crosses a wobbly suspension bridge.

Disney's biggest new project since Disneyland was first built, the Indiana Jones Adventure opened in the spring of 1995 and immediately became the most popular attraction at the park. If you haven't ridden with Indy, you haven't seen Disneyland as it exists today.

It seems that our intrepid archaeologist Indiana Jones has made yet another fabulous find, deep within a densely overgrown jungle. According to legend, the god Mara offers to all visitors one of three magical gifts: restoration from the Fountain of Eternal Youth, fabulous wealth from the Hall of Riches where all of the great treasures of history have been collected, or knowledge of all that is to come with the aid of a mystical amulet from the Observatory of the Future. In fact, says the legend, Mara is so powerful that she can peer into your soul to choose the one gift that is best for you.

But the legend also tells of a terrible curse for any visitor who is so foolish as to look directly into Mara's eye.

Unfortunately, funding for continued excavation is running out. To raise cash, Dr. Jones and his assistant Shallah have agreed to conduct tours. That's you, folks. Step right up!

As you approach the entrance to the temple, almost certainly accompanied by thousands of other visitors, you'll pass through a reconstructed pre-World War II world, including trucks, generators, phones, typewriters, books, and more. You'll also see a loading dock stacked with treasures waiting to be picked up by one of the Jungle Cruise boats that pass nearby.

You'll make your way into the temple through an appropriately creepy torchlit waiting area that includes caverns, an old well, and a makeshift movie

Money matters. The Main Street Bank is a bank on, uh, Main Street and it provides basic, uh, banking services to visitors on Main Street. You can also buy stamps, upgrade tickets, and buy "Disney Dollars" or gift certificates. There are also ATM banking machines (part of the Cirrus, PLUS, and Exchange networks) outside the park to the left of the entrance, on Main Street near the Penny Arcade, and in Tomorrowland and Frontierland.

Disney Dollars, by the way, are your chance to make an interest-free loan to the Walt Disney Company. Sold at face value without any discount, they are valid anywhere within the Disney properties and nowhere else. Do we sound unimpressed?

You will also be offered Disney Dollars at the ticket booths at the time you buy your ticket. The only reason we can think of to buy them is to obtain a free cash advance to spend in the park if you are short on real money.

The Indy-Disney connection. George Lucas has several other links to Disney, including Indiana Jones et le Temple du Péril, a roller coaster adventure at Disneyland Paris, The Indiana Jones Epic Stunt Spectacular and Star Tours at Disney-MGM Studios in Florida, Star Tours and Captain EO at Disneyland and Disneyland Paris, and the spectacular new Extra-TERRORestrial Alien Encounter at the Magic Kingdom of Walt Disney World.

Ancient art. Some of the original renderings for the Indiana Jones Adventure are on display at the Disney Gallery, located over the Pirates of the Caribbean in New Orleans Square. In addition to drawings that were eventually adapted for the ride as it now exists, you can also learn about some concepts that were not used, including a walk-through adventure and a high-speed mine car adventure within a temple. At one point Imagineers considered using Jungle Cruise launches to shuttle guests to the new ride.

theater where you'll learn some of the details of the discovery of Mara's temple.

This is not a ride for the timid. If the waiting line doesn't scare you, consider that the ride includes skulls and skeletons, bugs, snakes, explosions, a crumbling bridge, explosions, fire, and a car that will give you the shakes. And the waiting queue is not for the claustrophobic; some of the areas are very narrow and cave-like.

The ride handlers are very strict about enforcing the 48-inch minimum height requirement; adults don't want to take the ride if they have back problems or other health issues including pregnancy and heart conditions. This ride is wilder than anything else at Disneyland, and about as rough as the most severe roller coaster at other amusement parks.

About halfway through the waiting queue you will come to the Rotunda Room with a maze that circles a well—this point is about 15 minutes away from the end of the line. The sign warns against pulling the rope, but of course that is exactly what you are expected to do. "Leave off the rope, old fella!" comes a yell from below; every once in a while the words are even more extreme.

Another waiting area takes you through a screening room where you can watch a portion of the "Eye on the Globe" newsreel, flashed up on the screen by a rickety old projector. You'll learn how celebrities have been flocking to visit Professor Jones' latest discovery; one of the segments of the newsreel tells of a celebrated but aging actress who visited the temple of Mara and received the gift of eternal youth. "No more matronly roles for her," the breathless announcer reports. If you listen very carefully, you will also hear how not all of the visitors seem to have escaped.

Finally, you are boarded onto your 12-seater military transport and you are off. Buckle your seat belt and grab a firm hold on the handlebars in front of you.

There are three rows of four narrow seats across in the vehicle. The leftmost passenger in the front row gets to hold on to the steering wheel—it does not move, though.

In my experience, it seems that the wildest ride is given the passengers sitting in the back row and the mildest in the center row of the car.

Although you may be sorely tempted to try and take photographs or use a video camera on your trip, you are going to find that you will need both hands on that handle bar.

There are a total of 16 transports, each nicely decorated to look dirty and beaten up. Vehicles are dispatched every 18 seconds, and the ride can carry as many as 2,400 people per hour.

Beneath the shell of the transport is some of the highest technology of any ride at any theme park. Each vehicle has its own ride computer for sound and control. The troop transports use a Disney-developed technology called Enhanced Motion Vehicle which controls the movement of the transport forward and backward, up and down, and side to side, as well as the sounds and some of the special effects of the ride. Each vehicle can stop, back up, slow down, or go faster based on computer decisions.

It seems much larger. Disneyland occupies just 80 acres of land. In Florida, the Magic Kingdom takes up about 107 acres and the Disney-MGM Studios is spread over some 135 acres, while Epcot Center spreads over 260 acres (including a 40-acre lake). The sprawling Walt Disney World resort includes 28,000 acres or some 43 square miles of land, making it about the size of San Francisco or twice the size of Manhattan.

The ride is accompanied by John Williams' music from the Indiana Jones films, specially adapted and rerecorded by a 90-piece orchestra. To tell you the truth, we can't remember hearing it, though; we were very busy holding on for dear life and watching all the wild goings-on all around.

According to Disney, there are something like 160,000 possible combinations of sounds, motion, and events on any particular journey through the temple, and no two consecutive rides will be identical. In reality, the difference from one ride to another is actually rather minor, but it is interesting to remember that you are in the electronic hands of a computer throughout.

Carved over the door to the temple is a warning in a strange language: it translates as "Beware of the eyes of Mara." Other messages use the same language throughout the ride. You can pick up a small card that translates the characters, although you won't have much of a chance to do so as you move along through the temple. Actually, the characters are not that difficult to read once you realize that they are like our standard alphabet with a few missing parts here and there.

As your transport enters into the temple you will arrive at the Chamber of Destiny, where you will find three doors—one for each of the possible "good" gifts of Mara. Remember the warning against looking Mara in the eye, though. And that applies to everyone in the car.

You'll be offered the chance to decide together on the route you wish to take: the left door is Knowledge, the center is Riches, the right is Youth. (We don't want to spoil the illusion by pointing out that the computer will make the decision for you, so we won't.)

Of course, *somebody* in your transport just *has* to look in Mara's eye and

Free? Here's the best bargain in the park. You can obtain a free pair of aspirin or Tylenol to cure a headache at the First Aid Station at the top of Main Street. The cup of water costs $10, though. Just kidding. There's a registered nurse on duty at the station at all times, by the way, and special arrangements can be made to store medication there.

Aspirin and other common medicines can also be purchased at the Emporium on Main Street.

Baby biz. Walt Disney's baby picture adorns the wall at the Baby Care Center where you can change diapers, nurse a baby, warm a bottle, and do all of those other baby things. The baby center is located next to the First Aid Station at the top of Main Street. Next door is the Lost Children Center. (If you misplace a kid, contact the nearest cast member who will spread the word through the park by walkie-talkie and contact the center for a proper reunion.)

things go wrong. As you turn the corner from the Chamber of Destiny you'll meet Indy himself. "We've got a problem here," he might tell you. Or, more crankily, "Tourists! You had to look."

The transport careens into and out of a series of caves, across a shaking suspension bridge, through clouds of smoke and 60-mph winds, alongside bubbling lava pits, steam vents, and more. The best effect of the ride is the final one when your vehicle comes face to face with a huge rolling ball; at the last moment the jeep ducks under and out of the way. And then there is Indiana Jones himself to congratulate you on surviving the trip. Sometimes he's in a foul mood: "Next time you're on your own," he told us once. Another time he was in a more congratulatory mood: "Not bad for tourists."

And then it's over . . . and you can get back on line.

Disneyland planned for lengthy waiting lines for the ride, and they were not disappointed. When Indiana Jones first opened in the spring of 1995, early lines were as long as four hours in length; by Spring Break, typical midday waits were a still-unreasonable two hours.

The waiting line winds through the interior of the "excavation" that leads to the temple; if the queue ahead of you is full, there is about a 45-minute wait from the moment you enter into the building itself. Working backward, the line usually extends out into the main entrance of Adventureland between the Jungle Cruise and the back of the Golden Horseshoe Stage. If the line reaches past the Enchanted Tiki Room, the wait is about 90 minutes. From that point, the line can build up into a maze at the left side of the Central Plaza. On the busiest of days, it can work its way back down onto Main Street toward the entrance to the park; when the line touches Main Street, you're talking about a two-hour and longer wait.

The key to avoiding such lines is to get to the park as early as possible. If you have an early admission ticket that comes as part of a hotel package, take full advantage of the privilege and arrive at least 15 minutes before the time listed on that ticket, and then make a beeline to the Indiana Jones ride.

On Easter Sunday, waiting lines at noon were at least 90 minutes in a near-torrential downpour. That didn't bother us, since we had gone through the gates at 6:30 A.M. using an early admission ticket; by 7:30 A.M. we had gone through Indy's temple three times and were ready to stay away from significant lines for the rest of the day.

Isn't it a bit extreme to be at a theme park at 6:30 in the morning? Yes . . . and no. I consider it beyond acceptability to wait in line for several hours for almost anything, and especially for a relatively short ride. By 9 A.M., as most "early" visitors were arriving and preparing to stand on line, we were ready for a leisurely breakfast. By noon we had gone to all of our A-list attractions, and we headed back to our nearby hotel to rest and return later that night for the Fantasmic! show and Electrical Parade.

Swiss Family Treehouse. This is one of those "no accounting for taste" attractions—you'll either love it or hate it, probably depending upon how deeply the story of the Swiss Family Robinson is engraved upon your memory. Actually, this attraction is a remembrance of the 1960 Disney movie version of the classic novel *Swiss Family Robinson*, written by Johann David Wyss and completed by his son Johann Rudolf Wyss in 1813.

The treehouse winds 70 feet up and across a Disney simulation of a banyan tree (constructed of sculpted concrete and steel with several hundred thousand plastic leaves). There are a lot of stairs to climb and a few ropewalk bridges; on a busy day, your view may be mostly the backside of the tourist in front of you. It takes five to ten minutes to walk up, through, and down the tree; incredibly, there can sometimes be lengthy lines for the privilege. If there's a line and you're determined to climb this tree, come back late in the day.

WOW Jungle Cruise. Another Disney classic, this is an escorted boat tour through a simulated wild kingdom that somehow stretches from the African veldt to the Amazon rain forest to the Nile valley and the jungles of southeast Asia.

You'll see some of Disney's most famous special effects, like the automated hippos who lurk just below the water and the cavorting elephants who will

Gummed up. You cannot buy chewing gum at any store in Disneyland. The idea of sticky rubber underfoot was too much for Disney to bear, and it has always been banned. Cleaning crews search the walkways for contraband regularly.

When it rains . . . you will get wet. Most of Disneyland is outdoors and many of the waiting lines are open to the skies. When the rains come, vendors magically appear selling bright yellow plastic ponchos decorated with Disney characters; they are usually good for a few wearings before they tear.

If you fear the weather, you might want to shop before you travel, or stop at one of the discount stores nearby Disneyland and purchase raingear there; you may save a few dollars, end up with something a bit more durable, and make a non-Disney fashion statement.

Disabled guests.
Disneyland is pretty
accommodating to
visitors with special
needs; a list of
attractions with
wheelchair access is
available at Guest
Relations. Wheelchairs
can be brought into the
park or can be rented.

Visitors who are
disabled, together with a
limited number of family
members, can avoid
waiting lines and enter
directly onto certain
rides.

**How wet do you like
it?** Splash Mountain is a
watery place, and the
log cars make a huge
wave as they land at the
bottom of the big drop,
but the fact is that you
won't get very wet on
the ride. The two wettest
places seem to be the
very first row of seats
and the last—the wave
flies over the car. The
front row has the best
view of the drop; the last
row has the most
suspense.

spray water from their trunks. The shores are
lined with robotic zebras, lions, and giraffes. The
best part of the ride is the hokey but still entertaining patter of the tour guides in pith helmets.
("Be sure to tell all your friends about Jungle
Cruise," our guide told us on one trip. "It cuts
down the lines." He also apologized for some of
the worst one-liners: "I'd tell funnier jokes, but
they have to be Disney-approved.")

More, you want more? "On the right we have
plants," the guide said, pausing for effect. "On
the left we have more plants. Check out the
gigantic bamboo plants. That's something you
don't see every day. You don't, but I do."

Lately guides have begun encouraging riders
to laugh at the long, long line of people waiting
to enter the nearby Indiana Jones Adventure.

Amateur gardeners may be thrilled by the
amazing collection of plants, flowers, and trees—
most of them real—that Disney groundskeepers
manage to keep alive.

The ride is just short of ten minutes; the line
to get on board, alas, can sometimes wind
around and around the corral for more than an
hour. Go early or late on busy days.

Enchanted Tiki Room. In the Tiki, Tiki, Tiki,
Tiki, Tiki Room (you'll get the joke after you sit
through this squawking show), you'll find a collection of more than two hundred wisecracking,
wing-flapping, automated winged creatures,
along with a collection of singing flowers, totem
poles, and statues in a somewhat interesting
place with wood carvings and a bamboo lattice
roof. Your hosts are Jose, Michael, Pierre, and
Fritz.

Tropical Serenade is among the strangest of all
of the attractions at the Magic Kingdom, and you've got to be in exactly the
right frame of mind to enjoy the show. The birds were among Disney's first
attempts at Audio-Animatronics, representing the state of the art as it existed
around 1963.

We know some young children who have been absolutely enchanted by the
birds; the very young and the very cynical need not apply. Adults might want
to bring a Walkman.

Critter Country

Friendly bears in a hoedown, real canoes on a Davy Crockett tour, and a wet
and wild splashdown.

WOW **Splash Mountain.** Disney's "highest, scariest, wildest, and wettest" attraction is a wild ride to contemplate; you may have a long time to contemplate it as you wait your turn on a busy day. But don't get the wrong idea here: Splash Mountain is not anywhere near as wild or wet as it seems.

Here's one way to think of this place: it's a log flume ride with Pirates of the Caribbean and a bit of It's a Small World mixed in.

Splash Mountain has several false drops—including one with a little hump in the middle—before the big one that plunges about 52 feet at a 45-degree angle and a top speed of about 40 miles per hour. The big drop, visible to the crowds outside, makes it appear as if the log car has fallen into a pond. For the riders, though, the anticipation is much more intense than the experience itself—the drop is over in a few seconds.

Some of the best special effects take place within the mountain, with a story based on Disney's classic *Song of the South* cartoon, made in 1946. The ride follows Brer Rabbit as he tries to outwit Brer Fox and Brer Bear on a wild journey to the Laughin' Place.

Once you enter the Splash Mountain building itself, there are a few interesting exhibits including a series of placards that tell the Brer Fox story: "Some critters ain't never gonna learn" and "You can't run away from trouble. Ain't no place that far" among them.

More? "It was one of those Zip-a-Dee-Doo Days, the kind of day where you can't open your mouth without a song jumping right out."

And, "Everybody's got a laughing place—the trouble is most folks won't take the time to go look for it. And where it is for one, mightn't be for another."

The interior waiting line for Splash Mountain is not the place for claustrophobics; it's tight and dark in places, and especially confining when the lines move slowly.

One of a kind. The following attractions are found only at Disneyland and not at Walt Disney World:
Alice in Wonderland (Fantasyland)
Big Thunder Ranch (Frontierland)
Casey Jr. Circus Train (Fantasyland)
Great Moments with Mr. Lincoln (Main Street)
Indiana Jones Adventure, Temple of the Forbidden Eye (Adventureland)
Main Street Electrical Parade (Main Street)
Matterhorn Bobsleds (Fantasyland)
Mickey's Toontown
Motor Boat Cruise (Fantasyland)
Pinocchio's Daring Journey (Fantasyland)
Sailing Ship *Columbia* (Frontierland)
Sleeping Beauty (Fantasyland)
Storybook Land Canal Boats (Fantasyland)

Extra charge. When you get off Splash Mountain, you'll be greeted by a wall of video monitors that have color pictures of each log car as it goes down the big drop. You can buy a print that includes everyone in your car, strangers and all, for about $10.

You'll start by loading into your eight-passenger "log"; you may find the seats slightly wet. Be sure to protect cameras and other valuables from getting wet—you might want to travel with a plastic bag to cover them.

The logs will climb up into the mountain—you'll see the bottom of the big drop, and first-time riders will certainly be expecting a sudden sharp drop over the precipice they've seen from the ground. Just to build up the tension, there are a few small teasing drops.

But instead of the great fall, your log will move gently through a beautiful, tuneful, and peaceful water world filled with more than 100 Audio-Animatronic characters and lots of delightful details and insistently bouncy music. At the end of the first room there's a drop—but again it's not the big one.

Eventually you'll come to the big one, the spectacular waterfall you've seen from the walkway below. You're over . . . and down in about four seconds.

There is one final surprise at the very end—yet another pretty inside room with a "Welcome Home Brer Rabbit" party and the Zip-a-Dee Lady paddleboat. This is the scene you can also spy from the Disneyland Railroad as it passes through a portion of the Splash Mountain building.

All told, Splash Mountain is one of the longer rides at Disneyland at nearly 11 minutes. Despite the brevity of the final drop it does give you a lot more for your waiting time than Thunder Mountain or Space Mountain. If you can convince the kids (or the adults) to look past the short drop, they are sure to love the rest of the ride which is pure Disney. Try the ride in the day and in the night; the view of the park from near the top is worth the wait.

Be sure to ask a cast member about the length of the line. We'd suggest you come back another time—very early or late if the line is unreasonably long.

There are Splash Mountains at Walt Disney World and at Tokyo Disneyland; in California guests sit one behind another while the Japanese and Florida versions go side-by-side. Disney pros say that the Walt Disney World version of the ride is the most spectacular.

Country Bear Jamboree. A pun-derfully adorable show starring a cute cast of Audio-Animatronic characters including bears, deer, buffalo, and more. If you were ever curious about what bears do on their vacations, here's Disney's answer: "A loaf of bread, a jug of wine, and 7,000 ants."

The stage is located in a bit of a hideaway across from the entrance to Splash Mountain.

Stars of the show include Melvin the Mouse, Buff the Buffalo, and Max the Deer. Side-slapping hits include "Thank God I'm a Country Bear," "I Wish They All Could Be California Bears," and more.

For our money, we find this 15-minute attraction just barely (sorry) easier to take than the Enchanted Tiki Birds; youngsters and fans of Disney Audio-Animatronics will probably want to argue strongly in its favor.

Davy Crockett's Explorer Canoes. Do you remember Davy Crockett? If you do, you're probably well over the age of admission to Mickey's Toontown. The canoes are among the most realistic things in the park, large vessels that circle the Rivers of America around Tom Sawyer Island, in and among the river traffic of the Mark Twain Steamboat, the Mike Fink Keelboats, and the Sailing Ship, and across the path of the rafts to the island. The canoes, alas, are not operated every day and may be headed for permanent mothballs.

New Orleans Square

A favorite spot for the hearty of heart, New Orleans Square is home of the rollicking pirates and one of the world's largest collections of grim-grinning ghosts.

WOW **Pirates of the Caribbean.** Yo, ho, yo, ho . . . one of Disney's very best, a cruise into the middle of a pirate raid on a Caribbean island town.

The ride begins with a calm journey across a dark bayou that is among the most realistic settings in all of the park, right down to the robotic fireflies and recorded crickets. As you move deeper into the Caribbean Sea, hidden underneath the park, you'll meet a rollicking crew of pirates. "Thar be no place like home," one declares, but then he warns: "Keep a weather eye! There be squalls ahead."

The best of those squalls is the moonlit battle between a pirate ship and a government fortress across the harbor; cannonballs seem to land all around you in the cool water as your boat passes through the mist. Pay attention, too, to the jail scene where a group of pirates tries to entice a mangy dog to bring them the key. The ride includes a wondrous collection of Audio-Animatronic humans and animals, including robotic chickens and pigs. Our favorites are the mechanical crabs.

The famous "auction" of women in chains to the pirates occupies another central scene of the ride. The sign reads, "Take a Wench for a Bride." The pirate auctioneer tells one overly plump woman to turn and "show your larboard side."

Most serious Disneyphiles acknowledge that the older Disneyland version of Pirates of the Caribbean is superior to the flashier Walt Disney World ride in Florida. The California experience was enhanced in recent years with a new crystal-clear sound system.

The ride begins with a little bit of a watery drop; your boat is dropping below the Disney World Railroad tracks overhead.

Lines can be quite long throughout the day, especially in the afternoon after serious thrill-seekers have finished with Indiana Jones, Splash Mountain, and Space Mountain. If Pirates is a family favorite, you may want to head there early or at the end of the day. The ride itself takes just short of 15 minutes.

The Disney Gallery. A quiet and cool respite from the rest of the park, check out the changing exhibits of art and memorabilia. The entrance to the

Shiver me timbers. Some young children may be scared by the simulated cannon fire and the skulls and bones that are fairly liberally strewn about in some of the caves of **Pirates of the Caribbean.** Some adults may find bones of their own to pick—things like the depiction of women as objects for sale at auction. However, the ride just might offer an opportunity to discuss such unhappy elements of history with youngsters.

-- .. -.-. -.- . -.-- The telegraph operator working in the train station at New Orleans Square is clicking away in Morse code; the text is drawn from Walt Disney's speech on opening day at Disneyland.

Extra admission. Got a spare $20,000 or so for a ticket to Disneyland? That's about the price of admission to the very private and little-known Club 33, located upstairs at 33 Rue Royale in New Orleans Square. What's inside? Well, there's a bar (the only place in the park serving alcohol) and some real nice chairs.

Look for the green door with the number 33 just past the Blue Bayou restaurant next to the Gourmet; there is also an entrance between the pirate shop and the One of a Kind shop.

Club 33 was originally built as a private club for Walt Disney's guests; he died before it was completed. In case you're interested, there is usually a several-year waiting list for the right to plunk down about $20,000 for a corporate membership, $10,000 for an executive membership, or a mere $5,000 for an individual pass. Then you get to pay about $1,800 per year in annual dues.

Like I said, there are some real nice chairs inside. The club was another brainchild of Walt Disney, originally envisioned as a place where he could entertain visiting dignitaries. Disney was involved in its New Orleans design, but

gallery is by a stairway above the Pirates of the Caribbean. On recent visits the gallery has shown models and drawings for Disneyland Paris, the Indiana Jones ride, and some of the original sketches for Disneyland itself showing places with names like Holiday Land, Mickey Mouse Club, Frontier Country, the Hub, Fantasyland, Lilliputian Land, The World of Tomorrow, True Life Adventure Land, and Main Street. A scale model of the Disneyland Castle includes a tiny picture of Walt Disney walking in.

The suite of rooms that is now the Disney Gallery was originally planned as a private apartment in which Walt and Roy Disney could entertain business associates and foreign dignitaries. Although the rooms were never completed as originally envisioned, certain touches remain, including the stylized initials WD and RD woven into the wrought ironwork of the balcony.

The Disney Gallery is also the site of the most elegant place to view the nightly Fantasmic! show. For a cool $30 per person, you can rent one of 15 seats on the balcony of the gallery for the **Fantasmic Dessert Buffet.**

WOW **The Haunted Mansion.** Scare yourself silly in this masterpiece of an attraction with some of the most sophisticated special effects at Disneyland. The experience begins in the graveyard waiting line; before the tombstones make you feel too creepy, stop and read some of the inscriptions. They're a howl! (Speaking of howls, a recent addition is a pet cemetery.)

Recently, Disney wags parked an old horse-drawn hearse out front. The sign reads: "Reservations Accepted. Ghost Relations Disneyland. Please do not apply in person!"

Once you are admitted to the mansion itself, you will be ushered into a strange room with an interesting visual trick—is the ceiling going up or the floor going down? Either way, the portraits on the wall are a real howl. (Don't read this if you don't want to know. Okay, you have been warned: at Disneyland, the floor moves down and the walls are stationary; at Walt Disney World, the ceiling moves up and the floor stays where it is. The stretching room was put into place in California as a way to get visitors to the loading level which is on the other side of the railroad tracks. When the Florida house was built, there was no need to go down a level, but Imagineers wanted to keep the same illusion even if it was accomplished in a different way.)

The attendants, dressed as morticians, are among the best actors in the park, almost always staying in character. They may tell you to "fill in the dead space" in the line. When the elevator at the start of the ride fills up they may announce "No more bodies." They play their roles well—we've tried our best over the years to make them crack a smile, without much success.

You'll enter onto a moving set of chairs and settle in for a tour through a house that is in the control of the largest collection of spooks this side of the CIA. We've ridden the ride many times and see something different each time. Among the best effects are the dancing ghouls at the dinner party, the moving door knockers, and the face within the crystal ball.

This ride is probably the single best combination of Disney Audio-Animatronics, moviemaking, and scene setting.

There are all sorts of delightful details on the ride, enough to make it worth several rides if you have the time. Here are a few you might want to look for: the needlepoint that reads "Tomb Sweet Tomb," the legs sticking out from under the banquet table in the ghostly wedding reception, and the skull-shaped notes rising out of the top of the organ at the reception.

Some very young children may become a bit scared, although most kids of all ages can see the humor among the horrors. And speaking of humor, stop to read the inscriptions on the tombs at the exit.

Lines for this show vary greatly; the best times to visit are early or late in the day. The ride lasts about nine minutes, including a two-minute preshow.

Over recent years, Disney has been subtly raising the scarification level of the ride, perhaps in reaction to the overall explicitness of our society. The skeletons are just a

he died a few months before Club 33 was completed.

Within the door is an ornate grillwork elevator to the second floor. Upstairs are some equally-impressive oldstyle appointments, including an oak telephone booth with leaded glass panels, adapted from the one used in the Disney film, *The Happiest Millionaire*. The Lounge Alley is used for a buffet and sports a harpsichord decorated with a scene of a New Orleans harbor in the nineteenth century. The Main Dining Room is decorated in Napoleonic style, including three spectacular chandeliers.

The Trophy Room is the second dining room, a more informal place with cypress-plank walls. Hidden within the chandeliers are microphones installed at Walt Disney's suggestion; according to Disney historians, the intent was to allow a vulture in the room to converse with guests during dinner.

French doors on the upper level open out on a spectacular view of the Rivers of America and are a marvelous place to watch the Fantasmic! show . . . if you don't mind paying a bit extra for the privilege.

For better or verse.
The tombstones and pet cemetery are located in the upper waiting area for the Haunted Mansion. If the lines are not long you may not even pass in front of them, but they're worth a side trip. Here is a selection of some of the very worst of the verse.

"Here lies Good Old Fred. Great big rocks fell on his head."

"Rest in Peace Old Cousin Hewitt. We all know you didn't do it."

Some of the named tombstones include those of M. T. Tomb, I. L. Beback. U. R. Gone, and Rustin Pece.

And then there are the heartbreaking stories behind some of the gravestones in the pet cemetery:

"Here lies long-legged Jeb, he got tangled up in his very own web."

"Rosie was a poor little pig, but she bought the farm."

And there is the last resting place of Old Flybait the frog, who croaked on August 9, 1859.

bit more real, the ghosts are just a bit more ghoulish.

Actually, though, the first plans for the Haunted Mansion were more gruesome than what was actually built.

Because it was to be built near the New Orleans area of Frontierland, the idea was to make it look like an early 1800s Southern mansion; it actually ended up looking like an old home in Baltimore. Walt Disney himself vetoed a design that made the house appear to be derelict (Disney's first falling-down house would come some 30 years later with the construction of the Twilight Zone Tower of Terror at Walt Disney World).

The original plans also called for the tour to be a walk-through, with groups of about 40 visitors escorted through the house by a butler or maid who would tell the story. The first story line was quite different, too, and not at all sugarcoated: it told of a wealthy sea merchant who built a fabulous mansion for his new bride but then killed her in a rage after she learned he was really a bloody pirate. Her ghost came back to haunt him and tormented him so much that he finally hung himself from the rafters, giving the mansion two unhappy spirits. About all that is left of that gruesome story is the weathervane in the shape of a sailing ship on the top of the cupola of the mansion, some paintings with a seafaring theme, and a quick glimpse of a hanging body when the lights flash on in the "stretching room" in the preshow area of the ride.

The building was completed in 1963 but stood empty for nearly six years. The delay was in part caused by Disney's involvement in four major pavilions at the 1964–1965 New York World's Fair, including Pepsi's It's a Small World—A Salute to UNICEF ride, General Electric's Carousel of Progress, the Illinois pavilion's Great Moments with Mr. Lincoln, and Ford's Magic Skyway ride.

The first three World's Fair exhibits were later recycled for use at Disney parks: It's a Small World was moved to Disneyland and became the model for very similar and popular rides at Walt Disney World, Tokyo Disneyland, and Disneyland Paris. The GE Carousel was moved to Walt Disney World; it was updated a bit in 1994 but remains essentially unchanged. Great Moments with

Mr. Lincoln was Disney's first big success with Audio-Animatronics and was moved to Disneyland's Main Street.

The Haunted Mansion experience is accompanied throughout by a decidedly strange soundtrack that is among the more literate writings anywhere at Disneyland—that is, if you are able to hear it in the rather fuzzy sound system.

Here's part of the introduction from the stretching room:

> *When hinges creak in doorless chambers and strange and frightening sounds echo through the halls, whenever candlelights flicker where the air is deathly still, that is the time when ghosts are present, practicing their terror with ghoulish delight.*

> *Your cadaverous pallor betrays an aura of foreboding, almost as though you sense a disquieting metamorphosis. Is this haunted room actually stretching? Or is it your imagination? And consider this dismaying observation: this chamber has no windows, and no doors.*

> *Which offers you this chilling challenge: to find a way out! Of course, there's always my way.*

Says your Ghost Host: "We find it delightfully unlivable here in this ghostly retreat. Every room has wall-to-wall creeps and hot and cold running chills."

You'll meet Madame Leota, a disembodied guide who will help you attempt to make contact with the spirits within the mansion.

> *Rap on a table, it's time to respond, send us a message from somewhere beyond. Goblins and ghoulies from last Halloween, awaken the spirits with your tambourine. Wizards and witches wherever you dwell, give us a hint by ringing a bell.*

The best special effect of the ride is the wedding party scene, where guests move from mortal coil to diaphanous spirit and back. After the party, you'll meet the famous Grim Grinning Ghosts, captured within luminous globes. Through dozens of rides at the Magic Kingdom, Disneyland, and Disneyland Paris we were completely unable to figure out what they were saying until recently. Here's part of their song:

> *When the crypt doors creak and the tombstones quake, spooks*

Closed! Let's get this straight: we flew all the way across the country with two screaming kids, paid all that money, and ran all the way across the park, and Dumbo the Flying Elephant is *closed* for repairs? Yeah . . .

Because Disneyland is open every day, repairs and refurbishment have to be done in and among the visitors. Some minor jobs are done at night when the park is closed, but nearly every ride is closed for days, weeks, or even months every once in a while. Most of the closings take place during quieter times of the year; in other words, you can generally count on Space Mountain, Splash Mountain, and the Matterhorn Bobsleds being open around Christmastime and in the heart of the summer.

You can call (714) 999-4565 for the latest information on refurbishment of rides before you head out on your vacation.

*come out for a swinging wake. Happy haunts materialize and begin
to vocalize; grim grinning ghosts come out to socialize.*

*Now don't close your eyes and don't try to hide, or a silly spook
may sit by your side. Shrouded in a daft disguise, they pretend to ter-
rorize; grim grinning ghosts come out to socialize.*

As the ride comes to an end, Little Leota will urge you to hurry back. Make
final arrangements now; be sure to bring your death certificate.

Frontierland

The world of the Old West, with a nineteenth-century runaway mine train, the
Mark Twain paddle wheeler, and rafts to the kids' fantasies of Tom Sawyer
Island. Check out the quirky entertainment of the Golden Horseshoe Stage,
and stick around or come back later for the fantastic Fantasmic! show presented on a watery curtain in the Rivers of America.

WOW! **Big Thunder Mountain Railroad.** One of the best rides at the park
is at the same time much more than and much less than it appears.

Big Thunder is a Disneyfied roller coaster, one of only four "thrill" rides
in Disneyland (along with Space Mountain, Splash Mountain, and the new
Indiana Jones ride). As roller coasters go, it is fairly tame, with about a half
mile of track and a 3½-minute ride with a few short drops and some interesting twists and turns. But in the Disney tradition, it is the setting and the
attention to detail that make this one of the most popular places to be.

You will ride in a runaway mining train up through a quaking tunnel,
across a flooding village, and back down around and through an artificial
steel-and-cement mountain.

The mountain is bedecked with real mining antiques from former mines
out West. Look, too, at the Audio-Animatronic animals, birds, and an old coot
of a miner in a bathtub as you zoom by. The walls of the loading area are
lined with actual gold-bearing rock.

The trains have adventuresome names. We have spotted U. B. Bold, U. R.
Courageous, I. M. Fearless, I. M. Brave, and U. R. Daring. As the trains slow
down to enter the loading station they pass through a small Western town,
including the Big Thunder Saloon, an Assay Office, and the local newspaper,
the *Big Thunder Epitaph.*

Picking the right time to visit the railroad can make a real difference at
this very popular attraction; waits of more than an hour are common at midday in peak season. The shortest lines can be found early in the day or just
before dinnertime. The waiting line for Big Thunder Mountain Railroad is
about 15 to 20 minutes from the point at which you pass through the gates.

Coaster fans say the best ride (meaning the wildest) can be had with a seat
in the last row of seats. We also like the very front of any coaster ride since
it gives you a view of the perils ahead, over the top of the engine in front.

Thunder Mountain Railroad at night is another ride altogether. Like Space
Mountain, the fun is increased because the darkness hides the track ahead of
you.

Children under seven must be accompanied by an adult; no one under 40 inches is allowed to ride. Warn young children about the loud noises they will hear as their railway car is pulled up the first lift on the ride.

When you're through with the ride, listen to the talk coming from the bar in the little Western town, located above the ride next to the Mexican food place. At the big Thunder Saloon: "Do you know your toupee's on crooked?" "No, but if you hum a few bars I'll try to fake it."

Big Thunder Ranch. A small Disneyfied petting zoo set in a recreated horse ranch is located between Frontierland and Fantasyland behind Big Thunder Mountain. Keep alert: the tame goats, burros, horses, and other animals may try to chew on clothing, backpacks, cameras, and other possessions. Nearby is **Big Thunder Barbecue**, a Western chow hall offering barbecued chicken, ribs, and the like. By the way, there are some hidden pictures of Walt Disney inside the log cabin at the ranch.

Golden Horseshoe Stage. A longtime favorite, this is Disney's squeaky-clean version of a Western dance hall revue.

The original show included pretty can-can girls, corny comics, and strolling musicians to entertain visitors of all ages. A few years back, though, the show was closed and replaced with a country music show.

Shows are about 30 minutes in length. You'll need to arrive 30 to 45 minutes before showtime to make your way to your seat and place orders for drinks or snacks including chili and pickles (strictly optional, although it may be difficult to prevent kids from badgering you for something at the table).

In years past, admission to the show required a reservation made at the door, although on a recent off-season visit the doors were thrown open on a first-come first-seated basis for each show.

The Golden Horseshoe can eat up as much as two hours of your busy day; it may not make sense to visit if you are pressed for time.

WOW **Fantasmic!** The Fantasmic! show is like every other fabulous Disney entertainment, only more so. This is the highest tech portable singing, dancing, and pyrotechnical show we've ever known. A visit to Disneyland is not complete without a glimpse.

The 25-minute show is performed at the south end of Tom Sawyer Island on the Rivers of America from Frontierland to New Orleans Square. Shows are usually presented twice nightly on weekends and every night in the summer and in holiday periods. In off-season the park closes early and there is no show.

The show itself covers bits and pieces of Disney's illustrious history with the general theme of the battle for Mickey's imagination by some of the forces of evil including Ursula of *The Little Mermaid*, the Wicked Queen of *Snow White*, and Queen Maleficent of *Sleeping Beauty*. There are beautiful projected scenes on a water screen, fireworks, explosions, and surround-sound music. Mickey himself conducts the extravaganza from a podium on Tom Sawyer Island, and he is visited by dozens of characters including a pirate ship with the cast of *Peter Pan* (on board the redecorated *Columbia* sailing ship), and the stunning appearance of the Mark Twain riverboat packed with happy Disney characters at the finale.

Woodn't you? The petrified tree in Frontierland along the Rivers of America in front of the Golden Horseshoe was a gift from Walt Disney to his wife, Lillian. Mrs. Disney gave it back to the park in 1957.

It was taken from the Pike Petrified Forest in Colorado. According to the inscription, the section weighs five tons and measures seven-and-a-half feet in diameter. The original tree, a redwood or sequoia, is estimated to have been two hundred feet tall and was part of a sub-tropical forest 55 to 70 million years ago in what is now Colorado.

There are many places to stand and watch the show, including the waterfront near Splash Mountain, the bridge near the entrance to the Pirates of the Caribbean, the patios of the Cafe Orleans or the French Market Restaurant, and a tiered viewing area at New Orleans Square's Promenade.

The most elegant way to view the show is probably with the purchase of a ticket to a dessert and coffee buffet at the Disney Gallery near the Pirates of the Caribbean. Seats on the balcony sell for about $30 each. Reservations can be made at the Reservations Center on Main Street before noon, or at the Gallery in the afternoon.

Crowds for Fantasmic! can be quite large, especially for the first (or only) show; later shows are usually more approachable. The Main Street Electrical Parade, held on the other side of the park from Fantasyland to Main Street, will reduce the crowds if it is held at the same time as Fantasmic! (As we have noted before, the parade time is a good time to visit some of the more popular rides such as Splash Mountain, Indiana Jones, or Space Mountain.)

If you beat a quick retreat from the Fantasmic! show and move quickly back toward the Hub and toward Main Street, you should be able to catch the tail end of the Main Street Electrical Parade as it heads toward the Disneyland Railroad Station.

If you are heading for the second or third show, the insider's plan is this: approach the viewing area from the Splash Mountain side as the previous show is coming to an end. This way you won't have to fight the thousands of guests clearing out through Frontierland.

Disney pros say the best ground-level view of the show is along the river across from the entrance to the Pirates of the Caribbean and facing the shack on Tom Sawyer Island. There's a "Kodak Photo Spot" sign along the river, just to the left of the prime spot.

Warning: some of the mist from the fountains in the show drifts back into the faces of the closest viewers. This can become a bit uncomfortable on a cool evening. The show will be canceled in inclement weather or high winds.

WOW! Tom Sawyer Island. Another essential, at least for the youngsters, is the raft ride over to this little island in the middle of the Rivers of America. Based vaguely upon Mark Twain's classic book, you'll find dark caves, a dungeon, waterwheels, a barrel bridge, and a rope bridge to bounce on. At the far end of the island is Fort Wilderness, where kids can scramble around the parapets and fire air guns at passing sidewheelers.

Parents will appreciate the space to let their children burn off a bit of energy after standing in lines all day; be advised, though, that it is fairly easy to misplace a youngster in one of the simulated caves or on a trail. Discuss with your children a meeting place in case you become separated.

Go out on the front deck of Harper's Cider Mill to see some of the mechanisms for the Fantasmic! show. You can see spray heads in the water and underground lighting and projection platforms.

Nearby is a working replica of a water-powered mill. Across from the pontoon bridge is the back side of Big Thunder Mountain Railroad. Decorations include an abandoned mining train. Look closely at the cargo in the train—robotic chipmunks poke up their heads every once in a while.

Lines for the raft rarely require more than 10 minutes of waiting. The island closes at dusk and may not be open at all during the off-season and in bad weather.

Frontierland Shootin' Arcade. A durn-fancy shooting gallery, sort of a live video game, and not like any other shooting gallery you have seen at a county fair. For 50 cents, players aim huge buffalo rifles at a Disney replica of Boot Hill, a frontier town from the 1850s. The rifles fire infrared beams at targets on tombstones, clouds, banks, jails, and other objects; direct hits make the targets spin, explode, or otherwise surprise. Some of the signs on the objects tell a story: "Old Tom Hubbard died with a frown, but a grave can't keep a good man down." If you hit the skeleton of a steer, his horns will spin around.

More? "One last drink was in his hand, died a reachin', Red Eye Dan." Or: "Six-gun Tex lies in this grave, used his gun for a closer shave."

Mark Twain Steamboat. Reaching all the way back to the birth of Disneyland, this ⅝-scale paddle wheeler was built for the park. It has traveled uncounted thousands of miles without ever leaving the Rivers of America and without deviating from its underwater track.

The ride itself is no great shakes, but it is a pleasant reprieve on a hot day. The Mike Fink Keelboats, Davy Crockett's Explorer Canoes, and the *Columbia* make the same circle and see the same simulated Old West sights.

The ride takes about 15 minutes; lines rarely extend beyond a full boat load, so your waiting time should be 16 minutes or less.

Sailing Ship *Columbia*. A full-scale replica (110 feet long, with an 84-foot

Inside Fantasmic! Three projectors, located on Tom Sawyer Island, beam a 70 mm film onto three 30-by-50-foot "screens" of water mist. Natural gas jets feed a wall of flame that erupts from the water around the island.

Disney designers hid as much of the high-tech equipment as possible—much of the equipment is lowered into underground pits during the day. The elaborate 10-track audio system includes speakers in front of and behind the audience; some of the speakers are disguised as lampposts, and two large boats in the lagoon carry additional speakers.

Disney gives credit to a history pageant in Vendee, France, for the development of the mist screen technology.

main mast) of the three-masted merchant ship of the 18th century; famed for its beauty, it is also recognized for the discovery of the Columbia River in Oregon. The vessel was launched in Plymouth, Massachusetts, in 1787 and made many trips around Cape Horn to the northwest. It disappeared in the Orient.

The *Columbia* is definitely the classiest way to take a 15-minute tour of the Rivers of America. Below deck is a museum that depicts the lifestyles of the sailors.

The vessel operates only during daylight hours and only during the busiest days.

Mike Fink Keelboats. Small riverboats follow the same circuit as the Steamboat, the canoes, and the *Columbia*, a bit faster and a bit more personal with your own guide. Mike Fink, by the way, was a riverboat captain of legend who had an adventure with Davy Crockett. The small boats here, the *Bertha Mae* and the *Gullywhumper,* take about 10 minutes for a circuit. Because of the small capacity of the boats, we'd advise you to avoid joining a long line if there is one; we'd also suggest against duplicating a trip on the keelboats and one on the Steamboat. The keelboats run only during the day and may be closed during slow attendance days.

Fantasyland

This is the stuff of young dreams: Dumbo, Peter Pan, Alice in Wonderland, Snow White, and the toy riot of It's A Small World. Fantasyland is a bright and cheerful place, decorated in splashes of color and sprinkled with snippets of song. Over it all is Sleeping Beauty's castle.

Sleeping Beauty Castle. One of the emblems of Disneyland, more famous than most any real castle in the world, Sleeping Beauty Castle towers over the center of the park; well, it towers about 77 feet, but in true Disney fashion the forced perspective design of the building makes it look taller than it really is.

The Sleeping Beauty Walk Through is a somewhat obscure corner of the park, located within the castle between the Castle Christmas Shop and Tinkerbell's Toy Shop. Climb the stairs to see animated dioramas of scenes from *Sleeping Beauty*. This display has been closed from time to time over the years.

Dumbo, the Flying Elephant. Disney has taken a very ordinary amusement park ride and made it something special, at least for little visitors. Riders sit within fiberglass flying elephants that can move up and down as they circle around a mirrored ball and a statue of Timothy Mouse, the little guy who becomes Dumbo's manager in the classic Disney animated movie.

This ride has always held a tremendous draw for young children, with lines of up to an hour for the 90-second ride. If your kids insist on an elephant-back ride, head for Dumbo early or late in the day. One of the rites of passage for youngsters, we suspect, is the day they announce they're willing to skip the lines for Dumbo in favor of a second pass at Space Mountain.

King Arthur Carrousel. One of the few mostly "real" things in this world of fantasy and probably the oldest antique in use in the park, the carrousel was originally built in 1875. Disney reconstructed the ride with carved horses from Germany; no two are identical.

The lines for the two-minute ride ebb and flow; we'd suggest you wait for the times when you can walk right on board. And parents take note: the exit to the merry-go-round is in a different place than the entrance.

WOW **It's a Small World.** Every little girl's wildest dream: a world of beautiful dancing dolls from all over the world. There is nothing to get your heart beating here, but even the most cynical—including little boys and adults—will probably find something to smile about in this upbeat boat ride; teenagers are hereby excused from a mandatory visit. We especially enjoy the Audio-Animatronic can-can dancers. We only wish we could get the sugary theme song out of our heads.

This 11-minute ride was originally designed for the 1964–1965 World's Fair in New York.

The boats are large and the lines move pretty quickly, but we'd advise coming to this attraction early or late in the day. Be sure to check out the mechanical-doll parade every quarter hour on the clock outside the attraction.

It's a Small World was upgraded in 1994 with a digital sound system and a rerecorded soundtrack that features more instrumentals, originally produced for Disneyland Paris.

Peter Pan's Flight. A mellow excursion into some of the scenes from Disney's version of the story of the little boy who doesn't want to grow up. Riders sit in a small pirate ship that suspends them a foot or so off the floor. Everyone's favorite scene is the overhead view of London by night, which does a pretty good job of simulating Peter's flight. Strictly for kids.

At Disneyland Paris, a jazzed-up version of this ride is one of the more popular attractions; not so at Disneyland, although lines can still reach to 45 minutes or more on busy days for a two-minute ride.

Mad Tea Party. A Disney version of a rather common amusement-park ride in which circular cars move around a track and also spin around on platforms. If it sounds dizzying, that's because it is: the very young and others with sen-

What a bunch of characters. If you've ever wanted to see a child's eyes pop open like a cartoon character, watch carefully the first time a youngster comes face to face with a walking, talking Mickey or Minnie Mouse.

The characters are scattered throughout Disneyland; if your child has or you have a particular favorite, you can inquire at City Hall to check the day's schedule. You'll usually find them near the railroad overpass on Main Street, in and around the Castle, and in Toontown.

Don't be surprised if some very young children become frightened when their time in the spotlight arrives; the characters are large and usually surrounded by crowds. The cast members inside the suits (sorry to destroy the illusion) are pretty good at playing around with little ones, though.

Mickey, Minnie, Goofy, and most of the characters won't talk; they will, though, sign autographs if that is something you've always hoped for.

Travel plans. Stop and listen beneath the window between the entrance and exit to the Peter Pan ride. You'll hear Peter Pan and Wendy discussing a trip to Never Land.

sitive stomachs or ears might prefer the carrousel across the way. However, the riders have some control over how fast the cups spin; grab hold of the wheel in the center of the cup and don't let go for the least movement.

The ride has been designed like a scene from Disney's classic 1951 film, *Alice in Wonderland*. The ride itself is only about 90 seconds long; the wait can be much more than that. We'd recommend hopping on board only if lines are short.

Mr. Toad's Wild Ride. Not all that wild, but an entertaining ride based on one of Disney's more obscure films, *The Adventures of Ichabod and Mr. Toad,* which was in turn loosely based on the book *The Wind in the Willows.*

You will ride in an antique car on the road to Nowhere in Particular, crashing through fireplaces, into a chicken coop, and on a railroad track headed straight for an oncoming locomotive. It's light enough fare for most children, although the very young might become a bit scared by the Day-Glo devils and the somewhat loud sound effects. Adults will find this two-minute ride among the more ordinary at Disneyland; we'd recommend against joining a midday line unless a youngster is in charge.

Check out the titles on some of the books in the library as you enter into the ride.

Snow White's Scary Adventures. Read the sign over the door: see "Scary"? Now understand, this ride can't hold a fading candle to the spooks in the Haunted Mansion across the way in New Orleans Square, but there are a lot more skeletons and witches than very young children might expect. This ride emphasizes the grimmer parts of the Brothers Grimm fairy tale, as presented in Disney's 1938 animated movie.

Says the Wicked Witch: "One taste and the victim's eyes are closed forever." There's no real resolution of the threats presented in the ride except for a completely unexplained sign that reads: "And they lived happily ever after."

All that said, it's an interesting but short ride for children who can handle the dark side of the fairy tale; if your youngster is the sort who gets nightmares from Casper the Friendly Ghost, I'd suggest you go for two rides on Dumbo instead of one with Snow White.

By the way, over at the Magic Kingdom in Florida, a revision of the ride in 1994 rebuilt it as a kinder and gentler place.

Alice in Wonderland. A bit of this and a bit of that in a Disney version of the classic story: you'll climb into a four-seat caterpillar vehicle for a four-minute journey down the rabbit hole in a chase after the White Rabbit. A merry time is had by most; get there early or late to avoid lines during busy times. There's not a lot to the ride; it's like a roller coaster without the roll.

Pinocchio's Daring Journey. A trip to the scary side of Tobacco Road, the place where Pinocchio is sent when he disobeys Gepetto. (Have you realized by now how many of our favorite fairy tales have a dark side? Are you beginning to get the idea that many of the attractions at Fantasyland emphasize the scary elements of the story?)

Later, you'll enter Pleasure Island, which is a riot of Day-Glo colors, calliope music, and amusement-park rides. Eventually, we are rescued by Jiminy Cricket and reunited with Gepetto. At long last, we are reminded that "When you wish upon a star, your dreams come true."

The three-minute ride includes some of the more advanced technologies for the younger set, including fiber-optic fireworks and holograms. Lines are often slightly shorter than at other surrounding attractions in Fantasyland.

WOW **Matterhorn Bobsleds.** The Matterhorn is one of the reasons that Disneyland is a magic kingdom. The Matterhorn Bobsleds is just a rather small and not-all-that-fast roller coaster that was one of the earliest attractions at Disneyland, but, like Space Mountain which followed some two decades later, the Disney designers made it into something very special.

Here's the magic: these aren't roller coaster cars, they're bobsleds about to make a sharp ascent up the interior of the famous pointed Swiss peak. Almost 150 feet into the air, the bobsleds start their rapid descent within the mountain and out onto exposed tracks that—if you look quickly—present some spectacular views of the park. (This is one of those rides worth riding in the daylight and again at night to experience the different views.) And do keep your eyes open for a quick glimpse of the Abominable Snowman.

The left track, the one nearest the mountain at the turnstiles, has more turns and better views of the park, while the right track has sharper drops.

Within the mountain, near the large ice crystals, look for a box marked "Wells Expedition." This is a tribute to Frank Wells, president of the Walt Disney Company, a renowned mountaineer who died in a helicopter crash in 1993.

Lines for the bobsleds can become quite long, although the Matterhorn is no longer the number one draw at Disneyland; that honor goes to either the

Snow White is watching. Lean into the wishing well in **Snow White Grotto** to the right of the castle at the entrance to Fantasyland to hear Snow White singing "I'm Wishing" from the Disney movie. The song was rerecorded for the fiftieth anniversary of the classic cartoon by the original Snow White, Adriana Caselotti. You'll also find statues of Snow White, the seven dwarfs, and various woodland creatures.

And so is the evil Queen. Keep your eye on the windows above the entrance of Snow White's Scary Adventures. Every once in a while the curtains will part and the evil Queen will glare out at the visitors below.

And then be sure to make a visit to the Disney Villains Shop within Fantasyland next to the Peter Pan ride. Inside you'll find the evil Queen within a cage; if you pay her a little attention, she'll talk to you and try to convince you to set her free. (There's a button hidden behind the counter that turns on the speech when a cast member pushes it.)

Look up to see what's missing. The **Skyway,** one of the old landmarks of Disneyland, was dismantled near the end of 1994 and is apparently gone forever. According to Disney, the popular ride, which connected Tomorrow-land and Fantasyland, was taken down because it was out of compliance with current state safety codes including concerns about earthquakes. The ride had its troubles over the years, including a 1993 incident in which a teenager forced open the door and tumbled out.

new Indiana Jones ride, Splash Mountain, or Space Mountain. In any case, get to Matterhorn early or late to avoid lines.

Speaking of lines, the Matterhorn Bobsleds are somewhat unique at Disneyland in that the twin waiting areas can be seen from the walkway; it should be fairly easy to gauge how long the wait will be. By the way, the line that heads toward Fantasyland holds fewer people than the one that heads toward Tomorrowland; if the two lines are about the same length, go toward Fantasyland.

Like Space Mountain, the Matterhorn is nowhere nearly as wild as your average amuse-ment-park roller coaster; it's all in the setting.

The best time to ride the Matterhorn (other than at the very start of the day) is during one of the parades. Once crowds build, they usually set up two lines—one for each of the twin bob-sled runs. During parades the two lines are often combined into a single queue and routed away from the parade area. The single line looks long but moves twice as fast. Once you are inside the final waiting area, turn to your right instead of the left for a slightly shorter wait.

Each afternoon, look for Mickey Mouse and Goofy to climb up the sides of the mountain where Minnie is waiting for them with a picnic lunch.

Storybook Land Canal Boats. A kinder, gentler, smaller jungle cruise in and among some lovely miniatures taken from great fairy tales and Disney films, this is another of the early entertainments of Disneyland and a sup-posed favorite of Walt himself. Boats begin their journey with a trip into the mouth of Monstro the Whale from Pinocchio.

Guides point out some of the tiny scenes on a 10-minute tour which has something for most everyone. The very young will enjoy spotting scenes from Alice in Wonderland, the Seven Dwarfs Mine, and more; adults will revel in the details including tiny bonsai forests. As with the Jungle Cruise in Adventureland, some of the guides are about as lively as the bonsai while oth-ers put a bit of acting into their spiels.

Storybook Land has received some overdue attention, with models of scenes from some of Disney's recent animated films including *Aladdin, Beauty and the Beast,* and *The Little Mermaid.* A waterfall was added over the cave to Never Land. The improvements are derived from the Storybook created for Disney-land Paris.

Casey Jr. Circus Train. Dumbo comes to life in a mini-train with ani-mal cages and a caboose. The train circles Storybook Land on a three-minute trip that your very daring youngsters may want to ride all by themselves. Adults can squeeze in, too, or can view the same displays from the Storybook Land Canal Boats.

Fantasyland Theatre: "The Spirit of Pocahontas" Stage Show. Disney's animated retelling of the Pocahontas story comes to tuneful life on a colorful set. Actors sing and act to a recorded score. The show is aimed at the younger visitors, but is an entertaining diversion and a place to sit down. But speaking of sitting, seats in the outdoor stadium fill up regularly and no standing room is available.

In the summer and holiday seasons, the show is presented five or more times a day; at other times of the year it is offered on weekends only.

Mickey's Toontown

Disneyland, Walt Disney World, Disneyland Paris, Tokyo Disneyland, and the entire Disney empire were built upon the ears of the most famous rodent of all, but until just recently Mickey Mouse didn't have a place of his own. At Walt Disney World he got his own land (first a Birthday Party and then Mickey's Starland). At Disneyland, the Mickster shares the spotlight as emcee of Mickey's Toontown, a village based on some of the characters and locations of the Disney animated film, *Who Framed Roger Rabbit.*

As you enter into Mickey's Toontown, check out the civic signs on the railroad overpass: there's a chapter of the DAR (the Daughters of the Animated Reel), the Loyal Knights of the Inkwell, the Optimists In Toon National, and the Benevolent and Protective Order of Mouse.

This section of the park is definitely for the youngest visitors, like Fantasyland but without the crossover rides like Matterhorn and It's a Small World. If you're not traveling with kids, you're excused.

Note that this is a rather small area and can become very crowded, leading to lines that will please neither you nor your youngsters. Get there early or late in the day to avoid the lines.

This is one place where you are almost certain to find one or more Disney characters walking about. Listen for bells, horns, and whistles from Toontown City Hall for the changing of the guard. Other funny touches include the sign outside Goofy's Gas that asks, "Did we goof up your car today?" Goofy also offers: "If we can't fix it, we won't." The gas pump has fish floating around in the dispenser.

Finally, note that around the side of Daisy's Diner you will find The Third Little Piggy's Bank.

Mickey's House, Mickey's Movie Barn, and **Mickey's Dressing Room.** If you have kids, or ever were one, then there's not a whole lot of doubt about this: you've got to pay a personal visit to Mickey Mouse. What we've got here is a series of displays within the mouse's house (including some interesting memorabilia and lots of touch-me stuff) and a waiting area where you can see old MM cartoons. It all leads up to the big enchilada: an audience with the mouse himself. Groups of one or two families are ushered into the dressing room where Mickey will pose for photos, sign autographs, and stand still while he is hugged, poked, prodded, and otherwise inspected. One thing he won't do, though, is talk.

Minnie's House. Next-door is the home of Mickey's mouse-girlfriend; check out the strange stuff in her kitchen. Minnie herself, though, is not often in her own house; you'll more likely find her out walking the streets of Toontown. (No, she's not that kind of girl; she's just hard to tie down.)

WOW! Roger Rabbit's Car Toon Spin. Training wheels for the up-and-coming thrill rider. Not for the easily dizzied, this ride is based on the wild taxicabs in Roger Rabbit's Toontown. Your cab goes out of control when one of the weasels throws Judge Doom's toon-dissolving solution on the road. You're then headed off on a wild, spinning trip through special effects and Audio-Animatronic characters. Like the Mad Tea Party, you can control the speed of your spins by grabbing the wheel.

The lines for this three-minute ride can become quite long in midday; come early or late. The line you may see outside is only a hint at the interior queue that takes you through the back alleys of Toontown to your waiting cab. The waiting queue at Toontown is a lot longer than it seems. Figure on about 30 minutes from the entrance to the building until you are seated in a cab; if the line reaches to near the railroad underpass at the entrance to Toontown, the wait is at least one hour, and you may want to make other plans.

The waiting area, though, offers some entertainment of its own, as visitors can peek through holes in a fence to see the spinning cabs. You'll walk past Baby Herman's apartment, catch a glimpse backstage at the Ink and Paint Club, and learn about the invidious plot to literally wipe out the population of Toontown with a deadly concoction of paint solvents called *dip*.

Along the way, you can even learn the formula for dip: one part acetone, one part benzene, and one part turpentine, mixed well. That actually is a real solution that might be used for dissolving ink used by a cartoon artist.

There are lots of other interesting details to be learned as you wait in line. Check out some of the license plates right inside the entrance: I M LATE, CAP 10 HK, 3 LIL PIGS.

You'll come to the door of the Ink and Paint Club and the slider will open; a hideous face will appear with one of several menacing messages, including "Beat it before I call a cop on you," or "Hey, who do you think you are, Mickey Mouse?"

You can also see Jessica Rabbit's very round shape passing by in silhouette on the window.

There is a casting bulletin board outside of Jessica's dressing room announcing an audition for an upcoming Disney pic. They're looking for men, women, and animals; no giants, please.

Another sign: "Lost one magic feather. If found, please contact Dumbo c/o Timothy Mouse, Walt Disney Studio, Hollywood, CA."

More threatening is a "wanted" poster: "Wise Guy Weasel wanted in 13 states for toon napping, assault with a silly weapon, petty larceny, grand larceny, and really grand larceny."

When you finally board your two-person taxi, you'll follow behind Roger

Rabbit as he tears through town, pursued by Weasels who dump dip in the path of vehicles. You'll spin through Ferdinand's China Shop and an electrical storm in the Power Plant, and eventually you'll crash through the roof of the Gag Warehouse for a showdown with the Weasels.

The concept of the ride is supposed to allow drivers to control the spin of their cars as they move through the ride. We found the steering wheel a bit stiff and difficult to control and suspect that some young children will need the assistance of an adult in driving.

Gadget's Go-Coaster. A very short and not-very fast kiddie coaster. In Disney fashion, though, it's been made very attractive; the bad news is that lines can become unreasonable for a ride that lasts less than a minute.

If the line is more than a hundred kids long, I'd suggest you bribe the kids with an ice cream and skip any line longer than your kid's attention span or your willingness to stand around and do nothing.

Jolly Trolley. A slow trip around Toontown. Walking is faster and there are no lines for that; keep that in mind if time is an issue.

Disneyland Railroad. The vintage railroad that circles Disneyland has a station near the entrance to Mickey's Toontown, a good way to deliver kiddies at the start of the day or extricate them at the end.

Playgrounds

Chip 'N Dale's Treehouse and Acorn Ball Crawl. A Disneyfied playground with a climbing tree and slide and a room carpeted with plastic acorn-balls; let the kids burn off the energy while Mom and Dad collapse on a bench. Kids must be over the age of three and shorter than 48 inches to enter the ball room.

Miss Daisy. Donald's boat is docked nearby, and kids are welcome to scramble all over it. Up the rigging, down the slides, ring the bells.

Goofy's Bounce House. Just like it says, a place to take off your shoes and bounce. A basic amusement-park play area with a Goofy theme. Kids must be older than three and less than 51 inches tall; keep an eye on the shoes they must leave behind. Lines can become quite long and move slowly at midday.

Tomorrowland

Every Disney visitor with a bit of spunk—and his or her mom and dad—has got to visit Tomorrowland at least once to catch a lift on the DL-200 Intergalactic Probe, also known as **Space Mountain.** And then there's the rare chance to journey into deep space with a rookie pilot in **Star Tours.** Other modes of transportation at Tomorrowland include submarines, monorails, rocket jets, and a slow-speed PeopleMover.

The long-awaited renovation of Tomorrowland got underway in early 1996 when work began on converting the former Carousel Theater into a West Coast version of Innoventions, a popular exhibit at Disney's Epcot Center in Orlando, Florida. Innoventions is like a permanent World's Fair, featuring technology and product displays from major international companies. Innoventions at Disneyland is intended to be the centerpiece of New Tomorrowland.

The former Carousel of Progress has been closed since 1989, and was used for Disney offices.

The Captain EO show, starring the supremely strange Michael Jackson, will close and be replaced by "Honey, I Shrunk the Audience," a spectacular multimedia film that is also a major attraction at Epcot in Florida.

The area will include a new thrill ride called "Rocket Sled" that is the first of its kind at any Disney park; it will replace the venerable PeopleMover.

The $100 million reconstruction of Tomorrowland will be accomplished in phases through 1998, with some sections closed off to visitors. However, Disney officials promise that Space Mountain and Star Tours will remain open throughout the project, although both may be updated.

WOW Space Mountain. The big enchilada, the highmost high, the place where hundreds of Disneyland visitors have dropped their eyeglasses, cameras, and hairpieces. It is also one of the most popular of all of the attractions at all of the Disney parks (the Walt Disney World version is similar but not identical; at Disneyland Paris another version, called Discovery Mountain and based on Jules Verne's book, *From the Earth to the Moon,* opened in 1995).

Space Mountain is a masterpiece of Disney Imagineering, merging a relatively small and slow (top speed of about 28 mph) roller coaster with an outer space theme. The small cars zoom around indoors in near-total darkness, the only light coming from the projected images of stars and planets on the ceiling. The ride is a triumph of scene-setting, the amusement park equivalent of a big-budget movie's special effects.

The cars feel like they are moving much faster than they are because you have no point of reference in the dark. And no, the cars don't turn upside down.

The waiting line for Disney's famous Space Mountain wends its way through an imaginative maze designed to make the visitors feel like they truly are embarking on an intergalactic journey. A recent update includes television monitors that broadcast spoof ads and weather reports; Federal Express boasts about overnight delivery to anywhere in the galaxy; Crazy Larry, the used Weather Satellite dealer (with 27 convenient locations around the universe) hawks his wares loudly; and there are promos for "Lifestyles of the Rich and Alien." You'll walk through corridors decorated with satellite pictures of other planets, pass through beams of colorful pulsating light, and then descend upon a walkway into a busy launching pad packed with technicians and engineers loading the DL-200 Intergalactic Probe.

Professional Space Mountain riders—and there are tens of thousands of them—will argue over which seat affords the best ride. The last row of seats seems to benefit from a "whip" effect as the cars make sharp turns; we prefer the very front row, where you don't have the back of someone else's head to mar the illusion of space travel and there is a terrific blast of onrushing air as you move on the track. At busy times, you probably will not be able to cajole an attendant into allowing you to select the seat of your choice; late at night or on the occasional slow day you might be in luck.

The cars have two seats per row, with three rows per car and two cars in a train. Do keep a hand on your personal belongings; wrap camera and purse straps around your feet and make sure that children are properly placed beneath the restraining bar. (Disney launch technicians will double-check the safety arrangements, too.)

Now, speaking of waiting lines: they can easily extend to 90 minutes or more on a busy afternoon. Space Mountain is still one of the major draws of the park, even with newer attractions like Splash Mountain and Indiana Jones. The general rule to avoid long lines especially applies here. Get to the ride when the gates first open and you may be able to stroll right on board, or come back to the ride at the end of the day. Another somewhat quiet time is during the dinner hour or during major parades.

The ride is about 2 minutes, 40 seconds in length. If both tracks are operating and the doors are open, a crowd backed up to the front door means a wait of about one hour; sometimes, though, attendants will build up the line outside while the inside queues clear out. This is often done at the end of the day to discourage huge crowds as closing hour approaches.

Children under three cannot ride Space Mountain, and those under seven must be accompanied by an adult; all riders must be at least 40 inches tall, and pregnant women and others with back or health problems are advised against riding.

Space Mountain, along with other major rides like Big Thunder Mountain Railroad and Splash Mountain, offers a "switch off" arrangement if not all of the people in your party want to ride the coaster or if you are traveling with a child too young or too small to ride. Inform the attendant at the turnstile at the launching area that you want to switch off; one parent or adult can ride Space Mountain and change places with another at the exit.

WOW **Star Tours.** Whenever your plans call for intergalactic travel, say the Disney travel posters, consider flying Star Tours to the vacation moon of Endor.

Disney builds the atmosphere and excitement beautifully from the moment you walk beneath the huge space machine outside and continuing as you walk through the indoor waiting area that simulates a gritty space garage. Our favorite flaky robots, R2D2 and C3PO, are the mechanics.

Listen carefully to the announcements on the public address system. You'll hear a call for Egroeg Sacul (Star Wars creator George Lucas, spelled backward) and a summons to the owner of landspeeder THX-1138 which has been illegally parked in a "No-Hover" zone.

When your time comes, you will enter into a 40-passenger simulator cabin and meet your pilot, Captain Rex. The doors will be closed and your seat belts tightly cinched before he informs you that this is his first trip. Too late— you're off. You'll make an uneasy takeoff and then blast (accidentally) into and then through a frozen meteor, stumble into an active intergalactic battle zone, and finally make a wild landing at your goal, the vacation moon of Endor.

This is quite a wild ride, about seven minutes and a bit rough for the very young; pregnant women and those with health problems are advised to sit this one out.

Much of the waiting line for the ride is within the building, which is a good news–bad news situation: expectant riders are sheltered from bad weather and entertained a bit by the displays, but it's hard to gauge how long the wait will be from outside. If the interior is filled to the doorway, you can expect as much as an hour on line. Remember the rule: Go early or late to the most popular attractions.

Children must be at least 40 inches to ride; tall youngsters under seven years old must be accompanied by an adult.

PeopleMover. Trains of 20-passenger cars circle slowly above Tomorrowland, allowing riders to take a quick peek into a part of Space Mountain and Star Tours. The PeopleMover was a pet project of Walt Disney, demonstrating an unusual means of propulsion: the linear induction motor. The track and the car form a motor together, as magnetic pulses pull the car down a flat coil. The train is due to be removed as part of the update for New Tomorrowland.

Astro Orbiter. A basic amusement-park ride with rotating rockets and an up/down lever, but in typical Disney fashion it seems like much more. Nowhere near as threatening (to some) as Space Mountain and offering a nice view of Tomorrowland, it nevertheless is not for people with fear of heights.

Originally called Rocket Jets, this ride was renovated as part of the makeover of New Tomorrowland. Astro Orbiter is a slightly faster and somewhat higher version of Dumbo, the Flying Elephant. It is especially impressive at night.

Tomorrowland Autopia. Every kid we know dreams of getting behind the wheel of Daddy's car; most adults we know dream of taking a spin around a Grand Prix Racecourse. Perhaps that's why this attraction, which doesn't have much to do with Tomorrowland that we can think of, is such a popular destination. Adults, alas, will probably find the trip rather boring; children will often beg for another go around the course.

The little race cars have real gasoline engines that will propel them forward at up to a zippy seven miles per hour. The steering gear works, too, allowing the driver to move the car left and right down the course, although there is a center rail that will keep the car from completely leaving the track.

Children must be at least 50 inches tall to ride in one of the cars alone; otherwise their feet won't reach the gas pedal. Mom or Dad, though, can sit alongside and press the pedal while junior happily steers.

Waiting lines can reach to nearly an hour on the most crowded days; visit the track early or late to make the best use of your time. A circuit takes about four minutes, and there is no reason to rush; you can't pass the car in front of you.

Toy Story Funhouse. A new outdoor playground, to the left of the entrance to Space Mountain, opened early in 1996. It re-creates some of the themes and brings in some of the characters from Disney's *Toy Story* movie, which was the first completely computer-animated cartoon. And tucked under the loading ledge for Space Mountain is **Hamm's All Doll Revue**, with seating for small children only. The show is an adaptation of the live theater presentation that debuted at Disney's El Capitan Theater in Hollywood.

Submarine Voyage. We love the idea of a submarine ride, but if that's what you are looking for, this is not a very fine example. Actually, Disney put a great deal of effort into this attraction, including the creation of a six-million-gallon lagoon filled with fish, giant clams, coral, icebergs, caves, and more—all of it fake. Oh, did we neglect to mention the lost city of Atlantis and the polar ice cap?

The attraction is loosely based on the Jules Verne book *Twenty Thousand Leagues Under the Sea*, and in particular the 1954 Disney movie. The subs at Disneyland are of modern design; the similar ride at Walt Disney World tricks up the boats to look like the *Nautilus* of Verne's book.

> **One-way monorail tour.** On busy days, the line to take a trip on the monorail can become rather long. Here's one way to avoid the queue. Exit the park (have your hand stamped and hold onto your ticket!) and take the shuttle tram from the parking lot to the Disneyland Hotel. It's not as elegant as the monorail, but it goes to the same place. Visit the hotel, which is an attraction by itself, and then ride the monorail back to the park.

Passengers clamber down ladders into the narrow confines of the sub and sit alongside underwater windows; some riders may find the loading and unloading very difficult. The ride also showcases one of the strangest jobs at Disneyland: the pilot of the submarine stands on a little platform with just his lower torso sticking out into the cabin with the seated passengers.

Despite repeated warnings from those in the know, this is one of the more popular attractions of the park. The 10-minute ride moves rather slowly, and loading is even slower; long lines build up by midday and may not disappear at all until late. Personally, we'd rather watch the plastic grass on Main Street grow . . .

Disney insiders hint of a major reworking of this ride in the future.

Starcade. It's a bit of a concession to the outside world, but then again Disney is not known for leaving too many nickels on the table; actually, we're talking half dollars and dollars and more at this high-tech video-game arcade located on the lower level of Space Mountain. Every successful rocket rider has to pass the enticements of the machines.

You'll find just about every major arcade game here, including many violent offerings that are not in keeping with the rest of the theme of Disneyland. Centerpiece is the Sega R360 jet simulator, which looks like and acts like a NASA trainer; the pilot is strapped in and rotates in any of 360 degrees.

Most rides are priced between 50 cents and a dollar, with the exception of the R360, which costs $4.

Captain EO. Let's stay out of the debate about whether Michael Jackson is the King of Pop or the Sultan of the Strange. Instead, we can all enjoy the fantastic 17-minute movie put together by director Francis Ford Coppola (*The Godfather*, *Apocalypse Now,* and other films).

It's a loud, flashy rock 'n' roll science fiction opera that combines two Jackson songs ("We Are Here to Change the World" and "Another Part of Me") with spectacular 3-D effects and laser beams.

Jackson's reign at Disneyland is scheduled to end soon to be replaced by the wild and wacky "Honey, I Shrunk the Audience."

WOW **Honey, I Shrunk the Audience.** Coming soon: A spectacular 3-D thriller that takes off where the two shape-altering Disney films (*Honey, I Shrunk the Kids* and *Honey, I Blew Up the Baby*) left off. In this case, it's the audience that shrinks instead of the kids. This is a theatrical performance that is simply not to be missed.

The show has been playing to full audiences for more than a year at Epcot in Walt Disney World, and is due to be installed at Disneyland in 1997 or 1998.

We find ourselves as honored guests at the presentation of the "Inventor of the Year" award to Wayne Szalinski, played by actor Rick Moranis. Other members of the film cast also appear in the feature, and are joined by funnyman Eric Idle of *Monty Python's Flying Circus.*

As far as what happens next, we don't want to spoil the fun or play a cat-and-mouse game with you; oops, disregard that last hint.

The wild conclusion of the show comes when one of the machines goes berserk and ends up shrinking the entire audience down to toy size. "Stay in your seats and we will blow you up as soon as possible," says Wayne.

The auditorium conspires with the 3-D images to complete the illusion with moving seats, spectacular lighting, special film effects, and unusual effects that will tickle your fancy and sprinkle you with laughter.

Disneyland Monorail System. Yet another mode of transportation, but unlike all the others in this corner of the park, the monorail has a purpose: it is a quick and easy way to leave the park and zip over to the Disneyland Hotel. If you are staying at the hotel, this is the way to enter Disneyland. Day-trippers or those staying at other hotels can use the monorail to take a break for lunch or dinner outside of the park.

When the monorail was first built in 1959, it was quite a novelty: the first full-time monorail transit authority in the country. (Walt Disney World has a much more extensive system with several tracks.)

The two-and-a-half-mile trip gives some interesting views of Tomorrowland and Fantasyland. On an average day there are two monorail trains running; on an especially busy day they might add a third set of cars to the line, but the short track won't take more than that. The trains are capable of 70 miles per hour, but stay at 35 miles per hour or less.

For a minor thrill, you can maneuver yourself into one of the five seats in the front of the monorail with the driver; tell the attendant loading the monorail of your wishes and move to the first gate to wait your turn.

Circle-Vision. Disney's patented film system projects images all around you in a circular theater. If you're on a train, look over your shoulder to see where you've been or to either side to sightsee. At the start of 1996, the theater was showing the spectacular *Wonders of China* film, the centerpiece of the China pavilion at Epcot Center in Walt Disney World, and *American Journeys*, another epic which explores our own country. Both are highly recommended.

At Walt Disney World in Florida, the Circle-Vision theater there was converted to the Transportarium to showcase "Time and Again," with Jules Verne, H. G. Wells, and a few modern-day stars leading visitors on a stunning multimedia exploration of time and space.

Parade Schedule. The beloved Main Street Electrical Parade strutted down Main Street for the last time in the summer of 1996; Disney promises a spectacular replacement.

Meanwhile, the wondrous **Lion King Celebration** steps off twice or three times daily in the afternoon all summer and in most holiday periods; at other times of the year the parade is held only on weekends. The parade steps along to the bouncy tune, "Just Can't Wait to be King," stopping four times between Fantasyland and Main Street to perform the "Circle of Life" song. The best spots to see this parade are Main Street Plaza, along Main Street, at the Hub in the center of the park, and in Fantasyland between Alice in Wonderland and It's a Small World.

The Lion King parade is lead by a pair of overly friendly rhinos with great eyelashes and by Zazu, the hornbill guardian of Simba, and Rafiki, the baboon counselor to Pride Rock. (The recorded voice of British comedian Rowan Atkinson gives life to Zazu, and American actor Robert Guillaume speaks for Rafiki.)

The 75 dancers and drummers—and they are very talented and spirited even after nearly two years of the same show—are accompanied by monkey-actors swinging from trees and a robotic alligator. (At least it appeared to be a blunt-nosed alligator like the ones that live in Florida, rather than the pointy-nose crocodiles native to Africa.)

To the bouncy beat of "The Circle of Life," dancers plant poles in holes in the street and swing from them; drummers pound out a live beat on African drums, rain sticks, shakers, and other noisemakers, and one of the floats turns into a living carrousel before your eyes. We especially enjoy the lifelike birds that the dancers swing from sticks in the finale; real white pigeons are released at the very end of the show.

The **Fantasy in the Sky** fireworks with Tinkerbell is usually performed on nights when the park is open late.

When a parade is underway there are only a few marked places where you can cross the traffic; crossing zones north of the Matterhorn are usually less congested than those near Main Street. With the closure of the Skyway, the only alternative is to take the Disneyland Railroad, which circles the park in a clockwise direction.

The best advice on getting a prime spot to see a parade is to get in place early, as much as 30 minutes or more before the start. One of the best spots is from the central plaza near the railroad station above Main Street; it's no secret, though, and this is usually one of the first places to fill up. There's both good and bad news about this, though. For the first parade of the day, the beginning of Main Street marks the end of the parade route, and it can take 15 to 20 minutes for the entertainment to arrive; the second parade begins at Main Street and moves toward Fantasyland.

Check the parade schedule listed in the Disneyland Today flyer you will receive as you enter the park.

Disney Characters

Mouse Tracks. Face it: the real reason you flew a thousand miles and spent a thousand dollars and endured ten thousand people in line was to get a picture of yourself with your arm around Mickey or Minnie, with Goofy's mouth engulfing your head, or with Roger Rabbit standing on your feet. (Don't try and convince me that it's your kids who want the pictures.)

There are three ways to obtain the precious mementos: by chance, by investigation, or by plan.

The characters stroll about the park throughout the day, often accompanied by handlers who help them navigate or help them escape from the occasional attacking hordes of children of all ages.

If you are willing to take things by chance, you can often find one or another character on Main Street near the railroad station and Great Moments with Mr. Lincoln, regular visits at the Hub near the castle, and strolling characters in Toontown.

If you're lucky, you may find yourself in the middle of what Disney calls a **Character Flood**, a sudden deluge of characters. On busy days, you can expect a double-decker bus full of characters to flood the Hub near the castle, often around noon.

Planners can count on finding Mickey and friends in Mickey's House at Toontown, where His Mouseness meets his adoring public in small groups. One of Mickey's assistants is usually available to use your camera to take your picture, if you'd like. On busy days there are (sorry to destroy any illusions) four Mickeys in Mickey's House, in different "movie sets": Fantasia, the Band Concert, Steamboat Willie, and Through the Mirror. You're not supposed to have a choice, although you may be able to sweet-talk one of the cast members into steering you to the room and the Mickey of your dreams.

Finally, you may be able to enlist the assistance of a cast member with a walkie-talkie, or a representative at City Hall, who can tell you where characters are scheduled to be that day.

Eating Your Way Through Disneyland

It's my opinion that there are three types of restaurants at Disneyland: overpriced and bad, overpriced and barely acceptable, and overpriced and almost good. Well, okay, there are a few meals that are overpriced and good. In any case, we'd recommend that you not consider meals to be an important part of your experience at the park.

You do, though, have to eat. Disney has a rule against bringing your own sandwiches or other food into the park. In dozens of visits to Disney parks, though, we have never seen an attendant search a backpack or shoulder bag for tuna fish on rye, and you certainly can bring a baby's formula and a few candy bars for the kids.

If you don't pack your own, it is possible to pick and choose among the offerings at the park. Disney does offer a few nonstandard and more healthful offerings, like pasta salads, turkey hamburgers, and smoked turkey legs, at some of its stands.

You'll also find fruit stands at several places around the park, offering oranges, apples, bananas, and other real food; some also sell dill pickles. The stands also sell plastic bottles of soda, which are easier to seal up and drink between rides than paper cups.

Another very valuable strategy is to plan on taking an afternoon break and leaving the park to go to a real restaurant for lunch and then returning for a second visit in the evening. Your parking ticket allows you to exit and return on the same day, as does your park pass (with a hand stamp).

If you do eat in the park, you should try to avoid lines by eating early; arriving for lunch at 11:30 A.M. instead of noon can save an hour of your time.

Many restaurants offer a small-portion and limited-selection children's menu for $2.99.

Reservations for Aladdin's Oasis and The Blue Bayou can be made at the restaurants themselves or on weekends and holiday periods at the Reservations Center, located next to Great Moments with Mr. Lincoln on Main Street.

Although some visitors like to start their day with breakfast at the park, most of us feel that's not a particularly good use of time or money. Breakfast is pretty expensive, and the early morning is the best time to visit the most popular attractions at the park. We have found a secret high-carbohydrate start to the day: a plate of hash brown potatoes (hold the egg and bacon) from Tomorrowland Terrace, sold for about $2.

Main Street

Blue Ribbon Bakery. Pastries and sweets, and gourmet coffees. A good place to grab breakfast as you press on into the park.

Carnation Ice Cream Parlor and Restaurant.

Carnation Plaza Gardens. Burgers and fries, plus ice cream desserts.

Plaza Inn. An attractive, moderately priced hideaway on the main plaza, it was renovated in 1996.

Plaza Pavilion. Pasta specialties.

Refreshment Corner. An old-fashioned eatery offering hot dogs (turkey and regular), chocolate-chip cookies, and sodas. It leads right into the candy shop and connects into the arcade.

Adventureland

Aladdin's Oasis. A lunch or dinner show based on the Disney smash *Aladdin* that brings the audience into the wild and silly plot while they eat. Open seasonally, and subject to change.

The meal is a bit unusual for a Disney entertainment, a fairly realistic Middle Eastern offering of exotic breads and crackers including pita and *lavosh*, followed by steak, chicken, shrimp, or vegetable kabobs, rice pilaf, and stir-fried vegetables. For less adventuresome children, there's a more conventional offering of chicken fingers, corn on the cob, and fries. And all of the audience receives a super-secret dessert.

At most times of the year, there are two seatings per day, priced at about $30 for adults and $25 for children for dinner, and $24 and $18 for lunch. Reservations and prepayment are required at the restaurant itself or at the Reservations Center.

The restaurant is located in the former Tahitian Terrace.

Bengal Barbecue. Beef, chicken, and vegetable kabobs.

New Orleans Square

Royal Street Veranda. Counter service for clam chowder, fritters, and snacks.

Café Orleans. An informal eatery with lunch and dinner offerings priced from about $5 to $15, including prime rib and Cajun Boule (spiced chicken in a bread bowl). The menu also includes soup and salad choices.

Blue Bayou Restaurant. One of the prettiest spots in the park, this restaurant is within the dark bayou scene at the opening of Pirates of the Caribbean. Dinner entrees, priced from about $18 to $25, include prime rib of beef, grilled tournedos of beef, chicken Spartenique, Mardi Gras prawns, and salmon Paragon. Lunch is served from 11 A.M. to 4 P.M. and dinner from 4 to 9 P.M.

French Market Restaurant. An attractive outdoor patio with a view of the river and railroad and a simple buffeteria menu.

La Petite Patisserie. A somewhat hidden gem on Royal Street, this walk-up window serves decent turkey or ham sandwiches, pastries, and sweets and is usually not very crowded.

Fantasyland

Village Haus Restaurant. Pizza, pasta, burgers, and salads.

Yumz. Pizza and snacks.

Critter Country

Brer Bar. A small restaurant hidden away at the exit to Splash Mountain and often less crowded than others in the area. Offerings, priced from about $2.50 to $4, include a turkey-cheese sandwich, a quarter-pound hot dog, and a Mickey Mouse pretzel. You can also take the chill off your Splashed clothes with hot chocolate, coffee, cappuccino, or espresso.

Harbour Galley. Seafood and snacks at the counter.

Hungry Bear Restaurant. Burgers, sandwiches, and salads from the counter. The dining platform offers an attractive view of the area.

Frontierland

Big Thunder Barbecue. Barbecue offerings including chicken and beef from a buffeteria line. Some visitors consider this the best fast eatery in the park. The very nice setting in the shade of large trees is like a campsite. Prices range from about $6 for a barbecue chicken or beef sandwich, and $9 to $10 for platters of beef or pork ribs or chicken with beans, coleslaw, and biscuit.

Casa Mexicana. Buffeteria tacos, enchiladas, and more.

River Belle Terrace. An attractive setting near the Swiss Family Tree House and Pirates of the Caribbean. Complete breakfasts of scrambled eggs, bacon or sausage, and potatoes for about $6; Mickey Mouse pancakes with bacon or sausage for about $4.55. Luncheon fare, priced from about $4 to $7, includes Huck Finn's chicken meal, Mississippi vegetable stew, the Showboat ham sandwich, and Aunt Polly's turkey sandwich. Children's hot dog or chicken meals are offered for $2.99.

Stage Door Café. Burgers, hot dogs, and chicken-breast sandwiches.

Mickey's Toontown

Daisy's Diner. Counter snacks.

Pluto's Dog House. Hot dogs and snacks.

Tomorrowland

Lunching Pad. Hot dogs and snacks.

Tomorrowland Terrace. Burgers, fried chicken, salads, and more.

Disneyland Hotel

There's a whole other piece of Disneyland across West Street from the park: the 60-acre Disneyland Hotel. It includes 11 restaurants and lounges, nightly entertainment, amusements for the children, and 1,131 rooms and suites.

The entire area is connected to Disneyland by the monorail, making it very convenient for guests to commute to the fun every day. The monorail also offers the opportunity for Disneyland guests to zip out of the park for lunch or dinner and a change of pace. (Be sure to have your hand stamped and hold onto your admission ticket to gain readmittance to the park.)

Room rates start at about $150 per night and go up to about $230; special package rates available from travel agents or Disney Travel can reduce the prices considerably.

Restaurants at Disneyland Hotel

The hotel offers a range of eateries from goofy to elegant.

Goofy's Kitchen offers a breakfast buffet from 7 to 11:30 A.M. daily, plus lunch and dinner coffee-shop fare. **The Monorail Cafe** is also an early-morning place, with breakfast from 6:30 A.M., plus quick lunch and dinner items.

Granville's Steak House is the fanciest place at the hotel, with specialties in steaks, chops, and lobster; dinner is served from 6 to 10 P.M. **The Shipyard Inn** offers seafood dinners from 5 to 10 P.M. overlooking the hotel's marina. **Cafe Villa Verde** has Italian specialties with indoor or boardwalk seating, with lunch from 11:30 A.M. to 2:30 P.M. and dinner served from 5 to 10 P.M. **The California Wine Cellar** offers California wines and champagnes and more than 20 international beers for late-night entertaining.

Neon Cactus is pretty much like it sounds, a country-music lounge offering "cowboy karaoke" and other entertainment.

Entertainment at the Disneyland Hotel

Fantasy Waters. A mini version of Fantasmic!, presented each night at 9 and 10 P.M. at a small amphitheater in the back corner of the hotel grounds. Fountains are choreographed to music, with high-tech lighting effects and Disney toons.

Koi Fish. Two large ponds of overgrown goldfish with walkways allowing you to get up close; check the schedule for the daily feedings, usually in the morning and afternoon.

Pedal Boats. Rent a foot-powered boat in season for a leisurely tour of the marina.

Queen's Berth. Coin-operated remote-control boats. You sail your boats in and around a model of the *Queen Mary* and other structures, including a house on fire, and through tunnels.

Off-Road Raceway. Remote-control race cars on an upper-deck raceway.

Shopping at Disneyland

You can get just about anything you want in a store at Disneyland . . . at a price, of course.

You will see more Mickeys, Minnies, Goofys, and other Disney characters on shirts, hats, jackets, mugs, and other merchandise than anywhere else. Nearly all of Main Street is a retail store, and there are dozens of other shops in nearly every corner of the park; there is also a mall full of shops at the nearby Disneyland Hotel.

The shops within the park can become quite crowded in the afternoon; the best time to shop is usually in the morning or late in the day.

You don't have to carry around your purchases all day. Most of the stores in the park offer a package pickup service; you'll be given a claim stub and your purchases will be delivered to a package pickup location between the Disneyland Showcase and the Mad Hatter shops on Main Street, near the exit to the park. Allow at least one hour for the packages to be delivered to the pickup location.

Guests at the Disneyland Hotel can arrange to have packages delivered directly to their rooms.

You can also arrange to have your purchases shipped directly to your home, or as a gift to others.

There is also a huge gift shop at the Disneyland Hotel which is usually a lot less crowded than the gift shops at the park.

DISNEYLAND

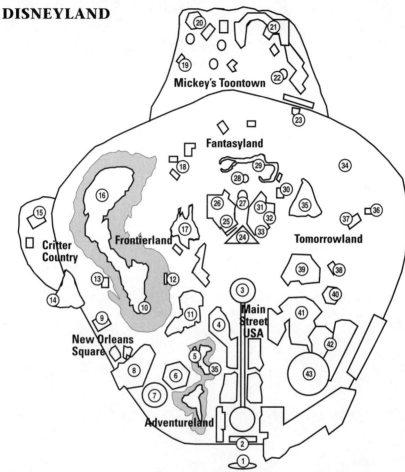

Mickey's Toontown

Fantasyland

Frontierland

Critter Country

Tomorrowland

Main Street USA

New Orleans Square

Adventureland

① Tickets	⑯ Tom Sawyer Island	㉛ Mr. Toad
② Main	⑰ Big Thunder Mountain	㉜ Alice
③ Central Plaza	⑱ Big Thunder Ranch	㉝ Peter Pan
④ Tiki Room	⑲ Gadget's Go Coaster	㉞ Tomorrowland Utopia
⑤ Jungle Cruise	⑳ Mickey's House	㉟ Matterhorn
⑥ Indiana Jones	㉑ Roger Rabit's Car Toon Spin	㊱ Submarine Voyage
⑦ Swiss Tree	㉒ Jolly Trolley	㊲ Monorail Station
⑧ Pirates of the Caribbean	㉓ It's A Small World	㊳ PeopleMover
⑨ Haunted	㉔ Sleeping Beauty Castle	㊴ Circle-Vision
⑩ Fantasmic!	㉕ Snow White	㊵ Rocket Jets
⑪ Golden Horseshoe	㉖ Pinocchio	㊶ Star Tours
⑫ Mark Twain Riverboat	㉗ Carousel	㊷ Magic Eye Theatre
⑬ Rafts to Island	㉘ Dumbo	㊸ Space Mountain
⑭ Splash Mountain	㉙ Storybook Land	
⑮ Critter Bear Playhouse	㉚ Tea Cups	

Chapter 4
Disneyana

You're not paranoid; they *are* chasing after you. The Walt Disney Company is on a tremendous roll in recent years, expanding its operations in California, Florida, Paris, Tokyo, and most every place in between.

Here's a sampling of some other corners of the world of Disney.

Who's Counting?

According to *Amusement Business* magazine, Disney owned the top four spots among American amusement and theme parks in 1995. For the first time in many years, though, Disneyland in California edged ahead of the Magic Kingdom in Florida mostly on the strength of the fabulously successful Indiana Jones ride in Anaheim.

The magazine estimated that Disneyland drew about 14.1 million visitors in 1995, up 38 percent from the year before. The Magic Kingdom drew about 12.9 million, a 15 percent boost. In third place was Epcot, and the fourth spot went to Disney-MGM. Universal Studios Florida owned fifth place.

Overall, Disney parks accounted for about 30 percent of all theme park visitors in the United States.

Of all the Disney parks around the world, though, Disneyland Tokyo holds the number one position for attendance, the magazine says.

Pacific's El Capitan Theater

A gem of a moviehouse jointly operated by the Walt Disney Co. and Pacific Theaters, the El Capitan specializes in Disney and Touchstone films, sometimes premiering movies a few weeks before general release.

The El Capitan was built in the 1930s for stage and opera performances. When it was converted for use for movies in the 1940s, the opera boxes were removed, but in 1991 the boxes were returned and the spectacular gold-leaf ceiling was restored. The screen lies behind no less than three curtains which open one after another to musical fanfare. Thoroughly modern touches include a THX sound system.

For special events, including premieres and some retrospective shows, the films are accompanied by short stage shows featuring singing ushers, dancers, and Disney characters.

The El Capitan is on Hollywood Boulevard, across the street from Mann's Chinese Theater. For information on prices and current engagements, call (213) 467-7674; advance tickets can be reserved by credit card by calling (213) 777-3456.

Coming Soon: Disney's Animal Kingdom

It all started with a mouse, so it seems perfectly logical that Disney should extend its Walt Disney World empire in Florida to include its own fanciful animal park.

According to the Imagineers, Disney's Animal Kingdom will celebrate all animals that ever or never existed. It is scheduled to open in the spring of 1998 with a combination of thrill rides, exotic landscapes, and close encounters with wild animals—real and imagined.

Construction was due to begin in September of 1996 on 500 acres on the western edge of Walt Disney World.

Centerpiece of the park will be the giant Tree of Life, 14 stories tall—about the height of Spaceship Earth at Epcot. It will be hand-carved by Disney artists with a tapestry of animal forms representing the diversity of animal life on Earth.

Guests will visit three major sections of the park: the real, the mythical, and the extinct.

The "real" world will include herds of live animals, including giraffes, zebras, lions, hippos, and elephants; there will be links to Disney stories, of course. Most of the animals will be born in zoological parks or rescued from endangered habitats, according to the company.

The "mythical" world is home to unicorns, dragons, and other magical creatures from legends, fairy tales, and storybooks.

The world of the extinct animals, of course, will use Disney's Audio-Animatronics to bring back the giant dinosaurs of the Cretaceous era for a thrill ride. (The Cretaceous era follows the Jurassic era in geological dating; across town, Universal Studios Florida will introduce its Jurassic Park theme area as part of its massive Universal's Islands of Adventure expansion due to open in 1999.)

Sports Shorts

Not content to own only the dreams of the youngsters, Disney has been increasingly moving into the world of adult fantasies. No, not sex: sports. Disney was negotiating to assume majority ownership of the California Angels major league baseball team in 1996, adding it to its Mighty Ducks hockey franchise in Anaheim, each located a deep fly ball away from Disneyland itself.

In Florida, Disney's massive sports complex is well underway, including the Spring Training home of the Atlanta Braves, an Indy Car racetrack, track and field facilities, and much more. A bid for an upcoming Summer Olympics is rumored.

Disneyland Paris

It's Disney's newest theme park, yet it feels like an old favorite. It's in a country where they don't speak English, yet everyone understands each other. Its financial problems have been front-page news around the world, yet it can offer some great bargains for the careful traveler. Disney renegotiated the financing package in 1994, which seems to have saved the park for the foreseeable future. In that same year it sold about 25 percent of ownership of the park to Saudi Prince Al-Waleed bin-Talal al-Saud; Disney retains 40 percent ownership.

Mouse mouths. Walt Disney himself performed the voices of Mickey and Minnie in the earliest cartoons, including *Steamboat Willie,* which was the first Mickey Mouse cartoon with sound—but not the first movie starring the rascally rodent. That honor went to *Plane Crazy.* The current voice of the Mickster is Wayne Allwine, the third mouse mouthpiece.

I visited Disneyland Paris (originally called Euro Disneyland) in Marne-la-Vallée near Paris in the spring of 1994; my wife and I were able to convince our preteen son and daughter to come to Europe for a week in London and a week in Paris with the promise of two days at Disneyland Paris as a reward for good behavior. (As it turned out, the kids absolutely loved London with its museums and theaters and were intrigued by incredible sights such as the Cathedral of Notre Dame in Paris, the palace of Versailles, and the ancient city of Provins, all within an hour of Marne-la-Vallée. Oh, and they liked Disneyland Paris real well, too.)

The cost of the trip in off-season (similar to Walt Disney World, with lowest prices in winter and parts of the fall and spring) was just slightly more than a trip to Orlando.

Disneyland Paris is not a big draw for Americans, with only a small percent of visitors from this country. However, enough visitors from the United Kingdom and other non-French-speaking nations, plus the international allure of Disney, makes it possible to get around the park without speaking French. The staff at the hotels within the park is multilingual, and guidebooks and signs are available in English.

If you do speak French, though, it's a bit of fun to see Disney frenchified: the centerpiece of the park is *Le Château de la Belle au Bois Dormant* (Sleeping Beauty's Castle); favorite rides in Fantasyland include *Blanche-Neige et les Sept Nains* (Snow White and the Seven Dwarfs).

There are some significant differences at the park; European tastes call for less subtle entertainment, sometimes much more explicit than at the American parks.

Beneath the castle is *La Tanière du Dragon* (The Dragon's Lair), with a rather scary, mechanical creature who comes to life every few minutes. *Indiana Jones et le Temple du Péril* in Adventureland is Disney's first real roller coaster, a wild ride through an archaeological dig among the ancient ruins of the Lost City. Phantom Manor in Frontierland is scarier than its cousins

Disney on ice. Walt Disney was pageantry chairman for the VIII Winter Olympic Games at Squaw Valley in 1960. Among his jobs were the opening and closing ceremonies and creation of the snow and ice statues that lined the Avenue of the Athletes in the Olympic Village.

in Florida and California. And Big Thunder Mountain is faster and wilder, disappearing into a tunnel under the river at one point.

But there are also some very refined, European touches in the park. We were enthralled by *Le Visionarium*, a Cinematronic 360-degree theater presenting a beautifully produced film about French science fiction author Jules Verne, in a spectacular time-travel adventure that soars through Europe. A version of that film opened as *From Time to Time* at the Transportarium in Walt Disney World's Tomorrowland in 1995.

It was also a hoot to see the familiar Star Tours, with a French-speaking R2D2 and C3PO.

Space Mountain: De la Terre à la Lune (From the earth to the moon) blasts visitors to the top through the barrel of a cannon mounted on top of the building; the cars descend through the tracks within the building. The French ride applies a Jules Verne theme and includes some spirals and twists and turns that are well beyond anything at an American Disney park.

Just outside the gates to the park is Festival Disney, a little bit of home in a cross between Pleasure Island at Walt Disney World, Church Street Station in Orlando, and CityWalk at Universal Studios in Hollywood. Under a starfield made up of tiny lights on wires, you'll find a collection of restaurants (Annette's Diner, Key West Seafood, and Los Angeles Bar & Grill among them), nightclubs, bars (Billy Bob's Country Western Saloon, Hurricanes, Rock 'n' Roll America, and The Sports Bar), and boutiques, all with an American theme.

Absolutely not to be missed is Buffalo Bill's Wild West Show, one of the best dinner theaters I have ever seen. The show is loosely based on an actual touring company brought to France by Buffalo Bill Cody. Four ranches compete in competitions with herds of buffalo, longhorn steer, and dozens of cowboys on horseback. Included is an Old West meal featuring chili, barbecued chicken and beef, and dessert. The show is located next to Festival Disney, and there are two performances per night at busy times.

We chose to make Disneyland Paris our base, venturing north to Paris and Versailles and southwest to Provins; you could also stay in Paris and commute down to the park quite easily. We were able to purchase off-season airfare of about $400 and a hotel room within the park for a bargain basement price of about $45 per night. Car rentals are slightly more expensive in Europe than in America; you can save money by renting a vehicle with standard transmission.

Tickets to Disneyland Paris are priced slightly higher than those at the American parks, but there are also more frequent special promotions that in the past have included free admission for children and discounted tickets for adults. Some of the restaurants offer free "early bird" meals for children.

Disneyland Paris is located about 20 miles east of Paris in Marne-la-Vallée; direct shuttle bus service is available from Orly or Charles de Gaulle airports in Paris. You can drive from Paris on the A4 motorway or take the new high-speed railway line that leads to a station directly at the entrance gate to the park.

Disney in Tokyo

Hai, Mickey-san. If ever proof was required of the global impact of American popular culture, it came with the opening of Tokyo Disneyland in 1983. The park, which is owned by a Japanese company under license to Disney, is located six miles outside of Tokyo. It includes familiar Disney attractions as well as new shows such as Pinocchio's Daring Journey, the Eternal Seas, and Meet the World.

Suspended animation. A recurring rumor about dear old Walt Disney is that he chose to be cryogenically frozen when he died of lung cancer in 1966, in hopes of a defrost in another day and age. Actually, according to the company, he went to the other extreme and was cremated before burial at the famous Forest Lawn Memorial Park in California.

Instead of Main Street, U.S.A., you'll find World Bazaar as the gateway to Adventureland, Fantasyland, Tomorrowland, and Westernland. Adventureland attractions include the Jungle Cruise, Enchanted Tiki Room, and Pirates of the Caribbean. In Westernland you'll find the Mark Twain Riverboat, Tom Sawyer Island, the Golden Horseshoe Revue, and Country Bear Jamboree, among other lures.

Fantasyland includes the Pinocchio ride, plus It's a Small World, Haunted Mansion, Snow White's Adventure, and the Mickey Mouse Revue. There are also venerable favorites like Dumbo, the Flying Elephant and Cinderella's Golden Carrousel.

Tomorrowland includes yet another Space Mountain as well as Meet the World, an attraction based on Japanese history and the country's influence on the rest of the world.

UNIVERSAL STUDIOS

1. Ticket Booths
2. Universal CityWalk
3. Waterworld
4. The Flintstone's Show
5. Back to the Future
6. Beetlejuice's Graveyard Revue
7. Animal Actors Stage
8. The Wild Wild Wild West Stunt Show
9. Escalator to Back Lot Tram Tour
10. Backlot
11. Escalator to Studio Center
12. E.T. Adventure
13. AT&T at the Movies
14. The World of Cinemagic
15. Backdraft
16. Sound Stages (off limits)
17. Lucy: A Tribute
18. Universal Hilton Hotel
19. Universal Sheraton Hotel
20. Universal Amphitheatre
21. Jurassic Park—The Ride

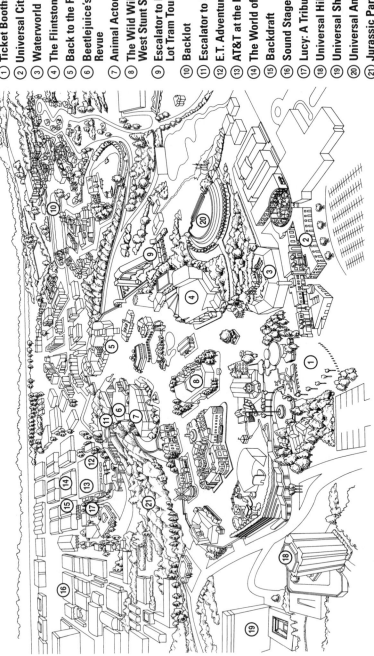

III
Universal Studios Hollywood and Universal CityWalk

Chapter 5
Universal Studios Hollywood

Universal Studios is a place of great history in the relatively short life of the motion picture industry. Its films and television shows have gone back in time to *Jurassic Park* and Bedrock, home of the Flintstones; to ancient Rome and Greece for *Spartacus* and Mel Brooks in a toga; to the classic antiwar theme of *All Quiet on the Western Front* and the more comedic *McHale's Navy*; to the chilling horror of *Psycho* and the technological terror of *Backdraft*; and way into the future and then back again in *Back to the Future*.

Each of these films and many more are celebrated at Universal Studios Hollywood, with exhibits, rides, stage shows, and guided tours.

There are four main areas at the theme park; plan on a full day to see them all.

In mid-1996, Universal celebrated its long history with a new entrance to the park that evokes the great movie palaces and themes of the past and leads into the upper-level Entertainment Center that is home to the stage shows including "Waterworld" and most of the park's eateries as well as the astounding Back to the Future . . . The Ride. Off to the right and down a long escalator is the loading area for the Back Lot Tram Tour. At the back, left corner is the first of a series of four long escalators that take you down to the Studio Center for more rides including the spectacular new Jurassic Park—The Ride.

Finally, there is the Universal CityWalk, a collection of unusual shops, clubs, and restaurants well worth a visit for lunch, dinner, or late-night entertainment. You don't even need an admission ticket to visit there.

A Universal History

Universal Studios was established in 1912 with the founding of the Universal Film Manufacturing Company, started at the time of the nickelodeon in a cluster of tiny offices in New York. Under the leadership of Carl Laemmle, the company became a major force in the industry.

When Laemmle decided to consolidate production facilities from both coasts to one site, he purchased a 130-acre chicken ranch in North Hollywood and construction of what was to become Universal City began in 1914.

Because the property in Cahuenga Pass was far removed from what passed for the modern conveniences of Los Angeles at the time, the company installed its own power, water, and other facilities.

At the grand opening on March 15, 1915, Thomas Edison was on hand to officially start the studio's electrical equipment, and showman Buffalo Bill Cody was an honored guest at the proceedings. Some 10,000 sightseers were also on hand to view the creation of the motion picture industry on the West Coast, presaging Universal's current role as a tourist magnet.

Universal quickly became the world's busiest motion picture studio, with some of its early filmmakers including the legendary John Ford, Eric von Stroheim, and Irving Thalberg.

A burst of expansion took place during World War II; government regulations prohibited excess profits during wartime, so the company poured its cash into two new soundstages and other construction.

In 1946, Universal merged with International Pictures. In the years that

Universal Studios Hollywood
©1995 Universal City Studios, Inc.

followed, the studio was home to director Alfred Hitchcock; later would come Steven Spielberg and George Lucas.

The Music Corporation of America (MCA) purchased the Universal studio facilities and land in 1959 and Universal Pictures itself in 1962. Over the next two decades, MCA opened the Universal Studios Hollywood theme park, 14 new soundstages, the Universal Amphitheatre, and many other facilities including office buildings, hotels, and restaurants.

Universal Studios Hollywood, Today

Since public tours were established at Universal Studios Hollywood in 1964, more than 80 million guests have come to the former chicken farm as paying guests. Today, more than five million visitors come to Universal Studios Hollywood each year.

Universal Studios Hollywood is located in Universal City between Hollywood and the San Fernando Valley, just off the Hollywood Freeway (Interstate 101), at either the Universal Center Drive or Lankershim Boulevard exits.

Tickets. Ticket prices, which include tax, were in effect in 1996 and are subject to change. *Discount coupon in this book.*
Adults: $34
Seniors (60 and above): $29
Children (3 to 11): $26
Two-day pass, adults: $48
Two-day pass, children: $37
Season pass, adults: $60
Season pass, seniors: $49
Season pass, children: $49
Parking: $6 for cars, **$7** for RVs

The park is open daily except for Thanksgiving and Christmas. Operating hours in the summer are generally 8 A.M. to 11 P.M., and for the rest of the year from 9 A.M. to 7 P.M.

Celebrity Annual Pass holders receive a number of special privileges. In addition to unlimited visits to the park for a year and free parking in Universal City, they are also entitled to 15 percent discounts on ticket purchases for up to six guests per visit, 10 percent off selected merchandise, 10 percent discount at some park and area restaurants, and "Red Carpet" tram boarding privileges, which may be especially valuable on crowded days.

The annual pass also offers discounts at the Sheraton Universal Hotel and the Universal City Hilton and Towers. Other discounts include reduced prices at several other major California attractions.

Should you buy an annual pass? No, if you plan on making only a one-day visit to Universal Studios Hollywood and do not expect to return within a one-year period. But if you expect to visit the park twice in one vacation, or if you plan to come back within a year's time, consider the advantages of the discounts and the "Red Carpet" privileges. There are too many combinations of numbers of visits and numbers of visitors to lay them out here, but a few minutes with a piece of paper will tell you whether it makes sense to buy an annual pass for yourself and everyone in your family. Another possible plan is to buy an annual pass for yourself and then treat the members of your party to a 15 percent discount.

MUST-SEES

Jurassic Park—
The Ride

Back Lot Tram Tour
(includes King
Kong and
Earthquake)

Back to the Future
. . . The Ride

The Flintstones
Show

Waterworld—
A Live Sea War
Spectacular

The Wild Wild Wild
West Stunt Show

Beetlejuice's
Graveyard Revue

Backdraft

E.T. Adventure

The World
of Cinemagic

Power Trip #1:
The Jurassic Dash

The new **Jurassic Park—The Ride** attraction will be the biggest magnet at Universal Studios for several years, and you can expect long lines there for most of the day. One strategy to avoid standing around and waiting for the chance to get up close and personal with an angry dinosaur clone is to arrive early—at least 30 minutes before the gates officially open, and make a beeline through the Entertainment Center and immediately head down the four sets of escalators to Studio Center. Go directly to Jurassic Park.

When you get out of dino-land, stay on the lower level and visit **E.T. Adventure**, **Backdraft**, and The **World of Cinemagic**. Then head up the escalator and visit **Back to the Future**.

You might want to grab an early lunch and then descend the other side of the hill to the **Back Lot Tram Tour**.

In early afternoon, consult the daily schedule and visit the shows including **Waterworld**, **Beetlejuice's Graveyard Revue**, **The Flintstones Show**, and **The Wild Wild Wild West Stunt Show**. By early evening you should be able to revisit the attraction of your choice.

Power Trip #2:
The Contrarian
Approach

The theory behind this schedule is that everyone else will try Power Trip #1. You still should attempt to arrive early at the park, but this time head for your second-favorite goal—anything other than Jurassic Park. Here's one schedule: Go first to the Entertainment Center and ride **Back to the Future . . . The Ride**. Then stumble your way to the escalator down to Studio Center and visit **E.T. Adventure**, **Backdraft**, and **The World of Cinemagic**.

Keep an eye on the waiting line for Jurassic Park; if it ever drops below a 30-minute wait you should seize the moment. (Estimated waiting times are posted near major attractions.)

By now, most of the early visitors will have taken the tram tour and will be heading your way. Grab an early lunch, and then go against the flow, back up the escalator to the Entertainment Center and then down the other side of the hill to the **Back Lot Tram Tour**.

In early afternoon, consult the daily schedule and visit the shows including **Beetlejuice's Graveyard Revue**, **The Flintstones Show**, and **The Wild Wild Wild West Stunt Show**.

By early evening the lines at **Jurassic Park— The Ride** should be manageable, and this may be your best chance to go back to the past.

〔WOW〕 **Back Lot Tram Tour**

Front Lot Soundstages
Colonial Street
Industrial Street
Old Mexico
Old West
Prop Storage
Psycho House
Spartacus Square
Little Europe
Earthquake
Courthouse Square
King Kong
New York Street
Collapsing Bridge
Vehicles
Bedrock and Jurassic Park
Flash Flood
Jaws
Wilderness/Avalanche

When it rains . . . you will get wet. Most of Universal Studios Hollywood is outdoors. The Back Lot Tram is exposed to the elements, and most of the shows are also uncovered.

Flimsy plastic rain jackets appear magically at shops, priced at $6.95; umbrellas are priced at $16.95. If the skies are at all threatening, I'd suggest you make a stop at a discount store outside of the park and pick up parkas or umbrellas to bring with you.

Some of the shows may be canceled because of rain.

Sit down and relax for a guided motorized tour through a large part of the famed back lot of Universal Studios, a place where many of the most celebrated movies and television shows of all time have been made.

Universal Studios Hollywood is unusual among theme parks in that the audience is delivered by chauffeured tram to the attractions for about half of its exhibits. There's just a single line to wait in; once you are loaded onto the large tram you'll be driven to and through sets and props for movies and TV shows including *Back to the Future*, "Murder, She Wrote," *Psycho*, *Jurassic Park*, and much more. And you'll go right into exciting re-creations of thrillers such as *Earthquake* and *Jaws*.

The loading queue for the tram is located down the hill at the back of the main Entertainment Center level of the park. Lines are shortest when the park first opens, and usually again in early afternoon; the last tram departs about two hours before the park closes. The length of each tour can vary depending on how busy the park is and shooting schedules that may affect parts of the back lot, but is generally about 60 to 90 minutes.

When you load onto the tram, try to avoid sitting too far forward, or you will end up breathing a fair amount of diesel fumes on your journey. Despite what the guide might say, don't worry about a "wet" or "dry" side of the tram; not much water makes its way into the tram on the tour. For the record, the right side (facing forward) of the tram is closest to the cascading waters in the *Earthquake* set, and the left side is nearest the flash flood in the back lot.

Cameras are welcome throughout the tour; there are no rest room stops, and there is no way to get off the tram short of an emergency.

The order of the tour as presented here may be different when you visit the park because of television or movie production schedules, and sometimes entire sections have to be skipped because the cameras are rolling.

Front Lot Soundstages

In 1996, the **Back Lot Tram Tour** added a detour into the Front Lot for the first time. If you're lucky you may see a television or movie star strolling by, or perhaps grab a quick glimpse inside the open door of one of the large soundstages there; otherwise, you're going to see a lot of blank walls.

Universal's facilities are in almost continuous use for television series; in recent years the heavy hitters produced here have included "Murder, She Wrote" and "Coach."

Stage 27 housed Houston Mission Control for *Apollo 13* and later was used for a number of scenes in the *Sergeant Bilko* remake. Stage 28 holds the historic Paris Opera House set used in the classic *Phantom of the Opera* and many other films since. The Sultan of Strangeness Michael Jackson (and sister Janet Jackson) installed a flying saucer in Stage 24 for the "Scream" music video.

Colonial Street

Where else but in Hollywood could you expect to find a neighborhood that includes the homes of Beaver Cleaver, Herman Munster, Jessica Fletcher, the Hardy Boys, Elvis Presley, Casper, and many more? And where else will you find The Best Little Whorehouse in Texas at the end of the street?

The official address is Colonial Street, and your tour guide will point out such sites as Frank and Joe Hardy's house from the Hardy Boys TV mysteries of the 1970s. Next-door to the Hardys is the home occupied by James Garner and Doris Day in *The Thrill of It All*. Just a bit farther down the road is an old Colonial mansion that among other roles served as the sanitarium in James Stewart's beloved *Harvey* film.

At 1313 Mockingbird Lane is the home of the Munsters, nearby to one of Faber College's sorority houses from *Animal House*.

Then we're on to a portion of the town of Cabot Cove, made famous in the "Murder, She Wrote" television series, one of Universal's most valuable ongoing properties. The brick building on the street has served as both the Cabot Cove Savings Bank and the Cabot Cove Town Hall; back in the sixties it was where the Beaver went to school in "Leave It to Beaver."

Many of the homes on Colonial Street were used in the film, *The Burbs*, starring Tom Hanks and Carrie Fisher. And then the same street became Memphis, Tennessee, for an episode of "Quantum Leap" in which Sam leaps into the body of the King himself, Elvis Presley. Yet another remake made it one of the homes of Casper the Friendly Ghost.

The Texas whorehouse was created within Stage 12 and the movie was filmed there; the set was later moved to its outdoor location.

Industrial Street

Many of the homes in this area are actual residences that were purchased for as little as $1 each and moved to the back lot to be used in the classic film, *To Kill a Mockingbird* starring Gregory Peck and a then-unknown actor named Robert Duvall.

Off to the side you'll catch a glimpse of the small body of water that stands in for Cabot Cove; the Universal megahit "Murder, She Wrote" has also filmed some scenes on Industrial Street as well as in Old Mexico.

Old Mexico

In addition to standing in for some scenes in "Murder, She Wrote," this area has been used for many old films and contemporary television shows. It was home of many scenes in the comedy *Three Amigos* with Steve Martin, Martin Short, and Chevy Chase.

Old West

Across the border from Mexico is the oldest section of the Universal Studios back lot, a filmmaker's recreation of the Old West, also known as Six Points, Texas. Many of the buildings which appear to be made of brick or stone are actually constructed of wood, chicken wire, and modern products such as foam rubber or fiberglass.

Note that some of the doors seem out of scale. Small doors were used to make small actors appear bigger and more threatening than they really were; large doors served to shrink tall cowboys and cowgirls down to size for the camera.

Old West was the home of stars including John Wayne, Tom Mix, Hoot Gibson, Audie Murphy, Ken Maynard, and others. Among the television series made there was "Wagon Train." More recently, it was used in the United Artists' film, *Wild Bill*.

At its height, there could be six films underway on the six streets at the same time; since the movies were silent, all the directors had to worry about was the possibility of an actor making a wrong turn from one film to another.

Old West's basic setup includes a hotel, bar, bank, and sheriff's office. In other words, a bad guy could stroll into town, get a drink, spend the night, rob the bank, and end up in jail.

Prop Storage

A prop on a movie set is just about anything that isn't nailed down. Some are small and some are huge; some are ordinary and some are unlike anything else.

More than a million of the studio's props are kept in the property warehouse at the back corner of the back lot, but many of the larger pieces are scattered outdoors.

Along the course of the tram tour you'll pass by bits and pieces of the past and future from *Back to the Future*, fossils and props from *Jurassic Park*, and various vehicles from dozens of familiar movies.

In the middle of the props area is a tiny lake—more of a pond, really. This body of water served as the entire Pacific Ocean every week in the popular TV series "McHale's Navy."

The pond was also used for some of the shooting in the 1977 film *Midway*. Scale models of battleships and cruisers made war on the pond; in fact, some of the vessels were painted in Allied colors on one side and Japanese colors on the other so that they could serve double duty in the war.

After you exit Sound Stage 50 later on in the tour you'll have another view of the pond. It was also used as the home of *The Creature from the Black Lagoon* in 1954.

You will also see a large metal tank that has been used in many underwater scenes, including the original *Jaws*. The actors and props are placed within the tank while cameras and crew are outside, looking in through windows.

Changing times and places, you may see some of the old wagons used in "Wagon Train" and "The Virginian." Nearby on one of my trips was a gigantic football helmet and a huge shopping cart, both from the film *The Incredible Shrinking Woman* with Lily Tomlin. Another time the tram caught a glimpse of a chariot from *The Ten Commandments*.

Psycho House

Is there any house more famous than Mrs. Bates' pleasant Victorian up on the hill over the Bates Motel?

You'll approach the house alongside the small swamp used by Norman Bates (Anthony Perkins) to bury the car of Marion Crane (Janet Leigh) in the 1960 Alfred Hitchcock classic, *Psycho*. Later on in the tour you'll approach Psycho House a bit closer.

The house was originally built to ¾ scale, which helped make Anthony Perkins look taller and more menacing as he posed in the foreground. When the house itself was pictured, it was always shot from below to look larger.

The house is a shell with a complete outside but nothing within except for the beams that help keep it standing; well, okay, some wag did stick a dummy that looks like Norman's mom in the second floor window. It is a dummy, right? Indoor scenes were all shot on a soundstage.

Nearby is the Bates Motel, more or less as it was created for the original film. The archway entrance in front did not appear in any of the *Psycho* films but was added in 1986 for a television movie of the week called "Bates Motel."

Spartacus Square

Parts of the classic film *Spartacus* were filmed in the section that is named in its honor; the same section was again used as ancient Rome in the classic Mel Brooks spoof, *History of the World, Part I*.

Little Europe

This section of old buildings stood in for Greece in Brooks' *History of the World*. More recently, it was Pamplona, Spain, for the opening sequence of *City Slickers*.

When Brenda and Donna left "Beverly Hills 90210" to go to France, they actually went just across town to Little Europe. Other television shows that have used this area include "Sea Quest DSV" and, of course, the ubiquitous "Murder, She Wrote." The quirky television series "Moonlighting" filmed its takeoff of *The Taming of the Shrew* here.

Way back, Little Europe was home of the classic antiwar film, *All Quiet on the Western Front*.

Real film history can be glimpsed in the Court of Miracles, built in 1919 for the film *The Miracle Man* starring Lon Chaney. But it is most famous for the monster movie classics that followed, including Chaney again in 1923's *The Hunchback of Notre Dame* and again in 1925 for *The Phantom of the Opera*. In 1930, Bela Lugosi was Dracula here; later classics included *Frankenstein*, *The Bride of Frankenstein*, *The Son of Frankenstein*, *Abbott and Costello Meet Frankenstein*, *The Wolf Man*, *The Mummy*, and *The Invisible Man*.

Earthquake

Quiet, now: you've got a green light to drive right into Sound Stage 50, a real working soundstage. Well, it's sort of a real stage (and still in occasional use for special projects), but it's mostly given over to a spectacular re-creation of a scene from the 1974 disaster epic, *Earthquake*.

Bigger . . . (and certainly better) than the real thing, Universal's Earthquake unleashes an 8.3 temblor beneath your feet. The earth falls out from under tramloads of visitors, trapping them in an underground subway station with sparking wires, out-of-control trains, and even a fuel truck that crashes through the ceiling and onto the tracks. Just to cap it all, water pipes let loose and trigger a 15-foot-tall wall of water in a 60,000-gallon flood.

Every detail of the simulation was based on re-creation of real earthquakes. The soundstage was built to withstand 600,000 pounds of force, more than 200 times a day, with concrete pilings sunk 25 feet into the ground below the tram. The ceiling slab that falls into the subway station weighs 11,000 pounds.

The simulated earthquake is the equivalent of an 8.3 event on the Richter scale, which is the same level as the huge temblor that destroyed San Francisco in 1906. By comparison, the 1971 Sylmar quake measured 6.6, and the 1985 Mexico City disaster was an 8.1 event.

The simulation lasts for about two-and-a-half minutes. After your tram exits the soundstage, the entire set resets in 15 seconds.

If it makes you feel better, engineers say the soundstage is built to withstand a genuine 8.3 quake, making it one of the safest places in the world to be during a real earthquake.

The Earthquake set was used for a scene in *Beverly Hills Cop 3*, which took place in a fictional amusement park.

Just outside the Earthquake set is Sound Stage 747, which includes full-size mock-ups of airplane interiors used regularly as sets in films and television shows.

Courthouse Square

The year is 1955. The date is November 5. And the time is 10:03 P.M. Down this road—with the aid of a great deal of movie magic—Marty McFly drove Doc Brown's time-traveling DeLorean at precisely 88 miles per hour hoping to catch the lightning bolt just in time to go back to 1985.

You'll see the Hill Valley courthouse more or less as it appeared in the film *Back to the Future* and its sequel, *Back to the Future 2*. It has also been used in many other films over the years.

King Kong

One of the most realistic sets at Universal Studios Hollywood can be found within a soundstage just past the Courthouse Square. It's a re-creation of lower Manhattan . . . and it smells suspiciously like bananas.

Your tram driver will take passengers directly into an attraction that celebrates the spectacular 1976 version of the classic film. The remake starred Jeff Bridges, Charles Grodin, and an unknown actress by the name of Jessica Lange, who went on to be an Academy Award winner.

King Kong rises out of the East River, towers over the Brooklyn Bridge, rips down power lines, attacks a hovering news helicopter, and then even tries to throw Universal's trams into the river as they move across the bridge.

Kong comes within a few feet of the tram—so close you'll be able to smell the bananas on his breath.

Computers control 29 facial movements, from nodding his head to curling his lip to showing his vicious artificial teeth. (Movements are controlled mostly by pneumatic air pipes.)

The $6.5 million leading man really throws his weight around. He's seven tons of fur, steel, and computers standing 30 feet high.

New York Street

Welcome to an all-purpose downtown, home of scenes from "Columbo," "McCloud," "McMillan and Wife," "Kojak," "Ironside," "The Rockford Files," "The Streets of San Francisco," "The Mod Squad," "Baretta," "The Night Stalker," and many more.

In 1969, these streets were walked by Elvis himself for his final film role, in *A Change of Habit*, also starring Mary Tyler Moore. Four years later, New York Street became Chicago in the Academy Award-winning film *The Sting*, starring Robert Redford and Paul Newman.

In 1977, New York Street was used to film scenes from the Warner Bros. classic movie *Dirty Harry*, starring Clint Eastwood. A few years later, it was turned into modern-day Chicago for *The Blues Brothers*, which starred John Belushi and Dan Aykroyd. It became London for *Wayne's World 2*, and then transformed back to 1930s New York in many scenes from *The Shadow* starring Alec Baldwin.

Nearly all of New York was destroyed in a fire in 1991, but the re-creation of the Big Apple was re-created again.

Collapsing Bridge

A bridge somewhat like this one was built in 1915 for a silent film. More recently, it has been used in television shows including "The Six Million Dollar Man" and "Quantum Leap."

In the "Bionic Woman" series, star Lindsay Wagner was shown jumping up from the water to the bridge. Actually, a stuntwoman jumped backward from the bridge to the water and the film was reversed. If you ever see the scene, note the filmmakers' goof: her hair was not tied down and defies the law of gravity as she seems to fly upward.

These days the bridge has been fixed up so that it falls down . . . as the tram passes over the top. Don't worry, though: most passengers survive to make it to the souvenir shops.

Vehicles

The "boneyard" of the back lot includes dozens of vehicles from movies and television shows. You may spot one of several red Ferraris used in the television series "Magnum P.I.," starring Tom Selleck. Nearby on a recent visit was the much less impressive Mousemobile driven by John Candy as Uncle Buck in the film of the same name.

You may also see some small vehicles from *The Little Rascals*, some of the DeLoreans used in *Back to the Future*, and some retro-military gear from *Waterworld*.

Bedrock and Jurassic Park

Still standing on both sides of the road is a piece of Bedrock, as it was constructed for *The Flintstones*. You'll see Barney and Betty Rubble's house and their car. Check out the welcoming sign with the town's claim to fame: "Bedrock: First with Fire."

Parked alongside the road just past Bedrock is the jeep that was nearly torn to pieces by a T. Rex in *Jurassic Park*. Most of that film—the number-one commercial success of all time—was filmed inside soundstages at Universal Studios Hollywood, with just a small amount of exterior footage taken in Hawaii.

AAA S.O.S. Card-carrying members of AAA can claim a 10 percent discount at most shops within Universal Studios.

From 2001 to the future. The director of the film used in the Back to the Future ride was renowned movie special effects designer Douglas Trumbull, who created special effects for hits including *2001: A Space Odyssey,* and *Close Encounters of the Third Kind.* The four-minute, 70-mm movie portion of the ride took two years to make and cost as much as a feature film. Elaborate hand-painted miniatures were created for the filming.

Flash Flood

The road that leads down toward Old Mexico was covered with dirt to become the Appian Way for *Spartacus* in 1960; hundreds of Roman soldiers marched right into ancient Rome.

Today's tour-goers, though, are given a watery treat as movie special effects are used to simulate a raging flash flood that roars down the hill on the left side of the tram. Some 10,000 gallons of water drop down from the top of the hill; it's all pumped back up for the next visitors.

The flash flood scene was used in the film *Fletch Lives* in 1989.

Jaws

Welcome to Amity Island, the reconstructed scene of some of the action from the classic 1975 fish-food movie, *Jaws.*

Jaws Lake not only serves as the backdrop for the shark, but also stands in for Cabot Cove, Maine, in exterior scenes from (yes, again) "Murder, She Wrote." The hairpin turn that leads past the lake is where Jessica Fletcher rides her bicycle every week at the beginning of the show.

Past the lake you will come to the small home where Lansbury/Fletcher does her gardening. The same house has also been used in many other productions, including "Quantum Leap" and the mostly-forgotten film *Shout,* with John Travolta.

Nearby is a light-colored house with green trim that was the home of Ben Matlock from the "Matlock" TV series. Next to Matlock's house is the home used in the classic Vincent Price horror film, *The House of the Seven Gables.*

Some of the scenes from the *Casper* movie were also shot near the lake.

Wilderness/Avalanche

As your tram begins to approach the wilderness area you will come to a large log cabin that was used in *The Great Outdoors* and then later as an important element of the Paramount comedy, *Naked Gun 33⅓.*

The wilderness, covered with fake snow, became the Antarctic for the remake of *The Thing.* A large painted backdrop behind a small lake was used for the splashdown scene for 1995's *Apollo 13,* starring Tom Hanks and directed by Ron Howard.

You're in for a touch of the real fake thing as your tram drives into the phony snow-covered tunnel in the wilderness. The slightest little sound is likely to set off a special effect avalanche; it's a rather simple mechanical setup that spins the outside walls of the tunnel, but the effect is dizzying. The entire tram seems to turn first one way and then the other. If you're prone to dizziness, this is a good place to close your eyes and take a short nap.

The avalanche tunnel was used in a scene from "The Six Million Dollar Man," and according to studio legend, star Lee Majors had a major problem staying upright long enough to get through his part.

Entertainment Center

Back to the Future . . . The Ride
The Flintstones Show
Waterworld—A Live Sea War Spectacular
The Wild Wild Wild West Stunt Show
Beetlejuice's Graveyard Revue
Fievel's Playland

💥 Back to the Future . . . The Ride

Dive into the world of the record-breaking movie trilogy, *Back to the Future,* in Universal's incredible simulator adventure. It's a roller coaster of an attraction that never moves more than a few feet in any direction.

It seems that weird Doc Brown is back home conducting new time-travel experiments. He has created his newest vehicle—an eight-passenger Time Vehicle that is faster and more energy-efficient than anything before . . . or since. That's the good news. The bad news is that Biff Tannen has broken into the Institute of Future Technology and threatens to end the universe as we know it! It's up to you to jump into your own DeLorean and chase down Biff.

Surrounded by images and sound and buffeted by the realistic motion of your flight simulator, you will soar into Hill Valley in the year 2015, blast back to the Ice Age for a chilling high-speed encounter with canyons of sheer ice, explode into the Volcanic Era for a once-in-a-lifetime encounter with a Tyrannosaurus Rex, and then go through a volcano and over the edge of a molten lava fall.

This is a state-of-the-art attraction that combines a spectacular 70-mm Omnimax film with simulator ride vehicles. The 80-foot diameter dome-like screens of the Omnimax theaters occupy all of the viewer's peripheral vision, making the screen seem to vanish and taking the viewer into the scene.

The Institute of Future Technology in the waiting area features actual props from the *Back to the Future* movie series, including hoverboards (futur-

Don't say you weren't warned. Back to the Future is described as a "dynamically aggressive ride." Visitors suffering from maladies including dizziness, seizures, back or neck problems, claustrophobia, motion sickness, and heart disorders, or pregnant women, are advised to sit this one out. The ride also won't work for persons of a certain size or shape who cannot fit into the seats and safety harness. We suspect you know who you are.

Coming attraction. If you have really sharp eyes and a good sense of balance, keep an eye out during your wild Back to the Future ride for the movie poster on the wall in Hill Valley; it advertises *Jaws 19.*

istic skateboards without wheels) and the all-important flux capacitors for time travel.

Check out the bulletin board in the waiting area, where you will see the names of some of the visiting scientists with offices in the building. They include Thomas Edison, Albert Einstein, and Francis Bacon.

There are three levels of 12 eight-seater DeLorean cars in the theater dome. Universal insiders say that the very best experience can be had by sitting in the front row of the center car on the second tier. This particular vehicle is in the absolute center of the movie dome, and you cannot easily see any surrounding cars which might distract from the illusion.

If you are concerned about getting motion sickness, you may want to try to get onto the lower level of the ride. (I prefer a Dramamine in the morning and the middle car.)

Some of Doc Brown's inventions are found in the waiting area outside of the simulators. Check out the Time Man Personal Time Travel Suit prototype. There are lots of clocks on the walls, including Greenwich, Moscow, Tokyo, Sydney, Hollywood, Hill Valley, Mexico City, and Orlando. Hill Valley is set about five minutes ahead of Hollywood.

When you enter into the holding room for the simulator, try to maneuver next to the door to get a seat in the front of the car. (Some visitors find the small waiting room a bit confining; you can ask the attendant to leave the door open if you feel it necessary. Trust us: a much more intense experience is coming.)

As you wait to board your simulator, pay attention to the little movie about time-travel safety; we enjoyed watching crash dummies "Fender" and "Bender" at work. When you feel a rumble beneath your feet, you'll know the car is returning to its base.

The preshow film and the movie shown in the ride itself were made specially for the simulator. Doc Brown (Christopher Lloyd) and Biff Tannen (Thomas Wilson) took part in the movie, but Marty McFly (Michael J. Fox) is nowhere to be seen. According to rumors, Fox asked for too much money.

The glass case in the preflight waiting room includes some juicy little details for fans of the film. The cabinet in one of the rooms included communication devices such as telepathic projectors, a multilingual translator, a telekinetic projector, and emergency supplies including first aid, travel rations, and dog biscuits. Also within the waiting room there is a hoverboard that is being energized in case it is needed.

The DeLoreans themselves rise about eight feet out of their garages at the start of the movie. Once in the air, four actuators drive the car—three for vertical movement and one for fore-and-aft movement. Although it may feel as if your car is soaring and dropping hundreds of feet, the entire range of movement for the vehicle is about two feet.

To give the feeling of traveling through space, the cars are surrounded with a fog made from liquid nitrogen.

The Flintstones Show

Wilma!

The Flintstones Show celebrates the movie that enlarged the old television cartoon show, but what we've really got here is a fine example of stagecraft. You've got singing, dancing, fireworks, rain, and a sophisticated flying rig that brings the stars out over the audience. Most Broadway theaters are not equipped so well.

The show itself is a lighthearted musical about Fred Flintstone's dream of becoming a rock star. Rock . . . get it? That's only the first of a seemingly endless series of puns you'll endure. Want some more? Well, the whole thing is billed as a production of Universe Shell Pictures, with Oliver Stone as director, Steven Spielbird as his assistant, a Madonna look-alike named Mastadonna, a high-flying dancer named B. C. Hammer, and the New Kids on the Rock.

Some of the funniest moments come from the "television" broadcast to Fred and Wilma's home, including 22nd birthday greetings to George Burns.

When Fred heads off to Hollyrock, they fly on Pterodactyl Airlines, which uses a pterodactyl instead of a 757.

The show lasts about 25 minutes and is usually presented about once an hour; on busy days there are added performances. The huge theater will accommodate all of the people standing outside in the queue and about 10 to 15 feet more of visitors; if you find yourself in a line longer than that, you may want to come back for a later show.

The theater is very wide and very deep, so some of the seats are not as good as others. The worst seats are probably those off to the side. Some parts of the show are a bit loud for youngsters, and the guests down front will get slightly wet in the finale, but a good time is had by all.

Waterworld—A Live Sea War Spectacular

A seaplane crashes through a wall of jagged steel, exploding straight at terrified onlookers. Underwater warriors rise from the sea to battle invaders on jet skis. A fiery figure falls 50 feet, turning a lagoon into a blazing inferno.

And it's all presented live, at Universal's Waterworld stunt show, based on the spectacular but flawed movie of the same name. We don't have to worry about the movie, though: we can enjoy the spectacular live stunt show they've made here, including some 60 stunts and special effects and water vehicles including jet skis, motorboats, and air boats. Don't pay much attention to the corny script, though; it only gets in the way of the stunts and pyrotechnics.

Visitors will pass through a collection of some of the props in the movie into another century, after the polar cap has melted and turned planet Earth into Waterworld. They'll find themselves seated with a view of the atoll, a floating island of boats, barges, driftwood, and debris; it's a dangerous day to pay a visit, though. Roving pirates of the future are swarming about the atoll, led by the Hellfire Gunboat.

Alarms sound. Nets drop. Flares explode in the sky. And high-pressure water cannons blast past the audience at slaloming hovercraft and jet skis. A dive-bomber makes a low-level run, tearing off a chunk of the wall and showering the visitors with salt spray. Avoid the green-painted "wet seats" unless you are looking for a free shower with your clothes on.

Above it all, the Legendary Mariner and Deacon—the leader of the cut-throat pirates—struggle for the fate of the future in hand-to-hand combat that climaxes in a death-defying plunge and a firestorm that destroys the set . . . at least until the next performance.

Special effects in the show include a submerged catapult that slingshots a jet skier from beneath the water and onto the watery stage.

The 2,800-seat stadium, formerly the home of the "Miami Vice" show, will eat up lines pretty quickly, and plans call for as many as eight performances a day at busy times of the year, but lines are sure to grow lengthy at midday. Head for the show early on a busy day.

And be aware that the complex special effects and outside forces like high winds can sometimes cause cancelation of some of the stunts; on one of our visits the spectacular seaplane never got off the ground.

🅆🄾🅆 The Wild Wild Wild West Stunt Show

Yeeha! This is a very silly, very entertaining live show with some spectacular stunts, bad jokes, and enough gunfire and explosions to wake Beetlejuice next door.

The storyline goes something like this: the professional stunt coordinator rides onto the set aboard his trusty steed to introduce a demonstration of Western skills only to find that his cast of cowboys has been kidnapped by Ma Hopper and her mean and ugly sons. The Hopper family proceeds to wreak havoc with guns, dynamite, and gross and dumb jokes, culminating in a shootout that literally brings down the house.

The 20-minute show is well worth a visit. Parents be warned: the explosions and gunfire may upset young visitors.

🅆🄾🅆 Beetlejuice's Graveyard Revue

This is the ultimate in graveyard rock, a tuneful singing and dancing show starring everybody's favorite creep, Beetlejuice, and a monstrous cast of characters including Wolfman, Dracula, Frankenstein, the Phantom of the Opera, and the Bride of Frankenstein.

The background music is tape recorded, but the singing and dancing is live and very entertaining, although the very young and older adults may find it a bit loud. In 1995, the show was moved indoors to the former home of Conan the Barbarian.

Beetlejuice is a character on loan from Warner Bros., while the rest of the awful actors are from Universal classics.

Fievel's Playland

A small outdoor playground where the kids can burn off a bit of energy on some interesting props and slides related to the cartoon feature, *An American Tail*.

Studio Center

Jurassic Park—The Ride
Backdraft
E.T. Adventure
Lucy: A Tribute
The World of Cinemagic
AT&T at the Movies

The Studio Center is located down the hill from the Entertainment Center, at the bottom of a series of three long escalators, a 200-foot drop down a 1,200-foot-long cascade of moving stairs. The Studio Center is actually closer to the real soundstages of Universal.

The long trek down to the center is a good reason why you'll want to plan your day at Universal. It is not a minor thing to go from one area to another at the park. (There is, by the way, alternate transportation between the upper and lower parts of Universal Studios by shuttle for guests with disabilities.)

🌟 Jurassic Park—The Ride

A spectacular ride, millions of years (and $100 million) in the making: Jurassic Park—The Ride opened with a huge splash for the summer of 1996.

The attraction, perhaps the most expensive and technologically advanced theme park adventure ever, fulfills Universal's promise to allow visitors to "ride the movies," in this case Steven Spielberg's movie version of Michael Crichton's bestselling novel, the most popular motion picture of all time.

You'll enter through the 35-foot-tall wooden gates of Jurassic Park. As you wait your turn to board your exploration raft, you'll see a multimedia preshow presented on massive video walls. The film features John Hammond, founder and owner of Jurassic Park; as in the movie, Hammond is played by distinguished actor Sir Richard Attenborough.

The journey begins as a gentle exploration of Jurassic Park's dinosaur habitat. The rafts explore the misty fog banks, brilliantly colored foliage and exotic vegetation of "Herbivore Country," home of the vegetarians of the dinosaur world.

The park at Jurassic Park. The re-created world of *Jurassic Park* includes some spectacular greenery. There are some 353 palm trees of 11 species, including Sago, King, Queen, Kentia, and Canary Island Date. Gardeners put in 926 additional trees of 33 species, including Flame, Golden Rain, Orchid, Australian Tree Fern, Giant Bird of Paradise, and Dragon. Finally, there are 7,441 shrubs, plants, and flowers of 76 species, including Star Jasmine, Breath of Heaven, Rattlesnake Grass, Tasmanian Tree Fern, Shell Ginger, Mystery Gardenia, Sugar Bush, Bougainvillea, and Giant Burmese Honeysuckle. Scattered about are 300 bamboo plants of six varieties.

Not to worry, though: the swift Velociraptors and the ferocious Tyrannosaurus

Rex are securely contained nearby in Carnivore Canyon behind a sparking 10,000-volt electrified fence.

The boats gently cruise through radiant Ultrasaur Lagoon, with gentle waterfalls and clear tide pools. Just a finger away sits a gigantic 50-foot Ultrasaurus cooling off at water's edge. The boat is nudged by what seems to be a rock below the surface—it turns out to be a surprised baby Ultrasaurus who eyes the riders curiously.

As the rafts glide out of the river, two rambunctious Psittacosauruses frolic nearby, splashing water across the boat's bow. Erupting geysers spew billows of white steam as the boat arrives at Stegosaur Pond, where mother and baby Stegosauruses seem happy to have company. Small dinosaurs called "Compys" shriek their greetings.

Riding an increasingly swift current, the boat next moves into Hadrosaur Cove. Suddenly, the waters begin racing at speeds of nearly 50 miles per hour and the raft is driven dangerously off-course into Carnivore Canyon where guests come to the Velociraptor pen—and find a jagged, gaping hole in the electrified fence. The vicious Velociraptors are nowhere to be seen, and signs of danger surround guests on the raft as it continues to veer out of control and deeper into unknown territory. A wrecked land cruiser dangles perilously from a nearby guardrail. An empty raft drifts by, seemingly abandoned; suddenly a "Spitter" rears his multi-colored crown and bares his teeth in a sinister smile.

Jurassic Park's water pump station is bedlam. Blaring alarms sound as nearby catwalks begin to collapse and the station's pipes crack and give way, shooting scalding water in the path of the raft. A pack of clever and voracious Raptors spring forward and begin to pursue the runaway raft.

And then . . . well, we're not going to spoil all of the scary fun except to say that sooner or later the rafts plunge into an 84-foot drop in total darkness, splashing into the lagoon at speeds of nearly 50 miles per hour. (It's claimed to be the longest, fastest water plunge at any theme park.) To make things even more interesting, the drop includes a "vertical curve" (you might call it a bump) that makes riders feel that their boat is being lifted straight up before it nearly tips over and smashes to the lagoon below.

The technology of the ride includes some of the most advanced Animatronic dinosaurs anywhere, using a new technique called "compliant reactivity" to model the interaction of different parts of a body as it moves. Many of the dinosaurs are programmed to react to the presence of visitors, some attacking at speeds of up to 25 feet per second, the quickness of a striking rattlesnake.

Stars of the park include Ultrasaurus, tall as a five-story building; the armor-plated 18-foot tall Stegosaurus, 40 feet long from nose to tail, and the relentlessly pursuing Tyrannosaurus Rex.

The 25-passenger boats are the largest amusement ride watercraft ever built; they are free-flowing, not on tracks. The boats are paced by computer to travel at least 30 seconds behind the boat ahead, propelled along by 1.4 million gallons of rushing water.

The 16 boats are capable of moving about 3,000 visitors per hour through the park for the ride, which lasts about five-and-a-half minutes. That still won't be enough to eliminate long lines from mid-morning through dinner; arrive early or late. The minimum height to ride is 42 inches.

A restaurant, Jurassic Cove Café, and a retail shop, Jurassic Outfitters, are included in the compound.

【WOW】 Backdraft

A back draft is a fire that has burned out all of the oxygen in a room, leaving only superheated gas waiting for a fresh breath of air. *Backdraft* is also the name of a successful thriller by director Ron Howard and is celebrated in a spectacular demonstration.

You'll learn how the film included real blazes set in old warehouses in Chicago. Actor Scott Glenn tells about how the flame-retardant underwear he wore in one important scene only worked for a short while; he also exposes some of the secrets of the Ashmatic, a machine created for the movie that shot burning ash over the cast.

The attraction includes a climactic re-creation of some of the special effects from the movie; in fact, the effects in this show are a lot more real than some of the movie magic seen in the film.

As many as two hundred times a day, the Backdraft soundstage becomes a fiery furnace with ruptured fuel lines, superheated air, and scalding heat.

When you first enter the soundstage, you'll watch a backdraft flame spinning wildly around the fictitious Nikolas Randall and Company chemical building. That is, of course, merely the overture: suddenly there's a massive explosion of fuel drums, which in turn causes overhead pipes to burst and spew their flammable contents toward the audience. The flames become a firestorm, reaching more than two thousand degrees.

The soundstage was built as a completely fireproof building; a special invisible "air curtain" protects visitors from the flames which march toward them.

There's a control room at the back of the Backdraft room behind a glass window where a technician supervises the show for safety purposes, as well as abundant fire extinguishers and other safety equipment in the room. Construction of the building required special dispensation from the Hollywood Fire Department.

【WOW】 E.T. Adventure

Climb aboard a flying bicycle, feel the wind in your face, and venture across the universe with E.T. in an effort to save his dying Green Planet in a spectacular, $40-million re-creation of the wondrous movie.

The attraction begins with a preshow film with director Steven Spielberg introducing E.T. and the ride that awaits you. "He must go home, and only you can help him," Spielberg says.

You'll be stopped soon afterward at a check-in station where an attendant will ask you your name and give you your Interplanetary Passport; hold onto it for later on.

Then you will walk through one of the most imaginative, fully realized scene-setting waiting lines at any theme park, a forest where you can see the searchers for the extraterrestrial all around you. If the ride is not too crowded, or if you're not in a rush, take your time and look around. Smell the smells, feel the fog.

Following an urgent plea from E.T.'s teacher Botanicus, E.T. and his new-found friends—that's you—escape government agents in a spooky forest and take flight on bicycles on a tour above Los Angeles. You'll go with him, and eventually you'll arrive at the Green Planet.

Through a thick haze and a shower of volcanic ash, E.T. extends his magic finger to help his friends Orbidon, Maagdol, and Tickli Moot Moots. Restored, they'll celebrate with you.

Special effects in the E.T. show include thousands of fiber-optic stars, 50 robots, a life-size redwood forest, and white billowy clouds.

At the end of the ride, E.T. thanks you for your help . . . by name.

As you exit the E.T. ride and emerge from the building, look to your left next to the escalator to see a re-creation of E.T.'s transmitter as used in the movie; it's constructed from a "Speak and Spell" toy, a tinfoil-covered umbrella, a coffee can, and an old record player.

Lucy: A Tribute

Lucy, I'm home! The original TV show was unusual in that the creators worked with three or four permanent sets that stood side-by-side in the studio, avoiding the flimsy-looking sets typical of television shows at the time. The permanent setting also allowed for more advanced lighting, allowing cameras to move quickly from one area to another. All of the sets were painted in carefully chosen shades of gray to control the contrast of the finished black-and-white film.

If you are a fan of Lucille Ball and everyone around her, you'll be enthralled at this collection of photos, scripts, and memorabilia and a continuous showing of episodes from her television show. Among my personal favorites is Lucy as part of a barbershop quartet.

There is a diorama showing how the original television show was filmed in front of a live audience. The show was photographed (on 35-mm black-and-white film) on one large set; episodes were edited and combined for the final show.

You'll see part of the script from "Mame," which in 1974 marked Lucy's return to the big screen for the final time, and a display of her five Emmy awards.

There's also a "Lucy" trivia quiz including questions like, "What was the biggest laugh in Lucy history?" Here's a hint: the answer involves Lucy, Ricky, a bunch of raw eggs, and a wild and romantic dance. You figure it out.

On display are photos of Lucille Ball's home on Roxbury Drive in Beverly Hills where she lived for 35 years. Next-door neighbors were the Jack Benny family, and the Jimmy Stewart family lived across the street. There's also a selection of home movies narrated by Luci Arnaz and a collection of stereo-scopic slides of Lucy's family taken in the 1950s.

Desi Arnaz was born Desiderio Alberto Arnaz y de Acha III in Santiago, Cuba, in 1917. The son of a Cuban senator, he lived in great luxury until the Cuban revolution of 1933 when the family left the country. Arnaz worked at various jobs, including cleaning bird cages for 25 cents.

Eventually he got a job in a band and soon became one of the top band leaders in New York. Signed to the lead in the New York musical "Too Many Girls," he played a Latin football player. When he went to Hollywood to play his role in the movie version of the musical, he met the studio ingenue Lucille Ball, and in late 1940 they began a bicoastal marriage.

After World War II, looking for a way to work together in Los Angeles, Lucy and Desi hired the writers of Lucy's radio show "My Favorite Husband" and produced a pilot for "I Love Lucy." Their new company, Desilu Productions, became the largest television and film production company in Hollywood. Arnaz died in 1986. Lucy passed on in 1989.

Universal CityWalk, Universal Studios Hollywood
©*1995 Universal City Studios, Inc.*

Rapid cutting. The shower scene in Alfred Hitchcock's original *Psycho* is made up of 78 different shots, edited in rapid sequence to simulate the violence of the attack. However, the knife is never shown piercing the skin. Hitchcock chose to shoot the film in black and white to lessen the gore. The "blood" is actually chocolate syrup, since stage blood photographs as gray in a black and white print.

Doubles. One of Hitchcock's famous signatures was the fact that he always had a minor walk-on in his movies. In Anthony Perkins' film introduction to the *Psycho* set, pay close attention early on when the technicians start to remove the set and lighting equipment; there is a Hitchcock look-alike walking off in the distance.

WOW The World of Cinemagic

Back to the Future Show
The Magic of Alfred Hitchcock
Harry & The Hendersons Show

Here's a three-part instant graduate degree in the magic of moviemaking. You'll learn some of the secrets behind the extraordinarily popular *Back to the Future* movies, receive a course from master of thrillers Alfred Hitchcock, and finally hear for yourself how sound technicians add auditory special effects to "sweeten" a film.

The best segment is Hitchcock's. You'll learn a bit about how he filmed his most famous moment—the shower scene from *Psycho* (including the story that during the final scene in the shower, Hitchcock replaced the hot water in the pipes with icy cold to increase Janet Leigh's reaction of terror) and hear from Kim Novak about her experiences in making *Vertigo*. Novak says that though she never learned to swim, she was nevertheless filmed by Hitchcock jumping into San Francisco Bay to be rescued by Jimmy Stewart.

Two girls over the age of 14 are selected from the audience to participate in a simulation of another famous Hitchcock moment, from *Saboteur*, his first American film. In the movie the handsome hero and a Nazi agent fight it out at the top of the Statue of Liberty high above New York harbor. Using a model of part of the torch and a moving camera, the two volunteers are inserted into the scene.

The third part of the show is the sound effects demonstration. The host will ask for—or draft—five persons from the audience to help operate some of the noisemakers on stage. You'll learn how some sounds are created and also how difficult it is to exactly match a sound to an action on screen.

AT&T at the Movies

A collection of computer games and entertainments, all with television and motion picture themes. Located directly outside the entrance to the E.T. Adventure, it is easy enough to miss if you are intent on running between the major entertainments.

Among the digital toys are an interactive portrait puzzle, electronic finger painting, a computerized movie makeup device, and a phraser machine that allows you to make a machine talk for you. There is also a booth with a huge telephone where a family can make a conference call home.

Eating Your Way Through Universal Studios Hollywood

Credit cards are not accepted at most restaurants, *except* for Victoria Station and How Sweet It Is. Soft drinks at Universal Studios are priced pretty high, at about $2 for a regular-size cup and nearly $3 for a large drink. You'll also find beer wagons at several locations in the park.

Entrance

Country Star Restaurant. Country music, country cooking, and ownership by some country stars. Specialties include Wynonna's Chicken, Charlie Chase's Baby Back Ribs, Reba's Garden Vegetable Pasta, and other entrees priced from about $6 to $20. The Country Star BBQ Feast includes chicken, beef, ribs, and fixings including "Rattlesnake Sauce" for $17.

The restaurant is just outside the gate to Universal Studios Hollywood, between the theme park and CityWalk. Be sure to have your hand stamped for readmission if you leave the park for a meal.

Entertainment Center

Victoria Station. An outpost of the national chain, featuring prime rib, seafood, burgers, and salads. Many of the tables are in old railway cars. Have your hand stamped at the entrance to the restaurant so that you can re-enter the park later; visitors to CityWalk can eat at Victoria Station without buying a Studios ticket. Burgers are priced from $6.95, sandwiches from $6.95 to $8.95, and pasta dishes from $9.95. The restaurant also has an early-bird special from 4 to 6 P.M. priced at $11.95; typical offerings include prime rib, grilled roasted chicken, a pasta dish, or fresh fish.

How Sweet It Is. More than 200 varieties of candy, caramel apples, fresh roasted nuts, and other snacks near the entrance to the park.

Star Struck Cafe. Cappuccino, espresso, latte, hot chocolate, and Häagen-Dazs ice cream alongside Victoria Station.

Moulin Rouge Cafe. A pleasant hideaway within the simulated streets of Paris. Offerings include platters and sandwiches priced from about $6 to $10, such as roasted chicken with fries, roasted smoked turkey, honey-mustard-glazed ham, and smoked turkey sandwich. French bread pizza is about $3. (Open in season only.)

Mel's Diner. A remake of a 1950s diner reminiscent of the eatery in *American Graffiti*. Load up on burgers, cheeseburgers, fried chicken, hot dogs, and other fine fare, priced from about $3 to $6.

Hollywood Cantina. Fajitas, tacos, burritos, nachos, enchiladas, and other Mexican favorites, priced from about $4 for soft tacos to $6 for fajitas. Platters including rice and beans sell for about a dollar more.

Ristorante Italia. Pizza by the slice from $2.95 for cheese, $3.25 for pepperoni, and $3.50 for barbecued chicken or vegetarian toppings. Also available are spaghetti, ziti, Italian sausage, and other dishes from about $3 to $5.

Winston's Grill. An outdoor grill prepares barbecued chicken, beef, and more. Prices range from about $7 to $9 for entrees. (Open in season only.)

Doc Brown's Fancy Fried Chicken. Chicken dinners, biscuits, and corn on the cob. A three-piece basket of fried chicken is priced at about $6; a full dinner with potatoes and gravy is priced about a dollar higher. (Open in season only.)

Crepe de Paris. A collection of crepes, from the ordinary to the extraordinary, priced from about $5 to $7. Offerings include the California Surfer with avocado, cheddar, and bacon; the Louisiana Purchase with Cajun shrimp and crab; Chinese chicken with Asian greens; the Hamlet with honey-baked ham and cheddar cheese; and Mu-Shu-style chicken. Sweet crepes include a southern berry blush, pina colada, and banana rum runner. (Open in season only.)

River Princess. Set inside a simulation of a riverboat with a wheelhouse above, the restaurant offers burgers, hot dogs, heros, and cherry cobblers. Offerings priced at about $5 to $7 include barbecued chicken salad and a turkey and cheddar cheese sandwich on squaw bread. The super hero sandwich serves four to six people and is priced at about $18.

Alpha Inn Pub. An attractive little bar, serving imported beers and ales including Watney's and Bass, cappuccino, and cocktails. If you're lucky, perhaps you can park the young ones at Fievel's Playground across the way and enjoy a pint or a cup in peace. (Open in season only.)

Cyrano's. A soup-and-salad stop with a view of the valley below. Other offerings include a french bread pizza for $2.55, spaghetti bolognese for $5, and a french dip sandwich for $5.75.

Whistle Stop. Cobb salad, Chinese chicken salads, fish and chips, burgers, and more.

Studio Snacks. Deli sandwiches, sticky buns, and fruit salad.

Hill Valley Beverage Co. Frozen margaritas, daiquiris, sodas, and chips. (Open in season only.)

Caribbean Chill Yogurt. Frozen yogurt and other treats.

Studio Center

Studio Commissary. Philly steak sandwiches, tostada salads, pizzas, and desserts.

Margarita Bar. Margaritas, beer, and lemonade.

Universal CityWalk

In typical Hollywood fashion, Universal Studios saw a place where there should be a city—a clean, safe, and fun city—and so that was what they built. The $100 million Universal CityWalk sprouted in 1993.

The concept for the development was for a street that was not an imitation of any particular place or time period, but instead a sort of architectural collage of the images and traits of Los Angeles without duplicating any buildings. The two-block-long street occupies a hilltop between Universal Studios Hollywood and the Universal City Cinemas.

"The theme of Boston is gray nineteenth-century neoclassical buildings. The theme of Venice is fourteenth-century rich merchant buildings adorned with gold and jewels. The theme of Los Angeles is that there is no theme," said architect Jon Jerde, principal designer of the city. Jerde also designed the wild Treasure Island hotel and casino on the Las Vegas Strip.

The 200,000 square feet of space along two major boardwalks includes more than three dozen shops and specialty restaurants. CityWalk connects to the 6,200-seat Universal Amphitheatre, the 18-screen Universal City Cinemas, and the Universal Studios Hollywood theme park and tour.

Stores are open seven days a week, from 11 A.M. to 11 P.M., with longer hours at peak times.

By night, Universal CityWalk comes alive with lighting that includes crackle-tube neon, cove and accent lighting, towers with theatrical lighting, and light-reflecting panels which splash color throughout the plazas. In addition, the Museum of Neon Art displays 21 vintage neon signs along the street.

Universal City Cinemas, an 18-screen complex, has become the "local theater" for many residents of the San Fernando Valley. It is the nation's busiest movie theater complex.

Universal CityWalk is an easy five- to ten-minute walk from the Entertainment Center of Universal Studios, making it an attractive alternative to the fast food of the theme park for lunch or dinner. See if you can convince the kids to save some of their souvenir money for the neat shops here.

Retail Shops

Adobe Road. Native American artware including jewelry, belts, skins, and shirts. Artisans create some of the products in the store.

Captain Coconuts. A fabulous zoo of a store where all the animals are stuffed and many have computer chips for brains.

Crabtree and Evelyn. Food, teas, soaps, lotions, and more.

Crow's Nest. A bookstore for the kids, next-door to the adults section and eatery of the **Upstart Crow Bookstore and Coffeehouse.**

Current Wave. Fresh street fashions and all manner of shades.

Dapy. Originally from Paris, this unusual retailer opened its first American store in New York's Soho district in 1984. It offers an eclectic collection of toys and things, including a 1950s retro section.

Golden Showcase. A showcase of Western Publishing and Golden Books products including toys, games, books, and videos.

Jam's World. Bright and unusual casual wear for men and women; the tags read, "Color, Freedom, Difference, Love."

Martin Lawrence Museum Shop. Arts, crafts, hand-painted dolls, clocks, and more.

Museum of Neon Art. The only institution in the world devoted to the collection, preservation, and exhibition of neon art; there is, of course, a museum shop. You can also take part in a walking tour that helps visitors learn the history of the nearly two dozen vintage signs on the facades of CityWalk.

Nature Company. Take a breathtaking walk through a rain forest—inside the store. Rising 40 feet into the mist and fog, a banyan tree serves as the focal point of the forest at the store's entrance. Items for sale include nature gifts, educational playthings, garden accessories, and other earth-friendly products.

Out-Takes. Step into a scene of *The Wizard of Oz, Casablanca, Gone with the Wind,* or other classic films; computer-generated composite photography does the trick for movie, television, or still scenes. Souvenir photos are about $35, with additional persons in a scene charged $5 more.

P. T. Copperpott. A huge copper pot filled with candies hangs outside a reproduction of a turn-of-the-century store; inside, you'll find more candies and gifts.

Sam Goody Superstore. Your basic music store with a live rock and roll stage and a 27-foot gorilla standing guard outside. You'll also find a piano-shaped coffee café . . . with music, of course.

Scientific Revolution. Products that celebrate science and scientists.

Things from Another World. Everything of necessity for the science fiction lover, including games, books, videos, and comics.

UCLA Spirit. Books, merchandise, and souvenirs from the well-known university.

Upstart Crow Bookstore and Coffeehouse. The name says it all. You can come in for the books, the atmosphere, or the java.

Wizardz Wonders. Tricks and treasures for the amateur magician, with professionals to demonstrate how they work.

Restaurants and Entertainment

B. B. King's Blues Club and Restaurant. The Los Angeles version of the original club on Beale Street in Memphis. High-energy blues music and Delta food.

Cafe Puccino. Baked goods and cappuccino in huge cups.

Camacho's Cantina. Authentic Mexican cuisine from sopas to tamales, and music.

Country Star Hollywood. The total country experience, from music to barbecue.

Gladstone's. Fish doesn't get much fresher than this. Inspired by the Malibu original, the restaurant includes several huge saltwater tanks, sawdust on the floors, and an oyster tank. Out front is the San Pedro light buoy, which marked channels in and out of San Pedro Harbor from 1942 until its decommissioning in 1971. Entrees range from about $12 to $20. The Gladstone's salad bar, priced at $6.95, can be a full meal by itself with items from greens to bay shrimp to antipasto; it is also available as an accompaniment to entrees at $2.95.

Hard Rock Cafe. A major outpost of the national trendy eatery opened on the CityWalk in 1995.

Hollywood Athletic Club. A new extension of the 70-year-old original, once a males-only club that drew in many of Hollywood's greatest stars. A billiards room is among the main attractions. One of the fancier places at City-Walk, with a very nice terrace overlooking the central plaza. Entrees include meatloaf Cajun-style for $11.95, pasta from $10.50 to $11.95, and burgers starting at $5.95.

Hollywood Freezway. A real cool, most unusual ice cream parlor with decorations including a 1957 Chevy bursting through a Hollywood Freeway sign.

Island Nut Company. You've got to be nuts—or a nut lover—to want to go to this place. Roasted nuts, trail mixes, honeys, gourmet peanut butter made on the premises, and more, all served from a Caribbean-style shack.

Jody Maroni's Sausage Kingdom. A California specialty, the king of the haute dog. Sausages and hot dogs including hot and sweet Italian, Portuguese fig and pine-nut, Bombay curried lamb, orange-garlic-cumin, and boudin blanc (chicken and duck with shallots and tarragon).

KWGB. A radio station for burger lovers, the call letters stand for World's Greatest Burgers. Sit down at your table, pick up the phone, push a button, and talk to your "burger jock" to place your order. Push another button on the phone to talk to the disc jockey and order your favorite rock and roll tune to play while you eat. A broadcast booth at the restaurant is also home to one of Los Angeles' leading morning radio shows.

L.A. Juice. An all-natural juice and salad bar in an outdoor café setting.

Lighthouse Beach. Sun, palm trees, weight-lifting contests, Beach Boys music . . . munchies and drinks. A huge outdoor Astrovision screen across from the beach is used to broadcast sporting events.

Morisawa Sushi. Fresh sushi, some of it flown in daily from Japan. Check out the *omaka sei* (chef's choice) or order your favorite.

Tony Roma's. Through the glass of the open kitchen, you can watch your ribs being cooked.

Wizardz Magic Club and Dinner Theatre. A celebration of prestidigitation. Drinks are served in test tubes and beakers from the alchemists' lab. Up-close magic and comedy acts are performed. Inside the main theater, you can see a laser display or a full magic act. A luncheon buffet is available most days (adults $6.95, children $3.99), and the bar is open in the afternoon with a magician working alongside the bartender. *Discount coupon in this book.*

Wolfgang Puck Cafe. The originator of the famed Spago restaurant offers his famously unusual pizzas and other items including rotisserie chicken.

Yo'gert. A cafeteria-style yogurt shop with a dizzying palette of toppings.

IV
Knott's Berry Farm

Chapter 6
Knott's Berry Farm

It all started with a biscuit and jam. Today Knott's Berry Farm has more than 165 attractions, rides, live shows, restaurants, and shops spread across 150 acres—nearly twice the size of the entertainment area at Disneyland.

Knott's Berry Farm traces its history back to 1920, when Walter and Cordelia Knott began farming 20 acres of land they leased for $1,000 per year in Buena Park. They had spent the three years before unsuccessfully trying to homestead in the Mojave Desert.

Most of the family's savings went to purchase equipment and berry plants, and the business nearly died in the first year when a series of unusually heavy frosts nearly wiped them out. In the second year, berry prices plummeted.

What saved the business was Walter Knott's decision to market his produce by himself. He built a roadside stand to sell his berries to summer vacationers who drove past the farm on Grand Avenue, now known as Beach Boulevard or Highway 39.

There was competition, though, from other berry stands, and Knott combined his marketing skills with some agricultural engineering. In 1922, he read a newspaper article about an unusual berry that was larger than other berries; it was a cross between a dewberry and a loganberry and was called a *youngberry*. Knott tracked down the source to a farm in Alabama and imported them to Southern California for the first time, developing a business selling the berries to visitors and the plants to other area farmers.

By 1927, business was successful enough to allow Knott to purchase the land and build a home and a larger berry stand on the property. To make ends meet on their farm, Cordelia Knott began serving hot biscuits and homemade preserves to customers of the roadside berry stand.

The original berry farm stand was located at La Palma Avenue at Beach Boulevard, which today is in the first corner of the park you come to; the stand has been replaced by a statue of westward pioneers, visible from the road.

KNOTT'S BERRY FARM

About the same time, Knott's growing fame as a berry farmer brought him in contact with Rudolph Boysen of Orange County, the superintendent of the city park and an amateur botanist who had conducted some experiments with a cross between a blackberry, a raspberry, and a loganberry. Boysen had abandoned his experiment, and it took some searching to find the last six surviving vines; they were brought back to life and eventually transplanted to Knott's farm.

They were named boysenberries, and they were an immediate success at the Knott's Berry Farm roadside stand. In June of 1934, the momentous day came when Mrs. Knott expanded her menu to include country-fried chicken at 65 cents per full meal; the first day she served just eight meals on her own wedding china. Since then, Mrs. Knott's Chicken Dinner Restaurant has served some 20 million pounds of chicken, 116 million biscuits, 3.6 million pies, and 8 million pounds of mashed potatoes. Today the restaurant serves more than 1.5 million meals per year.

By 1940, visitors were standing in line for hours to enjoy plates of Walter's boysenberries and Cordelia's chicken.

As long as all those people were standing in line, why not find something else for them to spend their money on? In 1940, Knott built an Old West Ghost Town next door. The family started with an artistic "cyclorama" called the "Covered Wagon Show," a detailed mural enhanced with real objects in the foreground; it depicted the journey of the Knotts to California. Knott found the Old Trails Hotel in Prescott, Arizona, and moved the 1848 structure to the farm to hold the cyclorama. He added a saloon (without alcohol) and soon expanded with other buildings including a Kansas schoolhouse, a blacksmith's shop, and shacks from mining territories.

In 1952, Walter Knott purchased America's last operating narrow-gauge railroad, the Denver and Rio Grande, moving its rolling stock in its entirety to the farm. It originally traveled a 76-mile route from Denver to Colorado Springs. The steam-powered train was renamed as the Ghost Town & Calico Railroad.

Over the years, the ghost town grew into an important tourist attraction, and Knott's Berry Farm jams and jellies were packaged and sold across the country.

In 1954, the Bird Cage Theatre opened in Ghost Town as the home of the country's only daily melodrama troupe. A replica of the Bird Cage in Tombstone, Arizona, the theater was the training ground for many actors and actresses, including funnyman Steve Martin.

In 1955, though, the local tourist economy was altered forever when Walt Disney opened Disneyland in Anaheim. According to their official biography, Walter and Cordelia Knott attended the July 18 opening ceremonies of Disneyland and returned to find the Farm parking lot filled to capacity; their park went on to enjoy its best year ever.

Knott's Berry Farm and the Ghost Town continued to be an important tourist destination, though the park began to change, with a cable car ride,

Tickets. Prices were in effect in 1996, and are subject to change. *Discount coupon in this book.*

	All-Day	After 4 P.M.
Adults:	$29	$13
Children (3 to 11):	$19	$13
Seniors (60 and above):	$19	$13

Parking: $5 cars/$6 buses. Three hours of free parking available for restaurant diners or shoppers, or visitors to Independence Hall.

a puppet theater, and a man-made mountain with a simulated mine train ride within.

In 1960, Knott harvested the last berries from the Buena Park farm and began purchasing produce from other area farms.

In 1966, a brick-by-brick re-creation of Philadelphia's Independence Hall, including a 2,075-pound replica of the Liberty Bell, was added. The reproduction is so exact you can see fingerprints in the brick, just as in the original. When the real Independence Hall was restored for America's bicentennial in 1976, its original blueprints could not be found; the reconstruction committee in Philadelphia contacted Knott's Berry Farm and asked to borrow the park's plans.

In 1968, a single admission price was instituted for the park, and major development of Knott's Berry Farm as an amusement park was underway. Between 1968 and 1976, the Log Ride, Fiesta Village, and the Roaring '20s amusement area (now The Boardwalk) which includes the Gasoline Alley auto race, a 20-story parachute drop, and the Corkscrew roller coaster were added.

Cordelia Knott died in 1974 at the age of 84; Walter died in 1981, just short of his 92nd birthday.

Today, all the boysenberries in the world can trace their roots (pardon the pun) to Knott's Berry Farm. For old time's sake, several boysenberry vines are still grown behind the **Original Berry Stand** in Ghost Town. (From 1920 to 1927, the stand was the Farm's only structure.) All the produce for Knott's jams and jellies, though, are grown at outside farms.

Knott's Berry Farm allied itself with Charles Schulz' cartoon characters in 1983 with the opening of Camp Snoopy.

In 1992, Knott's Camp Snoopy opened in Bloomington, Minnesota, at the Mall of America, the nation's largest retail and entertainment complex. The park, Knott's first outside of California, is America's largest indoor entertainment park.

Discount ticket prices are available for non-ambulatory or pregnant guests, as well as residents of Southern California. Check also at area supermarkets and fast-food restaurants for discount coupons.

A Knott's spokesman said that visitors can call the park before a visit to check on availability of discount coupons; you can also use the coupon in this book.

In an unusual policy at theme parks, visitors to Knott's are permitted to bring picnic lunches; however, bottles and glass are not permitted.

Call (714) 220-5200 for updated information on hours and special events.

Hours of Operation

Summer Hours: Open every day from 9 A.M. to midnight. (The summer season runs from about June 16 to September 3.)

Winter Hours: Open from 10 A.M. to 6 P.M. during the week, 10 A.M. to 10 P.M. Saturdays, and 10 A.M. to 7 P.M. Sundays. Closed on Christmas. Extended hours during seasonal periods.

The Changing Face of Knott's

In the first complete overhaul of one of its six themed areas, Knott's Berry Farm has embarked on a plan to change the Roaring '20s into The Boardwalk, a colorful high-energy tribute to Southern California's beach culture . . . and the home of several new rides and attractions including a spectacular roller coaster with an ocean theme. The new coaster will replace the venerable but creaky Wacky Soap Box Racers and the Gasoline Auto Race attractions, although the car track may be reborn elsewhere in the park.

Host for The Boardwalk will be Hammer-Head Hank, a frisky shark.

The largest of the areas of the park, The Boardwalk's first major new ride will be **HammerHead**, a high-speed spinning ride that takes visitors from the surface of a sea grotto to a height of 80 feet. The grandstand seats will at times spin upside down and sideways to the ground.

Knott's Cloud 9 Theatre, which opened in 1976, will reemerge as the **Nu Wave Theatre**, the home of "Cyber Sports in 3-D," a permanent 15-minute experience combining filmed 3-D images and high-intensity music with lasers, smoke, and other theatrical effects.

The Capn. Kelly's restaurant will become **Airheadz**, an interactive music, food, and high-tech arcade center offering visitors the

MUST-SEES

Timber Mountain Log Ride

Bird Cage Theatre

Camp Snoopy
(unaccompanied adults excused)

Jaguar!

Montezooma's Revenge

Boomerang

Parachute Sky Jump

Kingdom of the Dinosaurs

Pacific Pavilion

Bigfoot Rapids

Mystery Lodge

opportunity to try out the latest in virtual reality games, see themselves on giant videoscreens, call each other on table-to-table telephones, and listen to the park's new in-house band, "KnottHeads."

Other changes include the revamped **HeadAche** and **HeadSpin** rides (formerly Greased Lightning and Whirlpool), and a new decorative scheme including a 50-foot-high "May pole" radiating streamers of color to various parts of the park.

Park favorites Boomerang and Parachute Sky Jump and Sky Tower will remain unchanged.

Driving Instructions to Knott's Berry Farm

From West Los Angeles: Santa Monica Freeway (I-10) East to Santa Ana Freeway (I-5) South. Stay on Santa South to the **Artesia Boulevard/Knott Avenue** exit. Stay in one of the two right-hand lanes of the off-ramp. Go straight, making no turns. You will be on Knott Avenue, which leads directly into the park.

From Orange County and Disneyland Area: Santa Ana Freeway (I-5) north to **Route 91** west to the **Beach Boulevard** exit, which leads into Knott's Berry Farm.

Here's an alternate route from Disneyland: Santa Ana Freeway (I-5) north to the **Beach Boulevard** exit. Bear right off the exit, and turn right (south) onto Beach Boulevard, which leads into the entrance to the park.

From Hollywood/San Fernando Valley: Hollywood Freeway (101) South to Santa Ana Freeway (I-5) South. Stay on Santa Ana Freeway South to the **Artesia Boulevard/Knott Avenue** exit. Stay in one of the two right-hand lanes of the off-ramp. Go straight, making no turns. You will be on Knott Avenue which leads directly into the park.

Power Trip for Adults and Older Children

Until the new ocean-theme roller coaster opens in The Boardwalk in mid-1997, the biggest draw at Knott's Berry Farm is the new **Jaguar!** ride. Lines will be long through the middle of the day. Arrive early at the park and ride it first; if you stay late, come back in the dark for a second trip. Another good time to head for popular rides is during nighttime entertainment.

Move on to **Boomerang, Montezooma's Revenge,** and **Mystery Lodge.** As it starts to get warm, move on to **Bigfoot Rapids.** You can dry off a bit at the **Log Ride.**

Use the afternoon to see some of the shows, including the **Stunt Show** and **Bird Cage Theatre.** Visit **Kingdom of the Dinosaurs,** the **Sky Jump,** and any other rides that strike your fancy.

If you are going to stay into the night, think about ducking out and visiting the **Chicken Dinner Restaurant** for supper and returning later; for the amount of food, the reasonable price, and children's menu, it's the best deal in the park.

Power Trip for Children

The big draws for kids are in **Camp Snoopy**, which will become crowded by mid-morning. Arrive there early if you can.

Many other amusement park rides will appeal to younger visitors. Working counterclockwise from Camp Snoopy, visit whichever of the rides in Fiesta Village your youngsters can handle. These might include **Gran Slammer, Tumbler**, and **Sling Shot**. The **Carousel** is in Fiesta Village, too.

Some young visitors will enjoy the **Sky Jump**. Amusement park rides that may appeal to some kids include **HeadAche** and **HeadSpin**; they make many adults dizzy. Most kids enjoy the **Bumper Cars** near the Good Time Theatre.

Children are sure to enjoy the dolphins and sea lions at **Pacific Pavilion** and the living fossils at **Kingdom of the Dinosaurs**.

Finally, Ghost Town will appeal to children of all ages. Youngsters will particularly enjoy the **Haunted Shack, Bird Cage Theatre**, and **Big Foot Rapids** on a warm afternoon.

Very young children will probably not enjoy Mystery Lodge; save it for school-age visitors.

Children will enjoy the **Ghost Town & Calico Railroad** and the **Butterfield Stage**.

Ghost Town

A rough-and-ready 1880s Old West boomtown of cowboys, stunt fights, can-can dancers, stagecoaches, a steam train, a log ride, old-time melodramas, and panning for real gold. Ghost Town is a fun place to walk about and explore.

Knott bought the California ghost town of Calico before he developed his own amusement park; the unofficial name for the ghost town is Calico because of that original purchase.

WOW **Timber Mountain Log Ride.** A Knott's Berry Farm classic, it was originally called the Calico Logging Company. When it opened in 1968, it was the first log flume theme ride in the country; today it is still considered one of the best. Traveling in hollowed logs, guests float through animated scenes of the inner workings of an old-time sawmill.

There is a false drop in the dark, and then you are in a wilderness scene with wildlife; the room smells like a pine forest. Your log will move out onto a track with a view of the outside world, with the tracks of the new Jaguar! ride coming very near.

Eventually the logs reach the end of their tour within Timber Mountain and plunge down a 50-foot waterfall. Riders receive only a tiny splash; the ride was developed when most visitors came to the park to go to a chicken dinner and didn't want to get wet.

The Old Trails Hotel. The first building erected in Ghost Town, the hotel was built in 1868 in Prescott, Arizona, and moved to the farm in 1940 to house the Covered Wagon Show, Knott's first attraction. The show was a "cyclorama," a combination of costumed figures and artifacts with a painted backdrop; the exhibit is still in place and is open to the public for a few hours each day. Inside the hotel is a mirror backed with diamond dust and a key rack missing a hook for unlucky Room 13.

The Bottle House. All 3,082 empty wine and whiskey bottles that form the walls of the Bottle House face inward; if they didn't, they'd whistle in the wind. Built at the Farm in 1946, the Bottle House was inspired by similar structures in turn-of-the-century mining towns throughout the West. While wood was scarce (it was used in the mines), empty liquor bottles were plentiful.

Haunted Shack. The crooked residence of Shifty Sam and Slanty Sadie, a place where water runs uphill, where chairs attach to the wall at seemingly impossible angles, where the ball on the pool table always travels uphill into the hole, and the home of the worst puns in the park. Your guide will probably remind you that he doesn't write the material. Our favorite: "Sam and Sadie are two of the park's finest preserves." The building first stood in Esmeralda, Nevada, and was reconstructed nail-for-nail at the park.

Old School House. Everything in this old building—books, desks, chalkboard, and potbelly stove—is authentic and dates from about 1875.

Gold Mine. For a small fee, you can take a pan to the sluice in Ghost Town and sift out a few grains of gold. Each year, guests take home more than $70,000 in real gold dust from Knott's Gold Mine in Ghost Town; more than $3 million has been taken from the stream since the park opened.

Out to pasture. Old Betsey is a wood-burning engine that had been used in the early days of borax mining on the desert in Death Valley. The locomotive was a distinct improvement over the 20-mule team that used to haul borax from the mines. The mineral borax has a number of industrial uses as a water softener and as part of the foundry process. The engine was retired to the park in 1941.

Ghost Town & Calico Railroad. Think the New York City subways are unsafe? The Knott's Berry Farm train line is held up by bandits more than 10,000 times a year. The train circles the park on a ½-mile tour that takes 15 minutes (including a scheduled robbery).

The GT&C operates two locomotives: #41, *Red Cliff*, from the Rio Grande Southern, and #40, *Green River*, from the Denver & Rio Grande and the Denver & Rio Grande Western.

Both engines were built by the Baldwin Locomotive Works in 1881, two of only twelve C-19 narrow-gauge freight locomotives built by Baldwin. The total weight of the engine and loaded tender is about 127,260 pounds. The engine's wheel configuration is 2-8-0.

The stable of coaches for the GT&C includes:

Combine #351. Built in 1880, and rebuilt in 1937 as a parlor-buffet car for service on the San Juan Express

Closed Vestibule Coaches #310, #325, and #326. Built by Pullman in 1887

Parlor Car #105, *Durango.* Built in 1880, one of only three narrow-gauge parlor cars still in operation

Special Car B-20, *Edna.* Used as a private business car for Otto Mears, president of the Rio Grande Southern. Originally lit by oil lamps, it included mahogany-wood finish and crimson plush upholstery. Includes sleeping space for six, a private bedroom with bathroom, kitchen, and dining room

In January and February, the two steam engines are given time off, and service on the GT&C is provided by the *Galloping Goose*, a gasoline-fuel railway car built in 1931 for the Rio Grande Southern. Originally powered by a Pierce-Arrow engine, it now uses a GMC Truck powerplant.

Western Trails Museum. A most eclectic collection of things more-or-less Western. Some of the materials began from Walter Knott's own gatherings, but over the years many of the items in the Western Trails Museum were donated by guests.

You'll see old china from the early mining ghost towns of Colorado and California, period photos of Bat Masterson and Annie Oakley, and many guns and knives. On the back wall, look for an unusual picture of the Rock Island Line train system; based on an original black-and-white photo from 1900, it was hand-colored on mother of pearl. The work was created in 1916 for E. J. Goreman, president of the railroad, for his office. Set near Colorado Springs, Pike's Peak is the snow-covered point at the right side of the range.

Another interesting exhibit is a display of cigarette-box cards that offer a glimpse at what were considered naughty pictures at the turn of the century; there's nothing there to shock a modern-day visitor, alas.

Butterfield Stage. The last regularly scheduled stagecoach line in America circles a portion of Ghost Town. Five of Knott's six stagecoaches are authentic and more than 100 years old; many were used on the Oregon Trail in the 1880s and 1890s. The one replica, the Knott's coach, was built on the Farm in 1956. Knott's maintains a stable of more than 50 horses for this attraction.

Medicine Show. Be on the lookout for Dr. I. Will Skinnem and his old-time medicine show; this fast-talking pitchman has a cure for whatever ails you.

WOW Bird Cage Theatre. A replica of the Bird Cage Theatre in Kingston, Arizona, near Tombstone, it is claimed by Knott's as the oldest continually operated melodrama theater in the United States, putting on as many as nine different plays every day; dedicated fans can come back to see the entire series on one visit.

The Bird Cage Theatre has a stone front and a canvas ceiling. In the Old West, many buildings were never really completed because towns sprang up and died so fast.

At the time of its opening in December 1881, the theater had not been named. A visitor looked around at the ornate boxes that flanked the footlights and the rows of tiny curtain boxes that hung suspended on either side of the length of the theater. "They are like bird cages," she said, and the theater got its name. The price of admission to front boxes was $25, a small fortune at the time, and the theater was crowded to capacity each night.

Before the show begins, a musician will help gather the crowd with a performance on the antique steam-powered calliope parked outside. When you enter the theater, try for a seat in the front center; the sound of the actors does not travel well within.

Shows include "Riverboat Revenge," "The Drunkard," "Cloak of Evil," and "Wreck of the Blue Bell Express." The shows are high camp, with damsels in distress, bad guys in black hats, and handsome heroes. They have names like Caldwell Cadwallader, Heather Harmony, and Dan Darby.

At one of the shows I attended, the bad guy came on the stage at the end to thank the visitors. "I hope you enjoyed the show," he said. "If you didn't enjoy it, be sure to tell your friends that you saw it at Disneyland."

A long line of actors have made their debuts at the Bird Cage, with comedian Steve Martin the most famous alumnus.

Check out some of the old playbills in the lobby. Among the ones we've seen are Maude Adams in J. M. Barrie's "What Every Woman Knows," from the Hollis Street Theatre in Boston from 1910. There was also "Alice Sit-by-the-Fire" with Ethel and John Barrymore from 1906.

By the way, the Bird Cage Theatre takes part in the Knott's Scary Farm festivities with a special series of gruesome shows. At Christmas there are holiday specials.

Main Street Windmill. A one hundred-year-old import from England, the windmill was originally intended by Walter Knott to serve as the boundary for the park. Today it stands in roughly the middle of the park. The mill was brought to California in the 1860s by an English syndicate that first laid out and subdivided Riverside.

Siege of Fort Knott Stunt Extravaganza. Knott's first permanent new stunt show in 17 years. Cheer on the ever-resourceful U.S. Agent Jebadiah Casy as he attempts to hold down the legendary Fort Knott from the gold-hungry likes of Welby Weed and his evil cohort, Frank Fargo.

Note that some of the seats are out in the sun; if you want to be sure of shade, arrive early and choose one of the covered stagecoaches which ring the top of the small amphitheater. There also are two stagecoaches and some seats on the stage itself; they are up close to some of the action but don't offer the best view for events going on at the other end of the stage.

Seated Statues. Knott's four sets of seated character statues—**Handsome Brady/Whiskey Jim** and the can-can girls in Ghost Town, the Mexican ladies in Fiesta Village, and the flapper girls in The Boardwalk—are favorite stops for visitors to the park. A fifth pair, **Cecilia and Marilyn,** sit in front of the Calico Saloon and were modeled after actual Saloon performers of the 1950s. They have a recorded patter that is remarkably suited to the actions of most of the males and some of the females who sit down beside them.

At one time, nearly all Kodak film was processed in one plant, in Rochester, New York, and Knott's began to get phone calls from Kodak wanting to know who these guys were and why they kept turning up in photographs.

Berry Stand. In a nod to local history, the original stand that launched the Knott's Berry Farm empire is preserved as a refreshment counter.

Attached to the side of the stand are some old photos. Alongside is a Ford Model A, the vehicle driven by Walter and Cordelia Knott when they came to California. Out back is a small patch of boysenberry plants, the only berries still grown within the park.

Boot Hill. Most of the grave markers in this boneyard across the way from the Western Trails Museum are authentic relics of the Old West; the graves themselves were left behind. The painted backdrop to Boot Hill is the backside of the Good Times Theatre.

Check out the grave of Hyram McTavish. Legend has it the heart will beat again after one hundred years—any visitor who places his or her foot on the grave will feel . . . something.

Our favorite epitaphs? "Butch Youngman 1857. Here lies Butch, we planted him raw. He was quick on the trigger, but slow on the draw." And, "Here lies Lester Moore. 4 slugs shot from a 44. No less and no more."

Camp Snoopy

WOW The official home of the Peanuts gang, a six-acre kids' paradise themed like a section of California's High Sierra. Camp Snoopy features 30 attractions for the youngest visitors.

At Camp Snoopy, check out **Snoopy's Animal Friends** to get close to tame forest animals and birds, including a timber wolf, raccoons, and an owl. There's also a koi pond and pony ride.

Camp Snoopy's **Bear-y Tales Playhouse** is a just-for-kids world that includes winding corridors and all sorts of unusual surprises.

Jaguar!, Knott's Berry Farm

Wild thing. Jaguars
figure prominently in
Mayan and Aztec
mythology and are the
subject of much pre-
Columbian sculpture and
pottery. Many of these
works depict
Tezcatlipoca, a mighty
Mayan deity who could
transform himself at will
into a powerful jaguar.

The largest and most
powerful of the American
members of the cat
family, jaguars are
especially abundant in
the dense forests of
Central America. The
mature animal measures
more than seven feet in
length and stands two
feet high at the shoulder.
The big cat's coat is a
rich yellow, spotted with
large black rosettes
consisting of a circle of
spots surrounding a
central spot.

Although greatly
feared, the jaguar rarely
attacks humans.

Rides at Camp Snoopy include the **Red Baron** plane ride, the **Twister** mini coaster, the **Ball Room**, the **Rocky Road** cars, and a kid-size Ferris wheel.

Thomas A. Edison Inventors' Workshop. The workshop includes California's only collection of Edison artifacts and memorabilia, including early experimental lightbulbs and handwritten notes by Edison. There are 10 hands-on exhibits demonstrating the invisible forces of electricity and magnetism.

Fiesta Village

A salute to California's Spanish legacy, Fiesta Village is also the prowling ground for Knott's new Jaguar! adventure.

WOW! Jaguar! Knott's unusual roller coaster prowls through a large portion of the park like a cat stalking its prey, speeding up and slowing down as it threads the needle through thrill rides and circles the lake.

Passengers board the coaster at the Temple of the Jaguar, a five-story Mayan pyramid in Fiesta Village. The temple was inspired by the architectural style of the famed Tikal pyramid, which included a decorative crown cap depicting a supernatural figure holding a jaguar mask.

According to Mayan and Aztec legend there exists in this temple a deity who could transform himself into a mighty fire-breathing cat. As you make your way through the queuing area inside the five-story Temple of the Jaguar you will hear and see evidence of the cat and feel his presence.

The waiting line passes through detailed corridors and chambers as it moves upward to the columned Hall of Egress. Still within the temple, passengers board sleek 24-seat trains. As you board the trains it will become obvious that you have become the cat.

Immediately after departure, riders climb 60 feet into the air and then dive back through the temple's crown tower to begin a twisting, spiraling expedition above Knott's Berry Farm. The Jaguar! is a very quiet ride and actually travels very low to the ground in most places.

Halfway through your journey you will come back through the temple tower through fire effects, strobe lights, and fog.

Along the way, Jaguar! passes right through the middle of the loop of another Knott's Berry Farm coaster, Montezooma's Revenge, and then careens within inches of the Timber Mountain Log Ride. The Jaguar! track winds its way through all of Fiesta Village and parts of Camp Snoopy. The structure crosses the tracks of the park-circling Grand Sierra Scenic Railroad in eight places.

The steel structure runs about 2,700 feet. There are no guardrails to block the view from the cars, which travel just fast enough to give a thrill in places and do not turn upside down; at some points Jaguar! is more like an aerial tour of the park. The trip, about two-and-a-half minutes, is a ride that most everyone in the family will enjoy.

The waiting line for the ride will build during the summer and on holidays to as much as an hour; come early or on an off-season day to avoid the crowds.

Jaguar! joins Montezooma's Revenge and Boomerang as major coasters at the park; Camp Snoopy's Timberline Twister offers gentler trips. Jaguar! is actually the sixth coaster in Knott's history; the park's first coaster, Corkscrew, opened in June 1975. After 14 seasons and more than 31 million riders, it was retired in 1989.

Calico Mine Train. Built in 1966, it was the first ride on Knott's Berry Farm and one of the first dark rides at any park.

Jaguar's vital statistics. Track length: 2,700 feet
   Height of first track drop: 60 feet
   Height of second track drop: 60 feet
   Maximum G force: 2.5 Gs
   Capacity: Three 24-passenger trains can accommodate a total of 1,500 guests per hour

Special Ks. Knott's Berry Farm's equivalent of Disney's "Hidden Mickeys" are the park's several dozen "Hidden Ks" that are woven into structures and decorations in the park. For example, look in the designs made out of twigs in the windows of the Art Gallery across from the Bottle House.

The walkway to the loading platform is decorated with some old mining equipment. The whole scene is reminiscent of Disneyland's Thunder Mountain Railroad, but trust us: this is not a thrill ride.

The train chugs its way into the Calico Mine. Among the first sights is an old mine elevator like the ones used in the diggings of the west. You'll visit some interesting animated dioramas of miners at work, and then arrive at the highlight of the trip: an otherworldly cavern of stalactites and stalagmites with a simulated cave organ as accompaniment.

The mine train cars seat about 10 persons, with five cars per train; traffic is pretty constant on a busy day.

WOW! Montezooma's Revenge. From zero to 55 miles per hour in 3.2 seconds, heading for two circles within a vertical loop.

Montezooma's Revenge welcomed its first passengers in 1978. Revenge transports riders through a 76-foot-high, 360-degree loop to the apex of a 148-foot tower; the train pauses for a moment at the top of the tower and then races backward through the loop and up a 112-foot tower at the opposite end of the track.

Tampico Tumbler. Two cars revolve around a center pivot forward and backward as they rotate around the central column. At the same time the entire ride climbs up and down the column. It sounds complicated, and it is,

Hammer time. Near the exit from the park to the Knott's Marketplace is a stone with an old inscription describing the winners of a drilling contest held at Tonopah, Nevada, on July 30, 1905.

According to the legend, the Double Hand contest was won by Malley and Cundy; using an eight-pound hammer they drilled 38.5 inches in 15 minutes. The Single Hand contest was won by Atha Richie, who used a four-pound hammer and drilled 22.5 inches in 15 minutes.

What a pain. Hidden alongside the Church of the Reflections is a place of discomfort. Dr. Walker's dentist office was hauled in from the Ozarks in 1953. Dating back to the 19th century, the walls of the office include some frightening tools.

but all you've got to do is ride. This medium-wild experience is nearby to the entrance to Jaguar!

Dentzel Carousel. The oldest working carrousel at any amusement park in the country, it was one of the first two-level carrousels built. It was created by Gustav A. Dentzel in 1902 at G. A. Dentzel Steam and Horsepower Carousel Builder in Germantown, Pennsylvania. Prior to coming to Knott's in 1955, it entertained guests at Hershey Park in Hershey, Pennsylvania, and before then at Brady Park in Canton, Ohio.

Of the 54 animals on the Carousel, 48 are original, hand-carved works of art. Collectors have paid up to $100,000 for original, hand-carved Dentzels. The animal menagerie includes lions, tigers, ostriches, camels, zebras, giraffes, pigs, cats, and horses with real horsetail hair.

Music is provided by two turn-of-the-century organs, a Wurlitzer and a Gavioli band organ, which can produce the sound of 22 instruments.

Church of the Reflections. Originally the First Baptist Church of Downey, California, the building was moved to Knott's in 1955 to provide a nondenominational respite for Farm employees and visitors. More than one hundred weddings are performed here each year. Bride and groom sometimes ride off on a stagecoach; Snoopy is available to serve as the best man.

Reflection Lake. Between Fiesta Village and Ghost Town, this is the site of the **Incredible Waterworks Show**, a sound, light, and water spectacle that explodes nightly in season.

The Boardwalk

Enjoy the looping action of Boomerang, the high-flying thrills of XK-1 and the Parachute Sky Jump, and the exciting Kingdom of the Dinosaurs.

WOW! Boomerang. A high-speed, high-energy European-designed thriller, Boomerang turns riders upside down six times—three times forward and three times backward—in less than a minute.

Boomerang replaced Corkscrew, the first inverted 360-degree looping coaster in the country; Corkscrew was moved to an amusement park in Coeur d'Alene, Idaho.

The blue tracks of Boomerang take off from a loading station next to the Sky Jump. Riders sit two abreast, held into place by overhead restraints.

The train is pulled backward up a hill; at the top, the cars are suddenly released. The train races down the hill, back through the loading station and into a twisting turn one way and then the other, into a 360-degree double loop, and up another hill. When you reach the top, you will drop back through the same course, this time backward.

Boomerang's tracks are very close to the walkways of the park in The Boardwalk; passersby can get right up close to wonder why people would pay good money to subject themselves to such an experience.

XK-1. The ride lifts visitors 70 feet in the air and then turns the controls over to you. If you're not too careful—or are pretty daring—you'll find yourself upside down. Little rocket ships are attached to arms that extend up and away from a central revolving column. Riders can use a motor to spin their cabin around the pivot at the rear of the cabin. The entire assemblage rises up and then descends the central column.

Slingshot. An old amusement park ride that still thrills; visitors sit in a swing suspended by chains from an overhead canopy. The whole apparatus spins, rises, and then tilts. Riders must weigh less than 230 pounds.

WOW Parachute Sky Jump. Inspired by the classic Coney Island landmark, the parachute ride lifts riders 235 feet into the air . . . and then lets them drop to earth beneath a billowing parachute canopy. (The cables on the platform's harness are there to break your fall at the bottom and in case of an emergency; most of the drop is a true parachute glide.)

The combined weight of the riders on the parachute is not supposed to exceed 385 pounds, which is easy enough to exceed with a family of four; you may end up having to split your party.

You can also take the easier and slower way up and down by riding the **Sky Cabin,** a slowly revolving enclosed cabin that climbs the parachute jump tower.

WOW Kingdom of the Dinosaurs. As your ride begins, you'll find yourself within the lab of Prof. I. F. Wells in the 1920s. (This is obviously a guy who is a few initials left and right of fame.) Check out the details in the antiques and mementos, but don't let your mind drift too far—you are about to find yourself strapped into a time machine that will take you back into the day of the Tyrannosaurus Rex. You'll see a prehistoric world in battle with an ancient ancestor of the elk. Pterodactyls flap by overhead. And you'll even catch glimpses of Ice Age humans huddling for warmth in ragged furs.

There is a great deal of detail in the ride, beginning with the outfits worn by attendants who load you onto your car; they're in period dress, with argyle socks and knickers.

The massive 15-ton sculpture at the entrance to the Kingdom of the Dinosaurs was carved from a block of Taiwanese marble by California sculptor John Cody. The dino's name, by the way, is Rocky.

When the ride opened in 1987, it was way ahead of Barney and the rest of the dinosaur craze that followed; today it's interesting but lagging behind thrill rides at Disney and Universal parks. Still it's a relaxing place out of the sun or rain, and young kids will love it.

Discovery Center at Kingdom of the Dinosaurs. As you exit the ride, the park's resident paleontologists are ready to answer questions about the wonders you have just experienced. A detailed chart shows stages in the earth's development. On display in the area are petrified wood, teeth, and tusks from prehistoric beasts, and priceless fossils—some as much as tens of millions of years old.

Buffalo Nickel Arcade. Beneath the Kingdom of the Dinosaurs is a video arcade which neither is in Buffalo nor involves nickels or pennies. You'll need lots of quarters to get through the modern electronic games and old-time skee-ball alleys.

Charleston Circle Fountain. The unusual waterworks located in the circular plaza that opens to Ghost Town, the Charleston Circle Fountain was originally part of the set for the 20th Century Fox movie, *Hello, Dolly!*, starring Barbra Streisand.

WOW! Pacific Pavilion. Marine-mammal trainers demonstrate the skills of the park's dolphins and sea lions. The first session of each day is a demonstration of training techniques with one or more of the animals; serious animal lovers will want to see that demonstration as well as a later show. Consult the park schedule for performances on the day of your visit.

Gates open about 15 minutes before the scheduled show. The seating area for the small outdoor amphitheater is covered with a mesh top which does not offer much protection from the sun.

Good Time Theatre. In the summer and Christmastime, the stage features a live Broadway-style musical extravaganza with dazzling lights, spangled costumes, and special effects. Admission to shows is usually free, part of the general ticket for the park.

The Christmas entertainment usually features a Snoopy ice show. Summer performances have included an Elvis review and other rock performances.

HammerHead. A high-speed spinning ride that takes visitors from the surface of a sea grotto to a height of 80 feet. The grandstand seats at times spin upside down and sideways to the ground.

Nu Wave Theatre. Home of "Cyber Sports in 3-D," a permanent 15-minute experience combining filmed 3-D images and high-intensity music with lasers, smoke, and other theatrical effects.

Wacky Soap Box Racers. When it opened in 1975 it was the only four-track simultaneous roller coaster in existence, a slow-speed race. Alas, time has passed it by and the ride is due to be removed to make way for Knott's newest roller coaster.

HeadSpin. A spinning ride inside a dark building, an experience that holds an unusual appeal for some riders and terrifies the rest of us.

HeadAche. A spinning carnival ride; cars turn on their sides going around an uneven track under a tent.

Wheeler Dealer Bumper Cars. A classic favorite, the ride is somewhat hidden past the entrance to the Kingdom of the Dinosaurs and near the Good Times Theater.

Indian Trails

A celebration of the lore, legends, crafts, music, and dance of Native American tribes. The 27-foot **Knott's Totem Pole** at the entrance to Indian Trails is said to be the largest totem ever carved from incense cedar. The pole's nine figures are a Native American with child, buffalo, burro, turtle, owl, Knott's pioneer with covered wagon, grizzly bear, and eagle.

At Knott's Indian Trails, Native Americans produce intricate arts and crafts. The architectural styles include an authentic Big House and tepees of the Blackfoot, Nez Percé, Cheyenne, Crow, and Kiowa tribes.

The Big House is in the style of the Kwak'wala-speaking people. The building's facade and the hand-carved house posts near its entrance were created by Richard Hunt, a Kwak'wala artist from British Columbia.

Children's Camp at Indian Trails. Young visitors can create traditional honor bonnets, as well as learning beadworking, and sand painting. Native American storytellers recount living history, and kids can have their faces painted in authentic tribal fashion.

Wild Water Wilderness

The **Wild Water Wilderness** recaptures the beauty of a California river wilderness park of the early 1800s. The trees, all indigenous to the Far West, include California black oak, coast redwood, and Torrey pines. Colorful wildflowers blossom throughout the Wilderness, including poppies, bluebells, daffodils, larkspurs, and lilies.

WOW! Bigfoot Rapids. How's this for a specialized record: the Wild Water Wilderness area's major body of water, Bigfoot Rapids, is California's longest man-made whitewater river. The raft ride is a lot of fun if you don't mind getting a bit wet; depending on your luck, you may even get soaked. There: you have been warned. Now go and have fun.

(By the way, a sign at the Rapids tells visitors that garbage-bag raingear is not allowed. It seems that everyone wants to be a fashion critic.)

Nature Center at Wild Water Wilderness. After your ride on Bigfoot Rapids, stop to ask park rangers about Sasquatch, the elusive creature known to some of his friends as Bigfoot. You'll see some photos and footprints that suggest that the huge beast really does exist. Rangers will also show displays of insects, tarantulas, scorpions, and native plants, plus a glassed-in apiary that puts you about as close as you ever may want to get to a buzzing beehive.

The ranger station is located in the old Maizeland School, the first school in the Rivera District constructed in 1868.

The **Wilderness Dance Hall** in Wild Water Wilderness once stood on the Burbank farm of Jim Jeffries, one-time American heavyweight boxing champion. Jeffries used the barn to train promising young fighters. Today the barn is home to an antic assortment of entertainers from bluegrass pickers to Smoky Mountain cloggers.

WOW! Mystery Lodge. Legends tell of a mystical place called Thunder Falls deep within the luxuriant green forests of the Northwest Coast. It's a place of miracles where grand waterfalls crash into a running river with such force that the canyon reverberates with the sound of thunder. Some say that the roar of the thunder brings forth mystic images of the distant past.

Visitors enter Thunder Falls through an ornate wooden archway, constructed from Pacific Coast cedar. They'll continue across a re-creation of a traditional Native American boardwalk, like the wooden walks that connect Northwest Coast tribal houses to the ocean.

The lights dim, and the sounds of a multimedia preshow set the scene. Suddenly, lightning fills the sky, and guests are invited into the lodge to take refuge from the approaching storm.

Deep within the lodge, a mystical old storyteller begins to spin his tale. It's a story of life, of birth and love and marriage and children and old age and the approach of eternal rest . . . and it presents a mystical calm to all who hear it. The message is that if we can share the mysteries of life with the wonder of a child, life will always be full of magic.

Master dancer Bill Cranmer, a hereditary Chief of the 'Namgis people and chairman of the U'mista Cultural Society, choreographed and performs the traditional dance movements in the show, and he serves as the voice of the presentation. Kwak'wala musicians, including drummers and singers, perform the show's musical score.

I'm not about to destroy the illusions of the Mystery Lodge with an explanation of the magic you see performed, but I will tell you this much: the show combines a real actor on stage with spectacular lighting and special effects.

The $10 million project opened in 1994. The preshow and main lodge presentations total 26 minutes; the hourly capacity is 1,440 visitors.

The facade of Mystery Lodge, designed by Native American artists, includes images from the lore and legend of the Northwest People. The stonework includes four towering waterfalls dropping into Thunder Lake. At night, bursts of fire, fog, and strange images issue forth from the building.

Aspects of the Mystery Lodge experience are based on traditions of the 'Namgis people of Alert Bay, Cormorant Island, British Columbia, Canada. The 'Namgis are one band of the Kwak'wala speaking people, the native North American group who live on the northeastern coast of Vancouver Island, the central coast of mainland British Columbia, and the small islands in between.

Before contact with European settlers, the Kwak'wala-speaking people numbered about 7,000. With the introduction of European diseases in the 19th century, the population was reduced to less than 1,900 by 1929. Today they number about 5,000.

Because of the groundbreaking work of the German-American anthropologist Franz Boas in the late 1800s, the Kwak'wala-speaking people's traditions are among the most completely documented of all North American Indian traditions.

Today the descendants of Boas' guide George Hunt are among the cultural leaders of their people, and the Hunt family of carvers produced some of the elements of Knott's Indian Trails area.

Skilled canoeists, fishers, and sea hunters, the Kwak'wala also excelled as carvers of totem poles, masks, and other ritual objects. They originated some of the most spectacular rituals of the Northwest Coast culture, including the potlatch ceremony. Potlach means "to give" and is a ceremony common to all tribes in the area.

Occasions for holding a potlatch include marriages, naming children, mourning the dead, and transferring rights and privileges from a retiring chief to his successors. Dancers dressed in dramatic masks and robes invoke theatrical magic to act out the legends and stories of their people in dances that are traditional to a particular family. The host distributes gifts as payment to his guests for witnessing the ceremony. By accepting the gifts, guests validate the host's claims to the dances.

Mystery Lodge Store and Museum. At the exit to the Mystery Lodge is an attractive shop offering a variety of handmade native crafts to view and purchase. A hand-carved Coast Salish canoe depicting a killer whale design hangs from the ceiling beams. The canoe was carved at Knott's Berry Farm during a canoe-making demonstration begun in 1992 to commemorate the opening of the Indian Trails area. Also on display are intricately carved house posts and other craftwork.

Items for sale include bentwood boxes made from a single piece of cedar and used to store blankets and prized family possessions; carvings in argillite, a slate-like stone; hand-woven baskets; and a selection of native silver jewelry.

Eating Your Way Through Knott's Berry Farm

Mrs. Knott's Chicken Dinner Restaurant. The winner and still local champion is the sprawling eatery which regulars and employees call the *CDR*. Today the restaurant seats more than a thousand people in eight separate dining rooms and employs as many as 375 people in the summer.

The classic dinner, served from 11 A.M., was priced at $9.95 in 1996 and includes four pieces of fried chicken, cherry rhubarb, mashed potatoes and gravy, vegetable, soup or salad, as many buttermilk biscuits as you can eat, beverage, and boysenberry pie. You can also order broiled chicken breasts, chicken and dumplings, chicken potpie, barbecued beef ribs and chicken, or chicken-fried steak for the same $9.95.

Today it is the largest single-location chicken restaurant in the country, and the single largest user of chickens in California. The part of the restaurant that faces Grand Avenue is the original restaurant which was built in and around the Knott's home. You can ask to sit in one of the straight wood-backed chairs under the paddle fans in the original dining room.

Check out the guest register in the waiting area on the wall. Among distinguished eaters in the early years were Eddie Fisher, Elizabeth Taylor, and Jane Russell.

The biggest days of the year are typically Mother's Day, Easter, and Thanksgiving. (The restaurant is closed on Christmas Day.) The biggest day on record at the restaurant was Mother's Day 1982, when 8,400 meals were served.

Hollywood Beanery. A basic fast foodery in a beautifully retro diner; actually, Knott's didn't have to restore anything at all—this place has remained unchanged for decades. Located in the back corner of the park near the Bumper Cars, the restaurant is decorated with a giant black kettle on the roof; every few minutes a huge waitress pops out of the top of the kettle bearing a tray with a drink, burger, and fries. The Bean Pot's menu today features pizzas, nachos, and tossed salads.

Knott's Family Steak House. Located in the California Marketplace, this restaurant is open from 11:30 A.M. for lunch and into the night for dinner. Offerings, priced from about $8 to $15, include steaks, lamb brochette with rice pilaf, and broiled salmon with sautéed tomato and capers.

Chicken To Go/Deli. You can buy a chicken and a boysenberry pie to go—or pack up a picnic basket of fried chicken, sandwiches, or salads to take into the park. Located in the California Marketplace.

Fireman's Barbecue. Chicken, ribs, corn on the cob, and more, in Ghost Town. A stand offers huge dill pickles to top off your meal.

La Cocinita and **Herdez Cantina.** Mexican specialties in Fiesta Village.

Special Events and Presentations

Independence Hall. A free exhibit outside of the gates of Knott's Berry Farm. Within the reproduction is a replica of the Declaration-signing chamber; you'll see live performances by actors portraying Ben Franklin, Thomas Jefferson, Patrick Henry, and others. (Many of the actors do double duty at the Bird Cage Theatre in the park.)

There is an exact replica of the Liberty Bell, down to its crack. The only real difference lies upstairs where there is a large auditorium that is used for guest orientations, private parties, and special events.

Easter EggMazeMent. A hands-on family event with elaborate walk-through adventure mazes. Held each year for a two-week period on either side of Easter Sunday.

Independence Day. An annual Fourth of July fireworks show and special events.

Knott's Scary Farm. The park is filled with elaborate walk-through mazes with ghastly storylines, live performances, and awesome special effects. Several of the rides are rethemed with disorienting special effects, music, and monsters. Among the special live shows are **The Hanging**, an annual satirical send-up in Calico Square. More than one thousand costumed and made-up performers haunt the park, mazes, and rides. The Scary Farm is a special-ticket event not covered by general admission, and tickets sell out in advance each year. Tickets go on sale in August at Knott's, and at Ticketmaster outlets throughout the West. Not recommended for young children. Held weekends in October, and Halloween night.

Knott's Scary Farm Halloween Haunt, first begun in 1972, is considered both the world's largest annual Halloween party and the largest annual event in the amusement park industry.

On the last two weekends of October, look for **Camp Spooky,** a daytime non-scare Halloween celebration for kids 11 and under, including trick-or-treating, costume contests, and other activities.

Knott's Merry Farm. The park is transformed into an 1880s Victorian Christmas shopping and entertainment village, complete with lavish decorations, dozens of artisans, special holiday foods, continuous Christmas shows, Santa's workshop, strolling carolers, choirs, and more. Held from about Thanksgiving to Christmas Eve. (The park is closed on Christmas Day.)

Classic Christmas Celebration. The annual party includes snow sledding on Beagle Hill, a holiday ice show, and other festivities.

Shopping

Knott's California Marketplace includes **Mrs. Knott's Chicken Dinner Restaurant**, the **Knott's Family Steak House**, the **Garden Terrace Cafe**, **Simply Grand Foods**, the **Farm Bakery**, **Knott's Ice Cream Parlor**, the **Berry Market and Farm Market**, and the **Candy Parlour.** Shopping at the marketplace includes **Virginia's Gift Shop** for decorative treasures and collectibles; **Marion's & Toni's** designer dresses; **Bob's Men's Shop**; **Leather, Suede and Boots**; the **International Shop** for clothing, gifts, and collectibles and a year-round Christmas store; **Inspiration House** for bibles, books, and religious gifts; and **Custom Hats and Shirts** for Knott's baseball hats, shirts, and items. There is also **Snoopy Snapshots**, headquarters for Snoopy and Peanuts souvenirs, fashions, and collectibles.

Visitors at Knott's Berry Farm can have their hands stamped and exit the park to shop at the marketplace or eat at the Chicken Dinner Restaurant, returning to the park later.

The **Farm Market** offers a complete selection of jams, jellies, preserves, and other Knott's Berry Farm products. You can also order products including gift baskets to be shipped back home.

SIX FLAGS MAGIC MOUNTAIN

1. Guest Relations
2. Baja Ridge
3. Viper
4. Revolution
5. Six Flags Plaza
6. Flashback
7. Bugs Bunny World
8. Log Jammer
9. High Sierra Territory
10. Rapids Camp Crossing
11. Roaring Rapids
12. Ninja
13. Samuri Summit
14. Jet Stream
15. Cyclone Bay
16. Psyclone
17. Freefall
18. Tidal Wave
19. Monterey Landing
20. Batman the Ride
21. Gotham City Backlot
22. Colossus Country Fair
23. Colossus
24. Pirate's Cove
25. Superman The Escape

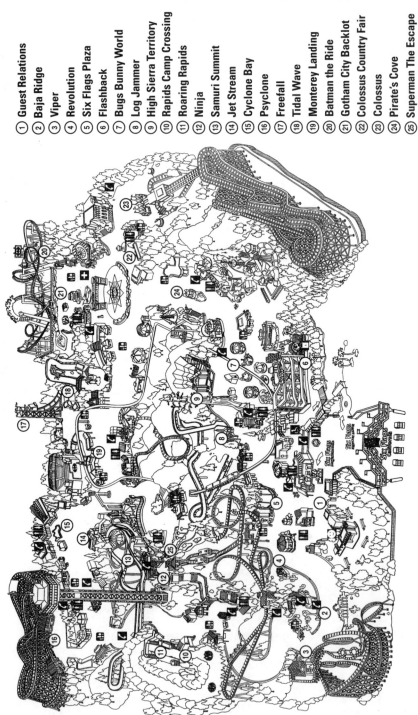

V
Six Flags California

Chapter 7
Six Flags Magic Mountain

Six Flags California is a thriller of a theme park, specializing in some of the most outrageous roller coasters, spinning rides, plunging cabins, and wet and wild water adventures anywhere.

Coaster aficionados go all soft and mushy as they recite the names of the park's world-class collection of roller coasters. They include **Viper**, the largest looping roller coaster in the world; **Flashback**, the world's only hairpin-drop roller coaster; **Psyclone**, a traditional boardwalk woodie; **Ninja**, the fastest suspended roller coaster in the West; **Goldrusher**, the park's first thriller; **Revolution**, the world's first 360-degree looper; and the spectacular **Batman The Ride**, which almost defies description. There's even the **Wile E. Coyote Coaster,** a mini-ride for the up-and-coming thrillseeker. And new for 1996 were a pair of unusual heart-stoppers: **Superman The Escape** and **Skycoaster**.

Also new was **Looney Tunes Nites**, Six Flags' first evening parade extravaganza. Grab a spot to watch cartoon superstars Granny and Tweety . . . with Sylvester not far behind, Wile E. Coyote, Foghorn Leghorn, the Tazmanian Devil, Yosemite Sam, and Daffy Duck. And there's also Superman and the Justice League of America and Batman. The parade begins in Gotham City Backlot and concludes with a spectacular fireworks finale over Six Flags Plaza.

It's a place where the vital statistics for rides include their "G" rating, something that visitors will share in common with jet fighter pilots and astronauts. One G is a measure of ordinary earth gravity; 3 Gs, for example, mean that the forces pulling on a rider are three times normal. You may also experience 0 Gs, or near to it, in drops.

It is also home to characters from Warner Bros. and Looney Tunes including Bugs Bunny, Foghorn Leghorn, Sylvester, Yosemite Sam, Wile E. Coyote, Pepe Le Pew, and Daffy Duck.

Six Flags California is the new name for the park that includes Six Flags

Tickets. Ticket prices were in effect for the summer of 1996 and are subject to change. Note that children over 48 inches tall must purchase a general admission ticket. *Discount coupon in this book.*
General admission: $32
Seniors: $19
Children under 48 inches: $15
Children two years and younger: Free
Two-park combo ticket: $45
Parking: $6

Can you name the six flags that have flown over Texas? They have been those of Spain, France, Mexico, the Republic of Texas, the Confederate States, and the United States.

Magic Mountain and the new Six Flags Hurricane Harbor water park, which opened for the summer of 1995.

The park is set in the beautiful Santa Clarita Valley, about 30 minutes north of downtown Los Angeles, at the Magic Mountain Parkway exit off Interstate 5 in Valencia.

Six Flags Magic Mountain is open daily from April through October. For the remainder of the year, the park is open on weekends and during school holidays. It is closed Christmas. Check the section on Six Flags Hurricane Harbor for spring and summer operating hours for that park.

Operating Schedule. In 1996, Six Flags Magic Mountain was open weekends and holidays from January through March, going to daily operations at the start of April through Halloween. The park was back on weekend hours through the end of the year, plus daily openings over the Thanksgiving and Christmas through New Year's Day holidays, with the exception of Christmas Day itself. Ordinary hours run from 10 A.M. to 6 P.M., with late closings of 10 P.M. or even midnight in the heart of summer and holidays. Call (818) 367-5965 to confirm hours.

Special events include **Spring Break Out** each April near Easter. A portion of the park is transformed into a gigantic Spring Break party, with a Velcro wall, human gyroscope, bungee run, mock sumo wrestling, and a zero-gravity space ball. Admission to the party is free to ticketholders, and a good and weird time is had by all.

On three weekends in October, Six Flags is transformed into a ghost town for **Fright Fest**, featuring strolling ghouls, goblins, and skeletons, as well as creepy graveyards, mazes, and live entertainment.

The Story of Six Flags

Land baron Henry Mayor Newhall bought the Spanish land grant known as the Rancho San Francisco in the mid-1800s. The Santa Clarita Valley was the site of California's first gold discovery in 1842 and of the state's first commercial oil well in 1875.

The amusement park opened its gates on May 29, 1971, a joint venture of subsidiaries of Seaworld, Inc. and the Newhall Land and Farming Company. Intended as a draw for the housing developments in the area, Magic Mountain originally featured 33 rides, attractions, and shows, as well as a local landmark, the 384-foot-tall Sky Tower. America's Bicentennial celebration in 1976 was the occasion for the introduction of the Great American Revolution—the world's first 360-degree looping roller coaster (now called the Revolution).

In 1979, the park was purchased by the Six Flags Corporation of Arlington, Texas. Under the new management, Roaring Rapids was added in 1981—the West's first white-water rafting ride on a quarter-mile-long man-made river.

Six Flags was the dream of a Texas oil man who came back from a trip to Disneyland in its early days, determined to create a mega-amusement park of his own. Angus Wynne, Jr., together with Hollywood director Randall Duell, created his first park in 1961: Six Flags Over Texas.

That first park, located between Dallas and Fort Worth, was divided into six "lands" that had the themes of the six national flags that had flown over Texas in its history.

Six Flags was subsequently purchased by Time Warner, whose properties include Warner Bros. Motion Pictures and Television (home of *Batman*), HBO, and *Time, People,* and *Sports Illustrated* magazines. The "cwazy wabbit" Bugs Bunny and his Looney Tunes cartoon compatriots joined the park as mascots in 1985. Now the whole bunch of them have taken up residence in Bugs Bunny World, a six-acre children's wonderland with 13 scaled-down rides and adventures designed exclusively for kids.

In 1995, Time Warner sold off about half the company to a venture capital company that included some of the executives of Six Flags among its investors.

Today, Six Flags claims the spot as the second largest theme park company in the world for its 12 properties: Six Flags Cal-

MUST-SEES

Flashback

Log Jammer

Colossus

Batman The Ride

Freefall

Skycoaster
(extra fee)

Psyclone

Superman The Escape

Ninja

Revolution

Roaring Rapids

Viper

ifornia (Six Flags Magic Mountain and Six Flags Hurricane Harbor); Six Flags Over Texas and Wet 'n Wild in Dallas/Fort Worth; Six Flags Over Georgia in Atlanta; Six Flags Over Mid-America in St. Louis; Six Flags Houston (Six Flags AstroWorld and Six Flags WaterWorld); Six Flags Great Adventure and Six Flags Wild Animal Safari Park in Jackson, New Jersey; Six Flags Fiesta Texas in San Antonio; and Six Flags Great America between Chicago and Milwaukee. All told, the parks draw more than 21 million visitors a year.

Times to Visit

In the busy summertime, the largest crowds are usually found from Wednesdays through Saturdays. Sunday is the least busy weekend day, and Monday and Tuesday are usually the quietest weekdays.

On a sunny Fourth of July, lines for signature rides like Superman The Escape and Batman The Ride can reach to three hours at midday.

Six Flags Magic Mountain is open on the weekends during the winter, which is a great time to come to the park to avoid crowds. Other off-season openings including Thanksgiving weekend and the two-week period leading up to Christmas and New Year's Day. Winter weather in Southern California can vary greatly, but usually ranges between 40 and 50 degrees with an occasional breakthrough to between 60 and 70.

Power Trip: Superman and Batman for Breakfast

There's no way around the fact that the new **Superman The Escape** ride will be the biggest draw at the park, followed closely by the venerable **Batman The Ride**. Your goal for a Power Trip is to arrive at the park early—aim for 15 to 30 minutes before the gates officially open—and make a beeline to Samurai Summit to be among the first to ride with Superman.

Watch your back. As we have noted, Six Flags Magic Mountain is a thriller of an amusement park, and many of the rides carry with them safety and health restrictions. Pregnant women and anyone with back, heart, or other health problems are advised against riding some of the wilder roller coasters and other rides. Other rides have height restrictions; these are intended to make sure that passengers are safely held in place by safety bars, belts, or other restraining devices.

Must be at least 54 inches to ride:
Batman The Ride
Superman The Escape
Viper

Must be at least 48 inches to ride:
Colossus
Flashback
Goldrusher
Psyclone
Revolution

Must be at least 42 inches to ride:
ACME Atom Smasher
Freefall
Gordon Gearworks
Ninja
Roaring Rapids
Sandblasters
Sierra Twist
Skycoaster
Swashbuckler
Tidal Wave

When you are back on earth, head immediately to Gotham City to visit Batman The Ride. With luck you will have accomplished your two major goals by the time the crowds begin to arrive at the park. Catch a quickie on **Colossus**. Then cut across the park to Baja Ridge and ride **Viper** and **Revolution**. As the crowds begin to move toward you, go against the flow to **Psyclone**, **Jet Stream**, and **Freefall**. Catch lunch early or late and complete your tour of the park.

Power Trip: Super Heroes for Lunch

This plan will work on days when the park is not overly crowded; on a holiday weekend it probably won't help much. The theory here is to go against the flow. Arrive at the park early. Insiders head to the back of the park first, riding most of the big roller coasters in quick succession: **Psyclone**, **Freefall**, and then **Gold Rusher**. Now work your way over to **Colossus**. Catch an early quick lunch and then move to Samurai Summit for **Superman The Escape** and then into Gotham City to ride **Batman The Ride** after the other early visitors have moved into other parts of the park. Now cut across the park to Baja Ridge and complete your coaster pilgrimage with **Viper** and **Revolution**. For the rest of your day, circle the park to the other attractions; by dinnertime you should be able to ride one of the major coasters a second time with only a reasonable wait.

Six Flags Plaza

Just past the entrance to Six Flags Magic Mountain is a mini-history of amusement parks in this century. To your left is a classic 83-year-old merry-go-round; to your right is a modern stomach-dropping stacked roller coaster. It's like that throughout much of the park, with old and new, machine and nature side by side.

WOW **Flashback.** This is the world's only hairpin-drop roller coaster, with six head-over-heels dives and a 540-degree upward spiral. It's all packed into a relatively small area with 1,900 feet of track stacked above each other. The drops are severe, producing a freefall experience on the plunges; fast steel switchbacks connect the turns just before trains fly into the gravity-defying upward spiral. Trains reach a maximum of 35 miles per hour, with a 3 G force on the one-and-a-half-minute ride. Flashback debuted in 1992.

Grand Carousel. A lovingly restored and maintained 1912 merry-go-round with moving wooden horses. Built by the Philadelphia Toboggan Company, it was operated at the Savin Rock Amusement Park in West Haven,

Connecticut, for 50 years before it was brought to California. The carrousel has 66 seats including 64 horses and two carriages; rides last three minutes.

Orient Express. At the back left corner of the plaza is an inclined railway up the mountain to the rides and observation tower on Samurai Summit. The people mover is a much easier route up the hill than the stairs and ramps that lead from the back of the park.

Palace Games. A skeeball and arcade game center. Nearby is the **Palace Hoop Shoot**, a basketball carnival stand.

Valencia Falls. A favorite picture spot in the park, with fountains and waterfalls cascading down the mountain. The **Valencia Falls Pavilion** is home of the popular Bugs Bunny in Rabbit Hood stage show, presented in an outdoor amphitheater; check the entertainment schedule for hours.

Maingate Bandstand and **Carousel Bandstand.** Check the park schedule for concerts and special events.

> **Rock news.** Bugs Bunny World is home to the "Weather Man Rock," a tongue-in-cheek example of folk art. (We've seen similar displays at several other places around the U.S.) The legend on the rock explains how it works: if the rock is hot and dry, the weather is sunny. If the rock is wet, it's rainy. If the rock is white, it's snowing. If the rock is not visible, it's foggy. And then there are the disaster warnings: if the rock is underwater, there's a flood. If the rock is moving, there is an earthquake going on. And if the rock is missing, the legend warns, there is a hurricane.

High Sierra Territory

One of the prettiest spots in a pretty park, the High Sierra Territory is beautifully landscaped with trees and plants of the mountains. All that said, the entrance to the area is through the **General Sam Tree**, a 140-foot-tall artificial Sequoia tree—a world-record holder for such replicated greenery, according to the park.

WOW **Log Jammer.** A log-ride classic, dating from the early days of the park and featuring a pair of straight-down drops.

Metro High Sierra Territory Station. A stop on the Six Flags aerial monorail system, connecting to stations at Colossus County Fair, Samurai Summit, or round-trip for a bird's-eye tour of much of the park.

Sierra Twist. A fast-spinning sled ride on an inclined platter.

Yosemite Sam Sierra Falls. Splash down 760 feet of twisting, turning water slides aboard two-person rafts. Warning: you will get wet, or even soaked. The heavier the riders, the more the water will fly.

Bugs Bunny World

A corner of the High Sierra is devoted to a children's play area. The rules are reversed here; children must be *short* enough to ride, and parents can only watch.

Wile E. Coyote Coaster. Training wheels for the under-48-inches set, this is the place to begin a career as a roller coaster rider.

Echo Cave/Rock Maze. A world unto the children, with a twisty-turny maze shrouded in the mist and a cave that talks back to visitors. Warning: visitors will be wetted by the mist.

Baron Von Fudd. Mini prop planes circle the field.

The Carousel. Another classic merry-go-round, in a mini version.

Daffy Duck Duners. Dune buggies on a kid-sized, kid-speed track.

Elmer Fudd Orchard. Round and round a big red apple on the back of a wacky worm.

Granny Gran Prix. Electrically powered minicars on a scenic track; young visitors need no driver's license.

Lady Bugs. This time it's ladybugs, and they're going round and round a big mushroom.

Road Runner Racers. The miniest of mini–grand prix racing cars.

Tasmanian Devil Cycles. Three-wheelers . . . going round and round.

Tweety Bird Cages. Now you're in a bird cage, going round and round just outside of the reach of that silly puddy cat, Sylvester.

Wile E. Coyote Critter Canyon. Here's your chance for the time-honored pursuit of tame sheep, goats, ducks, and other pettable critters. Display areas feature more than 50 species of rare and exotic animals.

Animal Star Theatre. Animals from exotic to household friends perform in a stage show presented in a mini 250-seat outdoor amphitheater in season.

Trainers demonstrate the tricks they have taught their menagerie, which includes dogs, birds, snakes, and more. A large part of the very popular show is devoted to educating the young audience about animals. Check the performance schedule on the day of your visit.

Golden Bear Theatre. A 3,200-seat amphitheater. Name entertainers and special events including cheerleader competitions and ice shows (1996 featuring the Russian Ice Skating Team). Some events require payment of an additional fee.

Wascal Terrace. A stage for special entertainment events. Check the park schedule.

Pirates Cove

A 15-foot volcano rumbles to life and blankets this swashbucklin' area with fog, almost obscuring your basic neighborhood six-foot skulls and seven-foot mermaids. This area is also the home of several classic carnival rides.

Buccaneer. A rocking pirate ship swings back and forth, gathering momentum until it finally turns completely upside down.

Jolly Roger. A classic tilt-a-whirl, sending riders around a wobbly, spinning turntable.

Swashbuckler. A spinning swing set.

Colossus County Fair

WOW! Colossus. The county fair serves as the backdrop for the colossal **Colossus** coaster, one of the largest dual-tracked wooden roller coasters in the world with nearly a mile of track times two courses.

An old-style speed demon, the Colossus features cars that reach speeds of up to 62 miles per hour and experience G forces of up to 3.23 on the 3.5-minute ride. That's a long ride in roller coaster terms.

Colossus covers 10 acres of land, climbing to 115 feet above the ground at its highest point. There are 14 hills in all, with two drops of more than 100 feet each (a world record at the time of its construction in 1978) and a climactic triple jump near the end.

There are two six-car trains on each of the two tracks; each car seats four riders. The maximum capacity of the ride is about 2,600 guests per hour. That's among the largest capacities of any thrill ride in the world. Colossus is a good place to head when lines are long elsewhere.

After dark, Colossus becomes a multicolored light show. A computer-controlled lighting system bathes the entire ride in color; as many as 128 different color combinations can be created.

Circus Wheel. Round and round you'll go; only the operator knows where you'll stop.

Metro Colossus County Fair. A stop on the park-circling monorail, which also has stations at Six Flags Plaza and Samurai Summit.

Boardwalk Arcade, Center Ring Games, Recording Studios of America, and **Shoot the Hoop.** Video machines, carnival games, and your chance to cut your own audio or videotape singing with a professional backup group.

Magic Moments Theatre. Home to a high-energy theatrical review in season, usually from mid-April through the end of September. A show called Carnaval du Futur has settled in for a long-term run; it is described as mixing bits of the roller-skating rock and roll of "Starlight Express" and the celebrated strangeness of Cirque du Soleil.

There are upper and lower levels to the one thousand-seat theater; visitors in the bottom half are closer to the action and sometimes surrounded by it, while the first row of the top section offers the best view of all the goings-on.

Gotham City Backlot

The dark world of the Caped Crusader is recreated in Gotham City Backlot, the newest of Six Flags California's theme areas. You'll know you're in town when you hear the rumble of the awesome Batman ride and the screams of the visitors who paid good money to climb on board.

You'll enter through the portals of the city and into Bruce Wayne's beautifully landscaped Gotham City Park. As you move a bit further into the park, though, you begin to hear some strange sounds and see some unsettling sights, including a crashed police car, a broken fire hydrant, and other indicators that all is not well with Gotham City. And then you are into the somewhat menacing tunnels beneath Gotham City, tunnels that lead up to Batman's newest crime-fighting device, The Ride.

WOW **Batman The Ride.** You'll clamber aboard one of two sleek black ski-lift-style trains, each carrying 32 passengers sitting four across. Unlike standard roller coasters, though, the trains are missing something: the floor! You'll be locked into place with padded over-the-shoulder and belt-locking harnesses.

Traditional roller coaster trains travel atop a track and inside of loops; Batman The Ride sends you soaring 360 degrees around the outside of a loop, a very different sensation.

Passengers experience a maximum of 4 Gs on the 2,700-foot track. Reaching speeds of up to 50 miles per hour, the trains enter into two vertical loops (77 feet and 68 feet tall), two single corkscrews (each 40 feet long), and a one-of-a-kind 224-foot "heartline" spin with a zero-gravity weightless force and nothing but air below your feet.

The heartline spin comes after the first loop when riders go through a twisting spin centered around the middle of your body. It's a quick trip from a 4G loop into a zero-gravity roll, which is something you don't do everyday unless you are a professional coaster rider.

Is Batman the ultimate in roller coasters? Well, the experts point out that there are faster, higher, and wilder coasters—including the Viper at Six Flags Magic Mountain—but Batman is unusual because the lower bodies of the riders are hanging free. Think of it as a ski lift gone crazy and you get the idea.

In the world of amusement park technology, the Batman ride is called an inverted coaster, while the Ninja is called a suspended coaster because it has enclosed train cars hanging from an overhead track.

The capacity of the Swiss-made ride is about 1,400 passengers per hour.

ACME Atom Smasher. A whirling, wobbly turntable ride set within the industrial walls of the ACME factory.

Gordon Gearworks. Let centrifugal force plaster you to the wall as the platform spins at a 45-degree angle.

Monterey Landing

WOW **Freefall.** Here's an elevator ride you won't soon forget: your car will rise to the top of a 10-story (98-foot) tower, move out onto a platform . . . and then drop straight down. You'll reach 55 miles per hour in about two seconds and then zoom out on a curved rail at the bottom.

Each of the eight cars carries four passengers per trip; one car drops every 12 seconds. A state-of-the-art system applies brake pressure according to the weight of each car plus its passengers at 40 different sensor locations along the slow-down pathway.

By the way, professional and amateur theme park enthusiasts consider this ride to be a roller coaster, albeit in a class of its own.

Goldrusher. The first roller coaster at Six Flags, this runaway mine train was built in 1971. By comparison to the big coasters, it's rather tame with a top speed of 35 miles per hour, but it still has its share of thrills. The half-mile track is built into the hillside, with its track very close to the ground—an excellent beginner coaster ride lasting about two-and-a-half minutes.

Sandblasters. Every amusement park worth its name has a bumper car ride; if that's what you're looking for, here's a fine example.

Scrambler. A human eggbeater, two-seat cars spin around on an uneven platform.

Spin Out. As the cage spins faster and faster, the floor drops out below you.

Tidal Wave. The wettest water flume, 20-passenger boats plunge over a 50-foot waterfall.

Batman Forever Stunt Show. The show at the one thousand-seat **Monterey Bay Theatre** presents a behind-the-scenes look at the making of the *Batman Forever* movie, including versions of some of the stunts in the film. The show was developed from the script for the movie and includes the new Batmobile.

Batman Nights Fireworks, Laser, and Special Effects Show. The legend of the Caped Crusader bursts into the evening skies in a display of fireworks, lasers, and special effects at the Monterey Bay Theatre in Monterey Landing.

Remote Control Boats. Coin-operated model boats patrol a miniature harbor on the back side of the Monterey Bay Theatre.

Cyclone Bay

A Southern California equivalent of a beachfront boardwalk, much more attractive than Coney Island in New York; alongside the Psyclone wooden coaster.

WOW **Skycoaster.** New for 1996 is the Skycoaster, a strange cross between a gigantic backyard swing, bungee jumping, hang-gliding, and skydiving, and you get to pay for the privilege!

The ride apparatus consists of a soaring 173-foot-tall steel arch from which four steel cables are suspended; alongside are a pair of launch towers. At the end of each pair of cables is an attachment for up to three flight suits.

The volunteer riders are placed in the suits and stretched out parallel to the ground, and then the fliers are pulled by cable behind the arch to the top of the launch towers, about 152 feet off the ground. When one of the riders pulls a ripcord, the fliers swoop down in free fall about 50 feet before they zoom past their starting point—when they reach the bottom of the fall, they will be about six feet off the ground and moving about 60 miles per hour.

The forward motion of the fliers will carry them about 90 to 100 feet up in the air in front of the arch, reaching a weightless free-fall stall in midair before they swing back the other direction. The fliers will swing back and forth about a dozen times before they come to a stop at the bottom.

In order to ride Skycoaster, you'll have to fork over an additional fee. For flights with three fliers in the harness, admission will be about $14.95 per flier; for two-person flights, the charge will be about $19.95; and for solo flights the fare will be about $24.95.

Skycoaster is located at Cyclone Bay, across from the Batman Forever Stunt Show and the exit from Jetstream. Riders must be at least 42 inches tall.

WOW **Psyclone.** A traditional wooden coaster opened in 1991, Psyclone is a replica of the legendary 1927 Cyclone in Coney Island, New York. How realistic? Well, in addition to the feel of the steep drops and high-banked twists and turns, you'll also hear the somewhat unnerving sounds of creaking wood and screaming steel wheels.

There is more than a half-mile of steel track, 11 hills, and five high-speed banked turns; the track also drops into a 183-foot-long pitch-black tunnel. Riders are treated to a maximum G force of 3.

Built in 1991, the ride required 450,000 board-feet of treated Southern pine, unpainted to emphasize the ride's natural beauty. It's held together with 16,000 pounds of nails and 125,000 pounds of bolts. One more useless but interesting factoid: the ride required something like 40,000 manhours to build; if one carpenter had done the job by himself, it would have taken him 20 years to finish the job.

Psyclone features a 95-foot first drop angled at 53 degrees, 10 additional steep hills, five high-speed banked turns, and average speeds of up to 50 miles per hour; just to set the scene, the ride begins with a drop into a 183-foot-long dark tunnel.

Jet Stream. A pleasant tour aboard a jet boat with a splashy 57-foot-plunge finale. There is a bit less chance of getting wet on Jet Stream than on the Log Jam ride, but don't count out the possibility of a damp touchdown.

The loading platform for the ride is a circular turntable that is synchronized to the speed of the moving boats.

Entertainment at Cyclone Bay includes **Sharkey's Shooting Gallery** and the **Boardwalk Bandstand.** Check the daily schedule for performances.

Samurai Summit

WOW **Superman The Escape.** Look, up in the sky: that roller coaster is accelerating from 0 to 100 miles per hour in just 7 seconds and delivering 6.5 seconds of weightlessness. Only Superman The Escape could perform such feats. In fact, Six Flags claims its new ride is the first to reach 100 miles per hour.

We're not going to quibble over a few miles per hour or notches on the G-force belt; we do know that this ride is Super-Awesome.

The L-shape dual-track ride travels more than 900 feet (three football fields) from its launchpad on Samurai Summit on a track that suddenly curves into a climb straight up a 415-foot-tall tower.

The Superman adventure begins in the Fortress of Solitude, a crystalline ice cavern high atop the mountain ridge at Six Flags. Confronted by enemy forces inside the Fortress, the only escape for guests is to board 15-passenger aerodynamically designed vehicles. Electromagnetic motors blast the six-ton vehicles out of the Fortress through a special effects tunnel; the cars accelerate to 100 miles per hour and 4.5 Gs and then climb the 41-story tower reaching near-total weightlessness when they reach the top and freefall straight down the skyscraper.

The high speed of the ride requires huge wheels—a pair of 24-inch front wheels and two 30-inch wheels at the rear.

The construction of the Swiss-designed ride—at a cost of about $10 million—changes the look of the park. Other alterations to the scene include a bridge over the lift for the venerable Goldrusher coaster which circles all around the loading station for the Superman ride.

Metro Samurai Summit Station. A stop on the Six Flags aerial monorail system, connecting to stations at High Sierra Territory, Samurai Summit, or round-trip for a bird's-eye tour of much of the park.

WOW! Ninja. The Black Belt of coasters, West Coast's fastest suspended roller coaster. Trains swing 180 degrees side-to-side while hanging from an overhead track and traveling at speeds of up to 55 miles per hour. Riders are treated to a nearly 4 G positive gravity force in the second spiral of the ride.

Completed in 1988, the ride takes about two minutes to travel 2,700 feet of track. Each of three trains carries a total of 28 riders sitting two abreast. The maximum capacity of the ride is about 1,600 riders per hour.

Orient Express. The people mover down the mountain to Six Flags Plaza.

Muscle Beach Arcade. A video-game parlor.

Viper, Six Flags Magic Mountain

Sky Tower. The 38-story landmark offers a spectacular view of the entire park and much of the Santa Clarita Valley. The elevator ride to the top is part of the thrill.

Oriental Gardens. A tranquil garden for contemplation of all that lies below; a wise old Buddha lives there, too.

Rapids Camp Crossing

WOW: Revolution. You say you want a revolution? This giant looping steel roller coaster was the first of its kind when it was built in 1976. It included the world's first 360-degree vertical loop, towering 90 feet above the Grand Carousel.

The Swiss-made white steel track is built into the park's lush hillsides and features a fast-and-furious series of steep dips and serious dives inspired by old-fashioned wooden roller coasters.

The two-and-a-half-minute ride travels 3,457 feet of track; each train carries 20 riders in five cars sitting two abreast. The maximum capacity is about two thousand riders per hour.

Riders experience a maximum positive G force of 4.94 entering the vertical loop, which soars 90 feet high in a 45-foot diameter loop. The difference between the rider's lowest point at Valencia Falls and the highest point at the top of the lift is 113 feet.

WOW: Roaring Rapids. America's first man-made white-water river. Twelve-passenger boats splash through waves, crosscurrents, and rapids.

Entertainment at Rapids Camp Crossing includes the **Mining Town Arcade** and **Mining Town Games.**

Baja Ridge

WOW: Viper. The largest looping roller coaster in the world, with a top speed of 70 miles per hour, three vertical loops, a double-barrel boomerang, and a classic corkscrew. Some roller enthusiasts consider the Viper among the most frightening rides on the planet.

Riders turn completely upside down seven times and change elevation 16 times; the height of the first drop is 188 feet, seven stories taller than the colossal Colossus.

The two-and-a-half-minute-long ride travels a 3,830-foot track; each of the three trains carries 28 riders in seven cars, seated two abreast. The maximum capacity of the ride is about 1,700 riders per hour.

About those vertical loops: the first one rises and falls 114 feet, making it perhaps the world's tallest; the second is a mere 90 feet in height, and the last 62 feet tall. The boomerang turn, which rotates riders upside down twice, is 60 feet from its lowest to highest point. And the corkscrew is 40 feet high and 200 feet long.

If you need a bit of reassurance before you strap yourself into the over-the-shoulder locking harness for the ride, consider that the Viper required one million pounds of steel and 600,000 tons of concrete for its construction in 1990.

Speedy Gonzales Mouse Racers. Circle a giant Swiss cheese in tiny mice.

Eating Your Way Through Six Flags Magic Mountain

Eateries at Six Flags run from the most basic of fast food—a McDonald's in Cyclone Bay—to a talking moose head to a sit-down family restaurant with a spectacular mountaintop view.

Soda prices in the park are about $1.75 for a regular drink, or about $4 for a souvenir bottle. A better deal is offered by machines that sell cans of soda for $1 in some of the corners of the park. Also available are "icee" frozen drinks.

Six Flags Plaza

Chicken Plantation. Crispy fried chicken with all the fixings.

Plaza Cafe. A casual outdoor sidewalk bistro serving croissants, fruits, and specialty coffees alongside Valencia Falls in Six Flags Plaza.

Suzette's Bakery. Funnel cakes, hot and cold drinks.

High Sierra Territory and Bugs Bunny World

Mooseburger Lodge. The mooseburgers aren't really made from a moose, and the restaurant isn't really a hunting lodge in the High Sierras, but you could be fooled by both. This is an attractive, fun family restaurant that features a trio of robotic moose heads who are aided and abetted by singing waiters and waitresses who will be glad to perform the Moose Muffle Shuffle just for you. In addition to the big burgers, you'll also find ribs, a buffet, and special desserts including (of course) chocolate mousse.

Wascals. A kiddie-oriented burger and fries stand.

Monterey Landing

Cantina. Mexican specialties.

Waterfront. A burger and fries and chicken strips eatery in Monterey Landing. Prices range from about $5 to $7, including a drink.

Rapids Camp Crossing and Baja Ridge

Katy's Kettle. Hamburgers, turkey burgers, and fries.

Cyclone Bay and Samurai Summit

Dockside Deli. Sandwiches and pizza.

Laughing Dragon Pizza Company. A fun eatery alongside the entrance to the thrilling Superman The Escape ride atop Samurai Summit. (Before the arrival of Superman, the restaurant had been called Four Winds.)

Surfside Grill. What else would you expect from a restaurant under a jumbo hot dog? Frankfurters, chili dogs, icees, and more.

Colossus County Fair and Pirates Cove

Colossus Cookery. Burgers and fries.

Food Etc. An indoor food court offering a wide range of delectables, including Mexican food, pasta, pizza, and more.

Frum D'Trees. Fresh fruit and juices under a thatched roof with a great view of the local volcano.

Gotham City Backlot

Gotham City Pizza Factory. Like the sign says.

Six Flags Hurricane Harbor

Whoosh! A hurricane of a water park swept into Six Flags in 1995 with the first season of Six Flags Hurricane Harbor. The successful second park was expanded for 1996.

The 22-acre park tells the watery story of a lost lagoon in a forgotten world. Set amidst the fringes of a tropical jungle, you'll find the remains of a disappeared civilization, hidden pirate treasures, playful sea creatures, ancient ruins, shipwrecks, girls in bikinis, guys in muscle shirts, kids in wave pools, suntan lotion, hot dogs, ice cream . . . you get the idea.

Tickets. Hurricane Harbor ticket prices were in effect in the summer of 1996 and are subject to change.
General admission: $16
Children under 48 inches: $10
Children two years or younger: Free
Seniors 55 and above: $10
Magic Mountain/ Hurricane Harbor combo ticket: $45
Parking (same lot as Magic Mountain): $6

The water park is in the shadow of Colossus and Flashback, two of the biggest, baddest roller coasters at the park.

Six Flags expects that most visitors will make it a day at either Magic Mountain or Hurricane Harbor. Combination tickets for separate days are available. Some visitors, though, might choose to visit the water park in the day and cross through to the theme park at night. Both parks share the same parking lot.

The operating schedule for Hurricane Harbor is dependent upon the weather, but plans call for it to be open on weekends only from early May and then daily from Memorial Day through Labor Day from 10 A.M. to 6 P.M.; the park will stay open until 8 P.M. on summer weekends. After Labor Day, Hurricane Harbor will remain open on weekends only through the end of September.

Be sure to call to confirm the schedule; call (818) 367-5965.

Rafts are required at Lightning Falls, Tiki Falls, Lost Temple Rapids, and the River Cruise. All visitors can use free tubes provided by the park; on busy days it may make sense to rent a personal tube for an additional charge.

Changing rooms are located in the entrance plaza, Buccaneer Village. Locker rentals are $3, plus a $2 deposit. Inner tubes are provided for the water slides; personal tubes for the Lazy River are available for $4 for a single and $6 for a double.

Castaway Cove. Designed exclusively for the littlest swashbucklers (under 54 inches tall), Castaway Cove is one of the largest children's water play areas in California. Adventures include a variety of pint-size water slides, including a pair of cannon slides. Little visitors will also find waterfalls, a bamboo raintree, friendly sea creatures, an organ that squirts water as guests play the keys, hidden pirate treasures, and a kiddie fortress loaded with waterfalls, gadgets, swings, slides, and more.

Youngsters can also enjoy splashing in the secluded tide pools of Octopus Island, where a giant eight-legged creature stands guard.

Shipwreck Shores. The place where Red Eye the Pirate first dropped anchor is now a splashy lagoon with more than 32 family activities, including a huge skull which dumps thousands of gallons of water on intruders every few minutes, and weeping sails shed continuous streams. Visitors enter through the rickety remains of Red Eye's ship, mysterious ancient ruins from a lost civilization. Around the shoreline are eight 11-foot-tall water-spraying statues and the old temple entrance to the volcano.

Geyser Peak. Towering 45 feet above the harbor between Castaway Cove and Shipwreck Shores is the volcano where Red Eye the Pirate once hid his plunder.

The River Cruise. Guests board rafts that circumnavigate Castaway Cove and Shipwreck Cove on a 1,300-foot-long lazy river at the center of the park. The three-foot-deep river moves at about two miles per hour, and a complete circuit takes about eight minutes. Along the river banks are nine 15-foot-tall tikis, replicas of the famous statues of Easter Island, as well as the Rainbow Reef, an overgrown tropical rain forest.

Forgotten Sea. Hurricane Harbor's tide pool, with a constant tide of two-foot waves. The 480,000-gallon pool slopes down to a depth of six feet.

Taboo Tower. The park's showcase attraction—visible from Interstate 5—is the crumbled remains of an ancient temple; three speed slides—including a completely dark tube—are built into the 65-foot-tall ruins. They include the 300-foot-long **Daredevil Plunge**, with a 45-degree straight drop; the bumpy, 260-foot-long **Escape Chute**; and the **Secret Passage**, an enclosed 325-foot spiraling slide.

Lightning Falls. Three twisting, turning, 400-foot-long open tube slides named after island storms drop about 42 feet; look for **Typhoon Tube, Tornado Twist,** and **Thunder Trough.**

Tiki Falls. Visitors splash down through the mouths of Hurricane Harbor's three most famous tikis: **Old Shut Eye,** a 395-foot enclosed slide; **Stone Face,** a 385-foot closed-tube slide; and **Bright Eyes,** a semi-enclosed 400-foot tube.

Lost Temple Rapids. A 560-foot-long, six-person family rafting adventure down the island's ancient aqueduct.

Eating Your Way Through Hurricane Harbor

Red Eye's Kitchen in Buccaneer Village features rotisserie chicken, hamburgers, hot dogs, salads, and more. **Trade Wind Treats** in Castaway Cove offers fresh fruit and snacks. **Paradise Snacks** next to the Forgotten Sea wave pool serves ices, churros, and pretzels.

VI
Sleeping and Eating for Less

Chapter 8
Negotiating for a Room

Notice the title of this section: it's *not* called *buying* a room. The fact of the matter is that hotel rooms, like almost everything else, are subject to negotiation and change.

Here is how to pay the highest possible price for a hotel room: walk up to the front desk without a reservation and say, "I'd like a room." Unless the "No Vacancy" sign is lit, you're going to pay the "rack rate," which is the published maximum nightly charge.

Here are a few ways to pay the lowest possible price:

1. Before you head for your vacation, spend an hour on the phone and directly call a half dozen hotels that seem to be in the price range you'd like to spend. (We recommend membership in AAA and use of their annual Tour Books as starting points for your research.)

Start by asking for the room rate. Then ask them for their *best* rate. Does that sound like an unnecessary second request? Trust us, it's not: we can't begin to count the number of times the rates have dropped substantially when we ask again.

[Here's a true story: I once called the reservation desk of a major hotel chain and asked for the rates for a night at a Chicago location. "That will be $149 per night," I was told. "Ouch," I said. "Oh, would you like to spend less?" the reservationist asked. I admitted that I would, and she punched a few keys on her keyboard: "They have a special promotion going on. How about $109 per night?"

Not bad for a city hotel, I reasoned, but still I hadn't asked the big question: "What is your best rate?" "Oh, our best rate? That would be $79," said the agent.

But, wait: "Okay, I'll take it. I'm a AAA member, by the way." Another pause, and then the reservationist said, "That's fine, Mr. Sandler. The nightly room rate will be $71.10. Have a nice day."]

When you feel you've negotiated the best deal you can obtain over the phone, make a reservation at the hotel of your choice. Be sure to go over the

Here's my card. Membership in AAA brings some important benefits for the traveler, although you may not be able to apply the club's usual 10 percent discount on top of whatever hotel rate you negotiate. (It doesn't hurt to ask, though.) Be sure to request a Tour Book and a California map from AAA, even if you plan to fly to California; they are much better than the maps given by car rental agencies.

Weekly, not weakly. Are you planning to stay for a full week? Ask for the weekly rate. If the room clerk says there is no such rate, ask to speak to the manager. He or she may be willing to shave a few dollars per day off the rate for a long-term stay.

dates and prices one more time, and obtain the name of the person you spoke with and a confirmation number if available.

2. But wait: when you show up at your hotel on the first night stop, look at the marquee outside and see if the hotel is advertising a discount rate. Many of the hotels in the Disneyland area adjust their prices based on attendance levels at the park. It is not uncommon to see prices change by $10 or more over the course of a day.

Here's where you need to be bold. Walk up to the desk as if you *did not* have a reservation, and ask the clerk: "What is your best room rate for tonight?" If the rate they quote you is less than the rate in your reservation, you are now properly armed to ask for a reduction in your room rate.

Similarly, if the room rate advertised out front on the marquee drops during your stay, don't be shy about asking that your charges be reduced. Just be sure to ask for the reduction *before* you spend another night at the old rate, and obtain the name of the clerk who promises a change. If the hotel tries a lame excuse like "that's only for new check-ins," you can offer to check out and then check back in again. That threat usually works; you can always check out and go to the hotel across the road that will usually match the rates of its competitor.

3. Here is the way to make the most informed choice, in the low-season only. Come down without a reservation and then cruise one of the motel strips near Disneyland. Check the outdoor marquees for discount prices and make notes. Find a phone booth and make a few phone calls to the hotels whose rates you found attractive. Once again, be sure to ask for the best price. The later in the day you search for a room, the more likely you are to find a hotel ready to make a deal.

Dialing for Dollars

As we cited in our true story, you must be aggressive in representing your checkbook in negotiations with a reservation agent. Sometimes you will also need to be persistent.

A few years back, *Condé Nast Traveler* magazine conducted a survey of hotel rates and found wide discrepancies between the prices quoted by central toll-free services, by a clerk called directly at a particular hotel, and by a travel agent. The survey was decidedly indecisive: no one source consistently yielded the lowest prices.

The magazine's recommendation: use the services of a travel agent you trust, and request that the agent verify the lowest rate with a direct call. The agent can check the computer first and then compare that rate against the hotel's offer.

Where Should You Stay?

Except for the busiest days of the year—Christmas through New Year's and the heart of summer among them—you're not going to have *any* trouble locating a place to stay somewhere near Disneyland. In fact, the biggest problem facing most visitors is choosing among the various places to stay.

Anaheim Area

(Price ranges are approximate and subject to change and adjustments in busiest seasons; ratings are relative for the area.)

$	Budget: less than $30
$$	$30–$60
$$$	$61–$90
$$$$	Luxury: $91–higher

Anaheim Angel Inn. 800 East Katella Avenue: (714) 634-9121. Shuttle, pool. **$$**

Anaheim Carriage Inn. 2125 South Harbor Boulevard: (714) 740-1440 or (800) 345-2131. Continental breakfast, shuttle, pool. **$$**

Anaheim Cavalier Inn and Suites. 11811 South Harbor Boulevard: (714) 750-1000. Shuttle, pool. **$**

Anaheim Center Inn and Suites. 505 West Katella Avenue: (714) 774-8639. Shuttle, pool. **$$$**

Anaheim Conestoga Hotel. 1240 South Walnut Street: (714) 535-0300 or (800) 824-3459. Shuttle, pool. **$$**

Anaheim Days Inn and Suites. 1111 South Harbor Boulevard: (714) 533-8830. Pool. **$$**

Anaheim Desert Inn and Suites. 1600 South Harbor Boulevard: (714) 772-5050 or (800) 433-5270. Continental breakfast, shuttle, pool. **$$**

Anaheim Desert Palm Inn and Suites. 631 West Katella Avenue: (714) 535-1133 or (800) 635-3423. Shuttle, pool. **$$**

Wrong numbers. Be sure you understand the telephone billing policy at the motel. Some establishments allow free local calls, while others charge as much as 75 cents for such calls. (We're especially unhappy with service charges for 800 numbers.) Be sure to examine your bill carefully at checkout and make sure it is correct. We strongly suggest you obtain a telephone credit card and use it when you travel; nearly all motels tack a high service charge on long distance calls, and there is no reason to pay it.

Safety first. The small safes available in some hotels can be valuable to the traveler, but be sure to inquire whether there is a service charge for their use. We've been in hotels that apply the charge regardless of whether we used the safe or not; look over your bill at check-out time and object to any charges that are not proper. In any case, we'd suggest that any objects that are so valuable you feel it necessary to lock up should probably be left home.

Anaheim Hilton and Towers. 777 Convention Way: (714) 750-4321 or (800) 222-9923. Shuttle, pool. **$$$$**

Anaheim Inn at the Park. 1855 South Harbor Boulevard: (714) 750-1811. Shuttle, pool. **$$$$**

Anaheim International Inn and Suites. 2060 South Harbor Boulevard: (714) 971-9393 or (800) 231-2345. Continental breakfast, shuttle, pool. **$$**

Anaheim Jolly Roger Hotel. 640 West Katella Avenue: (714) 772-7621 or (800) 446-1555. Shuttle, pool. **$$$**

Anaheim Marriott Hotel. 700 West Convention Way: (714) 750-8000 or (800) 228-9290. Shuttle, pool. **$$$$**

Anaheim/Orange Hilton Suites. 400 North State College, Orange: (714) 938-1111 or (800) 445-8667. Continental breakfast, shuttle. **$$$$**

Anaheim Plaza Hotel. 1700 South Harbor Boulevard: (714) 772-5900 or (800) 228-1357. Shuttle, pool. **$$$**

Anaheim Ramada Inn. 1331 East Katella Avenue: (714) 978-8088. Shuttle, pool. **$$**

Anaheim Super 8. 415 West Katella Avenue: (714) 778-6900 or (800) 777-7123. Pool. **$**

Anaheim Travelodge at the Park. 1166 West Katella Avenue: (714) 774-7817. Pool. **$$**

Best Western Anaheim Inn. 1630 South Harbor Boulevard: (714) 774-1050 or (800) 854-6175. Shuttle, pool. **$$$**

Best Western Anaheim Stardust. 1057 West Ball Road: (714) 774-7600. Shuttle, pool. **$$**

Best Western Courtesy Inn. 1200 South West Street: (714) 772-2470 or (800) 233-8062. Shuttle, pool. **$$**

Best Western Park Place Inn and Mini Suites. 1544 South Harbor Boulevard: (714) 776-4800 or (800) 854-8175. Continental breakfast, pool. **$$–$$$**

Best Western Pavilions. 1176 West Katella Avenue: (714) 776-0140. Shuttle, pool. **$$**

Best Western Raffles Inn and Suites. 2040 South Harbor Boulevard: (714) 750-6100 or (800) 654-0196. Shuttle, pool. **$$$**

Best Western Stovall's Inn. 1110 West Katella Avenue: (714) 778-1880 or (800) 854-8175. Shuttle, pool. **$$$**

Buena Park–Hampton Inn. 7828 Orangethorpe Avenue: (714) 670-7200. Shuttle, pool. **$$**

Buena Park Hotel. 7675 Crescent Avenue: (714) 995-1111. Shuttle, pool. **$$$$**

Candy Cane Inn. 1747 South Harbor Boulevard: (714) 774-5284. Shuttle, pool. **$$$**

Capri Laguna Inn on the Beach. 1441 South Coast Highway: (714) 494-6533. **$$$**

Carousel Inn and Suites. 1530 South Harbor Boulevard: (714) 758-0444 or (800) 854-6767. Continental breakfast, shuttle, pool. **$$**

Castle Inn and Suites. 1734 South Harbor Boulevard: (714) 774-8111 or (800) 227-8530. Shuttle, pool. **$$$**

Comfort Inn. 1251 North Harbor Boulevard: (714) 635-6401. Shuttle, pool. $$

Comfort Inn Maingate. 2200 South Harbor Boulevard: (714) 750-5211. Shuttle, pool. $$$

Comfort Suites. 16301 Beach Boulevard, Huntington Beach: (714) 841-1812 or (800) 714-4040. Shuttle, pool. $$

Comfort Suites at the Park. 2141 South Harbor Boulevard: (714) 971-3553. Shuttle, pool. $$$

Convention Center Inn. 2017 South Harbor Boulevard: (714) 740-2500 or (800) 521-5028. Continental breakfast, shuttle, pool. $$

Country Side Inn and Suites. 325 South Bristol Street: (714) 349-0300 or (800) 322-9992. Pool. $$$

Crown Sterling Suites. 3100 East Frontera: (714) 632-1221. Shuttle, pool. $$$$

Crown Sterling Suites Orange County Airport. 1325 East Dyer Road, Santa Ana: (714) 241-8300. Pool. $$$$

Crystal Suites Hotel. 1752 South Clementine Street: (714) 535-7773 or (800) 992-4884. Shuttle, pool. $$$

Days Inn Anaheim/Fullerton. 1500 South Raymond Avenue, Fullerton: (714) 635-9000. Shuttle, pool. $$$$

Days Inn Maingate. 1604 South Harbor Boulevard: (714) 635-3630 or (800) 634-8005. Shuttle, pool. $

Disneyland Hotel. 1150 West Cerritos Avenue: (714) 956-6400. Monorail, pool. $$$$

Doubletree Hotel Orange County. City Drive at Chapman: (714) 634-4500 or (800) 222-8733. Shuttle, pool. $$$$

Econolodge Maingate. 1570 South Harbor Boulevard: (714) 772-5721. Shuttle, pool. $$

Embassy Suites Hotel–Disneyland/Knott's Berry Farm. 7762 Beach Boulevard, Buena Park: (714) 739-5600 or (800) 362-2779. Shuttle, pool. $$$$

Four Seasons Hotel Newport Beach. 690 Newport Center Drive, Newport Beach: (714) 759-0808 or (800) 332-3442. Pool. $$$$

Good Nite Inn. 101 North State College Boulevard, Orange: (714) 634-9500 or (800) 544-6991. Shuttle, pool. $$

Hampton Inn. 300 East Katella Way: (714) 772-8713 or (800) 231-6034. Continental breakfast, shuttle, pool. $$$

Heritage Inn. 333 East Imperial Highway, Fullerton: (714) 447-9200. $

Holiday Inn Anaheim at the Park. 1221 South Harbor Boulevard: (714) 758-0900. Shuttle, pool. $$$

Holiday Inn–Buena Park. 7000 Beach Boulevard, Buena Park: (714) 522-7000. Shuttle, pool. $$$

Holiday Inn Express. 1600 East First Street, Santa Ana: (714) 835-3051 or (800) 959-4654. Shuttle, pool. $$

Holiday Inn Express–Anaheim. 435 West Katella Avenue: (714) 772-7755 or (800) 833-7888. Shuttle, pool. $$$

Holiday Inn–Fullerton. 222 West Houston Avenue: (714) 992-1700 or (800) 553-3441. Shuttle, pool. **$$$**

Holiday Inn–LaMirada/Buena Park. 14299 Firestone Boulevard, La Mirada: (714) 739-8500 or (800) 356-6873. Shuttle, pool. **$$$**

Holiday Inn–Maingate. 1850 South Harbor Boulevard: (714) 750-2801 or (800) 624-6855. Continental breakfast, shuttle, pool. **$$$**

Howard Johnson Hotel. 1380 South Harbor Boulevard: (714) 776-6120 or (800) 422-4228. Shuttle, pool. **$$**

Hyatt Newporter. 1107 Jamboree Road, Newport Beach: (714) 729-1234 or (800) 232-1234. Pool. **$$$$**

Hyatt Regency Alicante. Harbor and Chapman: (714) 750-1234 or (800) 972-2929. Shuttle, pool. **$$$$**

Hyatt Regency Irvine. 17900 Jamboree Boulevard, Irvine: (714) 975-1234 or (800) 283-1234. Pool. **$$$$**

Irvine Marriott at John Wayne/Orange County Airport. 18000 Von Karman, Irvine: (714) 553-0100. Shuttle, pool. **$$$$**

Magic Carpet Motel. 1016 West Katella Avenue: (714) 772-9450. Pool. **$**

Magic Lamp Motel. 1030 West Katella Avenue: (714) 772-7242. Pool. **$**

Marriott Norwalk Hotel. 13111 Sycamore Drive, Norwalk: (310) 863-5555 or (800) 553-1666. Continental breakfast, shuttle, pool. **$$$**

Mission Inn. 3649 Seventh Street, Riverside: (909) 788-0300 or (800) 344-4225. Pool. **$$$$**

Motel 6–Anaheim. 100 West Freedman Way: (714) 520-9696. Shuttle, pool. **$**

Newport Beach Marriott Hotel and Tennis Club. 900 Newport Center Drive, Newport Beach: (714) 640-4000. Pool. **$$$$**

The Pan Pacific Hotel. 1717 South West Street: (714) 999-0990. Shuttle, pool. **$$$$**

Park Inn International. 1520 South Harbor Boulevard: (714) 635-7275 or (800) 828-4898. Shuttle, pool. **$$$–$$$$**

Peacock Suites Hotel. 745 Anaheim Boulevard: (714) 535-8255 or (800) 992-4884. Shuttle, pool. **$$$**

Quality Hotel–Maingate. 616 Convention Way: (714) 750-3131 or (800) 231-6215. Shuttle, pool. **$$$$**

Radisson Plaza Hotel–Orange County Airport. 18800 MacArthur Boulevard, Irvine: (714) 833-9999 or (800) 353-3333. Pool. **$$$**

Ramada Limited. 921 South Harbor Boulevard: (714) 999-0684. Shuttle, pool. **$$**

Ramada Limited Newport Beach/Costa Mesa. 1680 Superior Avenue, Costa Mesa: (714) 645-2221 or (800) 345-8025. Continental breakfast, pool. **$$**

Ramada Maingate Anaheim. 1460 South Harbor Boulevard: (714) 772-6777 or (800) 447-4048. Shuttle, pool. **$$$**

Red Lion Hotel Orange County Airport. 3050 South Bristol Street, Costa Mesa: (714) 540-7000. Shuttle, pool. **$$$$**

Residence Inn by Marriott. 1700 South Clementine Street: (714) 533-3555. Shuttle, pool. **$$$$**

Residence Inn by Marriott La Mirada/Buena Park. 14419 Firestone Boulevard, La Mirada: (714) 523-2800 or (800) 331-3131. Continental breakfast, shuttle, pool. **$$$$**

Residence Inn by Marriott–Orange. 201 North State College Boulevard, Orange: (714) 978-7700 or (800) 423-9315. Shuttle, pool. **$$$$**

The Ritz-Carlton, Laguna Niguel. 33533 Ritz-Carlton Drive, Dana Point: (714) 240-2000. Pool. **$$$$**

Rodeway Inn Anaheim. 1030 North Ball Road: (714) 520-0101 or (800) 331-0055. Continental breakfast, shuttle, pool. **$$**

Saga Inn. 1650 South Harbor Boulevard: (714) 772-0440. Shuttle, pool. **$$**

Sheraton Anaheim Hotel. 1015 West Ball Road: (714) 770-1700 or (800) 331-7251. Shuttle, pool. **$$$$**

Sheraton Cerritos Hotel at Towne Center. 12725 Center Court Drive, Cerritos: (310) 809-1500 or (800) 325-3535. Shuttle, pool. **$$$**

Station Inn and Suites. 989 West Ball Road: (714) 991-5500 or (800) 874-6285. Shuttle, pool. **$$**

Super 8–Anaheim Park Motor Inn. 915 South West Street: (714) 778-0350. Shuttle, pool. **$$**

Surf and Sand Hotel. 1555 South Coast Highway, Laguna Beach: (714) 497-4477 or (800) 524-8621. Pool. **$$$$**

Travelodge Apollo Inn. 1741 South West Street: (714) 772-9750 or (800) 826-1616. Shuttle, pool. **$$**

Travelodge Convention Side Inn. 733 West Katella Avenue: (714) 774-8065 or (800) 826-1616. Pool. **$$**

Travelodge Cornerstone Inn. 1765 South West Street: (714) 774-6427 or (800) 826-1616. Pool. **$$**

Travelodge Maingate. 1717 South Harbor Boulevard: (714) 635-6550 or (800) 826-1616. Shuttle, pool. **$$**

Travelodge Westgate. 1758 South West Street: (714) 774-2136 or (800) 826-1616. Pool. **$$**

Tropicana Inn. 1540 South Harbor Boulevard: (714) 635-4082 or (800) 828-4898. Shuttle, pool. **$$$–$$$$**

Vagabond Inn–Costa Mesa. 3205 Harbor Boulevard, Costa Mesa: (714) 557-6360. Shuttle, pool. **$**

Washington Suites Hotel. 720 City Drive South, Orange: (714) 740-2700 or (800) 278-4837. Shuttle, pool. **$$$$**

Waterfront Hilton Beach Resort. 21100 Pacific Coast Highway, Huntington Beach: (714) 960-7873 or (800) 822-7873. Pool. **$$$$**

Westin South Coast Plaza Hotel. 686 Anton Boulevard, Costa Mesa: (714) 540-2500 or (800) 228-3000. Pool. **$$$$**

Long Beach Area

(Price ranges are approximate and subject to change and adjustment in busiest seasons; ratings are relative for the area.)

$ Budget: less than $30

$$ $30–$60

$$$ $61–$90
$$$$ Luxury: $91–higher

Belmont Shore Inn. 3946 East Ocean Boulevard: (310) 434-6236. **$**

Best Western Golden Sails Hotel. 6285 East Pacific Coast Highway: (310) 596-1631 or (800) 762-5333. **$$$–$$$$**

Best Western of Long Beach. 1725 Long Beach Boulevard: (310) 599-5555. Pool. **$$$**

City Center Motel. 255 Atlantic Avenue: (310) 435-2483. Continental breakfast, pool. **$**

Comfort Inn Long Beach. 3201 East Pacific Coast Highway, Signal Hill: (310) 597-3374 or (800) 228-5150. Continental breakfast, pool. **$$**

Days Inn City Center. 1500 East Pacific Coast Highway: (310) 591-0088. Continental breakfast. **$$**

Days Inn Long Beach. 5950 Long Beach Boulevard: (310) 423-5950 or (800) 882-8883. Continental breakfast. **$**

Econo Lodge. 250 Alamitos Avenue: (310) 435-7621 or (800) 446-6900. **$$**

Edgewater Beach Motel. 1724 East Ocean Boulevard: (310) 437-3090. **$**

Friendship Inn. 50 Atlantic Avenue: (310) 435-8369. **$**

Holiday Inn Convention and World Trade Center. 500 East 1st Street: (310) 435-8511. Pool. **$$$**

Holiday Inn Long Beach Airport. 2640 Lakewood Boulevard: (310) 597-4401 or (800) 465-4329. Pool. **$$$–$$$$**

Hotel *Queen Mary*. 1126 Queens Highway: (310) 435-3511. Staterooms on *Queen Mary*. **$$$–$$$$**

Howard Johnson Plaza Hotel. 1133 Atlantic Avenue: (310) 590-8858 or (800) 442-1688. Shuttle, pool. **$$$**

Hyatt Regency Long Beach. 200 South Pine Avenue: (310) 491-1234 or (800) 233-1234. Pool. **$$$–$$$$**

Long Beach Airport Marriott. 4700 Airport Plaza Drive: (310) 425-5210 or (800) 228-9290. Pool. **$$$–$$$$**

Long Beach Hilton. Two World Trade Center: (310) 983-3400. Pool. **$$$–$$$$**

Long Beach Inn. 2900 East Pacific Coast Highway: (310) 494-4393. **$**

Long Beach Renaissance Hotel. 111 East Ocean Boulevard: (310) 437-5900 or (800) 228-9898. Pool. **$$$$**

Queen City Motel. 3555 East Pacific Coast Highway: (310) 597-4455. Continental breakfast, pool. **$$**

Residence Inn by Marriott. 4111 East Willow Street: (310) 595-0909 or (800) 331-3131. Continental breakfast, pool. **$$$–$$$$**

Sheraton Long Beach. 333 East Ocean Boulevard: (310) 436-3000. Pool. **$$$$**

Super 8 Motel. 4201 East Pacific Coast Highway: (310) 597-7701 or (800) 800-8000. Continental breakfast, pool. **$$**

Surf Motel. 2010 East Ocean Boulevard: (310) 437-0771. **$**

Travelodge Convention Center. 80 Atlantic Avenue: (310) 435-2471 or (800) 578-7878. Pool. **$$**

Travelodge Hotel Resort and Marina. 700 Queensway Drive: (310) 435-7676 or (800) 255-3050. Pool. **$$$$**

Vagabond Inn. 185 Atlantic Avenue: (310) 435-3791. Continental breakfast, pool. **$$**

Los Angeles Downtown

(Price ranges are approximate and subject to change and adjustment in busiest seasons; ratings are relative for the area.)

$ Budget: less than $60

$$ $60–$89

$$$ $90–$149

$$$$ Luxury: $150–higher

Best Western Dragon Gate Inn. 818 North Hill Street: (213) 617-3077 or (800) 282-9999. **$$**

Best Western The Mayfair. 1256 West Seventh Street: (213) 484-9789 or (800) 821-8682. **$$–$$$**

The Biltmore. 506 South Grand Avenue: (213) 624-1011 or (800) 245-8673. Continental breakfast. **$$$$**

City Center Motel. 1135 West Seventh Street: (213) 628-7141. Afternoon tea. **$**

Figueroa Hotel–Convention Center. 939 South Figueroa Street: (213) 627-8971 or (800) 421-9092. Outdoor pool. **$$**

Good-Nite Inn. 1903 West Olympic Boulevard: (213) 385-7141. Outdoor pool, free parking. **$$**

Holiday Inn City Center. 1020 South Figueroa Street: (213) 748-1291 or (800) HOLIDAY. Outdoor pool, free parking. **$$$**

Holiday Inn Crowne Plaza Los Angeles Downtown. 3540 South Figueroa Street: (213) 748-4141 or (800) 872-1104. Outdoor pool. **$$$**

Holiday Inn LA Downtown. 750 South Garland Avenue: (213) 628-5242 or (800) 465-4329. Outdoor pool, free parking. **$$$**

Hotel Inter-Continental at California Plaza. 251 South Olive Street: (213) 617-3300 or (800) 327-0200. Outdoor pool. **$$$$**

Hyatt Regency Los Angeles. 711 South Hope Street: (213) 683-1234 or (800) 233-1234. Outdoor spa. **$$$–$$$$**

The Inn at 657. 657 West 23rd Street: (213) 741-2200 or (800) 347-7512. Full breakfast. **$$$**

InnTowne Hotel Los Angeles. 925 South Figueroa Street: (213) 628-2222 or (800) 528-1234. Outdoor pool. **$$$**

Kawada Hotel. 200 South Hill Street: (213) 621-4455 or (800) 752-9232. **$$$**

Los Angeles Athletic Club. 431 South Seventh Street: (213) 625-2211 or (800) 421-8777. Continental breakfast, indoor pool. **$$$**

Los Angeles Hilton and Towers. 930 Wilshire Boulevard: (213) 629-4321 or (800) 445-8667. Outdoor pool. **$$$–$$$$**

Metro Plaza Hotel. 711 North Main Street: (213) 680-0200 or (800) 223-2223. Free parking. **$$**

Milner Hotel. 813 South Flower Street: (213) 627-6981 or (800) 827-0411. Continental breakfast. **$–$$**

Motel de Ville. 1123 West Seventh Street: (213) 624-8474. Outdoor pool. **$**

The New Otani Hotel and Garden. 120 South Los Angeles Street: (213) 629-1200 or (800) 421-8795. Japanese garden. **$$$$**

Orchid Hotel. 819 South Flower Street: (213) 624-5855. **$**

Oxford Palace Hotel. 745 South Oxford Avenue: (213) 389-8000 or (800) 532-7887. Continental breakfast, free parking. **$$$**

Park Plaza. 607 South Park View Street: (213) 384-5281. Indoor pool, free parking. **$–$$**

Quality Inn. 7330 Eastern Avenue: (310) 928-3452 or (800) 228-5150. Complimentary breakfast, outdoor pool, free parking. **$$**

Radisson Wilshire Plaza. 3515 Wilshire Boulevard: (213) 381-7411 or (800) 333-3333. Outdoor pool. **$$$–$$$$**

Ramada Inn Commerce. 7272 Gage Avenue, Commerce: (310) 806-4777 or (800) 547-4777. Outdoor pool, free parking. **$$**

Royal Host Motel. 901 West Olympic Boulevard: (213) 626-6255. Outdoor pool, free parking. **$**

The Sheraton Grande. 333 South Figueroa Street: (213) 617-1133 or (800) 325-3535. Outdoor pool. **$$$$**

Stillwell Hotel. 838 South Grand Avenue: (213) 627-1151 or (800) 553-4774. **$–$$**

Travelodge Suites. 7701 Slauson Avenue: (213) 728-5165. Continental breakfast. **$**

USC Summer Conference. 620 West 35th Street: (213) 740-0031. Summer lodging, indoor/outdoor pools. **$–$$**

Vagabond Inn Figueroa. 3101 South Figueroa Street: (213) 746-1531 or (800) 522-1555. Continental breakfast, heated pool, free parking. Pets welcome. **$$**

The Westin Bonaventure Hotel and Suites. 404 South Figueroa Street: (213) 624-1000 or (800) 228-3000. Outdoor pool. **$$$$**

Wyndham Checkers Hotel. 535 South Grand Avenue: (213) 624-0000 or (800) 426-3135. Outdoor pool. **$$$$**

Hollywood Area

(Price ranges are approximate and subject to change and adjustment in busiest seasons; ratings are relative for the area.)

$	Budget: less than $60
$$	$60–$89
$$$	$90–$149
$$$$	Luxury: $150–higher

Banana Bungalow–Hollywood Hotel. 2775 Cahuenga Boulevard: (213) 851-1129 or (800) 446-7835. Free airport pickup. Beach and Disneyland shuttle, outdoor heated pool, free parking. **$**

Bel Age Hotel. 1020 North San Vicente Boulevard, West Hollywood: (310) 854-1111. Pool. **$$$**

The Westin Bonaventure Hotel, Los Angeles

Best Western Hollywood. 6141 Franklin Avenue: (213) 464-5181. Outdoor pool. **$$**

Best Western Hollywood Plaza. 2011 North Highland Avenue: (213) 851-1800 or (800) 232-4353. Outdoor pool. **$$**

Best Western Sunset Plaza Hotel. 8400 Sunset Boulevard: (213) 654-0750. Pool. **$$**

Beverly Garland's Holiday Inn. 4222 North Vineland Avenue, North Hollywood: (818) 980-8000 or (800) 238-3759. Transportation to Burbank Airport and Universal Studios, outdoor pool, and lighted tennis courts. **$$$**

Days Inn–Hollywood. 7023 Sunset Boulevard: (213) 464-8344. Heated pool. **$$**

Dunes Motel–Sunset. 5625 Sunset Boulevard: (213) 467-5171. **$**

Holiday Inn–Hollywood. 1755 North Highland Avenue: (213) 462-7181. Pool. **$$$**

Le Montrose Suite Hotel De Gran Luxe. 800 Hammond Street, West Hollywood: (310) 855-1115. Pool. **$$$**

Le Parc Hotel. 733 North West Knoll Drive, West Hollywood: (310) 855-8888. Pool. **$$$**

Le Reve Hotel. 8822 Cynthia Street, West Hollywood: (310) 854-1114. Pool. **$$$**

Mikado Best Western Motor Hotel. 12600 Riverside Drive, North Hollywood: (818) 763-9141. Pool. **$$**

Mondrian Hotel. 8440 Sunset Boulevard, West Hollywood: (213) 650-8999. Pool. Modern art collection. **$$$–$$$$**

Orchid Suites Hotel. 1753 North Orchid Avenue: (213) 874-9678. **$–$$**

Park Sunset Hotel. 8462 Sunset Boulevard: (213) 654-6470. Pool. **$$**

Radisson Hollywood Roosevelt Hotel. 7000 Hollywood Boulevard: (213) 466-7000. Pool. **$$**

Ramada Limited Hollywood. 1160 North Vermont Avenue: (213) 660-1788. Pool. **$**

Ramada–West Hollywood. 8585 Santa Monica Boulevard, West Hollywood: (310) 652-6400. Pool. **$$$**

Summerfield Suites Hotel. 1000 Westmount Drive: (310) 657-7400. Pool. **$$$**

Sunset Marquis Hotel and Villas. 1200 North Alta Loma Road, West Hollywood: (310) 657-1333. Private villas available. Pool. **$$$$**

Travelodge–Sunset/La Brea. 7051 Sunset Boulevard: (213) 660-1788. Pool. **$–$$**

Chapter 9

Eating Your Way Through Orange County and Los Angeles

Orange County Restaurants

California Cuisine

Foxfire. 5717 East Santa Ana Canyon Road, I-91 at Imperial Highway: (714) 974-5400. Salads, pastas, seafood, and steak. Moderate.

   Ozzies. 512 East Katella Avenue, Orange: (714) 633-3280. Moderate.

   Planet Hollywood. 1641 West Sunflower, Santa Ana: (714) 434-7827. Moderate.

   T.G.I.Fridays. Two locations: 3339 City Boulevard East, Orange: (714) 978-3308. 935 East Birch, Brea: (714) 256-2390. Moderate.

Chinese

Lotus Court. 181 East Commonwealth Avenue, Fullerton: (714) 738-3838. Moderate.

   Ming Delight. 409 West Katella Avenue, Anaheim: (714) 758-0978. Moderate.

   Wok Inn. 13055 Chapman Avenue, between Crystal Cathedral and Harbor Boulevard, Orange: (714) 750-3511. Moderate.

French

Aurora Ristorante. 1341 South Euclid Avenue, Fullerton: (714) 738-0272. Continental to exotic, including alligator, venison, and elk. Moderate to expensive.

   Cellar Restaurant. 305 North Harbor Boulevard, Fullerton, in the Villa del Sol: (714) 525-5682. Expensive.

   La Vie En Rose. 240 South State College Boulevard, Brea: (714) 529-8333. Expensive.

About the listings.
Price categories are relative to the type of restaurant and area, but in general a *Budget* restaurant has offerings priced below $10, while *Moderate* eateries have entrees in the range of $10 to $20, and *Expensive* restaurants have entrees that start at or near $20 and go up from there.

   Be sure to call restaurants to check on hours and the possible need for a reservation.

German

Gustav's Jagerhaus. 2525 East Ball Road, Anaheim: (714) 520-9500. Moderate.

Italian

Angelo's & Vinci's Ristorante. 550 North Harbor Boulevard, Fullerton: (714) 879-4022. Set in a reproduction of an Italian town square. Moderate.

   Foscari. 5645 East La Palma Avenue, Anaheim Hills: (714) 779-1777. Northern Italian. Moderate.

   Mulberry Street Ristorante. 114 West Wilshire Avenue, Fullerton: (714) 525-1056. Moderate.

   Thee White House. 887 South Anaheim Boulevard: (714) 772-1381. Northern Italian. Moderate.

Japanese

Koisan Japanese Restaurant. 1132 East Katella Avenue, Orange: (714) 639-2330. Moderate.

Seafood

The Catch. 1929 South State College Boulevard, Anaheim: (714) 634-1829. Steaks, too. Moderate.

   McCormick & Schmick. 2000 Main Street, Irvine: (714) 765-0505. Old Boston–style fish house. Moderate.

Fast Food

The Train McDonald's. 7861 Beach Boulevard, Buena Park. Just like every other McDonald's on the planet, although this one also includes a flight-simulator ride, a train set, and a souvenir shop. One block north of Knott's Berry Farm. Budget.

Los Angeles Restaurants
American

Brasserie. Hyatt Regency, 711 South Hope Street: (213) 683-1234. Budget.

   Checkers. Wyndham Checkers Hotel, 535 South Grand Avenue: (213) 891-0519. Expensive.

   Engine Co. No. 28. 644 South Figueroa Street: (213) 624-6996. Steaks, seafood, and salad in a renovated firehouse. Moderate.

   Fountain Court. Wells Fargo Center, 350 South Hope Street: (213) 621-2155. Budget.

   Garland Cafe. Holiday Inn L.A. downtown, 750 Harland Avenue: (213) 628-5242. Budget.

   Nicola. 601 South Figueroa Street: (213) 485-0927. Moderate.

   Original Pantry Cafe. 877 South Figueroa Street: (213) 972-9279. 24 hours. Moderate.

Otto Rothschild's Bar & Grill. The Music Center, 135 North Grand Avenue: (213) 972-7322. Budget.

Pacific Dining Car. 1310 West Sixth Street: (213) 483-6000. Classic steakhouse and seafood. 24 hours. Moderate.

Philippe the Original. 1001 North Alameda Street: (213) 628-3781. Where the "French Dip" was invented; cafe food with 9-cent coffee. Budget.

Sidewalk Cafe. The Westin Bonaventure Hotel & Suites, 404 South Figueroa Street: (324) 624-1000. Under the atrium, along the indoor lake, for salads and sandwiches. Budget.

Stepps on the Court. Financial district; shuttle to Music Center: (213) 626-0900. Moderate.

Argentine

Grand Avenue. The Shark Club, 1024 South Grand Avenue: (213) 747-0999. Budget.

California

Azalea. The New Otani Hotel & Garden, 120 South Los Angeles Street: (213) 253-9255. California and Continental cuisine; breakfast and lunch buffets. Moderate.

Back Porch. The Sheraton Grande, 333 South Figueroa Street: (213) 617-1133. Budget.

City Grill. Los Angeles Hilton & Towers, 930 Wilshire Boulevard: (213) 629-5828. Budget.

Grand Cafe. Hotel Inter-Continental, 251 South Olive Street: (213) 356-4155. Nearby to the Museum of Contemporary Art, Music Center. Moderate.

The Pavilion. Atop the Dorothy Chandler Pavilion at the Music Center, 165 North Grand Avenue: (213) 972-7333. Moderate.

Top of Five Grill. The Westin Bonaventure Hotel & Suites, 404 South Figueroa Street: (213) 624-1000. Beef, seafood, and a 35th-floor view. Moderate.

Chinese

Mon Kee's Restaurant. 679 North Spring Street: (213) 628-6717. Moderate.

Continental

Bernard's. The Biltmore, 506 South Grand Avenue: (213) 612-1580. Expensive.

Epicentre. Kawada Hotel, 200 South Hill Street: (213) 621-4455. Earthquake motif. Moderate.

Orchid Gardens. Best Western The Mayfair, 1256 West Seventh Street: (213) 484-9789. Lunch buffet. Budget.

Rendezvous Court. The Biltmore, 506 South Grand Avenue L: (213) 624-1011. Afternoon tea. Budget.

The Tower. 1150 South Olive Street: (213) 746-1554. Peppered salmon, Louisiana crab cakes, linguine with mussels. Moderate.

Tulips Garden. Radisson Wilshire Plaza, 3515 Wilshire Boulevard: (213) 381-7411. Pasta and salad bar. Moderate.

Velvet Turtle. 708 North Hill Street: (213) 489-2555. Moderate.

Cuban

El Colmao. 2328 West Pico Boulevard: (213) 386-6131. Budget.

French

Taix. 1911 Sunset Boulevard: (213) 484-1265. Country cooking since 1927. Moderate.

Indian

The Clay Pit. Figueroa Hotel–Convention Center, 939 South Figueroa Street: (213) 627-8971. Budget.

Gill's Cuisine of India. Stillwell Hotel, 838 South Grand Avenue: (213) 623-1050. Budget.

Italian

Cardini. Los Angeles Hilton & Towers, 930 Wilshire Boulevard: (213) 227-3464. Moderate.

Ciao Trattoria. 815 West Seventh Street: (213) 624-2244. Budget.

La Bella Cucina. 949 South Figueroa Street: (213) 623-0014. Northern Italian. Budget.

Little Joe's. 900 North Broadway: (213) 489-4900. Los Angeles' oldest Italian restaurant, in Chinatown. Moderate.

Massimo Trattoria. CaliforniaMart, 110 East Ninth Street: (213) 689-4415. Northern Italian, in the fashion district. Moderate.

Pavan. Hyatt Regency Los Angeles, 711 South Hope Street: (213) 683-1234. Italian/California mix. Moderate.

Rex Il Ristorante. 617 South Olive Street: (213) 627-2300. Expensive.

Scarlatti. Sheraton Grande, 333 South Figueroa Street: (213) 617-1133. Free limousine to Music Center. Moderate.

Smeraldi's. The Biltmore, 506 South Grand Avenue: (213) 612-1562. Italian/California cafe mix. Budget.

Japanese

A Thousand Cranes. The New Otani Hotel & Garden, 120 South Los Angeles Street: (213) 253-9255. Sushi, tempura, and more. Moderate.

Garden Grill. The New Otani Hotel & Garden, 120 South Los Angeles Street: (213) 253-9255. Teppan grill. Moderate.

MCC Yoshiz. World Trade Center, 350 South Figueroa Street: (310) 518-5904. Moderate.

Restaurant Horikawa. 111 South San Pedro Street: (213) 680-9355. Gourmet fare, sushi, Teppan grill. Expensive.

Saka-E. Radisson Wilshire Plaza, 3515 Wilshire Boulevard: (213) 381-7411. Tempura, Teppan grill, chirashis, and sushi. Moderate.

Take Sushi. Oxford Palace Hotel, 745 South Oxford Avenue: (213) 389-8000. Japanese, Korean, and American. Moderate.

Tokyo Kaikan. 225 South San Pedro Street: (213) 489-1333. Sushi, tempura, shabu. Expensive.

Mexican/Spanish

Back Door Pub. The Milner Hotel, 813 South Flower Street: (213) 627-6981. Budget.

El Cholo. 1121 South Western Avenue: (213) 734-2773. Budget.

El Paseo Inn. 11 East Olvera Street: (213) 626-1361. Budget.

Gaslighter Restaurant. The Milner Hotel, 813 South Flower Street: (213) 627-6981. Budget.

La Golondrina. 17 Olvera Street: (213) 628-4349. Mariachi dinner entertainment. Budget.

Palma Terrazas. Holiday Inn L.A. City Center, 1020 South Figueroa Street: (213) 748-1291. Moderate.

Seafood

McCormick & Schmick's. First Interstate World Center, 633 West Fifth Street: (213) 629-0997. Classic seafood. Moderate.

Water Grill. 544 South Grand Avenue: (213) 891-0900. Oyster bar, Northwestern specialties. Moderate.

Southwestern

Kachina Grill. Wells Fargo Center, 330 South Hope Street: (213) 625-1989. Grilled salmon in corn husk, tamales, and more. Free shuttle to Music Center. Budget.

Sonora Cafe. 445 South Figueroa Street: (213) 624-1800. Mexican, Californian, and Southwestern cuisines; outdoor section. Moderate.

Vegetarian

Country Life Vegetarian Buffet. 888 South Figueroa Street L: (213) 489-4118. Budget.

Long Beach Restaurants

Californian/American Cuisine

Americana Restaurant. 210 Atlantic Avenue: (310) 435-4030. Budget.

Belmont Brewing Company. 25 39th Place: (310) 433-3891. Budget.

Cafe 456. 456 Elm Avenue: (310) 590-8790. Budget.

Cafe Terrace. Long Beach Airport Marriott, 4700 Airport Plaza Drive: (310) 425-5210. Moderate.

Ciro's Cafe. 407 Shoreline Village Drive, #F: (310) 436-5719. Waterfront dining. Budget.

City Grill. One World Trade Center: (310) 499-7040. Moderate.

Comedy Club Cafe. 49 South Pine Avenue: (310) 495-2807. Moderate.

Courtyard Cafe. 401 East Ocean Boulevard, #208: (310) 590-8108. Budget.

Denny's. 601 Long Beach Boulevard: (310) 437-1992. 24 hours. Budget.

E. J. Malloy's. 3411 East Broadway: (310) 433-3769. Moderate.

Emerald Cafe. Hyatt Regency Long Beach, 200 South Pine Avenue: (310) 491-1234. Moderate.

555 East. 555 East Ocean Boulevard: (310) 437-0626. Steakhouse. Moderate.

Grand Prix Cafe. 211 Pine Avenue: (310) 436-1882. Budget.

Grille 91. Sheraton Cerritos, 12725 Centre Court Drive, Cerritos: (310) 403-2030. Moderate.

The Grill/Sheraton Long Beach. 333 East Ocean Boulevard: (310) 499-2060. Moderate.

Grinder Restaurant. 301 West Broadway: (310) 436-2111. Budget.

Hornblower Dining Yachts. 100 Golden Shore: (310) 519-3100. Expensive.

Johnny Rebs' Southern Smokehouse. 4663 Long Beach Boulevard: (310) 423-7327. Budget.

Kelly's Prime Burger. 311 Pine Avenue: (310) 435-3334. Budget.

Kim's Buffeteria. 444 West Ocean Boulevard: (310) 437-9326. Budget.

Lighthouse Cafe. 30 Pier Avenue, Hermosa Beach: (310) 372-6911. Moderate.

Long Beach Cafe. 615 East Ocean Boulevard: (310) 436-6037. Budget.

Lunch Box. 700 Pine Avenue: (310) 436-3802. Budget.

Mirage. 100 Oceangate, #P295: (310) 437-6850. Soup, salad, sandwiches. Budget.

The Omelette Inn. 108 West 3rd Street: (310) 437-5625. Budget.

Phillips Chicken Pie Shop. 730 Pacific Avenue: (310) 432-1419. Budget.

Razzberries. 300 Oceangate, #100: (310) 437-4792. Budget.

The Reef. 880 Harbor Scenic Drive: (310) 435-8013. Steaks, seafood. Moderate.

Sizzler. 225 West 3rd Street: (310) 432-6433. Budget.

System M Caffe Gallery. 213-A Pine Avenue: (310) 435-2525. Budget.

Tony's Famous French Dips. 701 Long Beach Boulevard: (310) 435-6238. Budget.

Williamsburg Restaurant & Bakery. 355 East 1st Street: (310) 590-0220. Buffet. Budget.

World Trade Cafe. One World Trade Center: (310) 435-7226. Budget.

Caribbean/African-American

Cha Cha Cha. 762 Pacific Avenue: (310) 436-3900. Moderate.

The Golden Frog. 205 East Broadway: (310) 432-8787. African-American. Budget.

Chinese/Thai

August Moon. 6417 East Pacific Coast Highway: (310) 596-8882. Moderate.

China Queen Buffet. 141 East Third Street: (310) 436-0136. Mandarin fare. Budget.

Chong's by the Sea. 405 Shoreline Village Drive: (310) 436-1848. Budget.

Ciao Chow Express. 245 Pine Avenue, Suite 290: (310) 495-9022. Italian/Chinese. Budget.

Golden Chopsticks. One World Trade Center, #109: (310) 495-8008. Budget.

King Tu Restaurant. 340 East 3rd Street: (310) 437-5352. Budget.

Minkquan Thai. 802 Long Beach Boulevard: (310) 432-7868. Budget.

Wa Wa. 155 Long Beach Boulevard: (310) 437-5986. Budget.

Continental

Cannon's Restaurant. 600 Queens Way Drive: (310) 436-2247. Moderate.

Eastenders. 425 East Broadway: (310) 437-7037. A taste of Britain. Budget.

La Grotte Restaurant. 300 Oceangate, #150: (310) 437-2119. Expensive.

Maison de France. 301 Cedar Avenue: (310) 436-0663. French cuisine, tearoom. Moderate.

Sir Winston's Restaurant. *Queen Mary* Seaport, 1126 Queens Highway: (310) 435-3511. Expensive.

Greek

Ciro's Greek Cafe. Shoreline Village, 407 Shoreline Drive: (310) 436-5719. Moderate.

Mykonos. 5374 East 2nd Street: (310) 434-1856. Moderate.

Papadakis Taverna. 301 West 6th Street: (310) 548-1186. Moderate.

Italian

Andiamo. 217 Pine Avenue: (310) 435-1255. Budget.

Ascari Restaurant. Two World Trade Center: (310) 983-3400. Budget.

Expresso Cafe. 320 Elm Avenue: (310) 437-1464. Sandwiches, pasta. Budget.

Floreale. 111 East Ocean Boulevard: (310) 437-5900. Pasta, veal, beef. Moderate.

Gazzella. 525 East Broadway: (310) 495-7252. Lamb, steak. Moderate.

Giorgio's Restaurant. 300 Oceangate, Suite 150: (310) 432-6175. Budget.

L'Opera. 101 Pine Avenue: (310) 491-0066. Moderate.

La Trattoria. 111 East Ocean Boulevard: (310) 437-5900. Open air cafe. Budget.

Mamma Tina's Cucina. 329 Pacific Avenue: (310) 432-9718. Budget.

Mum's. 144 Pine Avenue: (310) 437-7700. Northern Italian/Californian. Moderate.

Pasta Presto. 200 Pine Avenue: (310) 436-7200. Budget.

Japanese

Tanpopo. 445 East 1st Street: (310) 432-2123. Budget.

Jazz Clubs

Birdland West. 105 West Broadway: (310) 436-9341. Moderate.

Mexican/Spanish

El Charro. 695 Locust: (310) 495-0447. Burritos, tacos, quesadillas. Budget.

El Sunzal Restaurant. 603 Atlantic Avenue: (310) 436-4737. Salvadoran fare. Budget.

El Trebol Restaurant. 351 Pacific Avenue: (310) 432-5388. Mexican. Budget.

J & R's Cookery. 70 Atlantic Avenue: (310) 437-4583. Budget.

La Salsa. 245 Pine Avenue: (310) 491-1104. Moderate.

Mardi Gras-International Onion. 401 Shoreline Village Drive: (310) 432-2900. Moderate.

Patio del Sol. *Queen Mary* Seaport, 1126 Queens Highway: (310) 435-3511. Budget.

Salsa Boy. 2109 East Broadway: (310) 433-3180. Moderate.

Sancho's Place. 225 East Broadway: (310) 590-8077. Budget.

Super Mex. 732 East 1st Street: (310) 432-9164. Budget.

Moroccan

Babouch Moroccan Restaurant. 810 South Gaffey Street: (310) 831-0246. Moderate.

Seafood

The Chelsea Restaurant. *Queen Mary* Seaport, 1126 Queens Highway: (310) 435-3511. Moderate.

Parker's Lighthouse. 435 Shoreline Village Drive: (310) 432-6500. Moderate.

Pine Avenue Fish House. 100 West Broadway: (310) 432-7463. Moderate.

Rainbow Pier Fish Market. 423 Shoreline Village Drive, #A: (310) 436-1295. Moderate.

Simon & Seaforts. 340 Golden Shore: (310) 435-2333. Fish, chop house. Moderate.

Vegetarian

Papa Jon's Natural Market and Cafe. 5006 East 2nd Street: (310) 439-1059. Budget.

VII
Beyond the Theme Parks

Chapter 10
Festivals

January

Tournament of Roses Parade. New Year's Day through the streets of Pasadena. It dates all the way back to 1890 and then, like now, was meant as a proclamation to the world about southern California's temperate climate. Today the parade is broadcast around the world, and don't you think that makes the Chamber of Commerce happy?

Sponsoring organizations and companies spend hundreds of thousands of dollars constructing their floats. Floats must be completely covered with flowers, greenery, or some other organic material, with an average float requiring up to 100,000 blossoms. It's all accompanied by the traditional trappings of modern parades: marching bands, second-tier celebrities, horses and television cameras.

The parade starts pretty early in the day, and many spectators spend the night or arrive at the crack of dawn to grab the best curbside viewing places. Overnight parking on some Pasadena city streets near the route is permitted beginning at noon on the day before the parade; observe posted signs. There are also a limited number of grandstand seats available for sale; they're usually spoken for well before the parade begins.

For information, contact the Tournament of Roses Association at (818) 449-4100 or (818) 449-7673, or write to the association at 391 South Orange Grove Boulevard, Pasadena, CA 91184.

Tickets for the parade and for some overnight parking spaces may be purchased from companies that include:

A-1 Tickets, Inc. (818) 968-6070
Al Brooks Rose Bowl Tours. (213) 626-5863
Encore Ticket Service. (213) 257-7530
Murray's Tickets & Tours. (213) 234-0123
Pasadena Ticket Agency. (818) 441-5141
Sharp Seating Company. (818) 795-4171
Southern California Ticket Service. (818) 577-2557
Ticket Time. (818) 440-9700
Tour Connection. (818) 440-9700

Tyson Choice Ticket Service. (800) 367-8497

Kingdom Day Parade. Exposition Park, downtown Los Angeles: (213) 298-8777. Parade honoring Dr. Martin Luther King, Jr., from Crenshaw to the Natural History Museum.

Native American Film Festival. Southwest Museum, Highland Park, Los Angeles: (213) 221-2164. Late January.

Oshogatsu. Japanese-American Cultural and Community Center, Little Tokyo, Los Angeles: (213) 628-2725. Japanese New Year celebration with food, music, dance, and crafts.

Winter Wonderland. Brand Park, Glendale: (818) 548-2000. Sledding on mountains of man-made snow.

Tet Festival. Golden West College, Huntington Beach: (714) 895-8367. A celebration of the Vietnamese New Year with entertainment, food, and crafts.

February

Chinese New Year. They celebrate the Lunar New Year (usually a few weeks after January 1) with firecrackers, dragons, and a colorful parade in Chinatown. For dates and information, contact the Chinese Chamber of Commerce at (213) 617-0396.

Whiskey Flats Days. An Old West festival in Kernville: (619) 376-2629.

African-American History Month Celebrations. Various locations in Los Angeles: (213) 295-0521.

Black History Month Exhibit. Watts Towers Arts Center, Watts, Los Angeles: (213) 569-8181.

Mardi Gras. El Pueblo de Los Angeles Historic Monument, downtown Los Angeles: (213) 687-4344.

Festival of the Whales. Dana Point: (714) 496-1555. The annual migration of the California gray whales is celebrated with a parade, a street fair, whale-watching cruises, exhibits, lectures, and an art show. Call for locations.

Laguna Beach Winter Festival. Festival of Arts Grounds, Laguna Beach: (714) 494-1018. A four-day event showcasing more than 100 artists.

Mardi Gras. Downtown Los Angeles: (213) 687-4344.

Long Beach Marathon. A 26-mile jaunt that begins at the Long Beach Convention Center. For information, call (310) 494-2664.

March

Beverly Hills St. Patrick's Day Parade. A very tony, somewhat upscale parade that runs down Rodeo Drive to Wilshire Boulevard and beyond. Grandstand seats are available for a charge. For information, call (310) 271-8126.

Return of the Swallows to Capistrano. A celebration of the miraculous return of thousands of swallows to the ruins of Mission San Juan Capistrano each March 19: (Of course, some swallows also come on March 18 and March 20, but there's no party for them.) For information, call (714) 493-1111.

Academy Awards. Your chances of getting tickets for the ceremony itself are about as good as your chances of winning an Oscar, but there is a lot of excitement each March in the streets of Los Angeles and Hollywood. Bleachers are set up near the award site itself for those who want to ogle the stars as they arrive. For information, call (213) 972-7211.

American Indian Festival and Market. Natural History Museum of Los Angeles County, Exposition Park, Los Angeles: (213) 744-3488. Folk arts and dance and a crafts market.

Azalea Festival. South Gate Park, South Gate: (213) 563-5443. Carnival, parade, crafts, entertainment.

Los Angeles Marathon. Yet another 26-mile jog, starting at the Los Angeles Memorial Coliseum. For information, call (213) 747-7111 or (310) 444-5544.

Saint Patrick's Day Parade. Avenue of the Stars, Century City: (310) 275-2214.

Fiesta de las Golondrinas. Mission San Juan Capistrano, San Juan Capistrano: (714) 248-2048. A parade, music, food, and entertainment celebrate the return of the swallows to the mission.

Golden City 5K and Half-Marathon. Centennial Park, Santa Ana: (714) 647-6561.

Intercultural Festival of Friendship. Golden West College, Huntington Beach: (714) 895-8367.

Irish Faire. Festival of Arts Grounds, Laguna Beach: (714) 493-9643.

Patriots Day Parade. Laguna Beach: (714) 494-1018. Call for location.

Spring Festival. Civic Center Gardens, Westminster: (714) 895-2860.

Spring Orchestra Festival. Chapman University, Orange: (714) 997-6871.

Museum of Television & Radio Los Angeles Festival. Los Angeles County Museum: (213) 621-6600 or (213) 857-6110. Three weeks of retrospectives and tributes sponsored by New York's Museum of Television and Radio.

April

Blessing of the Animals. El Pueblo de Los Angeles Historic Monument, downtown Los Angeles: (213) 628-7833.

Brentwood Art Show. San Vicente Boulevard between Bundy Drive and Bringham Street, Brentwood: (818) 797-6803.

Easter Sunrise Service. Hollywood Bowl, Hollywood: (213) 850-2000.

Feria de los Niños. Hollenbeck Park, Los Angeles: (213) 261-0113. Hispanic folk festival for children.

Fiesta Broadway. Broadway and Hill and Spring streets between 1st Street and Olympic Boulevard in downtown Los Angeles: (310) 914-8315. Hispanic block party with music, food, and entertainment.

UCLA Powwow. UCLA, Westwood: (310) 825-7315. Native American festival.

Art Festival. Coastline Community College, Fountain Valley: (714) 241-6154.

Asian Heritage Festival. UC Irvine: (714) 856-7215. Call for locations.

Celebration UCI. UC Irvine: (714) 856-5182. Call for locations.

Coast Days. Orange Coast College, Costa Mesa: (714) 432-5507. Games, food, entertainment, and arts and crafts. (Also in October.)

Easter Egg Hunts. Estancia Park, Costa Mesa: (714) 645-4985. Santa Ana: (714) 647-6561. Columbus Tustin Park, Tustin: (714) 544-8890, ext. 220.

The Glory of Easter. Crystal Cathedral, Garden Grove: (714) 544-5679.

Newport to Ensenada Race. Newport Beach Harbor, Newport Beach: (714) 640-1351.

Orange County Muscle Classic. Disneyland Hotel, Anaheim: (714) 533-3159. An annual bodybuilding contest.

Shakespeare Festival. Irvine Barclay Theatre, UC Irvine: (714) 865-6616.

Spring Festival. Westminster Civic Center, Westminster: (714) 895-2860.

May

Cinco de Mayo Celebration. Dancing, singing, eating, and more in a moveable Mexican feast around Los Angeles, including Olvera Street. For information, call (213) 628-0605 or 625-5045.

La Fiesta Broadway is held in and around Broadway in downtown Los Angeles; for information, call (818) 793-9335. For information about celebrations in LaPalma Park, Anaheim, call (714) 254-5191; for 4th Street in Santa Ana, call (714) 558-6869.

Festival of Philippine Arts and Culture. Dance, arts, and crafts at various locations. For information, call (213) 485-2437.

Topanga Banjo/Fiddle Contest, Dance, and Folk Arts Festival. Paramount Ranch, Agoura Hills: (818) 594-1742. Usually held first Sunday in May.

Strawberry Festival. On the Village Green in Garden Grove: (714) 638-0981 or 638-7950. Strawberries, a parade, strawberries, music, strawberries, and more. Did we mention the strawberries?

UCLA Mardi Gras. Wild and somewhat wacky. UCLA Athletic Field. For information, call (310) 825-4321.

Long Beach Carnival. Long Beach Promenade, Long Beach: (310) 436-7794. Memorial Day weekend. Music, entertainment, carnival, and food.

Asian Pacific–American Heritage Month. Various locations. For information, call (213) 485-3404.

Pacific Islander Festival. Harbor City Regional Park, Harbor City: (310) 926-6707. Celebration of dance and music from islands of the Pacific including Hawaii, Tonga, Guam, Marshall, Tahiti, and Cook.

Los Angeles Asian Pacific Film and Video Festival. Various locations: For information, call (310) 206-8013.

Children's Day. Japanese-American Cultural and Community Center, Little Tokyo, downtown Los Angeles: (213) 628-2725.

Museums of the Arroyo Seco Day. Various locations in Highland Park, Los Angeles: (213) 221-2164.

Urban American Indian Art Expo. Southwest Museum, Highland Park: (213) 221-2164.

Very Special Arts Festival. Music Center of Los Angeles County, downtown Los Angeles: (213) 972-7389. Art, music, and dance by disabled children.

Art Show and Sale. Coastline Community College, Fountain Valley: (714) 241-6174.

California Wine Exposition. Seaside Lagoon, Redondo Beach: (310) 376-6911.

Gay Pride Festival. Shoreline Aquatic Park, Long Beach: (310) 987-9191.

Irvine Camerata. Irvine Barclay Theatre, UC Irvine: (714) 856-6616.

Orange County Youth Symphony Orchestra. Chapman University, Orange: (714) 997-6871.

United Scottish Society Highland Games. Orange County Fairgrounds, Costa Mesa: (714) 751-3247.

June

Follows Camp Family Bluegrass Festival. Follows Camp, 23400 East Fork Road, Azusa: (818) 700-8288 or 910-1100. First weekend in June, and again in October.

American Film Institute Los Angeles International Film Festival. Various locations: For information, call (213) 856-7707.

Christopher Street West Gay and Lesbian Pride Celebration. West Hollywood Park, West Hollywood: (213) 656-6553. Parade, entertainment, and crafts show.

Irish Fair and Music Festival. Santa Anita Racetrack, Arcadia: (818) 985-2223.

Playboy Jazz Festival. Hollywood Bowl, Hollywood: (310) 659-4080 or 450-9040. Father's Day weekend.

South Gate Street Fair. Tweedy Boulevard, South Gate: (213) 564-4431.

Summer Solstice Folk Music, Dance, and Storytelling Festival. Soka University, Calabasas: (818) 342-7664.

Summerfest. George Izay Park, Burbank: (818) 953-8763.

Chili Cook-Off. El Camino Real, Tustin: (714) 544-8890, ext. 220.

Concours d'Elegance. Talbert Avenue and Golden West Street, Huntington Beach: (714) 960-8839. A display of antique and exotic cars.

Kids' Auction. Anaheim Marriott Hotel, Anaheim: (310) 691-2413. Proceeds from this annual event are donated to Boys and Girls Club of La Habra/Brea.

A Taste of Orange County. Irvine Spectrum, Irvine: (714) 753-1551. Cuisine from local restaurants, wine tasting, live music, and children's activities.

Wooden Boat Festival. Newport Harbor, Newport Beach: (714) 642-5031.

Summer Solstice Folk Music and Dance Festival: Various locations on Father's Day weekend. For information, call (818) 342-7664.

July

Laguna Beach Arts Festival. July–August. Displays of work by local artists, plus the Pageant of the Masters, a re-creation of classic works of art using live models. For information, call (714) 494-1146.

Malibu Summer Festival and Art Show. Malibu Civic Center: (310) 456-9025.

Orange County Fair. Orange County Fair and Exhibition Center, Costa Mesa: (714) 751-3247. Rides, exhibitions, and entertainment.

Marina del Rey Arts and Crafts Fair: For information, call (310) 821-0555.

Hollywood Bowl Open House. Children's performing arts festival. For information, call (213) 850-2000.

Anifest. Beverly Garland Hotel, North Hollywood: (818) 842-8330. A celebration of the art of animated films.

Dance Kaleidoscope. Ballet, modern dance, jazz, tap, folk, and more, presented at various locations. For information, call (213) 343-5124.

Garlic Festival. Federal Building, Westwood: (213) 937-4850.

Ho'olaule'a Hawaiian Festival. Alondra Park, Lawndale: (310) 329-9794.

Lotus Festival. Echo Park Lake and Recreation Center, Los Angeles: (213) 485-8744. Asian-Pacific cultural festival.

Santa Monica Independence Art Festival: For information, call (310) 393-9825.

Fountain Valley Fiesta and Chili Cook-Off. Mile Square Regional Park, Fountain Valley: (714) 668-0542.

Fourth of July Celebration. Peralta Park, Anaheim: (714) 254-5191. Huntington Beach High School, Huntington Beach: (714) 960-8899. Newport Dunes, Newport Beach: (714) 729-3863. Centennial Park, Santa Ana: (714) 647-6561.

Lifeguard Competition. Huntington State Beach, Huntington Beach: (714) 536-1454.

Tustin Concerts in the Park. Peppertree Park, Tustin: (714) 544-8890, ext. 220.

Dance Kaleidoscope. California State University, Cal State Playhouse, 5151 University Drive, Los Angeles: (213) 343-5124 or 343-4118. Weeklong festival of dance.

McCabe's Annual Variety Day Summer Festival. Lincoln Park, Santa Monica: (310) 828-4497. Third Sunday in July. Folk, jazz, classical music.

Grove Shakespeare Festival. Garden Grove: (714) 638-7950. July–August.

World Frisbee Championships. La Mirada Park, La Mirada: (310) 943-6978.

August

Nisei Week. Parade and celebration of Japanese culture in America, in Little Tokyo (1st and 2nd streets near Alameda in Los Angeles). For information call (213) 628-2725 or (213) 687-7193.

Long Beach Sea Fest. Two weeks of water and beach sports and activities. For information, call (310) 436-3636.

Old Spanish Days. Weeklong celebration of Spanish culture in Santa Barbara. For information, call (805) 962-8101 or (805) 965-3021.

Santa Monica Sports and Arts Festival. Palisades Park: (310) 458-8311.

Jewish Summer Festival. West Los Angeles Civic Center Mall: (310) 828-3433.

San Fernando Valley Fair. Devonshire Downs, Northridge: (818) 373-4500. Three days of exhibits, carnival rides, entertainment and the Los Angeles County Beauty Pageant.

Venice Beach Rathayatra Festival. Ocean Front Walk, Venice. Parade and festival celebrating Indian and Buddhist culture.

Westwood Sidewalk Arts and Crafts Show. August and October. Westwood Village, Los Angeles: (310) 475-4574.

African Marketplace and Cultural Fair. Rancho Cienega Park, Crenshaw, Los Angeles: (213) 734-1164.

Children's Festival of Art. Barnsdall Art Park, Los Angeles: (213) 485-4474.

Folk and Traditional Arts Festival. California Plaza, downtown Los Angeles: (213) 485-6759.

International Sea Festival. Long Beach: (310) 421-9431. A monthlong series of maritime-related competitions and entertainment.

Pasadena Jazz Festival. Various locations in Pasadena. For information, call (800) 266-2378.

Shakespeare Festival. Citicorp Plaza, downtown Los Angeles: (213) 489-1121.

Watts Summer Festival. Various locations in Watts. For information, call (213) 789-7304.

County Fair Jamboree. Stanton Recreation Department, Stanton: (714) 379-9222.

Indian Powwow. Orange County Fairgrounds, Costa Mesa: (714) 543-0221. A three-day festival with Native American arts and crafts, food, and entertainment.

Laguna Beach Muscle Classic. Call for location. Laguna Beach: (714) 533-3159.

Mission Rancho Days. Mission San Juan Capistrano, San Juan Capistrano: (714) 248-2048.

Southern California Home and Garden Show. Anaheim Convention Center, Anaheim: (714) 978-8888.

September

San Bernardino County Fair. Victorville: (619) 245-6506. Old-style agricultural and crafts fair.

Los Angeles County Fair. County Fairgrounds, Pomona: (909) 623-3111. The largest agricultural fair in the country, plus rides, racing, and entertainment.

Danish Days. Solvang: (805) 688-3317. Third weekend of September. Parade, dance, and music.

Greek Festival. Santa Anita Racetrack, Arcadia: (818) 574-7223.

Day in the Park. Rancho Cienega Park, Crenshaw, Los Angeles: (213) 732-9742. Celebration of Belizean Independence Day with calypso and reggae music, dancing, food, and crafts.

Day of the Drum Music and Arts Festival. Watts Towers Arts Center, Watts, Los Angeles: (213) 847-4646.

Festival of Philippine Arts and Culture. Los Angeles City College: (213) 485-2473.

Korean Festival. Korean Community Center, Koreatown, Los Angeles: (213) 730-1495.

L.A. Classic Jazz Festival. LAX Marriott, Westin Hotel Los Angeles Airport: (310) 521-6893. Labor Day weekend.

Los Angeles Birthday Celebration. El Pueblo de Los Angeles Historic Monument, downtown Los Angeles: (213) 680-2525.

Mexican Independence Day Celebrations. Bristow Park, Commerce: (213) 269-5603. El Pueblo de Los Angeles Historic Monument, downtown Los Angeles: (213) 628-7833. Belvedere County Park, Los Angeles: (213) 268-9391. South Gate Park, South Gate: (213) 563-5443. Santa Ana: (310) 695-5222.

Moon Festival. Chinatown, downtown Los Angeles: (213) 617-0396. Held on the 15th day of the eighth moon.

International Street Faire. The Traffic Circle, Orange: (714) 532-6260.

Lively Arts Festival. Hilcrest Park, Fullerton: (714) 738-6575.

Long Beach Blues Festival. Long Beach: (310) 985-5566. Call for locations.

Seafest. Newport Beach: (714) 729-4400. Call for locations.

Simon Rodia Watts Tower Music and Arts Festival/Day of the Drum Festival. Jazz, gospel, and R&B festival, held at the end of September. For information, call (213) 485-2437 or 569-8181.

October

Follows Camp Family Bluegrass Festival. Follows Camp, 23400 East Fork Road, Azusa: (818) 700-8288 or 910-1100.

Oktoberfest. Alpine Village, Torrance: (310) 327-4384.

Great Bear Oktoberfest. Big Bear Lake: (714) 866-5877.

Oktoberfest. Old World Village, Huntington Beach: (714) 895-8020.

Calico Days. Calico Ghost Town, Yermo: (619) 254-2122.

Knott's "Scary" Farm. Knott's Berry Farm, Buena Park. A Halloween conversion of the amusement park. See the chapter on Knott's Berry Farm in this book for information.

East Village Celebration of the Arts. East Village, Long Beach: (310) 432-3322.

Halloween Festival. Cudahy Park, Cudahy: (213) 773-5143.

Halloween Street Festival and Parade. Santa Monica Boulevard, West Hollywood: (310) 854-7471.

Halloween Party. Tustin: (714) 544-8890, ext. 220. Call for locations.

International Festival of Masks. Hancock Park, mid-Wilshire, Los Angeles: (213) 937-5544.

Los Angeles Poetry Festival. Various locations. End of October. For information, call (213) 660-4306.

Fall Concerts. Chapman University, Orange: (714) 997-6871.

Fall Fair. Orange Coast College, Costa Mesa: (714) 432-5880.

Irvine Harvest Festival. Irvine: (714) 552-7336. Call for location.

Pumpkin Festival. Blakey Park, Westminster: (714) 895-2860. A pumpkin pie contest, a cooking contest, games, entertainment, and a barbecue.

Silverado Days. William Peak Park, Buena Park: (714) 521-0261. A carnival, a parade, entertainment, food, and arts and crafts. Proceeds benefit local nonprofit organizations.

Tustin Tiler Day. Columbus Tustin Park, Tustin: (714) 544-8890, ext. 220. Food, games, crafts, and entertainment.

Scandinavian Festival. Colorado Place, 2425 Colorado Avenue, Santa Monica: (213) 661-8137. The music, arts, and culture of Scandinavia.

November

Hollywood Christmas Parade. Sunday after Thanksgiving. Sunset and Hollywood Boulevards, Hollywood: (213) 469-8311.

Parade of Masks. November 1. Wilshire Boulevard, Los Angeles: (213) 937-5544.

Doodah Parade. Starts at Colorado Boulevard and Fair Oaks Avenue, Pasadena. The countercultural response to the Rose Parade with some of the silliest and most useless assemblages of marching groups and floats ever to grace the streets of Pasadena; that is, until the next Rose Parade. For information, call (818) 796-2591.

Farmer's Market Harvest Festival. Plummer Park, West Hollywood: (310) 854-7471.

Festival of Jewish Artisans. Temple Isaiah, West Los Angeles: (310) 277-2772.

Harvest Festival. Los Angeles Convention Center, downtown Los Angeles: (707) 778-6300.

Hollywood Christmas Parade. Hollywood and Sunset Boulevards, Hollywood: (213) 469-8311.

Intertribal Marketplace. Southwest Museum, Highland Park, Los Angeles: (213) 221-2164.

Tribal and Folk Art Show. Santa Monica Civic Auditorium, Santa Monica: (310) 455-2886.

Christmas Fantasy. Rogers Gardens Nursery, Newport Beach: (714) 640-5800. Seven acres of lighted trees and holiday displays.

Christmas Tree Lighting Celebration. South Coast Plaza, Costa Mesa: (714) 241-1700. City Hall, Tustin: (714) 544-8890, ext. 220.

Fiesta Marketplace Christmas Celebration. Fiesta Marketplace, Santa Ana: (714) 558-6869.

Holiday Happening. Civic Center: (714) 895-2860. A two-day event with over 100 vendors.

Rainbow Festival. UC Irvine: (714) 856-6345. A celebration of ethnic diversity. Call for locations.

Times/Orange County Holiday Parade. Santa Ana: (714) 571-4260. Call for locations.

December

American Indian Festival. Los Angeles County Museum of Natural History: (213) 744-3414.

Beverly Hills Perrier 10K Run. Beverly Hills: (310) 550-4816.

Las Posadas. Olvera Street, Los Angeles: (213) 625-5045. Nightly procession from mid-December through Christmas Eve.

Beverly Hills Lighting Ceremony. Regent Beverly Wilshire Hotel, Beverly Hills: (310) 275-5200.

International Los Angeles Art Fair. Los Angeles Convention Center, downtown Los Angeles: (310) 271-3200.

Las Posadas. El Pueblo de Los Angeles Historic Monument, downtown Los Angeles: (213) 687-4344. Candlelight procession depicting the journey of Mary and Joseph to Bethlehem.

Western Hemisphere Marathon. Culver and Oberlin Boulevards, Culver City: (310) 202-5689.

Children's Holiday Party. Santa Ana Stadium, Santa Ana: (714) 647-6561.

Festival of Jewish Artisans. Temple Isaiah, West Los Angeles: (310) 277-2772.

Fiesta Marketplace Christmas Celebration. Fiesta Marketplace, Santa Ana: (714) 558-6869.

First Night Fullerton. Downtown Fullerton: (714) 738-6575.

The Glory of Christmas. Crystal Cathedral, Garden Grove: (714) 544-5679.

Holiday Faire. LaPalma Park, Anaheim: (714) 254-5191.

Holiday Wassail. Chapman University, Orange: (714) 997-6871. The Chapman University choir and chamber orchestra perform.

Madrigal Dinner. Fine Arts Village Theatre, UC Irvine: (714) 856-6616. An authentic Renaissance-style dinner with entertainment by King Henry VIII and his court musicians.

Many Moods of Christmas. Golden West College, Huntington Beach: (714) 895-8378. Christmas songs are performed by the Golden West Concert Band.

Newport Harbor Christmas Boat Parade. Newport Beach Harbor, Newport Beach: (714) 729-4400.

Tournament of Champions. Santa Ana Stadium, Santa Ana: (714) 647-6561. Southern California bands compete in this annual event.

Victorian Christmas and Candlelight Walking Tour. Heritage Hill Historical Park, Lake Forest: (714) 855-2028.

Los Angeles County Holiday Celebration. Dorothy Chandler Pavilion: (213) 972-7211. Annual free festival on Christmas Eve, in and around the Music Center.

Nutcracker Suite. Late December–New Year's Day at the Los Angeles Ballet, Music Center: (213) 972-7211. Early December at Ballet West and Long Beach Symphony, Terrace Theater, Long Beach: (310) 436-3661.

Chapter 11
Museums

Most museums charge admission unless noted. Operating hours are subject to change; call to confirm before heading out. Museums also of interest to children are marked with **KIDS** at the end of the listing.

Griffith Park

Griffith Park Observatory and Planetarium. Hall of Science, 2800 East Observatory Road, Griffith Park: (213) 664-1191.

Indoors is an eye-popping planetarium also used for laser light shows; outside is a rooftop observatory with spectacular views of the city on all sides and the heavens above; that is, when the smog clears.

To the right of the entrance to the observatory is a bust of James Dean, who died in 1955—the same year his most famous movie, *Rebel Without a Cause* was filmed in and around the observatory. Over the shoulder of the bust is the famous Hollywood sign on the hills behind it.

The backside of the observatory itself presents a terrace which looks out over Los Angeles over toward Hollywood.

The 12-inch Zeiss telescope, one of the largest public telescopes in the world, is open in the summer nightly from dark until 9:45 P.M.; in the winter the telescope is available every night except Mondays from 7 P.M. to 9:45 P.M. Call (213) 663-8171 to hear a recorded message about astrological events.

The 650-seat planetarium's 75-foot dome is used as the backdrop for hour-long presentations about the stars and planets. There are afternoon and evening shows year-round. Planetarium tickets are adults, $4; seniors, $3; and children (5 to 12), $2.

The Laserium uses dazzling krypton and argon lasers to paint pictures on the ceiling of the Planetarium to the accompaniment of rock music; it is Southern California's longest-running theatrical attraction. Shows in 1996 featured music by The Beatles and Pink Floyd. Tickets are available at the Observatory or in advance through Ticketmaster; general admission is $7, and children are charged $6.

Note that children under five years of age are not permitted at the Laserium or at most shows at the Planetarium; special children's Planetarium shows are offered weekend afternoons all year round and daily in the summer.

The Hall of Science within features a collection of meteorites and geological specimens. Lectures and exhibits explore principles of physics and astronomy. A popular exhibit is a working World War II periscope, which was originally used on the USS *Blenny*. The six-power periscope extends 37 feet up; it presents a nearly 360-degree view from the top of the observatory.

Admission to the hall is free. The Hall of Science is open every day in the summer from 12:30 P.M. to 10 P.M.; in the winter, it is open Tuesdays to Fridays from 2 P.M. to 10 P.M. and on weekends from 12:30 P.M. to 10 P.M.

In addition to *Rebel Without a Cause*, the observatory was used as a setting in *The Terminator* and as a backdrop for many other films from classic to forgettable. **KIDS.**

Travel Town Transportation Museum. Zoo Drive, Griffith Park: (213) 662-5874. An almost-secret and *free* treasure guaranteed to enthrall children of most ages. A large collection of steam locomotives, retired Los Angeles street

trolleys, antique railway cars, boxcars, cabooses, and old wagons; visitors can climb aboard most of the equipment including a Hawaiian sugarcane narrow-gauge train and a 110-ton Union Pacific locomotive.

One of the more spectacular engines is Engine No. 26 from the Western Pacific Railroad, which stands almost 12 feet tall. A set of steps leads you to the controls. You will also find a 1911 Metropolitan Transportation Authority streetcar and a 1902 Pacific Electric Electra car.

Among the oldest pieces is a wooden Railway Postal Car from the 1880s. The mail cars were used as rolling post offices on local and long-distance trains; they often included a car equipped with pigeonholes, sorting bags and tables, cancellation stamps, and frenzied clerks trying to sort a bag of mail picked up at one station before arriving at the next station. Metal arms hung from the sides of the cars to drop off or pick up bags of mail at stations where the train was not scheduled to stop. The last railway postal car ran between Washington, D.C., and New York on June 30, 1977.

An indoor section houses a collection of antique firefighting equipment dating back to 1869. Within the shed is the East Valley Line Model Railroad Club, which presents a very large model train layout. All of the rolling stock and engines are owned by individual members of the club, and much of it goes home every night, which explains why you'll seldom see the same trains running on any two visits.

Open daily from 10 A.M. to 5 P.M., and until 6 P.M. on weekends. Parking and admission to the museum is free; there is a $1.75 fee for train ride. Open daily. **KIDS.**

Pony and Stagecoach Rides. Crystal Springs Drive, near Los Feliz Boulevard in Griffith Park: (213) 664-3266. Three small pony tracks accommodate riders from infants to preteens. A replica stagecoach takes all comers. Open Tuesdays through Sundays from 10 A.M. to 5 P.M. Nominal fee. **KIDS.**

Merry-Go-Round. Griffith Park Drive, Griffith Park: (213) 665-3051. A lovingly maintained 1926 wooden carrousel. Open daily from 11 A.M. to 5 P.M. in summer, and on weekends and holidays in winter. Nominal fee. **KIDS.**

Gene Autry Western Heritage Museum. 4700 Western Heritage Way, Griffith Park: (213) 667-2000.

A significant collection of artifacts including possessions of some of the wagon train travelers who settled the west and the cowboys who worked the trails. Run as a nonprofit organization established by the Autry Foundation, the museum includes seven theme galleries with a permanent hands-on gallery for children. It's a hidden piece of Disneyland, too; Disney Imagineers helped create animated displays that celebrate and explain the real Old West.

The fine art collection includes work by painters including Frederic Remington and Seth Eastman. A museum store offers jewelry, clothing, books, posters, and gifts.

Gene Autry, born in 1907 in Tioga, Texas, has been a star of radio, Hollywood, music, and business. He began his radio career in 1928 as the result of a chance meeting with Will Rogers; his "Melody Ranch" show on CBS ran for 16 years from 1939. Autry appeared in 95 films, and recorded more than 635 records, selling more than 40 million copies. His most famous gold records include "Rudolph the Red-Nosed Reindeer," "Peter Cottontail," "Here Comes Santa Claus" (which he coauthored), "Tumbling Tumbleweeds," "Back in the Saddle Again" (coauthor), and "You Are My Sunshine."

Autry put some of his riches into business interests, owning four radio stations in Los Angeles and Seattle, the California Angels baseball team, and other properties. He sold off majority ownership of the Angels to the Walt Disney Company in 1996.

Open Tuesdays through Sundays from 10 A.M. to 5 P.M. Closed Mondays except for certain holidays; closed Thanksgiving and Christmas.

Adults, $7.50; seniors (over 60) and students (13 to 18), $5; and children (2 to 12), $3. **KIDS.**

Art Museums

Barnsdall Art Park. 4800 Hollywood Boulevard, Los Feliz: Architect Frank Lloyd Wright's first Los Angeles house was the Hollyhock House, built in 1918 for oil heiress Aline Barnsdall. Guided tours are offered Tuesdays through Sundays at noon, 1 P.M., 2 P.M., and 3 P.M. For information, call (213) 485-4581.

The Barnsdall Art Park on the grounds features the work of local and international artists as well as theater presentations. For information, call (213) 562-7272.

J. Paul Getty Museum, Malibu. 17985 Pacific Coast Highway at Coastline Drive, Malibu, between Sunset and Topanga Canyon boulevards. (310) 458-2003.

A spectacular building in a spectacular setting with a spectacular endowment. Collections established by oil billionaire J. Paul Getty include Greek and Roman antiquities, 18th-century European decorative arts, 14th- to 19th-century Western European drawings and paintings, Medieval and Renaissance manuscripts, sculpture from the Middle Ages to the 19th century, and 19th- and 20th-century American and European photographs.

The museum is set in a re-creation of a 1st-century Roman villa, built on a cliff overlooking the ocean and surrounded by manicured gardens. Its plan is based on the Villa dei Papiri, which stood outside the ancient city of Herculaneum, overlooking the Bay of Naples. The villa was completely buried by the eruption of Mount Vesuvius in A.D. 79, the same event that froze Pompeii in time. The villa was accidentally rediscovered in the 18th century and was explored by archaeologists and treasure seekers through a system of underground tunnels. Plans for the museum were based on drawings made at the time of that exploration.

The landscaping is supposed to duplicate the greenery that would have been found at the Villa dei Papiri in Southern Italy some two thousand years ago. The bronze statues in the gardens are modern casts of statues unearthed in the 18th century.

The collection of Greek and Roman antiquities includes marble and bronze sculptures, paintings, vases, and other objects from 3000 B.C. to A.D. 300.

Major works include the Cycladic harpist from about 2500 B.C. and the limestone and marble Aphrodite from the end of the fifth century B.C.

The collection of drawings and paintings includes Rembrandt's *Nude Woman with a Snake*, as well as works by Leonardo da Vinci, Raphael, Rubens, Goya, Cézanne, Gainsborough, Renoir, Munch, and van Gogh.

Open Tuesdays through Sundays from 10 A.M. to 5 P.M. Admission is free, but in true Southern California style, you'll need a reservation for your car for one of the limited number of parking spaces. No walk-in visitors are permitted without a special pass. The restrictions are in place because of limited parking in the neighborhood; at busy times of the year, it may be necessary to make reservations one to two weeks in advance.

You can take a taxicab to the museum or ride the RTD bus 434 from Santa Monica. The bus will let you off about a half mile away; be sure to obtain an admission pass from the driver to certify your mode of transportation and prove you are not a walk-in visitor.

Huntington Library, Art Gallery, and Botanical Gardens. 1151 Oxford Road, San Marino: (818) 405-2275 or 405-2100.

Another art-filled monument to Old Money, the extensive and wide-ranging collections of railroad magnate Henry E. Huntington are housed in a set of buildings on a 200-acre botanical garden in the San Gabriel Valley. The estate was built in 1919. The library, built in 1925, contains more than half a million books and five million manuscripts, including a first folio of some of Shakespeare's plays and a Gutenberg Bible. The art gallery, built in 1910 as Huntington's home, showcases famous works such as Thomas Gainsborough's *Blue Boy.*

The estate's botanical gardens include a large Japanese garden with a koi fish pond; the Desert Garden is the largest such collection in the world with more than 2,500 desert plant species.

Guided tours are available. Open Tuesdays through Fridays from 1 P.M. to 4:30 P.M. and weekends from 10:30 A.M. to 4:30 P.M. Reservations are recommended for Sundays. Free; donation suggested.

Long Beach Museum of Art. 2300 East Ocean Boulevard, Long Beach: (310) 439-2119. An intriguing mixture of old and new, with displays of modern art, sculpture, and videos in a 1912 mansion on a beach overlooking the Pacific. Open Wednesdays through Sundays. Call for hours.

Los Angeles County Museum of Art. 5905 Wilshire Boulevard, Los Angeles: (213) 857-6111.

A sprawling collection of art from around the world, including a fabulous collection of Tibetan, Indian, and Nepalese works, a gallery of Daumier prints, and a pavilion with one of the best gatherings of Japanese art outside of Asia.

The large museum includes four main buildings: the Hammer Building (photography, prints, drawings, and late 19th-century European art), the Bing Center, the Robert O. Anderson Building (primarily 20th-century art), and the Ahmanson Gallery. The Ahmanson includes ancient Egyptian, Asian, Middle

Eastern, pre-Columbian, and early American art and artifacts. The Bing Theater at the Bing Center offers a family film series.

Open Tuesdays through Fridays 10 A.M. to 5 P.M., Saturdays and Sundays from 10 A.M. to 6 P.M. Closed Mondays, Thanksgiving, Christmas Day, and New Year's Day. Adults, $5; students and seniors, $3.50; and children 6 to 17, $1.

Museum of Contemporary Art, Los Angeles (MOCA). 250 South Grand Avenue, Los Angeles: (213) 621-2766.

In the best traditions of grand museums, the building that houses the collection of modern art at MOCA is a work of art by itself; designed by Japanese architect Arata Isozaki and opened in 1986, it includes spectacular pyramidic skylights and geometric angles.

Interestingly, the more mundane **Temporary Contemporary** at 152 North Central Avenue in Little Tokyo, (213) 626-6222, opened while MOCA was under construction, has been kept in service as home to traveling exhibitions and some of the works from the main museum. Temporary Contemporary is housed within a converted Los Angeles Police Department garage.

Both museums are closed Mondays. Admission charge. Call for hours.

Newport Harbor Art Museum. 850 San Clemente Drive, Newport Beach: (714) 759-1122. 20th-century American art. Closed Mondays.

Norton Simon Museum of Art. 411 West Colorado Boulevard at Orange Grove Boulevard, Pasadena: (818) 449-3730. Only the best: modern 19th- and 20th-century classics from Picasso, Monet, vanGogh, Renoir, Degas, Cézanne, Klee, and more, and two thousand years of Indian and Southeast Asian sculptures. Open Thursdays through Sundays from noon to 6 P.M. Adults, $4; students with ID, $2; children under 12, free.

Pacific Asia Museum. 46 North Los Robles Avenue, north of Colorado Boulevard, Pasadena: (818) 449-2742. A somewhat incongruous sight in downtown Pasadena; housed within a replica of a Chinese imperial palace is an extensive collection of Pacific and Asian costumes, ceramics, textiles, ornaments, and paintings. The grounds include a koi fish pond and a Chinese garden. Open Wednesdays through Sundays. Nominal admission.

Armand Hammer Museum of Art and Cultural Center at UCLA. 10899 Wilshire Boulevard at Westwood Boulevard: (310) 443-7000. The 20th-century industrialist and deal maker's collection of Leonardo da Vinci drawings and caricatures by Honoré Daumier highlight the exhibition.

Folk Arts and Crafts

Angel's Attic. 516 Colorado Avenue, Santa Monica: (310) 394-8331. Every little girl's dream: a museum of dolls, dollhouses, toys, and more, set in a restored Victorian home that seems like a dollhouse itself. The former home, a Queen Anne Victorian built in 1875, is the oldest house in Santa Monica. Proceeds benefit autistic children. Open afternoons Thursdays through Sundays. Adults, $5; children under 14, $3. **KIDS.**

Margaret Cavigga Quilt Collection. 8648 Melrose Avenue, Los Angeles:

(310) 659-3020. Antique quilts, Victorian crocheted tablecloths, lace chris-
tening gowns, and more delicacies. Call for hours. Free.

Craft and Folk Art Museum. 5800 Wilshire Boulevard, Los Angeles: (213)
937-5544. Just like the name says, crafts and folk art from around the world.
The permanent collection includes more than 3,000 folk art, craft, and design
objects, focusing on the folk art of world cultures that have influenced southern California, and the work of local artists and designers. The museum is also
the sponsor of the International Festival of Masks each year near Halloween.
Open Tuesdays through Sundays from 11 A.M. to 5 P.M. **KIDS.**

Hobby City Doll and Toy Museum. 1238 South Beach Boulevard, Anaheim: (714) 527-2323. Several thousand antique dolls and toys in a small-scale
replica of the White House. Puppet shows. Open daily. **KIDS.**

Specialty Museums

Fowler Foundation Museum. 9215 Wilshire Boulevard, Beverly Hills: (310)
392-3313. An eclectic collection of artistic objects from Europe, Asia, and
America including carved ivory, model ships, firearms, and decorated silver.
Closed Sundays.

Frederick's of Hollywood Lingerie Museum. 6608 Hollywood Boulevard: (213) 466-8506. There's less to see here than at most any other museum
we've visited, and there's a lot of it. A private collection of flashy garments
including personal belongings of Madonna (of course), Cher, Judy Garland,
Mae West, the (err) Pointer Sisters, Zsa Zsa Gabor, Cybill Shepherd, . . . and
Milton Berle. The museum is open Mondays through Saturdays from 10 A.M.
to 6 P.M. and Sundays from noon to 5 P.M. Admission is free.

Max Factor Beauty Museum. 1666 North Highland Avenue, Hollywood:
(213) 463-6668. A salute to another of the foundations of Tinseltown.

Hollywood Guinness Museum. 6764 Hollywood Boulevard at Highland
Avenue, Hollywood: (213) 463-6433. A commercial collection of the strange
and amazing. Re-creations depict some of the denizens of the *Guinness Book
of World Records.* Open daily; call for hours. **KIDS.**

Museum of Neon Art. CityWalk, 1000 Universal Center Drive off
Cahuenga Boulevard, West Universal City: (213) 617-1580. Here's something
to get all aglow about: a collection of neon sculpture, art, and classic signs
from the 1920s to modern times. Closed Mondays. Call for hours.

Huntington Beach International Surfing Museum. 411 Olive Street,
Huntington Beach (exit I-405 at Highway 39–Beach Boulevard): (714) 960-
3483.

Far out, dude: a collection of wicked surfboards including a 1930 wooden
behemoth that measures more than 12 feet and weighs 135 pounds. Other
exhibits include posters, artwork, surfing music, and a Hall of Fame.

Open daily in summer from noon to 5 P.M.; open remainder of the year
Wednesdays through Sundays only. $1 admission.

Science Museums

Cabrillo Marine Aquarium. 3720 Stephen White Drive, San Pedro: (310)

548-7562. Saltwater aquariums, displays of sea plants, tide pools, and mud flats in and around a 1920s bathhouse. The museum also sponsors educational lectures and whale-watching trips. Annual Whale Fiesta in June and Autumn Sea Fair in October. Open Tuesdays through Fridays from noon to 5 P.M.; weekends from 10 A.M. to 5 P.M. Closed Thanksgiving and Christmas. Free; donations accepted. Beach parking fee $5.50.

California Museum of Science and Industry. 700 State Drive, Los Angeles: (213) 744-7400. A sprawling museum with hands-on explorations of science from railroads to outer space, from medicine to telecommunications. Second only in size to the Smithsonian in Washington.

You may well do a double-take as you approach one of the corners of the museum; on the lawn out front is a full-size United Airlines jet.

Hands-on and up-close exhibits include computer-assisted design and art machines, an agricultural section with egg hatcheries and plant genetics exhibits, and the Hall of Health.

The new Aerospace Museum includes historic airplanes, spacecraft, and other exhibits, and the **IMAX Theater** with a 50-foot-high, 70-foot-wide screen used to present science, nature, and travel films. Call (213) 744-2015 for IMAX schedules; tickets are about $6 for adults and $4 for children.

The museum is located next to the Los Angeles Memorial Coliseum and the area is often used for special events. There are quite a few parking lots in the area; it is probably not advisable to park on the street.

Open daily; call for hours. Free. **KIDS.**

Jet Propulsion Laboratory. 4800 Oak Grove Drive, Pasadena: (818) 354-4321. Exhibits include models of the *Viking*, *Mariner*, and *Voyager* spacecrafts. Tours given by reservation only; call for information and hours. Children under 10 not permitted.

Los Angeles County Museum of Natural History. 900 Exposition Boulevard, Los Angeles, in Exposition Park: (213) 744-3466.

A national treasure, with dozens of major displays from the age of the dinosaurs to modern-day mammals and most everything in between. You'll find an insect zoo, a Hall of Birds, a sparkling collection of gems and minerals, and even a display of ancient Mayan artifacts. The original museum was built in 1913 and has been added on to many times, most recently with the Ralph Parsons Discovery Center, a hands-on sight, sound, and smell experience. Closed Mondays. Admission charge. **KIDS.**

Next-door to the Natural History Museum is the **Exposition Park Rose Garden,** one of the largest such displays in the country. Open daily. Free.

Los Angeles Maritime Museum. Berth 84, 6th Street and Harbor Boulevard, San Pedro: (310) 548-7618. The next best thing to a life at sea: a collection of more than 600 ship models, including a matchstick re-creation of the *Titanic*, plus all manner of maritime equipment including diving equipment and artifacts from the old whaling and shipping days to modern times. The museum is located in a former ferry building with a view of the harbor. Closed Mondays; call for hours. Nominal admission. **KIDS.**

Nearby at Berth 94 is the **SS *Lane Victory*,** a restored World War II cargo ship. The ship is open for tours and makes six cruises a year to Catalina Island. Call (310) 519-9545 for information and schedules.

La Brea Tar Pits/George C. Page Museum of the La Brea Discoveries. 5801 Wilshire Boulevard, east of Fairfax Avenue, Los Angeles: (213) 936-2230. The La Brea Tar Pits are one of the most unusual elements of a downtown anywhere in the world, a little bit of the Ice Age in the shadow of the skyscrapers. La Brea dates back some 40,000 years; the museum is much more recent and has within it more than a million fossils of plants and animals taken from the tar pits since their discovery in 1906. Among the remains found in the tar are saber-toothed tiger skeletons, mammoth skeletons, and a nine-thousand-year-old skeleton of a woman. Don't promise your kids a view of dinosaurs, though: the pits are only about 40,000 years old, and the big guys had been gone tens of millions of years before then.

There are nine major tar pits in the park area. Summertime visitors can see an ongoing excavation of Pit 91, one of the richest fossil deposits in the world.

As you enter Hancock Park, home of the La Brea Tar Pits, you can smell tar and asphalt in the air. The first historic reference to the tar pools was recorded in the diary of Gaspar du Portola in 1769; the area was originally a portion of the Rancho La Brea granted by Governor Alvarado in 1840.

The Lake Pit along Wilshire Boulevard fills a quarry where asphalt was mined in the 19th century; life-size fiberglass models of an imperial mammoth family stand at the east end of the lake, which is covered with an oily slick. Bubbles of methane burst through the surface of the lake regularly.

The pools of thick oil became unique death traps for countless Ice Age animals and birds, making La Brea the richest deposit of ice age fossils in the world. More than 100 tons of fossil bones have been recovered.

The reconstructed Imperial Mammoth Bull alongside the Lake Pit is modeled after a nearly complete skeleton exhibited in the George C. Page Museum. The animal stood about 12 feet tall and weighed over 10,000 pounds.

On a nice Sunday, you will also likely find a collection of some of California's patented kooks. On one of my visits, I found a man exhibiting his pair of "psychic cats." If you held out a dollar bill, they would grab hold of it with their paws and push a lever on a cigar box to release a printed message.

Visitors can stroll through Hancock Park without charge. The park is landscaped to include plants that were present during the last Ice Age. Open Tuesdays through Sundays from 10 A.M. to 5 P.M.; first Tuesday of the month is free. Admission is $6 for adults and $3.50 for seniors and students. Children from 5 to 10 are charged $2. Parking at the museum is $4 with validation. **KIDS.**

History Museums and Historic Districts

California Afro-American Museum. Exposition Park, South Figueroa Street and State Drive, Los Angeles: (213) 744-7432. Art exhibitions, a library, and theater celebrating African-American culture. Closed Mondays. **KIDS.**

Carole & Barry Kaye Museum of Miniatures. 5900 Wilshire Boulevard, Los Angeles: (213) 937-6464. A big collection of little re-creations of famous places, people, and things. There's some wild stuff here including a complete tea set that could fit on a quarter, Victorian dollhouses, and a tiny reproduction of the Hollywood Bowl, complete with a pantheon of musical stars from Louis Armstrong to Michael Jackson. Open Tuesdays through Saturdays from 10 A.M. to 5 P.M. and Sundays 11 A.M. to 5 P.M. Adults, $7.50; seniors (60 and older), $6.50; students (12 to 21), $5; children (3 to 12), $3. Validated parking half price. **KIDS.** *Discount coupon in this book.*

William O. Douglas Outdoor Classroom. Franklin Canyon Ranch, north of Beverly Hills: (310) 858-3834. Nature center, family and children's hiking trails, and special educational and ecological programs. Free.

Heritage Park (El Monte). 1918 North Rosemead Boulevard, El Monte, within the Whittier Narrows Recreation Area: (818) 442-1776.

An unusual collection of military equipment, including tanks, jeeps, cannons, and other devices. Open weekends from noon to 4:30 P.M. Nominal admission.

El Monte Historical Museum. 3150 North Tyler Avenue, El Monte: (818) 580-2232.

A small museum that celebrates El Monte's history as the end of the Santa Fe Trail, which extended some 780 miles from Independence, Missouri, to Santa Fe, New Mexico, and from there on to California. Hundreds of wagon trains made the 40- to 60-day trip to New Mexico from about 1822 until 1880 when the Santa Fe Railroad reached the area.

The adobe-style building, a former WPA-built library, includes Victorian-era settings and a children's section with antique toys that the kids can play with.

Open Wednesdays through Saturdays from 10 A.M. to 3 P.M. Donations are accepted. **KIDS.**

Hebrew Union College Skirball Museum. 3077 University Avenue, Los Angeles: (213) 749-8611. Jewish history and art from around the world and across time. Closed Saturdays and Mondays. Free.

Heritage Square Museum. 3800 Homer Street at Avenue 43, Lincoln Heights: (213) 449-0193. Eight Victorian-era and older buildings have been restored into a living museum with shops and displays; they are open for tours by costumed guides Fridays through Sundays. Buildings include the Palms Railroad Station, which has been restored and filled with railroad artifacts, plus several homes and a church from 1897. Special events include old-fashioned Fourth of July celebrations and Christmas festivals. Admission charge.

Japanese-American National Museum. 369 East 1st Street at Central Avenue, Los Angeles: (213) 625-0414. The story of Japanese immigrants to America, told in artifacts, photos, art, and recordings. Closed Mondays.

Korean Friendship Bell. Angel's Gate Park, San Pedro, on Gaffey Street. What is said to be the largest bell in America was a gift from the Republic of Korea to the United States for the 1976 Bicentennial celebration. The one-ton bell is rung three times a year: on New Year's Day, the Fourth of July, and Korean Liberation Day, August 15.

Los Angeles Flower Market. 700 Wall Street. The wholesale market for florists and decorators, opens in the middle of the night for commercial clients. The public is admitted after 9 A.M. on weekdays and Saturdays. Get there early to browse and buy from the spectacular leftovers.

Martyrs Memorial and Museum of the Holocaust. Jewish Community Building, 6505 Wilshire Boulevard, Los Angeles: (213) 651-3175. A commemoration of the martyrs of the Holocaust, including photographs, diaries, artifacts, and oral histories. Closed Saturdays.

Masonic Hall. 416–418 North Main Street: (213) 626-4933. Furnished with some of the items brought back on sailing ships that went around Cape Horn. Open for free tours Tuesdays through Fridays from 10 A.M. to 3 P.M.

Museum of Tolerance, Simon Wiesenthal Center. 9786 West Pico Boulevard at Roxbury Drive, Century City: (310) 553-8403. Never again: exhibits on 20th-century genocide, war, and oppression, from the Holocaust to the 1992 Los Angeles riots. Some of the exhibits can be rather intense, including the Whisper Gallery where visitors walk through an audio gauntlet of racial and ethnic slurs, and the Hall of Testimony, where you will hear stories of survival and sacrifice from the Holocaust in Europe. Visitors are escorted through the museum; call for tour hours.

Pacific Stock Exchange. 233 South Beaudry: (213) 977-4700. A viewing gallery overlooks the second largest stock trading floor in America. Open weekdays from 8:30 A.M. to 1:30 P.M.

Petite Elite Miniature Museum. 11355 West Olympic Boulevard, Los Angeles: (310) 277-8108 or 268-0066. It's all summed up in the name: an unusual collection of miniatures, scale models, and historical settings. Closed Sundays and major holidays.

Southwest Museum. 234 Museum Drive, near Highland Park in Los Angeles: (213) 221-2163. An impressive collection of artifacts and crafts of Native Americans of the West, as well as elements of the Spanish colonization of California. Closed Mondays. Admission charge. **KIDS.**

Lummis Home. 200 East Avenue 43, Highland Park, near the Southwest Museum: (213) 222-0546.

Writer Charles Lummis, who chronicled some of the early days of the Wild West, built his home with telegraph poles from the Santa Fe Railroad and other bits of memorabilia. Inside are rare photos of Native Americans and other artifacts. Open Thursdays to Sundays from 1 to 4 P.M. for free tours.

Wells Fargo History Museum. 333 South Grand Avenue at 3rd Street in the Wells Fargo Bank Center, Los Angeles: (213) 253-7166. A history of the rough side of development of the West, including stagecoaches, the Pony Express, mining equipment, gold nuggets, and a replica of a 19th-century Wells Fargo office. Visitors can try their hands at a telegraph key and examine early photos and documents that trace the history of Wells Fargo Bank from its founding in 1852 into the electronic age. Open weekdays from 9 A.M. to 5 P.M. Free. **KIDS.**

Transportation Museums

Lomita Railroad Museum. 2135 250th Street, at Woodward Avenue, Lomita:

(310) 326-6255. Step back to the turn of the century and explore a 1902 Southern Pacific locomotive, an old train station, an antique caboose, and other equipment. Closed Mondays and Tuesdays. Nominal admission. **KIDS.**

Museum of Flying. 2772 Donald Douglas Loop North at 28th Street, Santa Monica: (310) 392-8822. On the grounds of the Santa Monica Airport, a working museum of military and commercial aviation, with more than 65 vintage aircraft including the 1924 Douglas World Cruiser biplane *New Orleans*, the first aircraft to fly around the world; World War II planes; and modern jets. There's also a model of the Mercury space capsule. A theater shows films about aviation. Closed Mondays and Tuesdays. Adults, $4; seniors, $3; students, $2; children 3 to 12, $1.

Planes of Fame Air Museum. Chino Airport, 7000 Merrill Avenue, Chino: (714) 597-3722. Rare aircraft from the dawn of flight to the space age. Open daily.

Entertainment Industry Museums

Hollywood Studio Museum. 2100 North Highland Avenue, Los Angeles, near Hollywood Bowl: (213) 874-2276. Memorabilia, costumes, and equipment from the early days of moviemaking. The museum is located in the barn where Lasky's Feature Play Company, with Cecil B. DeMille as director, made *The Squaw Man*, the first feature-length film made in Hollywood. Objects on display include the chariot from *Ben Hur*. Open weekends only throughout the year; weekdays by appointment. Call for special hours. Adults, $3.50; seniors and students, $2.50; and children 6 to 12, $1.50.

Hollywood Bowl Museum. 2100 North Highland Avenue, Hollywood: (213) 850-2058. Changing exhibits about the arts and the Hollywood Bowl. Open daily in summer, Tuesdays through Saturdays the rest of year. Free.

Hollywood Wax Museum. 6767 Hollywood Boulevard, Hollywood: (213) 462-8860 or 462-5991. Get up close and personal with more than 200 of Hollywood's greatest stars; just don't expect them to give you an autograph. The museum also includes a Chamber of Horrors with residents including Frankenstein's Monster, Dracula, the Wolfman, Pinhead, Elvira, and the Phantom of the Opera, and a movie theater that shows films celebrating the old hometown. Open daily. **KIDS.**

Chapter 12
Hollywood Movie and Television Studios

In Los Angeles on any given day, a film or television crew is likely to be shooting scenes on the streets or within a public building. They're not that difficult to spot: a film crew usually travels with a phalanx of several dozen trucks with equipment, mobile dressing rooms, caterers, and carloads of technicians, film crew, production assistants, and more. They are often accompanied by police cars.

On one of my trips, there were no less than two movies being filmed in and around my hotel room at the Westin Bonaventure Hotel in downtown Los Angeles. In the lobby, a crew worked on *Nick of Time*, a political kidnapping story. Outside my window, Al Pacino and Robert DeNiro ran up and down the street with machine guns as a huge crew shot action scenes for *Heat*.

Moviemaking takes place mostly behind closed doors or in remote sets. But several major studios offer tours—from simple peeks behind the curtains to elaborate theme-park-like attractions such as Universal Studios.

Fans of television from game shows to sitcoms to talk shows may have good luck in obtaining tickets to television studios.

Paramount Pictures

860 North Gower Street between Santa Monica Boulevard and Melrose Avenue, Hollywood. This historic movie studio—where classics including *The Godfather*, the Bob Hope and Bing Crosby *Road* pictures, many of Elvis Presley's "vehicles," and hundreds more were filmed—is now mostly used for television production. The Paramount empire includes the holdings of the former Desilu Production Studio formed by Lucille Ball and Desi Arnaz and RKO-Pathé (home of many of the Fred Astaire–Ginger Rogers films).

Paramount Studios is not a theme park; the two-hour Paramount Tour is a real visit to working parts of the historic movie and television factory, including soundstages, sets, and production departments.

Most film sets are closed while in production, but you may be able to take a peek at the stages when they are quiet. Television shooting for series is usually done on Mondays and Tuesdays, but additional action can be scheduled for any day. "Entertainment Tonight" is in production daily, while talk shows are usually taped in clusters with several episodes shot on one day.

The entrance to the tour is through a small marked door on Gower Street. Through the gates on your left is Stage 29, part of the original RKO lot and the onetime home of "The Brady Bunch."

Some of the other soundstages you will pass include Stage 30, where parts of *Forrest Gump*, including the famous Oval Office scene, were shot; Stage 28, home of "Entertainment Tonight"; and Stage 32, where many of the classic dance-musicals were made, including *Top Hat*. Stage 25, once the home of "Here's Lucy," and later the "Cheers" set, is now used for "Frasier." Stages 19 and 20 were used for much of the shooting for both *Addams Family* films; the television sitcom "Wings" uses part of the stage now.

When Desilu Studios owned the RKO lot, Desi Arnaz's office overlooked a little park designed to look like Lucy and Desi's upstate New York vacation home. Near a kiosk at the park are the unauthorized but still appreciated handprints and names of "Cheers" stars Ted Danson and Woody Harrelson, added in 1989.

The "Hard Copy" set is little more than a desk in front of a large wraparound blue screen; video technology replaces the blue color with an image of a busy newsroom. (The newsroom scene was shot at the Spanish-language Telemundo studios in Florida.)

Across from the Marlene Dietrich Building is a small trophy case that displays some Academy Awards, Emmys, Golden Globes, and other trinkets. Among the most historically noteworthy is the 1927 Academy Award for the classic motion picture *Wings*; it was the first Best Picture winner.

Nearby is Production Park, a small, grassy area once used by Bing Crosby and Bob Hope as a putting green; in a well-remembered episode of "Cheers," Diane Chambers (Shelley Long) played croquet on the grass as she recovered from a nervous breakdown.

The famed Paramount Gate is gone, replaced in recent years by a smaller reproduction. Hollywood superstition still calls for young would-be stars to hug the wrought-iron gate, stare at the Hollywood sign in the distance, and declare the line from *Sunset Boulevard*, which was filmed on the lot: "I'm ready for my close-up, Mr. DeMille." Atop a soundstage at Melrose and Gower you can see the remains of the famous RKO globe and transmitter tower.

A large parking lot near the Production Park doubles as a "tank" for water shots; walls around the lot can hold several feet of water, and there are deeper pits that can be opened for special effects. A blank wall at the back of the tank can be painted as a backdrop or used as a blue screen for video productions. In 1995, the tank was used for some of the scenes from *Waterworld* and *Congo*.

The Property Department is like a gigantic attic, holding bits and pieces of props from thousands of movies and television shows. In one corner is a room full of creepy artifacts from *The Addams Family*; around the corner you'll find Marcia Brady's Debating Team plaque.

Within the Bing Crosby Building is Paramount's Scoring Stage, where musical soundtracks are recorded. At the time of my visit, a 100-piece orchestra was recording revisions to the score for *Congo*; the film had been reedited prior to release based on comments from test audiences.

The studio is also occasionally used for record making because of its reputation as the best "string room" on the West Coast. Among albums made there was Barbra Streisand's *Evergreen*.

The end of the tour is often a stroll through the massive New York City back lot, which stands in for downtowns anywhere in the world.

The best time to visit is from mid-summer through mid-April when television sitcoms and dramas are in production. Feature films can be shot at any time and may be inside on soundstages or on an outdoor set.

The tours are conducted by studio pages and are limited to 15 persons at a time; the tours involve a great deal of walking, and there is little shelter in bad weather.

Tours are held Mondays through Fridays from 9 A.M. to 2 P.M. every hour on the hour; reservations are suggested during the summer and in holiday periods. Tickets were priced at $15 in 1996; visitors must be 10 or older. Call (213) 956-1777 for information. *Discount coupon in this book.*

Universal Studios

100 Universal City Plaza, Universal City, Hollywood Freeway. (US 101) at Lankershim Boulevard: (818) 508-9600.

From the very start of the studio in 1915, when legendary filmmaker Carl Laemmle charged 25 cents to watch movies being made, Universal has welcomed visitors.

Of course, in true Hollywood style, things have gotten a whole lot flashier and more grandiose over the years. Universal Studios Hollywood is now a major theme park, mixing glimpses of working elements of the studios with re-creations of some of recent filmdom's greatest hits, including *E.T.*, *King Kong*, *Back to the Future*, and *Backdraft*. See Chapter 5 on Universal Studios Hollywood for more information.

Warner Bros. Studios VIP Tour

Follow in the footsteps of Humphrey Bogart, Bette Davis, and Jimmy Cagney; walk down the same dirt road trod by Gary Cooper and Maverick, and step into the soundstage that once housed *The Old Man and the Sea*, *My Fair Lady*, *Camelot*, and part of *Jurassic Park*.

The two-hour Warner Bros. tour is a real chance to go behind the scenes at a working studio. No two tours are the same because of production schedules; with a bit of luck, visitors will get to see a film in production or see a rehearsal or taping of a television sitcom or series. The 12-passenger trams, led by a knowledgeable guide, go through the famous back lot of the 110-acre studio and visit some of the soundstages.

The tour begins at the Visitor Center. You are invited into the small the-

Warner Bros. Studios VIP Tour. 4000 Warner Boulevard, Hollywood Way and Olive Avenue, Burbank (Gate 4).

Tickets $29 for all visitors. Children under 10 are not permitted. *See discount coupon in this book.*

For information and reservations, call (818) 972-8687.

Free parking is available at the Visitors Center, at the corner of Olive Avenue and Hollywood Way in Burbank.

The tour is offered weekdays on the hour from 9 A.M. to 4 P.M.; in the summer, trams leave every half hour. The studio is closed on holidays and weekends. Reservations may be necessary at busy times; they are accepted by telephone several weeks in advance.

Photography is permitted on the back lot—the famous outdoor sets—but not allowed at the soundstages.

ater by the recorded voice of announcer Gary Owen, welcoming you to "beautiful downtown Burbank."

The 13-minute film—updated regularly—is an entertaining collage of some of Warner Bros. most famous stars and some of the best-loved punch lines from classic films. You'll see James Cagney, Henry Fonda, Clint Eastwood, Bette Davis, Ronald Reagan, and many others at work and play. Strung together are Michelle Pfeiffer's Catwoman "meow"; a very young Mickey Rooney as Puck in *A Midsummer Night's Dream* declaring "What fools these mortals be"; Jack Nicholson's "Here's Johnny!," and Bugs Bunny's "What's up, doc?" Among the favorite lines is the one delivered by doe-eyed starlet Bette Davis: "I'd like to kiss you, but I just washed my hair." The biggest laughs come from an assemblage of outtakes and flubs by famous stars.

The Warner Bros. Story

Warner Bros. Studios is among the oldest motion-picture centers to be continuously occupied by the same company. Warner films have brought home more than 100 major Academy Awards, including six Best Picture Oscars, for the films *The Life of Emile Zola* (1937), *Casablanca* (1943), *My Fair Lady* (1964), *Chariots of Fire* (1981), *Driving Miss Daisy* (1989), and *Unforgiven* (1992).

The studio was originally built for First National Pictures on farmland purchased from Dr. David Burbank, a dentist and rancher after whom the city of Burbank was named. The property was acquired in 1929 by the Warner brothers, two years after they had revolutionized movies with their release of the first "talkie," Al Jolson's *The Jazz Singer*. Soon the brothers were turning out movies at a feverish pace—86 features in 1929 alone.

By the late 1930s, Warner Bros. Studios had constructed nine new soundstages, all of which are still in use today, with Darryl F. Zanuck as head of production and Busby Berkeley bringing his musical extravaganzas to theaters.

The studio also developed its own zany brand of animation at a rundown Hollywood annex somewhat affectionately known as "Termite Terrace," and after 1940 at the main studio. From the drawing boards of Tex Avery, Chuck Jones, and Friz Freleng sprang such classic and enduring characters as Bugs Bunny, Daffy Duck, Yosemite Sam, Sylvester and Tweety, the Road Runner, and Pepe Le Pew. All of the voices for the original characters were performed by Mel Blanc.

The 1940s saw the studio add three more soundstages and many more classic titles, including *Casablanca, Yankee Doodle Dandy,* and *The Treasure of the Sierra Madre.*

During the 1950s, Warner became the first studio to switch part of its operation to television. At first Jack Warner tried to fight the advent of television with major hits like *A Streetcar Named Desire, A Star is Born,* and *Mr. Roberts.* But by the 1950s, Warner had become the most successful major producer of series television in Hollywood, creating shows including "Maverick," "The Lawman," "77 Sunset Strip," "Cheyenne," and "Hawaiian Eye."

The studio was purchased by the Kinney National conglomerate in 1969, and the whole company became known as Warner Communications Inc. In 1972, Warner Bros. and Columbia Pictures joined forces to create a single production facility, called The Burbank Studios. The studio now was like a small city with its own fire department, mail service, parks, bank, and bicycle shop. (In 1990, Sony purchased Columbia Pictures and moved the company off the Burbank Studios property.)

In 1980, Warner Bros. purchased the Samuel Goldwyn Studios in Hollywood, renaming it Warner Hollywood Studios. In 1988, the company acquired Lorimar Products and moved it to the Burbank lot.

Finally, in 1989, Time-Life merged with Warner Bros., creating Time Warner Inc., one of the largest and most powerful media companies in the world.

Exterior Sets

Midwestern Street. Smalltown, USA, complete with village green, gazebo, and town square. The residential section was built in 1941 for *King's Row* with Ronald Reagan, and the storefront section was constructed in 1945 for *Saratoga Trunk* with Gary Cooper and Ingrid Bergman.

Later the set was used for *Pollyanna,* and more recently for television series including "The Dukes of Hazzard," "Growing Pains," and "Sisters."

The street still includes the gazebo where Robert Preston declared there was trouble in River City in *Music Man.* And, Paul Newman was arrested nearby for cutting down parking meters in *Cool Hand Luke.*

New York Street. Around the corner from the Chicago set is New York, used in many famous scenes. The New York of the 1920s was seen in *The Great Race* and in *The FBI Story* with Jimmy Stewart. On the road was the courthouse used in the 1960s "Batman" television series. It was also decked out in neon for the futuristic main drag of *Blade Runner* and later for scenes in *Batman Returns.*

Hennesy Street. Designed by Dale Hennesy for *Annie,* it was transformed into Kansas of the 1930s for *City Heat,* and was also seen in *Dick Tracy, Peewee's Big Adventure,* and the television series "Scarecrow and Mrs. King."

Nearby to Hennesy Street is the exterior of the emergency room entrance to "ER"'s County Hospital; overhead is a simulated stretch of elevated train tracks. Depending on the shooting schedule, you may also see Doc Magoo's

Diner, the greasy spoon eatery favored by the "ER" cast; the diner is mounted on wheels and is moved into position when that particular set is needed.

Laramie Street. Laramie Street was constructed in 1941 for Westerns and served as the location for some of the best-loved films of all time, including *High Noon* with Gary Cooper. A less-serious classic, Mel Brooks' *Blazing Saddles* was shot there. Television series that used Laramie included "Bonanza" in its last five years, the original "Maverick" series, "F Troop," "Kung Fu," and "Little House on the Prairie."

The buildings on the Western set are constructed at ⅞ths scale, allowing filmmakers to exaggerate the height of cowboy-actors; camera operators have to shoot from a low angle anyway to avoid including power lines and skyscrapers located just outside the Warner Bros. lot.

Laramie is actually the last of three Western sets that at one time were located on the lot.

Jungle Set. This versatile set was seen in *Camelot, The Great Race, Finian's Rainbow* with Fred Astaire, *Green Berets* with John Wayne, and in the television series "Fantasy Island" and "China Beach."

1930s Set. Built in 1938 for *Angels with Dirty Faces* with James Cagney and Humphrey Bogart, the area has been maintained since for a long string of gangster movies and stories never envisioned at the time. For example, it was used as Gotham City for the Batman movies; in *Batman Forever*, it was where Robin stole the Batmobile and took it for a spin through the street. It has also served as Metropolis for Superman movies, as Atlanta for the TV series "The Client," and as Chicago for "Sisters" and "ER."

With some special set dressing, the same streets stood in for Tokyo in *Karate Kid Part 2*, and as Havana in *The Mambo Kings*.

The set is made up almost entirely of facades; only a few structures have any interior spaces.

Kings Row. Used for the Ronald Reagan classic of the same name, it also was featured in *Rebel Without a Cause*. On the same street you'll find the home of Marion the Librarian from *The Music Man*, the *Gremlins* house, the heart of Hazzard County, and the place where Elvira, the Mistress of the Dark, filmed some of her high-camp scenes.

The Jungle. The forested area was created in 1930 and was the home of Tarzan. It also served as Sherwood Forest for Errol Flynn as *Robin Hood* and for parts of *Camelot* and *Finian's Rainbow*. Scenes from the "Fantasy Island" television show were also shot there, and a small pond in the jungle was Walton Pond in "The Waltons."

More recently, the jungle was Vietnam in the television series "China Beach" and the movie spoof *Hot Shots Part Deux*.

And a moment of high drama from the "ER" series was also shot in the small pond; it was here that actor George Clooney struggled to pull a small boy out of a drainage pipe while floodwaters raged all around him.

Costume Warehouse. The huge Costume Warehouse on the back lot is a regular stop of the tram tour. The new building includes no less than 8 miles of hanging rack space and 3.4 miles of shoes. One section holds nothing but wedding gowns. There are aisles of straw boaters and fedoras, Roman gladiator outfits, and maternity and fat pads.

There's a small museum display at the warehouse that on one visit included part of the *Batman Forever* wardrobe. The producers of that film spent $6 million on costumes; a great deal of that money went for latex rubber suits worn by Batman and Robin, and examples of the expensive duds are on display at the warehouse.

> Warner Bros. claims the largest collection of antiques west of the Mississippi. During the Depression years of the 1920s and 30s, Warner Bros. sent its art directors to Europe to buy up antiques for its production needs.

Indoor Soundstages

Warner Bros. has 37 soundstages, the largest collection in Hollywood. Thirty-two are on its lot and five others are down the street. Most were built in the 1930s.

Most of the stages do not have dressing rooms, and movable trailers are parked outside most of the buildings.

"ER"'s operating rooms are within Stage 11, which lies next door to the giggly digs of "Family Matters" in Stage 10. Nearby is the Little Brown Schoolhouse, used by school-age children involved in productions on the lot; state law requires young actors to attend four hours of school per day.

Stage 16. The tallest full-time soundstage in the motion picture industry, it was raised to its present height of 98 feet in the 1930s by William Randolph Hearst, who had moved his production company to the lot in hopes of creating pictures for Marion Davies.

Stage 16 was later used for films including *My Fair Lady*, *Camelot*, *Key Largo*, *Gremlins 2,* and *Batman Returns*.

Also called the "lake stage," it can hold an entire "sea" of water, as seen in *The Old Man and the Sea* and *PT 109*. Steven Spielberg installed a waterfall for a scene for Universal's *Jurassic Park* shot at the stage.

And a glass-and-chrome office building was constructed within for the rise and fall and rise of Michael Douglas and the rise and fall of Demi Moore in *Disclosure*.

Stage 19. The home of the spectacular dancing scenes from *Yankee Doodle Dandy*, it was also used in *The Story of West Point* with Jimmy Cagney, *Gypsy,* and a number of Doris Day musicals including *Calamity Jane*.

Stage 4. Today used to shoot the popular television sitcom "Murphy Brown," it was where Bette Davis once filmed *Now, Voyager*. The stage was also home to the musical *Mame* with Lucille Ball, and was transformed into the fifth floor of the *Washington Post* for *All the President's Men*.

Stage 9. This stage once held the entire set of Rick's Café Americain for *Casablanca*. It was also used for the famous egg-eating scenes in *Cool Hand Luke*, and served for ten years as home to the television comedy "Night Court." In 1996, it was the home of the "Hanging with Mr. Cooper" show.

Stage 8. Most recently used for the television series "Sisters," this stage also

A one-hour television show requires about eight long days to shoot; filming usually takes place only on weekdays. Half-hour sitcoms take four or five days for each episode.

Visitors on the tour sometimes get to see rehearsals for shows. Tour guides can sometimes arrange for tickets to television tapings on the day of your visit. Most regular series go on "hiatus" from mid-spring through mid-summer, resuming production in July and August.

housed memorable scenes from *Who's Afraid of Virginia Woolf?* with Richard Burton and Elizabeth Taylor.

Stage 24. The home of "Friends," which despite its name is not very accommodating to visitors. Tickets to tapings of the show are among the most difficult to obtain in Hollywood.

Other Film Studios

Burbank Studios (Warner Bros. and Columbia). 4000 Warner Boulevard, Burbank: (818) 954-6000. "Gower Gulch" is named after the gathering of would-be actors who would gather outside the gates in hope of gaining a job in one of the many classic silent Westerns shot there in the 1920s. The original Columbia lot is now called Sunset-Gower Studios and is used primarily by ABC Television.

Culver Studios. 9336 West Washington Boulevard, Culver City: 836-5537. Among various owners was Cecil B. DeMille. It later became RKO-Pathé. *King Kong* was filmed here; the studio's white mansion on Washington Boulevard was used for some of the scenes for *Gone with the Wind.* Today the studio is used mostly for television productions.

Hollywood Center Studios. 1040 North Las Palmas Avenue, Hollywood: (213) 469-5000. At one time the home of Harold Lloyd's company, it was used by Howard Hughes for his 1927 silent movie *Hell's Angels,* featuring the debut of Jean Harlow. Shirley Temple made her debut here, and the first episodes of "I Love Lucy" were made here in 1951. More recently it was the location of Francis Ford Coppola's Zoetrope Studios. It now rents out its facilities to various production companies.

Lorimar Telepictures. 3300 Riverside Drive, Suite 405, Burbank: (818) 954-5305. The former Metro-Goldwyn-Mayer studios, former home of Clark Gable, Greta Garbo, Katherine Hepburn, the Marx Brothers, and dozens of other icons of the day. The lot is not open to the public, but you may be able to catch a glimpse through the studio gates.

Raleigh Studios. 650 North Bronson Avenue, Hollywood: (213) 466-3111. Mary Pickford and Douglas Fairbanks made their films here in the 1920s and 1930s. They went on to use this location to form United Artists. Films made here included *Mark of Zorro, Hopalong Cassidy, Guys and Dolls,* and *The Best Years of Our Lives.* It was also the home of television's original "Superman" series.

20th Century-Fox Film Corporation. 10201 West Pico Boulevard, Los Angeles: (310) 277-2211. The much-reduced Fox Studio still includes major sets including the New York City set employed in numerous films including *Hello, Dolly!* and as an all-purpose downtown in many other films; you can see part of the set from the street. Films made at the lot include *The Sound of Music*, *Butch Cassidy and the Sundance Kid*, and *Planet of the Apes*.

Television Studios

There are three principal ways to obtain tickets to see a television taping or live broadcast: connections, planning, or luck. Connections with someone in the industry may work at any time. Planning a few months ahead of time may give you the tickets you'd like. The very lucky may be able to walk into a show on the day of taping.

ABC Television Network. 4151 Prospect Avenue, Los Angeles: (310) 557-7777. Handles tickets for various ABC theaters, including dress rehearsals and tapings.

Audience Associates. 7471 Melrose Avenue, #10: (213) 467-4697. Tickets to CBS, Fox, NBC, and Universal productions.

Audiences Unlimited. 100 Universal City Plaza, Building 153, Universal City: (818) 506-0043. An agency that supplies audiences for shows. Call to check on scheduled shows; send a self-addressed stamped envelope for up to six free tickets (zip code 91608). Allow several weeks for delivery.

CBS Television Network. 7800 Beverly Blvd, Los Angeles: (213) 852-2458. CBS and independent productions.

Fox Television Center. 5746 Sunset Boulevard: (213) 856-1520.

KCET-TV. 4401 Sunset Boulevard, Los Angeles: (213) 953-5242. Free 90-minute tour of one of the leading public television stations, offered Tuesday and Thursday mornings by reservation only. The location has been in continuous use as a studio since 1912, with owners including the historic Essenay Company, Monogram Pictures, and Allied Artists Studios. Under Monogram, the "East Side Kids" (Bowery Boys) series and the Charlie Chan movies were made here. In 1952, Allied filmed *Attack of the 50-Foot Woman* and *Invasion of the Body Snatchers* at the studio.

KTLA-TV. 5800 Sunset Boulevard, Hollywood: (213) 460-5500. Independent and Fox productions. The original home of Warner Bros. Studios. Al Jolson made the first "talkie," *The Jazz Singer*, here in 1927.

NBC Television Network. 3000 West Alameda Avenue, Burbank: (818) 840-4444 or 840-3537. The studio offers 70-minute guided tours of some of its facilities, including the home of "The Tonight Show." Tours depart at regular intervals weekdays from 9 A.M. to 3 P.M.; open weekends and extended hours during summer and holiday seasons. Closed Easter, Thanksgiving, Christmas Day, and New Year's Day. Tickets for the tour in 1996 were $6 for adults and $3.75 for children from 5 to 12. For tours, call (818) 840-4444, ext. 3537.

"The Tonight Show". Jay Leno took over the mantle as the King of Burbank when he took the helm of "The Tonight Show." For much of the year, he tapes his nightly talk and entertainment show from his custom-designed studio there.

If you want to be in the audience for taping of "The Tonight Show with Jay Leno," you can try for tickets at the NBC kiosk on Universal's CityWalk on the day of the show. (The booth may also have tickets for other shows.)

Or if you have a few weeks' advance notice, send your request by mail to NBC Tickets, 3000 West Alameda Avenue, Burbank, CA 91523; include the day or days you hope to see a show and the number of tickets you need, with a stamped self-addressed envelope.

Taping takes place about 5 P.M. Monday through Friday; with tickets in hand, you must be in line by 4 P.M.—even earlier if there is a particularly popular guest booked that night. Like it or not, the studio gives out more tickets than there are seats—on a typical day 30 to 50 people are turned away.

There is no parking lot for the studio, but early arrivals should find spaces around the corner at a location you could find only near Hollywood: Bob Hope Drive, across from Johnny Carson Park.

The slow and disorganized waiting line is annoying, but you might want to keep your eye out for strolling members of the crew looking for audience members to use in skits; on the night of one of my visits they were planting questions for "Iron Jay," Leno's dim-witted weightlifter alter ego. You may also be offered tickets to the taping of other sitcoms while you wait.

The only way to avoid standing in line is to pull whatever strings you can to obtain invited VIP tickets; these tickets guarantee entrance to the show but not necessarily the best seats in the house.

"The Tonight Show" studio seats just 320; there are only 30 seats on the "floor" of the studio. Lucky guests here are usually personally greeted by the host at the start of the show.

The excellent Kevin Eubanks band entertains the audience before the show and during the time when couch potatoes must suffer through commercials; some guests may wish there was a volume control, though.

Leno usually comes out to warm up the audience himself, and will pose for pictures and sign a few autographs. He seems to be much more approachable than many other "stars" in Hollywood.

The show is recorded straight through; in television terms it is "live on tape."

Universal Television. 100 Universal City Plaza, Universal City: (818) 777-1000. Most Universal television shows are not made before a live audience; you may be able to see glimpses of work underway as part of the Universal studio tour.

Chapter 13
Children in Los Angeles

There's a lot more than theme parks for kids in Los Angeles and Orange County. Here are some interesting tours, museums, and playhouses aimed at the younger set and the old folks lucky enough to accompany them.

Tours

Los Angeles Fire Department Open House. (213) 485-5971. On the second Saturday of May, all Los Angeles fire stations are open to the public for tours and demonstrations. Free.

Los Angeles Times. 1st and Spring Streets, Los Angeles: (213) 237-5000. Tour the newsrooms and printing plant. Mondays through Fridays 3 P.M. Free.

Navy Open House. Navy Public Information Office: (310) 547-6721. Tours of Navy vessels docked at Long Beach shipyards each weekend. Free.

Los Angeles Police Headquarters. Parker Center, 150 North Los Angeles Street: (213) 485-3281. Guided tours including the crime lab and jail. Call for appointment. Free.

Sheriff's Training and Regional Services (STARS) Center. 11515 South Colima Road, Whittier: (310) 946-7081. A museum and tour of some of the facilities of the Los Angeles County Sheriff's Department. Call for hours.

Children's Museums

See also the chapter on general museums.

Kidspace. 390 South El Molina Avenue, Pasadena: (818) 449-9143. Children try on some of the roles of adulthood in this innovative museum that insists that visitors touch the exhibits. Kids can walk through a human-scale anthill, play doctor, run a TV station, and much more. Children must be accompanied by an adult. Open weekends and some weekdays; call for hours. Nominal admission.

La Habra Children's Museum. 301 South Euclid Street, La Habra: (310) 694-1011. A converted train depot with hands-on exhibits and Grandma's Attic, with trunks full of clothing to try on. Closed Sundays.

Los Angeles Children's Museum. 310 North Main Street: (213) 687-8800 or 687-8226. The mother of all kid museums in Los Angeles: lots of exhibits to touch and lots of adult things to play with. Here kids can climb on board a police motorcycle, run the television cameras in a kid's studio, or play fire-fighter. An Ethnic LA exhibit spotlights the many different cultures of the region. An animation workshop contributed by Walt Disney Productions allows kids to lay hands on cartoon characters. Open daily. Admission charge.

Children's Theaters

Most listed theaters offer weekend performances of shows aimed at children. Call for hours and show titles.

American Cinematheque. Directors Guild Theatre, 7920 Sunset Boulevard, Los Angeles: (213) 466-3456 or 461-9622. Saturday movie matinees.

Blackstreet U.S.A. Puppet Theatre. 4129 West Washington, Los Angeles: (213) 936-6091.

Bob Baker Marionette Theater. 1345 West 1st Street, Los Angeles: (213) 250-9995. A local institution just for kids (and lucky adults); puppet show, backstage tour, and cookies and ice cream. Performances Tuesdays through Saturdays. Admission $8.

Brea's Youth Theatre. 1 Civic Center, Brea: (714) 990-7727 or 990-7722. For children, presented by children.

Century City Playhouse. 10508 West Pico Boulevard, Century City: (310) 478-0897.

Comedy & Magic Club. 1018 Hermosa Avenue, Hermosa Beach: (310) 376-6914 or 372-1193. Sunday afternoons.

Great American Children's Theatre. Touring company performs at various locations. For information, call (900) 852-9772.

Hans Christian Andersen Fairy Tale Festival. Solvang: (805) 688-5575. Two-day festival the week before Easter Sunday.

Imagination Celebration. Weeklong festival for children in Orange County in the spring. For information, call (714) 556-2787.

Jim Gamble Puppets. Various locations. For information, call (310) 541-1921.

La Cabaret Comedy Club. 17271 Ventura Boulevard, Encino: (818) 501-3737. Sunday family shows.

La Connection Comedy Improv for Kids by Kids. 13442 Ventura Boulevard, Sherman Oaks: (818) 784-1868. Sunday afternoons.

Laguna Playhouse Youth Theatre. The Laguna Playhouse, 606 Laguna Canyon Road, Laguna Beach: (714) 497-9244.

Let's Put on a Show. Roxy Theatre, 9009 Sunset Boulevard, Hollywood: (310) 276-2222.

Los Angeles Chamber Orchestra Family Concert Series. For information, call (213) 622-7001.

LULA Washington Children's Jazz Dance Ensemble. For information, call (213) 936-6591.

Magic Mirror Players. Third Stage Theatre, 2811 West Magnolia Boulevard, Burbank: (818) 508-4780 or 842-4755.

Mojo Ensemble Family Theatre. 1549 North Cahuenga Boulevard, Hollywood: (213) 957-0690 or 960-1604.

Odyssey Theatre Ensemble. 2055 South Sepulveda Boulevard, Los Angeles: (310) 477-2055. Saturdays.

Open House at the Hollywood Bowl. 1301 North Highland Avenue, Hollywood: (213) 850-2077 or 850-2000. Six-week festival in July and August, including music, dance, and theater.

Open House at the Music Center. Dorothy Chandler Pavilion, Los Angeles: (213) 972-7211. Saturday classical music program.

Santa Monica Playhouse. 1211 4th Street, Santa Monica: (310) 394-9779.

Silent Movie Theater. 611 North Fairfax Avenue, Los Angeles: (213) 653-2389. Nightly.

Symphonies for Youth. Dorothy Chandler Pavilion, Los Angeles: (213) 850-2000. Los Angeles Philharmonic in special shows for youngsters on Saturdays.

Theatre West Storybook Theatre. 3333 Cahuenga Boulevard West, Los Angeles: (213) 851-4839 or (981) 761-2203. Fairytales brought to life.

Wonderworld Puppet Theater. Various locations. Call (310) 532-1741 for information. Saturdays.

VIII
Sporting Activities

Chapter 14
Beaches, Water Parks, Parks, and Zoos

Can You Overlook the Pacific Ocean?

Strolling the make-believe streets of Disneyland or the concrete canyons of Los Angeles, it is easy enough to forget that you are within swimming distance of the Pacific Ocean and some of the most famous beaches on the West Coast. There are dozens of swimming, surfing, and sunbathing strands along the 75-mile coastline from above Malibu to Newport Beach.

LOS ANGELES AREA BEACHES

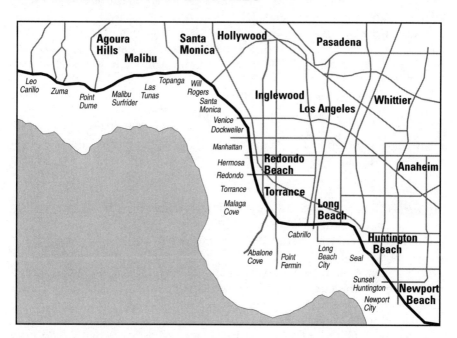

Los Angeles Area Beaches

Los Angeles County Beaches and Harbors Information Center. (310) 305-9545
Surfing and Weather Conditions:
Central Section: (310) 578-0478 or 451-8761
Long Beach City Beach: (310) 477-1463
Newport City Beach: (714) 673-3371 or 673-3373
Northern Section: (310) 457-9701
San Pedro/Cabrillo Beach: (310) 832-1130
Southern Section: (310) 379-8471

Northern Section

The beaches between Point Mugu and Malibu are among the less crowded in Southern California and offer excellent swimming, surfing, water sports, and fishing. There are public campsites at **Leo Carrillo** and **Point Mugu State Park**; there are also some spectacular hiking trails that lead into the foothills.

Leo Carrillo Beach. 36000 Pacific Coast Highway, Malibu: (818) 880-0350 or 706-1310. There's something for everybody at this 1,600-acre beach, named for actor Leo Carrillo (best known as Pancho on the television series "The Cisco Kid"). It's a fine swimming, surfing, and snorkeling beach (including a "clothing optional" section); there's also a nature trail that leads to tide pools and interesting rock formations, and Sequit Point, which contains sea caves and a natural tunnel.

Zuma Beach. 30000 Pacific Coast Highway, Malibu: (310) 457-9891. Like wow, man: a handsome beach carpeted with valley girls and surfer dudes. The surf can get rough. At the paved side of the beach are playgrounds, showers, restrooms, and concession stands.

Point Dume. South of Zuma and a little less well-known, it is still an excellent swimming and surfing site. From November to May the Point Dume Headland is a prime vantage point to observe migrating California gray whales just off shore.

Malibu Surfrider Beach. 23200 Pacific Coast Highway, Malibu: (818) 706-1310. This is the one you're thinking of, the one you've seen in the Gidget movies, the surfing competitions, and your dreams of hanging ten. There's nearly a mile of beach alongside the hulking Malibu Pier. There's also a marine preserve and a nature center.

Central Section

Las Tunas Beach. Below Malibu toward Santa Monica. A small beach with an offshore reef popular for diving and fishing.

Topanga Beach. Another mile-long sandy beach between Topanga Creek at the end of Topanga Canyon Road, popular for surfing and swimming.

Will Rogers Beach. 16000 Pacific Coast Highway: (310) 394-3266. Donated to the state by the famous author and commentator, this three-mile beach offers moderate surf, a playground, and gymnastics equipment.

Santa Monica Beach. Pacific Coast Highway at Colorado Boulevard, Santa Monica: (310) 451-2906. A broad, attractive beach with relatively gentle surf, it flanks the Santa Monica Pier which includes a turn-of-the-century carrousel, arcades, restaurants, and gift shops. The pier is also used for fishing.

Venice Beach. 1531 Ocean Front Walk, Venice: (310) 394-3266. The beach is quite nice, but the real attraction here is the Venice Boardwalk, the world capital of West Coast weird. The boardwalk is lined with food stands and shops; the roadway is populated with street performers and roller-bladers, and in and among the palm trees is the famous outdoor gym called Muscle Beach. You can rent roller skates or bicycles and join the circus.

Southern Section

Dockweiler Beach. Vista del Mar Boulevard, Playa del Rey: (310) 322-5008. This is not the beach of your dreams, but it is a very lively local favorite for some reason. It lies in the approach path of LAX and is alongside a sewage treatment plant and an oil refinery. There's a beach for swimming and surfing, a playground, and a bicycle trail.

Manhattan Beach. Highland and Manhattan boulevards: (310) 372-2166. A broad swimming, surfing, snorkeling, and fishing beach with two miles of broad beachfront. There are more than 100 volleyball courts. At the back of the beach is the Strand, a concrete promenade crowded with skaters, skateboarders, and joggers.

Hermosa Beach. A relatively quiet mile-long beach with a fishing pier and concession stands.

Redondo Beach. Esplanade at Knobhill Avenue, Redondo Beach: (310) 372-2166. A wide beach that extends from the Redondo Pier with restaurants, gift shops, and concession stands. Excursion and fishing boats depart from the pier.

Torrance Beach. A popular diving, surfing, and swimming beach with a bathhouse and playground.

Malaga Cove. Paseo del Mar at Via Arroyo, Palos Verdes: (310) 372-2166. A gazebo on the bluffs gives a great view of the cove; a path leads down to the sandy beach.

Abalone Cove. 5755 Palos Verdes Drive South: (310) 372-2166. On the Portuguese Bend of the Palos Verdes Peninsula, with a view of Catalina Island. No lifeguards.

Point Fermin Lighthouse. The lighthouse, built in 1874, sits on the bluff

Santa Monica Pier. (310) 458-8900. An out-to-sea amusement place that includes a Philadelphia Toboggan Company carrousel, built in 1922 and maintained and restored to its original splendor. The march of the hand-carved horses is accompanied by the incomparable sounds of an antique Wurlitzer organ. The pier also features some other more modern kiddie rides.

Sand Dune Park. 33rd Street at Bell Avenue, Manhattan Beach: (310) 545-5621. Just what it sounds like: a colossal, steep sand dune that kids can climb, slide on, and carry home in their bathing suits. There's also a playground and picnic area. Run by the Manhattan Beach Parks and Recreation Department. Open daily. Free.

with a view of Catalina Island; trails descend to the beach below. There's a playground and a small amphitheater.

Cabrillo Beach. A generally calm waterfront with a playground and snack bar. Nearby is the Cabrillo Marine Museum.

Long Beach Area

Long Beach City Beach. The seven-mile beach is within the harbor break-water and therefore generally offers calm water. The Belmont Pier offers fishing locations. East of Long Beach City Beach, the **Alamitos Bay Peninsula** reaches almost a mile into Alamitos Bay with calm waters on the bay side and surf on the ocean side.

Orange County

Seal Beach. (310) 430-2613. Swimming, surfing, and fishing (from the adjacent Seal Beach Pier).

Sunset Beach at Huntington Beach. Pacific Coast Highway at Beach Boulevard, Huntington Beach: (714) 499-3312 or 536-1454. A beachside entertainment area, with sand, water, volleyball courts, picnic areas, and a marina. A bicycle path runs along the three-mile length of the beach.

Newport City Beach. (714) 644-3047. Another one of the picture-perfect Southern California beaches. There's a famous sand castle contest each summer. The Dory Fleet returns each morning to sell its catch on the west side of Newport Pier.

Los Angeles Area Parks

Griffith Park. (213) 665-5188. This is the true back lot of Los Angeles and Hollywood, some 4,213 acres of mostly undeveloped hilly land in the eastern Santa Monica Mountains. The park ranges from 384 to 1,625 feet above sea level and includes semiarid foothills and heavily forested valleys.

It includes hiking trails, picnic areas, the first-class Griffith Observatory and Planetarium, the Los Angeles Zoo, a railroad and transit museum, the SR-2 Simulator ride, a western heritage museum, and the Greek Theatre, an outdoor amphitheater.

The park is regularly used by Hollywood filmmakers for location shooting, with some of the most famous scenes including parts of *Rebel Without a Cause* and *King Kong*. A wilderness area that includes a former rock quarry was the location of the Batcave in the television and film versions of *Batman*.

The land was originally part of Rancho Los Feliz, a land grant to scout and explorer Corporal Jose Vicente Feliz in 1796. Most of the park land was eventually given to the city in 1896 by Colonel Griffith J. Griffith, a gold speculator and somewhat shady character who had, among other recommendations, served a year in prison for attempting to murder his wife. City officials took the gift but refused to accept the money to build what became the Griffith Observatory until after his death.

When weather conditions are right—which, unfortunately, is not very often—it is well worth the short trip up the hill to the park to see the view of the city below. Take big city precautions if you make a visit to the park at night.

See Chapter 11 on museums for more details on the cultural facilities in the park.

Arriving by car, you can use any of eight entrances: Commonwealth Avenue, Ferndell Drive, Forest Lawn Drive, Riverside Drive, North Vermont Avenue, Interstate 5 (Griffith Park Drive or Zoo Drive exits), and Highway 134 (Victory Boulevard exit). MTA buses 96 and 97 connect downtown to the park.

The park is open from 6 A.M. to 10 P.M. daily; horseback and hiking trails and mountain roads close at sunset. The speed limit within the park is 25 miles per hour and is strictly enforced.

Regional Parks

California Department of Parks and Recreation. (818) 880-0350. MISTIX Campground Reservations: (800) 444-7275.

National Park Service. (818) 597-9192. MISTIX Campground Reservations: (800) 365-2267.

U.S. Forest Service. Angeles National Forest: (818) 574-5200. National Forest Recreation reservations: (800) 280-2267.

Angeles National Forest: (818) 574-5200, 335-1251
Chantry Flat Visitors Center: (818) 355-0712
Chilao Visitors Center: (818) 796-5541
Crystal Lake Visitors Center: (818) 910-1149
Henninger Flats Museum: (818) 794-0675
Mount Baldy Visitors Center: (909) 982-2829
San Gabriel Canyon Entrance Station: (818) 969-1012

If Griffith Park is the back lot of Los Angeles, then the Angeles National Forest is the outback. It's a gigantic preserve—some 695,000 acres—that sits like a shield over north Los Angeles, incorporating within it the San Gabriel Mountains.

The forest has nearly 600 miles of hiking and horse trails, nearly 200 miles of fishing streams, 400 miles of off-road trails and 64 campgrounds. Several lakes are available for swimming, fishing, and boating. The park rangers offer a variety of programs in the summer.

Entrances to the park include Highway 2 from Pasadena, which becomes the Angeles Crest Highway that traverses most of the park from west to east; Highway 39, which enters from near Azusa and proceeds north to Crystal Lake; Big Tujunga Canyon Road from near Sunland; and Mount Baldy Road from near Glendora.

Ernest E. Debs Park. (213) 225-3329.

An interesting piece of near-wilderness in northeastern Los Angeles, part of Arroyo Seco Canyon. The 300-acre park includes a fishing lake, hiking trails, and picnic areas. Enter the park off Monterey Road, north of Huntington Drive.

Kenneth Hahn State Recreation Area. (213) 291-0199.

The park includes an Olympic Forest planted with trees and shrubs representing each of the nations that competed in the 1984 Olympics in Los

Angeles. Recreational facilities include playgrounds, picnic areas, and hiking trails. Located on the western edge of Los Angeles, at 4100 South La Cienega Boulevard between Rodeo Road and Stocker Street.

Santa Monica Mountains National Recreation Area. (818) 597-9192.

A spectacular seaside preserve, stretching 55 miles from Santa Monica to Point Mugu and including favorite beaches such as Leo Carillo State Beach, Zuma Beach, Point Dume, and Malibu Surfrider Beach. The J. Paul Getty Museum is also within the park. See the section on beaches and the chapter on museums for more details.

Hiking and walking trails are marked. Stop by the Visitors Center off Highway 101 for information. The Center is located in Agoura Hills at 30401 Agoura Road, Suite 100, at Reyes Adobe Road, and is open daily except Sundays.

Verdugo Mountains. (800) 533-7275.

The Verdugo Mountains, a western reach of the San Gabriels, form the backdrop to Burbank and Glendale. The area includes spectacular hiking trails in La Tuna Canyon and less-taxing but still-thrilling picnic areas and trails in Wildwood Canyon Park.

You can enter the park from Glenoaks Boulevard, along the southern section, or from La Tuna Canyon Road from the west.

Will Rogers State Historic Park. 14253 Sunset Boulevard, Pacific Palisades: (310) 454-8212. The famous humorist and former cowboy's home and 187-acre estate were given to the public after his death in a plane crash in 1935. The home includes remembrances of Rogers' career and life; his private polo field is used for weekend games, and visitors are welcome. The park is open daily; call ahead for open times for the Rogers home. Free admission; parking $5.

Historic Ranches

Paramount Ranch. Cornell Road, Agoura Hills: (818) 597-9192 for Paramount Ranch and Peter Strauss Ranch. Not quite the real thing . . . this 300-acre ranch was once used by Paramount Pictures to film some of its classic Westerns; it was later used for early television horse operas. The remains of a false-front Western town from the TV years still stand, and there are hiking and nature programs available.

Nearby is the **Peter Strauss Ranch**, at 30000 Mulholland Highway, Agoura Hills. Originally developed as a lakeside resort, it was later owned by the actor whose name is now attached to it. There are hiking and nature trails and concerts and theatrical presentations at an outdoor amphitheater.

William S. Hart Park. 24151 Newhall Avenue, Newhall: (805) 259-0855. The cowboy world of former Western film star William S. Hart, about an hour north of Los Angeles and near the Six Flags California theme park. The collection includes saddles and gear, weapons, and artifacts. The 250-acre ranch is home to farm animals and a herd of buffalo, a gift to the public by Walt Disney. The Spanish colonial Revival-style mansion contains original furnishings, a collection of Western art, Native American artifacts, and mementos of early Hollywood.

William S. Hart was born in Newburg, New York, in 1864 and began an acting career in his twenties; at the age of 49, Hart came west to Hollywood to start his movie career. During the next 11 years, he made more than 65 silent films, the last being *Tumbleweeds* in 1925. Hart lived at the ranch nearly 20 years until his death in 1946; in his will, Hart gave the Horseshoe Ranch to the County of Los Angeles.

On Sundays you can visit the adjacent Saugus train station, restored to turn-of-the-century realism. For information, call (805) 254-1275.

The park is open daily; tours of the house are offered from mid-September to mid-June on Wednesdays through Fridays from 10 A.M. to 1 P.M. with the last tour at 12:30 P.M., and Saturdays and Sundays from 11 A.M. to 4 P.M., with the last tour at 3:30 P.M. In the summer tours are offered Wednesdays to Sundays from 11 A.M. to 4 P.M., with the last tour at 3:30 P.M. Admission is free.

Zoos and Animal Preserves

Los Angeles Zoo. 5333 Zoo Drive, Griffith Park, near the junction of the Golden State and Ventura freeways: (213) 666-4090.

The zoo began in 1912 with just 15 animals and was moved to its present location in 1966. Today it includes more than 2,000 mammals, reptiles, and birds in displays designed to resemble their natural environment. Unusual exhibits include the indoor Koala House, the China Pavilion which includes endangered snow leopards, and a display of emperor tamarins. A special children's section displays animals of the Southwest. A small petting zoo is at the Children's Zoo. Open daily from 10 A.M. to 6 P.M. Admission is $8.25 for adults and $5.25 for children ages 2 to 12.

Institute for Wild and Exotic Animal Studies. Moorpark College, Campus Road, Moorpark: (805) 529-2324. A small collection of exotic animals. Open Sundays only; call for hours.

W. G. Kellogg Arabian Horse Farm. California State Polytechnic University, 3801 West Temple Avenue, Pomona: (909) 869-2224. Purebred Arabian horses on display daily; shows presented first Sunday of each month from October to June. Token admission charge.

Santa Ana Zoo. Prentice Park, 1801 East Chestnut Avenue, Santa Ana: (714) 835-7484. Smaller mammals and birds plus a Children's Zoo with petting section and playground. Open daily; token admission.

Arboretums

Descanso Gardens. 1418 Descanso Drive at Foothill Boulevard, La Cañada Flintridge: (818) 952-4400. A wonderland of camellias, roses, orchids, and other flowers and plants. Camellias are in blossom over the winter, from October to March; lilacs and outdoor orchids are at their best in April; and roses and other glories own the summer months. Guided tours by tram are offered daily. The gardens are open every day except Christmas for a minimal admission charge.

Los Angeles State and County Arboretum. 301 North Baldwin Avenue near Colorado Boulevard, Arcadia: (818) 821-3222. More than 30,000 plants from around the world outdoors and in greenhouses on the historic Rancho Santa Anita. Also on the 127-acre grounds are a former Santa Fe Railroad depot, replicas of Indian homes, and a historic Queen Anne Cottage.

A large lagoon, hidden within a stand of huge palm trees, was the setting for many of the original Tarzan movies, At the far side of the lagoon is a restored adobe, dating from 1839.

Guided tours are conducted on Wednesdays. Open daily except Christmas; low admission charge.

Water Parks

Magic Mountain Hurricane Harbor. See the section in the chapter about Six Flags Magic Mountain in this book.

Raging Waters. In San Dimas where the 10, 210, and 57 freeways meet, about 25 minutes from Disneyland and 30 minutes from downtown Los Angeles: (909) 592-8181.

The largest water theme park west of the Mississippi, there are 23 rides and slides including the new Volcano FantaSea, a smoking volcano with water slides descending to a blue lagoon. Other attractions include a raft ride, a river ride, and a wave pool.

Open weekends from mid-April through Memorial Day, daily from about June 1 to mid-September, and weekends from mid-September to the end of the month. General admission, $19.99; junior ticket for children from 42 to 48 inches, $11.99. Small children free; discount tickets for non-sliders and seniors available. *Discount coupon in this book.*

Wild Rivers. 8800 Irvine Center Drive, Laguna Hills, off I-405 at the Irvine Center Drive exit: (714) 768-9453.

An artificial mountain of water slides and tube rides, plus the Thunder Cove wave pool and the Explorer's Island play area for children. The African theme picks up on the former identity of the park, the departed Lion Country Safari.

Open daily from 10 A.M. to 8 P.M. from mid-June to early September; from 11 A.M. TO 5 P.M. weekends and holidays from mid-May to early June and in mid-September until early October. Admission $18.95 for visitors age 10 and older; $14.95 for children from 3 to 9. *Discount coupon in this book.*

Chapter 15
Sporting News

Professional and Collegiate Sports Teams
Baseball

California Angels. Anaheim Stadium, 2000 East Gene Autry Way, Anaheim: (714) 634-2000. Major league baseball. Disney bought a majority interest in 1996 . . . cuteness awaits.

 Los Angeles Dodgers. Dodger Stadium, 1000 Elysian Park Avenue, Los Angeles: (213) 224-1400 or 224-1500. Major league baseball.

 UCLA—University of California, Los Angeles. For information on Bruins baseball games and tickets, call (310) 825-2106 or 825-2101.

 USC—University of Southern California. For information on USC Trojans baseball games, call the ticket office at (213) 740-2311 or 740-4072.

Basketball

Los Angeles Clippers. Los Angeles Sports Arena, 3939 South Figueroa Street: (213) 748-6131 or 748-0500. NBA basketball.

 Los Angeles Lakers. The Forum, Manchester Boulevard and Prairie Avenue, Inglewood: (310) 419-3100. NBA basketball.

 UCLA Basketball. Pauley Pavilion, UCLA Campus, Westwood: (310) 825-2106 or 825-2101.

 USC Basketball. Sports Arena, 3939 South Figueroa Street, Los Angeles: (213) 743-2620, 748-6136, or 740-4072.

Football

Los Angeles Raiders. LA Coliseum, 3911 South Figueroa Street, Los Angeles: (213) 747-7111 or (310) 322-5901. NFL football.

 Los Angeles Rams. Anaheim Stadium, 2000 East Gene Autry Way, Anaheim: (714) 535-7267 or 937-6767. NFL football.

 UCLA Bruins. The Rose Bowl, 1001 Rose Bowl Drive, Pasadena: (818) 793-7193.

 USC Trojans. LA Coliseum, 3911 South Figueroa Street, Los Angeles:

Hallowed ground.
Have you ever dreamt
of stepping up to the
plate at a huge baseball
stadium, trying out the
water fountain in the
dugout, or checking out
the dressing room where
Reggie Jackson hung his,
err, hat? Daily 45-minute
tours of Anaheim
Stadium are offered at
11 A.M., noon, 1 P.M.,
and 2 P.M.; no tours are
given on days of daytime
home games or events.
Adults, $3; children 5 to
16, $2. Call (714) 254-
3120 for information.

(213) 747-7111. For Trojans schedule, call (213)
740-2311.

Rose Bowl Football Game. The parade now
serves as prelude to the big football game, traditionally pitting the best of the Pacific Coast
Conference against the best of the Big Ten Conference. Tickets are hard to come by and are usually sold out well in advance of the game.
Contact the Rose Bowl at (818) 793-7193.

Ice Hockey

Anaheim Mighty Ducks. Anaheim Arena, 2695
East Katella Avenue at Douglass Road, Anaheim:
(714) 704-2701. NHL hockey. Not your basic
hockey club . . . owned by Disney.

Los Angeles Kings. The Forum, Manchester
Boulevard and Prairie Avenue, Inglewood: (310)
419-3100. NHL hockey.

Horse Racing

Hollywood Park. 1050 South Prairie Avenue, Inglewood: (310) 419-1500.
Thoroughbred racing April to July and November to December. Harness racing
August to October.

Los Alamitos. 4961 Katella Avenue, Los Alamitos: (310) 431-1361. Harness
and quarter-horse racing May to August.

Santa Anita. 285 West Huntington Drive, Arcadia: (818) 574-7223. Thoroughbred racing at one of the country's most famous tracks. Morning work-
outs open daily from 7:30 to 9:30 A.M. during racing season, which is
December to April and October to November. Free.

Stadiums and Arenas

Anaheim Arena. 2695 East Katella Avenue at Douglass Road: (714) 704-2500.
Capacity: 17,256. Anaheim Mighty Ducks of the National Hockey League, plus
other events.

Anaheim Stadium. 2000 Gene Autry Way near Katella Avenue: (714) 254-
3000. Capacity: 70,500. California Angels of the American League, Los Angeles Rams of the National Football League, concerts, and major events.

Dodger Stadium. 1000 Elysian Park Avenue, Los Angeles: information,
(213) 224-1500, and box office, (213) 224-1400. Capacity: 56,000 seats. Los
Angeles Dodgers of the National League.

The Great Western Forum. 3900 West Manchester Boulevard at Prairie
Avenue, Inglewood: information, (310) 673-1300, and box office, (310) 419-
3100. Capacity: 17,000–20,000. Los Angeles Lakers of the National Basketball
Association, the Los Angeles Kings of the National Hockey League, concerts,
and special events.

Hollywood Park. 1050 South Prairie Avenue, Inglewood: (310) 419-1500.
Thoroughbred and harness racing.

Long Beach Arena. 300 East Ocean Boulevard at Long Beach Boulevard: (310) 436-3661. Capacity: 14,500. Special events.

Los Alamitos Raceway. 4961 Katella Avenue, Los Alamitos: (310) 431-1361. Harness and quarter-horse racing.

Los Angeles Memorial Coliseum. 3911 South Figueroa Street, Los Angeles: (213) 747-7111. Capacity: 92,000. Site of some of the events of the 1932 and 1984 Olympics. Los Angeles Raiders of the National Football League, USC football team, special events.

The Coliseum offers tours of the stadium itself and the interior, including locker rooms, press box, and other hidden areas. Tickets are $4 for adults, $3 for seniors, and $1 for children under 12. For reservations and information, call (213) 748-6136.

Los Angeles Sports Arena. 3939 South Figueroa Street at Martin Luther King, Jr. Boulevard, next-door to the Los Angeles Memorial Coliseum: (213) 748-6131. Capacity: 16,000. Los Angeles Clippers of the National Basketball Association, USC basketball, concerts, conventions, and special events.

Pauley Pavilion. University of California, Los Angeles, 650 Westwood Plaza at Strathmore Place: (310) 825-2101. Capacity: 12,819. UCLA basketball.

Rose Bowl. 1001 Rose Bowl Drive at Arroyo Boulevard, Pasadena: (818) 577-3106 or 577-3100. Capacity: 100,184. UCLA football, the New Year's Rose Bowl game, concerts, and special events.

Santa Anita Park. 285 West Huntington Drive, Arcadia: (818) 574-7223. Thoroughbred racing.

Participation Sports

Ballooning

Adventure Flights. (714) 678-4334.

Oz Airlines Hot Air Balloon Adventures. (213) 464-6487.

Panorama Balloon Adventures. (800) 878-7292.

Plums Aircraft Balloon Adventures. (818) 888-0576 or (800) 843-7433.

Bicycle Tours

Breaking Away Bicycle Tours. 1142 Manhattan Avenue, Manhattan Beach: (310) 545-5118.

Boating

Port Royal Marina. 555 Harbor Drive, Redondo Beach: (310) 318-2772.

Rent-A-Sail Inc. 13179 Fiji Way, Marina del Rey: (310) 822-1868.

Westwind Sailing Inc. 4223 Glencoe Avenue, Marina del Rey: (310) 822-8022.

Ice Skating

Culver City Ice Rink. 4545 Sepulveda Boulevard, Culver City: (310) 398-5718. Daily public sessions.

Ice Chalets. 6100 Laurel Canyon Boulevard, North Hollywood: (818) 985-5555. Also 550 Deep Valley Drive, Rolling Hills Estate: (310) 541-6630.

Iceland. 90723 Jackson Street, Paramount: (310) 636-8066.

Pasadena Ice Skating Center. 300 East Green, Pasadena: (818) 578-0800.
Pickwick Ice Arena. 1001 Riverside Drive, Burbank: (818) 846-0032.

Motor Racing

Long Beach Grand Prix. (310) 436-1251. Formula One race through the streets of Long Beach.

Malibu Grand Prix. 19550 Nordhoff Place, Northridge: (818) 886-3252. Scaled-down versions of racing cars on a one-mile track. Racers must be over 52 inches.

Scuba/Skin Diving

A Blue Fantasy. Los Angeles: (213) 256-8554.
   Malibu Divers. 21231 West Pacific Coast Highway, Malibu: (310) 456-2396.
   Reef Seekers. 8612 Welsher Boulevard, Beverly Hills: (310) 652-4990.
   Scuba Haus. 2501 Welsher Boulevard, Santa Monica: (310) 828-2916.

Roller Skating

Beach Skatepath. Santa Monica and Venice beaches.
   Moonlight Rollerway Skating Rink. 5110 San Fernando Road, Glendale: (818) 241-3630.
   Skatepark Paramount. 16000 Paramount Boulevard, Paramount: (310) 630-4088.
   World on Wheels. 4645½ Venice Boulevard, Los Angeles: (213) 933-3333.

Skiing

Ski Reports, Southern California area: (310) 976-7873
   Ski Reports, Big Bear area: (714) 585-2519

Big Bear Lake Region.

Los Angeles' local ski region lies mostly due east in and around Big Bear City and Big Bear Lake in the San Bernardino National Forest. The resorts are about one hundred miles from Los Angeles, about a two-hour drive on Interstate 10 and State Route 18.

Bear Mountain. Big Bear Lake: (714) 585-2517. Vertical drop of 1,500 feet. Longest run, 2.5 miles. Five chairlifts, three tows. Tickets can be reserved through Teletron. Lodging information: (714) 866-5877 or 866-4601.

Mountain High. Wrightwood: (714) 972-9242. Vertical drop 1,600 feet. Eleven lifts. Tickets can be reserved in advance. Lodging: (619) 249-5477.

Mount Baldy. San Bernardino: (714) 981-3344. A smaller area closer to Los Angeles. Four chairlifts.

Ski Sunrise. Wrightwood: (619) 249-6150. Smaller area with one chairlift, three Pomas, and one rope tow.

Snow Forest. Big Bear Lake: (714) 866-8891. Novice-oriented area. Lodging: (714) 878-3000.

Snow Summit. Big Bear Lake area: (714) 866-5766. Vertical drop of 1,200 feet. Nine chairlifts. Longest run, 1.25 mile. Lodging: (714) 878-3000.

Snow Valley. Big Bear Lake area: (714) 867-2751. Vertical drop of 1,100 feet. Twelve chairlifts. Longest run, 1.25 mile. Lodging: (714) 878-3000.

La Canada (North of Pasadena)

Mount Waterman. La Canada: (818) 790-2002. Vertical drop of 1,100 feet. Small ski area. Three chairlifts. Longest run, ½ mile.

Skydiving

Air Adventures West: (800) 423-8908.

Blue Sky Adventure. 3017 Propeller Drive, Paso Robles: (805) 239-3483.

California City Skydiving Center. California City Municipal Airport, California City: (619) 373-2733.

Perris Valley Skydiving. Perris Valley Airport, 2091 Goetz Road, Perris: (800) 832-8818.

Skydiving California. 20701 Cereal Road, Skylark Airport, Lake Elsinore: (714) 674-2141.

IX
Theater

Chapter 16
West of Broadway

Major productions and traveling shows bear the same high price structure in Los Angeles as they do in any major city. However, Los Angeles also has a flourishing class of smaller shows—so-called *Equity Waiver* productions—that offer lower-cost tickets. The waiver refers to an agreement by Actors Equity to permit its members to work for much less than usual rates in small houses; most of the theaters have fewer than one hundred seats.

Many of these shows are cast with would-be stars who have moved to Hollywood, and not a few of today's major stars began their careers in such a theater. Some major current or fading stars keep themselves in acting form in smaller productions.

Los Angeles does not, though, have a centralized Theater District, although there are a few groupings of houses near the intersection of Hollywood and Vine, and in the North Hollywood district.

Theaters and Convention Centers

Alex Theatre. 216 North Brand Boulevard at Wilson Avenue, Glendale: (800) 883-7529 or (818) 792-8672. A 1920s movie palace, renovated for the 1990s with 1,452 seats. Glendale Symphony, musicals, and plays.

Ahmanson Theatre (Music Center of Los Angeles). 135 Grand Avenue, Los Angeles: (800) 762-7666 or (213) 972-7211. Broadway musicals, plays, and concert performances in a handsome theater that can be configured from about 1,500 to 2,100 seats.

Ambassador Auditorium. 300 West Green Street at South Saint John Avenue, Pasadena: (800) 266-2378 or (818) 304-6166. One of the best-looking and best-sounding rooms in the West, with 1,442 seats and a fantastic crystal chandelier in the lobby. Home of the Los Angeles Chamber Orchestra, world-class soloists, jazz festivals, dance events, and more.

Anaheim Convention Center. 800 West Katella Avenue, Anaheim: (714) 999-8900.

Beckman Auditorium. California Institute of Technology, 332 South

Michigan Avenue near Del Mar Boulevard, Pasadena: (818) 395-4052. A converted lecture hall, it offers 1,165 seats (all of them good) for concerts, plays, and special events.

Canon Theatre. 205 North Canon Drive near Wilshire Boulevard, Beverly Hills: (310) 859-8001 or 859-2830. A small movie house converted to an intimate theater with 382 seats. Musicals, plays, and special events.

Cast Theater. 804 North El Centro Avenue, Hollywood: (213) 462-9872 or 462-0265. Two tiny theaters—99 seats and 65 seats—that are home to innovative small productions. A longtime fixture in Hollywood, Charlie Chaplin directed some shows here in the 1940s.

Dorothy Chandler Pavilion (Music Center of Los Angeles). 135 North Grand Avenue, Los Angeles: (213) 972-7211. Los Angeles Music Center Opera, Los Angeles Philharmonic, and the Academy Awards. This is the Lincoln Center of Los Angeles, the hub of high culture. The theater seats about 3,250. (The complex of theaters at the Music Center will grow soon with the addition of the Walt Disney Concert Hall, which will become home base for the Philharmonic.)

Cerritos Center for the Performing Arts. 12700 Center Court Drive at Bloomfield Avenue, Cerritos: (310) 916-8510 or (800) 300-4345. An attractive, modern arts complex with an auditorium that can be configured from about 1,000 to 2,000 seats for plays, concerts, and special events.

Coronet Theatre. 366 North La Cienega Boulevard, Los Angeles: (310) 652-9199. An intimate 272-seat theater that presents plays and special events; home to the Serendipity Theatre Company, a children's theater group.

James A. Doolittle Theatre (Music Center of Los Angeles). 1615 North Vine Street, Hollywood: (213) 462-6666 or 365-3500. A Broadway-like theater with 1,021 seats, it is a converted 1920s movie palace.

East West Players. 4424 Santa Monica Boulevard at Vermont Avenue, Los Angeles: (213) 660-0366 or 660-8587. An Asian Pacific theater company.

Henry Fonda Theatre. 6126 Hollywood Boulevard, Hollywood: (213) 480-3232 or 464-0808. Plays and concerts in an old moviehouse with 860 seats.

John Anson Ford Amphitheatre. 2580 Cahuenga Boulevard at Barham Avenue: (213) 974-1343. A 1,200-seat outdoor stage used for a Shakespeare festival, concerts, and dance and jazz events.

Globe Playhouse. 1107 North Kings Road, West Hollywood: (213) 654-5623. A half-scale replica of the Old Globe Theatre, with 99 seats. Shakespearean plays, of course, but also other fine drama.

Great Western Forum. 3900 West Manchester Boulevard, Inglewood: (310) 419-3100. When the hockey ice is cleared and the basketball parquet removed, the Forum is used for major concerts.

Greek Theatre. 2700 North Vermont Avenue, Hollywood: (213) 665-1927 or 665-3156. A huge outdoor amphitheater in a green canyon in Griffith Park with a capacity of 6,197. Major concert events, shows, and dance events.

Hollywood Bowl. 2301 North Highland Avenue off Hollywood Freeway, Hollywood: (213) 850-2000. Capacity about 18,000. A spectacular amphitheater in a canyon, home to special musical and theatrical events.

Hollywood Palladium. 6215 Sunset Boulevard at Argyle Avenue, Hollywood: (213) 962-7600. A once-grand ballroom for the Big Bands of the 1940s, it was later Lawrence Welk's Saturday-night home from 1961 to 1976. Though a bit down-and-out today, it is still used for occasional concerts and special events.

Irvine Meadows Amphitheatre. 8800 Irvine Center Drive, Irvine: (714) 855-6111 or 855-2863. Seats and lawn space for 15,000 for the Pacific Symphony Orchestra, special events, and concerts.

Japan America Theater. 240 South San Pedro Street, Los Angeles: (213) 680-3700. From Kabuki to classical and modern Asian music, in an 841-seat theater.

Los Angeles Convention Center. 1201 South Figueroa Street, Los Angeles: (213) 741-1151.

Long Beach Convention and Entertainment Center. 300 East Ocean Boulevard, Long Beach: (310) 436-3661.

Long Beach University Theatres. 6101 East 7th Street, Long Beach: (310) 985-5526.

Los Angeles Theatre Center. 514 South Spring Street at 6th Street, Los Angeles: (213) 627-6500. Used as home base for a number of small local theater groups.

Matrix Theater. 7657 Melrose Avenue, Hollywood: (213) 653-3279 or 852-1445. Home to experimental theater and avant-garde productions, in a 99-seat house.

Melrose Theater. 733 North Seward Street, Hollywood: (213) 465-1885. A pleasant, small theater with 82 seats, used for original plays and revivals.

MET Theatre. 1089 North Oxford, Hollywood: (213) 957-1459 or 957-1152. New shows and revivals in a 99-seat house that sometimes draws big Hollywood names.

The Music Center of Los Angeles. See listings for Ahmanson Theatre, Dorothy Chandler Pavilion, Mark Taper Forum, and James A. Doolittle Theater.

Odyssey Theater. 2055 South Sepulveda Boulevard, West Los Angeles: (310) 477-2055. Three small stages with 99 seats each, presenting original, revival, and children's productions.

Orange County Performing Arts Center. 600 Town Center Drive, Costa Mesa: (714) 556-2787 or 740-2000. There *is* culture outside of Los Angeles, and spectacularly so at OCPAC. Broadway touring shows, symphony and chamber concerts, jazz, and theater events.

Pacific Amphitheatre. 100 Fair Drive, Costa Mesa: (714) 979-5944 or 546-4876. Sit down on the lawn with 10,000 of your closest friends, or join 8,000 others in seats for concerts and special events.

Pantages Theatre. 6233 Hollywood Boulevard, Hollywood: (310) 410-1062. A 2,705-seat former art deco movie palace of the 1920s, it was the former home of the Academy Awards; now used for touring shows, concerts, and special events.

Pasadena Civic Auditorium. 300 East Green Street near Euclid Avenue, Pasadena: (818) 449-7360. Musical theater.

Pasadena Playhouse. 39 South El Molino Avenue, Pasadena: (818) 792-7343 or 356-7529; also (800) 883-7529. Musicals and dramas presented within a national historic landmark, a restored 701-seat theater built in 1925 in a mission style.

Royce Hall. UCLA, Westwood: (310) 825-2953. On the campus of UCLA, home to orchestra, chamber, and solo performances, plays, and rock concerts.

San Gabriel Civic Auditorium. 320 South Mission Drive at Santa Anita Street, San Gabriel: (818) 308-2865 or 308-2868. The large stage was built for a pageant; now used for musicals and dramas and the San Gabriel Valley Civic Light Opera. 1,450 seats.

Santa Monica Civic Auditorium. 1855 Main Street at Pico Boulevard: (310) 458-8551. Capacity 3,000.

Santa Monica Playhouse. 1211 4th Street, Santa Monica: (310) 394-9779. An 88-seat intimate theater used by the Actors Repertory Theater Company, presenting plays, musicals, and children's theater.

Shrine Auditorium. 665 West Jefferson Boulevard at Figueroa Street, Los Angeles: (213) 749-5123. One of the largest theaters in the country, with 6,300 seats, a gigantic stage, and a stupendous pipe organ. Plays, musicals, ballets, and concerts.

Shubert Theatre. 2020 Avenue of the Stars, Century City: (800) 233-3123 or (310) 201-1500. Located within the ABC Entertainment Center. Home to the largest and splashiest touring Broadway musicals and other productions, with 2,150 seats.

South Bay Center for the Arts. El Camino College, 16007 Crenshaw Boulevard, Torrance: (310) 715-3715 or 329-5345. Plays, musicals, and concerts.

Mark Taper Forum (Music Center of Los Angeles). 135 North Grand Avenue, Los Angeles: (213) 972-7353 or 365-3500. Experimental plays and revivals presented in a 750-seat theater with a thrust stage that extends out into the audience.

Universal Amphitheater. Universal City Plaza, Universal City: (818) 777-3931. A covered amphitheater on the Universal Studios lot and theme park with 6,251 seats. Concerts and special events.

Variety Arts Theatre. 940 South Figueroa Street, Los Angeles: (213) 623-9100 or 362-0440.

Wadsworth Theater. UCLA, 650 Westwood Plaza, Westwood: (310) 825-2953.

Westwood Playhouse. UCLA, 10886 Le Conte Avenue, Westwood: (310) 208-6500 or 208-5454.

Wilshire Ebell Theatre. 4401 West 8th Street, Los Angeles: (213) 939-1128. Once a clubhouse for a private women's club, the 1,270-seat theater is used for special events and concerts.

Wiltern Theatre. 3790 Wilshire Boulevard at Western Avenue, Los Angeles: (213) 380-5005. Capacity: 2,200. A renovated art deco house of the 1930s.

Performing Arts Companies

Afro-American Chamber Music Society. (213) 292-6547. Various locations.

Aisha Ali Dance Co. (310) 474-4867. Music and dance of Middle East; various locations.

American Chamber Symphony. Gindi Auditorium, University of Judaism, 15600 Mulholland Drive: (310) 201-0045.

American Youth Symphony. (310) 476-2825.

Apsara Dancers of Cambodia. (818) 785-1498. Special events include Cambodian New Year in April and Cambodian Thanksgiving in September. Various locations.

Avaz International Dance Theatre. (818) 441-1630. Folk dance; various locations.

Bach Camerata. (805) 963-0761. Lobero Theater, Santa Barbara, and other locations.

Ballet Folklorico Ollin. (818) 894-5858. Mexican dance company; various locations.

Ballet Pacifica. (714) 642-9275 or 854-4646. From traditional works such as The Nutcracker to modern dance; various locations.

California Traditional Music Society. (818) 342-7664. Folk and dance performances, which include the Summer Solstice Folk Music and Dance Festival.

Chorale Bel Canto. Shannon Center for the Performing Arts, Whittier College, Whittier: (310) 907-4233.

Cypress Pops Orchestra. Cypress College, Cypress: (714) 527-0964. Free popular music concerts.

Danza Floricanto. (213) 223-2475. Mexican dance troupe; various locations.

Fuego Flamenco. (213) 663-2235 or 663-1525. Spanish dance troupe; various locations.

Glendale Symphony Orchestra. Alex Theatre, Glendale: (818) 500-8720.

Hermosa Civic Theatre. (310) 318-3452. Jazz, classical guitar, and more.

Hollywood Opera Ensemble. (213) 851-0271. Immanuel Presbyterian Church in Los Angeles and Temple Beth Ami in West Covina.

Karpatok Hungarian Folk Ensemble. (818) 363-2219. Eastern European folk dance; various locations.

Korean Philharmonic Orchestra. (213) 387-4632.

Koroyar Folklore Ensemble. (714) 736-9608. Folk dance and music from Armenia, Bulgaria, Greece, and Turkey. Various locations.

Lewitzky Dance Company. (213) 580-6338. Well-established dance troupe; various locations.

Long Beach Opera. Terrace and Center Theaters, Long Beach: (310) 596-5556 or 436-3661.

Long Beach Symphony. Terrace Theatre, Long Beach: (310) 436-3203.

Los Angeles Chamber Ballet. (310) 453-4952. Various locations.

Los Angeles Chamber Orchestra. (213) 622-7001. Various locations.

Los Angeles Civic Light Opera. (213) 468-1704.

Los Angeles Classical Ballet. (818) 564-0575. Various locations.

Los Angeles Korean Folk Dance Group. (213) 933-9661. Various locations.

Los Angeles Master Chorale and Sinfonia Orchestra. Dorothy Chandler Pavilion: (213) 972-7282 or 626-0910.

Los Angeles Mozart Orchestra. (213) 851-4256 or 851-7100. Wilshire Ebell Theatre and other locations.

Los Angeles Music Center Opera. Dorothy Chandler Pavilion: (213) 972-7219 or 972-7211.

Los Angeles Philharmonic. Dorothy Chandler Pavilion: (213) 850-2000 or 972-7398.

Master Chorale of Orange County. Orange County Performing Arts Center: (714) 556-6262.

Mexican Dance Theatre. (213) 267-0140. Various locations.

Music Guild. (310) 275-9040. Chamber music at various locations.

Nigerian Talking Drum Ensemble. (310) 398-2316. Various locations.

Opera a la Carte. (818) 791-0844. Gilbert & Sullivan light opera; various locations.

Opera Pacific. Orange County Performing Arts Center: (714) 546-7372.

Orange County Philharmonic Society. Orange County Performing Arts Center: (714) 553-2422.

Pacific American Ballet Theatre, Inc. (310) 302-9361. Various locations.

Pacific Chorale. Orange County Performing Arts Center: (714) 252-1234.

Pacific Dance Ensemble. (310) 839-8083. Various locations.

Pacific Symphony Orchestra. Orange County Performing Arts Center: (714) 474-2109 or 556-2787.

Pasadena Pops Orchestra. Ritz-Carlton Huntington Hotel, Pasadena: (818) 792-7677.

Pasadena Symphony. Pasadena Civic Auditorium: (818) 793-7172 or 449-7725.

Rhapsody in Taps. (714) 838-3318. Various locations.

Santa Barbara Symphony. Arlington Theatre, Santa Barbara: (805) 965-6596 or 963-4408.

Santa Monica Symphony Orchestra. (213) 850-5660 or 458-8551. Various locations.

Serendipity Theatre Company. (310) 652-9199.

Southwest Chamber Music Society. (818) 794-4799. Various locations in Orange County and Pasadena.

Swingbrazil Dance Company. (213) 957-4952. Brazilian folk dance.

Theatre Los Angeles Arts Hotline: (213) 688-2787.

USC Performing Arts. (213) 740-7111.

Tickets

There are three legal ways to get tickets to Los Angeles shows and events: discount bureaus, full-price with a service charge, and high-price ticket brokers.

Okay, there's a fourth way to obtain tickets, but we're not going to recommend the use of a ticket scalper; there are too many risks with doing business with someone on the street.

Discount Bureaus

Ticket Outlet is run by Theatre Los Angeles, a group of commercial and non-profit theaters in Greater Los Angeles offering same-day discounts of at least 40 percent. Call (213) 688-2787 between noon and 5 P.M. to purchase tickets for the same night; call Saturday for tickets for that night and for Sunday. You'll pay for your tickets by credit card and pick them up at the theater.

Times Art Tix. The San Diego Theatre League offers same-day tickets at half-price at its booth in Horton Plaza in downtown San Diego. Call (619) 238-3810 to hear a recorded listing of available shows; the booth is open Tuesdays through Saturdays from 10 A.M. to 7 P.M. Tickets for Saturdays, Sundays, and Mondays are sold on Saturdays. San Diego is about a two-hour drive south from Los Angeles.

Ticket Services

These companies contract with many theaters and stadiums to sell tickets over the phone. They add a service charge of several dollars per ticket; you'll need to use a credit card to prepay for your seats by phone. Tickets will be mailed if there is sufficient time or held at the box office.

Ticketmaster is the largest such company, with several phone lines: (213) 480-3232 and 365-3500; also (714) 740-2000. It also operates walk-up windows (cash only) at many locations in the Los Angeles area. The company's computer is supposed to automatically select the best available tickets, selling from the front to the back; the walk-up locations have seating charts for most theaters and stadiums. You can buy tickets—if available—for events up to 3 P.M. on the day of the performance.

Theatix handles some smaller productions as well as fundraisers and cultural events. The company's operators at (213) 466-1767 also have information on nearby restaurants and parking lots.

Tickets LA also specializes in smaller productions. They have a walk-up office downtown as well as phone service at (213) 660-8587.

Ticket Brokers

If you are absolutely determined to see a show and have some extra money to spend, check the Yellow Pages or the concierge at your hotel to find a ticket broker. These companies obtain tickets in various ways and charge a premium over listed price.

CHINATOWN–EL PUEBLO–LITTLE TOKYO AREA

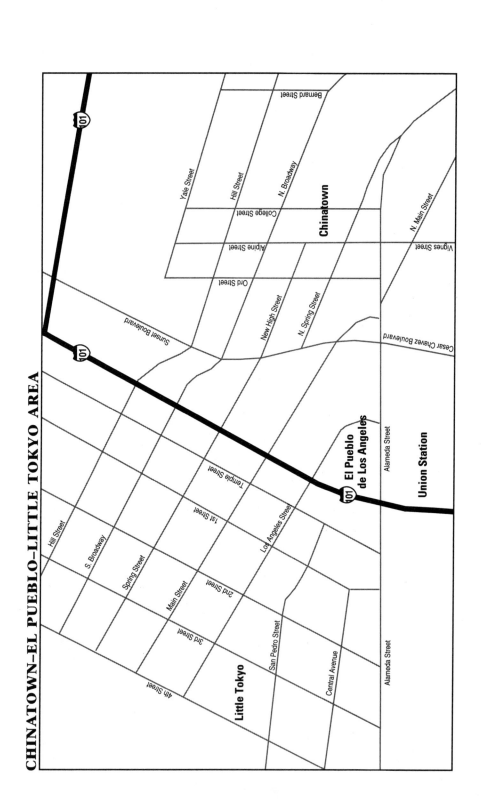

X
Touring Around
Southern California

Chapter 17
Downtown Los Angeles

El Pueblo de Los Angeles Historic Monument

El Pueblo is located within the area of Main Street, Sunset Boulevard, Macy Street, Alameda Street, and Arcadia Street. For information, call (213) 628-1274.

El Pueblo was a group of mud huts established in 1781 by 11 families from Mexico. Today a 44-acre park is the home of the city's first church, firehouse, theater, and other restored buildings from the original settlement of Los Angeles.

There's a visitors center in the 1887 Sepulveda House on Main Street. Other notable structures include the Garnier buildings used by Chinese immigrants at the turn of the century. Free guided walking tours are offered Tuesdays through Saturdays at 10 A.M., 11 A.M., noon, and 1 P.M. **KIDS.**

Nearby to El Pueblo are **Olvera Street** and the **Avila Adobe.**

Olvera Street is one of the oldest commercial streets of Los Angeles, now serving as a center for Mexican arts and business. Street vendors and color- ful shops line the area of Olvera between Alameda Street and North Main Street. South of Olvera is The Plaza, once the center of the pueblo and now the location of festivals and celebrations including Cinco de Mayo.

Avila Adobe, at 10 Olvera Street, is the oldest remaining home in Los Angeles. It was built in 1818 by Francisco Avila, who was mayor of the pueblo at the time. The ravages of time and earthquakes have been repaired and the restored adobe is furnished with period artifacts. Free tours are offered daily except Mondays. For information, call (213) 628-1274.

The **Old Plaza Firehouse** at 134 Paseo de la Plaza dates from 1884 as Los Angeles' first fire station. Restored as a museum of old firefighting equipment, the firehouse is open daily except Mondays.

El Mercado at 3425 East First Street is a three-story indoor Mexican mar- ket including a supermarket, restaurants, and stores.

Among the interesting restaurants along Olvera Street is **La Golondrina**, located within the Pelanconi House, Los Angeles' first brick edifice, dating

Maxi-service mini bus.
Traffic and the scarcity
(and high price) of
parking can present a
real problem to visitors
to El Pueblo, Chinatown,
Little Tokyo, and other
downtown areas. One
solution is to make use of
the RTD Downtown
MiniBus (Route 202),
which circles through
the area.

from 1850. Strolling mariachi musicians entertain outside.

Chinatown

Nearby to El Pueblo and historic Union Station, Chinatown is bordered by Alpine, Spring, and Yale streets and Bamboo Lane. Most of the shops and restaurants can be found on streets off Gin Ling Way, the "Street of the Golden Palace."

Chinese labor helped open California to the world and helped build Los Angeles. The Chinese did not, at first, share in the success of the Golden State.

Laborers cut an early wagon road through the mountains near Newhall, worked on the mines of the Comstock in Nevada, and dug the difficult San Fernando tunnel that brought the Southern Pacific to Los Angeles in 1876. Most of the Chinese chose to—or were forced to—live in a small area located close to Olvera Street. Living conditions were marginal, and anti-Chinese prejudice included what has become known as the Chinese Massacre of 1871, when 19 men and boys were killed.

The Chinese influence continued as Chinese immigrants became fishermen, cooks, and servants and established farms that provided most of the vegetables sold in Los Angeles.

The old Chinatown was torn down in the 1930s to make way for the construction of Union Station. The new Chinatown, off North Broadway, opened in 1939 with businesses to serve the several thousand residents and with an eye on tourism. Shopping is a major pastime, and most stores are open in the evening. For authentic Chinese markets and restaurants, North Spring Street is worth a visit. There is also a Chinese cinema. About 10,000 people reside in Chinatown today.

Although small in comparison to Chinatown in San Francisco, the Los Angeles version is just as lively and colorful, especially in February. During the celebration of the Chinese New Year, traditional parades take to the streets and the sounds of music and firecrackers fill the air as dragons wind their way along.

The main entrance to Chinatown is through the ornamental **Gin Ling Way** pagoda gate at 900 North Broadway near College Street. Facing the gate is a statue of Dr. Sun Yat-sen, who led the overthrow of the Manchu dynasty in 1911 and is regarded as the founder of the Republic of China. As you walk through the area, look at the roofs and upper structures of many of the buildings for images of animals and fish, considered good luck talismans.

Guided walking tours of the district are offered by the Chinese Historical Society of Southern California; call (213) 621-3171 for more information.

Over the years new waves of Asian immigrants have added to the mix. You'll find cuisine from China, Taiwan, Hong Kong, Vietnam, and more.

Several tightly jammed shopping arcades transport you thousands of miles once you are through their gates. On Broadway you will find **Dynasty Center**, **Chinatown Plaza**, and **Saigon Plaza**.

Wing On Tong, at 701 North Spring Street, is a Chinese herb store that dates back nearly one hundred years.

Further down the street is the **Capitol Milling Company** at 1231 North Spring Street. Originally established in 1855 as the Eagle Mills, it was one of the earliest flour mills in California; it was also one of the original seven telephone subscribers of the Los Angeles Telephone Company in 1881. It continues as a commercial mill.

Philippe the Original is one of those only-in-Los Angeles places, a turn-of-the-century delicatessen once located downtown (supposedly the place of invention of the French Dip sandwich) which moved to Chinatown in 1948. Go figure.

Little Joes is one of the oldest Italian restaurants in Los Angeles; it moved

Gateway to Chinatown Plaza

to Broadway near College before Chinatown was relocated all around it in the 1930s.

Mandarin Plaza at 970 North Broadway includes several dozen restaurants and stores. Near the intersection of North Broadway and Bernard Street is **Association Row**, home of many family and fraternal associations set up by Chinese immigrants.

F. See On Company at 940 Chungking Court is a renowned Asian art gallery.

Those with a literary bent may want to visit the **Chinatown Branch of the Los Angeles Public Library** at 536 West College Street. Its collections include materials on Chinese, Vietnamese, and Spanish cultures.

Little Tokyo

Bordered by 1st, Alameda, 3rd, and Los Angeles streets, **Little Tokyo** is the cultural and commercial center for Japanese-Americans of the Los Angeles region. This is the largest Japanese community outside Japan with a population of more than 100,000. Older enterprises can be found in the many small shops and restaurants; newer development includes several large shopping malls including the spectacular Yaohan Plaza at Alameda and 3rd streets. Yaohan includes a sprawling supermarket of Japanese foods and a branch of the Japanese toy store Hello Kitty. At Weller Court at Weller and 2nd streets is another grouping of interesting stores; the central mall includes a monument to Japanese-American astronaut Ellison Onizuka, one of the victims of the *Challenger* disaster.

Little Tokyo can be found within the area of Main, 1st, Alameda and 3rd streets. The Japanese American Cultural and Community Center at 244 San Pedro Street, (213) 628-2725, offers information on cultural events and festivals in Nisei Week in August, which celebrates American-born citizens of Japanese extraction. The center also offers traditional Kabuki theater performances and the Doizaki Gallery of Art.

The Little Tokyo Business Association offers guided tours during the week. Call for reservations: (213) 628-2725.

The **Higashi Hongwangi Temple**, at 8505 East 3rd Street, is an authentic Buddhist temple with a spectacular golden altar.

The **Japanese Village Plaza**, on 1st and 2nd streets between San Pedro and Central, includes Japanese food stores, Japanese and Korean restaurants, and other unusual outlets. (213) 620-8861.

City Hall

As Sgt. Joe Friday used to say as he drove past this place each week on his "Dragnet" beat: "Just the facts, ma'am." A mixed message of a building, unlike almost any other City Hall we know of, it has a pyramid at its top with an observation deck on the 27th floor, and a domed rotunda at the base. Tours are available weekdays. 200 North Spring Street. Open Mondays through Fridays from 9 A.M. to 5 P.M.

Los Angeles Farmer's Market

The Farmer's Market of Los Angeles is a bit of heaven for anyone who eats. Begun in the 1930s when farmers gathered in a field at what was then the edge of town, the market grew to include restaurants, food stands, art galleries, and shops. The stands sell items from all around the world.

Market stands include cheese, poultry, meats, breads, ice cream, fruits, vegetables, and health food.

One next to another you will find restaurants from Mexican to Chinese to Japanese to American. On one Sunday morning visit, I had some New Orleans gumbo and corn bread, washed down with fresh limeade, and topped off with a sinful slice of pie.

You'll also find some spectacular fruits and vegetable stands, although there are not as many as there used to be. Some interesting crafts and gift shops are located across the parking lot.

The Farmer's Market is located at 6333 West Third Street, off Fairfax between downtown Los Angeles and Hollywood. Three free hours of parking are allowed at the lot. The market is open daily except for major holidays, from 9 A.M. to 6:30 P.M. Mondays through Saturdays, and from 10 A.M. to 5 P.M. on Sundays. During the summer, the market stays open half an hour later. For information, call (213) 933-9211.

Koreatown

Olympic Boulevard between Crenshaw Boulevard and Vermont Avenue: (213) 936-7141. Another fascinating, far-flung outpost of an ancient Asian culture. Korean restaurants, grocery stores, and shops, as well as the Korean Cultural Center on Wilshire Boulevard at La Brea Avenue with a performance space, gallery, and library.

Watts Towers

1765 East 107th Street, Watts: (213) 569-8181. A world-renowned example of primitive art and a landmark of the Watts area, **Watts Towers** were built by hand over a 30-year period from the 1930s through the 1960s by Sabatino Rodia, an Italian tile setter. The towers are made up of steel rods decorated with pieces of tile, dishes, pieces of bottles, bedframes, and other objects including thousands of seashells. The park at the towers is open on weekends from 10 A.M. to 3 P.M. Admission charge.

The **Watts Towers Art Center** at 1727 East 107th Street, Watts, offers displays of art, poetry readings, and special exhibits that explore and celebrate the African-American culture of Watts and is open Tuesdays through Saturdays from 8 A.M. to 5 P.M.

Los Angeles Central Library

5th and Hope streets: (213) 612-3200. A Los Angeles landmark from the moment of its completion in 1926, the library was reborn and expanded in 1993 from the ashes of a disastrous fire seven years earlier. It is now the third largest library in the country. It sits beneath a somewhat fanciful colored-tile pyramid tower. Guided tours are available daily. The library is open Mondays, Thursdays, and Saturdays from 10 A.M. to 5:30 P.M.; Tuesdays and Wednesdays from noon to 8 P.M., and Sundays from 1 P.M. to 5 P.M.

Historic Walking Tours

The Los Angeles Conservancy offers one- and two-hour walking tours on Saturdays of historic neighborhoods and commercial areas, including the theater district, Union Station, and Pershing Square. Different tours are offered each day; tickets cost $5. Call (213) 623-2489 or 385-5600 for information.

Bonnie Brae Street

The 800 and 1000 blocks of South Bonnie Brae Street, near MacArthur Park, are beautifully preserved Victorian residences dating from the 1890s. They are regular locations for film shoots.

Broadway Theater District

Los Angeles' original theater district, cleverly named as Broadway, stretches from 3rd to 9th streets in downtown. The oldest of the legitimate theaters date to about 1910, and the first movie palaces opened in the 1920s.

Most of the movie houses have gone to seed, or at least to new roles as neighborhood homes to second- and third-rate films, but the exteriors and interiors remain interesting. Among the tired gems are the art deco Doremus Building at 9th Street; the Cameo Theater at 528 Broadway, built in 1910 as a nickelodeon; and the Million Dollar Theater at 307 Broadway, built in 1918 by impresarios Sid and D. J. Grauman, of Chinese Theater fame.

For more details about legitimate theater in Los Angeles, see Chapter 16.

University of Southern California (USC)

The largest private university on the West Coast, with more than 20,000 students, USC is near Exposition Park, home of the California State Museum of Science and Industry and the Los Angeles County Museum of Natural History.

Chapter 18

Los Angeles East to Beverly Hills, Hollywood, Burbank, Pasadena, Anaheim, San Bernardino, Riverside, and Palm Springs

Beverly Hills

From its very humble beginnings as a lima bean farm, Beverly Hills has grown to become a place where a different kind of bean is counted; the local sport is the barely disguised pursuit and display of wealth. How many other places do you know where the ZIP code (90210) can identify a television series, a line of clothing, and a way of life?

The small town (less than six square miles) lies within the City of Los Angeles but is an independent entity fiercely protected by its mostly upscale residents. First developed in 1906, the town was named after Beverly, Massachusetts; many of the early stars of Hollywood moved there, and the area became the center of attention in 1921 when Mary Pickford and Douglas Fairbanks built their famous mansion Pickfair in Beverly Hills.

Today many of the homes of the glitterati are hidden in the hills above the Hills, in the canyons above Sunset Boulevard, and behind massive hedges and imposing fences. You can, though, see the hangers-on of the lifestyles of the rich and famous: trendy and overpriced restaurants, overpriced and trendy clothing and jewelry stores, theatrical agents, production companies, stockbrokers, and more. The main street of all of this excess is Rodeo Drive, a short connector that runs between Wilshire Boulevard and Santa Monica Boulevard.

Other famous structures include the **Beverly Hills Hotel**, 9641 Sunset Boulevard: (310) 276-2251. Built in 1912, there is a pink Mission-style building as well as 21 bungalows on 12 lush acres. Howard Hughes rented Number 3 for years at a time; many other legends of Hollywood have made the cottages their temporary homes.

Burbank

Beautiful downtown Burbank, which is neither downtown nor particularly beautiful, is not quite Hollywood, but it is nevertheless the vital heart of the modern television and movie industry. It was built around the sprawling Warner Bros. Studios, where stars including James Cagney, Humphrey Bogart, Lauren Bacall, and others made many of their most famous films.

Today, major operations include Warner Bros., the Disney Studios at 500 South Buena Vista Street, and the NBC production facilities at 3000 Alameda Avenue.

Hollywood

Hooray for Hollywood, a state of mind as much as a place.

The area was first developed in the 1880s; the wife of the developer named the area Hollywood after an all-but-forgotten place of the same name near Chicago. Hollywood, California, began as a quiet fruit-farming community; things began to change soon after an early silent picture was filmed on a ranch there in 1906. The landscape and weather were perfect for tableau films including Westerns, and the infant moviemaking industry moved from its mostly East Coast origins to Hollywood.

The famed Hollywood sign that looms over much of the area, by the way, dates to 1923 when it was built to publicize a housing development called Hollywoodland. The "land" is gone, but the sign remains. The 50-foot-high, 450-foot-long advertisement underwent a restoration in 1978, and received a complete paint job again in 1995.

By the 1940s, nearly the entire American film industry was located in Hollywood. In the years that have followed, the rising price of real estate has resulted in relocation of large portions of the business a bit farther outside of Hollywood proper.

Here's an eclectic tour of eclectic Hollywood.

A&M Records. 1416 North La Brea Avenue. Located in the former Chaplin Movie Studios, operated since 1966 as one of the premier recording studios, A&M was founded by musicians Herb Alpert and Jerry Moss. Chaplin's footprints are immortalized in front of Stage 3.

The Brown Derby. Wilshire Boulevard at Alexandria. The hat remains from the original as built in 1926, although the interior has been completely rebuilt. The Brown Derby was the "in" restaurant and night spot of Hollywood in the 1930s. Owner Bob Cobb reportedly told his friends that food was all that matters—in fact, he said, his menu would be so good that people would eat out of a hat. He built his restaurant in the shape of a derby.

Capitol Records Tower. 1750 Vine Street. An unusual circular office building, likened by some to a stack of records when it was built in 1956 or perhaps, in this modern day, to a pile of CDs. A rooftop light flashes "Hollywood" in Morse code.

Crossroads of the World. 6671 Sunset Boulevard: (213) 463-5611. Called the world's first modern shopping center, it dates from 1936 and is now used for offices. The architecture is a strange mélange of French Provincial, Tudor,

Italian, Moorish, and Californian. The Crossroads was used as a scene in *Indecent Proposal* and as a model for part of the Disney-MGM Studios theme park in Orlando.

Egyptian Theatre. 6712 Hollywood Boulevard. Another creation of Sid Grauman, it was built in 1922 as the first of Hollywood's grand movie houses. A Middle Eastern predecessor to the Chinese Theatre, it suffered serious earthquake damage in recent years.

El Capitan Theatre. 6838 Hollywood Boulevard: (213) 467-7674. Built as a legitimate theater in 1922, it was converted in 1942 to become a showcase for Paramount films. Orson Welles' *Citizen Kane* opened here in 1939. See

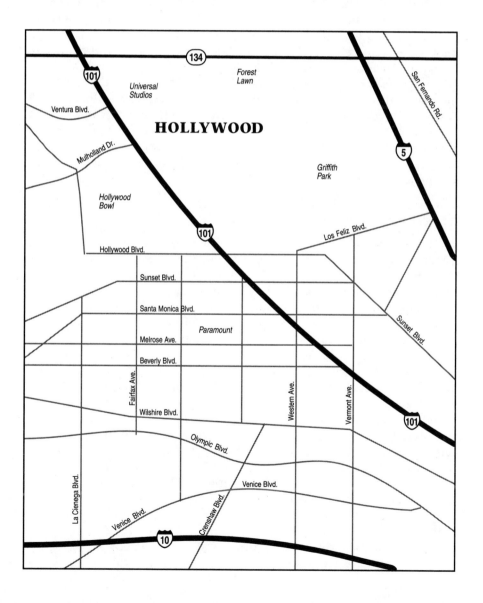

Chapter 4 for more details about its current operation as a joint venture with the Walt Disney Company.

Hollywood High School. 1521 North Highland Avenue: (213) 461-3891. The alma mater of stars including Carol Burnett, James Garner, Rick and David Nelson, Stefanie Powers, John Ritter, and Jason Robards. A small museum of memorabilia from former students can be visited by appointment. The famous ice cream shop where star Lana Turner was discovered was located across from the school at 1500 North Highland Avenue; despite Hollywood legends, it was *not* Schwab's Drugstore, which was located at 8024 Sunset Boulevard. In any case, both soda fountains have been torn down.

Hollywood Walk of Fame. Hollywood Boulevard between Gower and Sycamore streets, and Vine Street between Sunset Boulevard and Yucca Street. Nearly two thousand stars of the silver screen, early radio, and (lately) the television screen are memorialized with star-shaped plaques in the sidewalk.

Mann's Chinese Theatre. 6925 Hollywood Boulevard. Over the years the theater has been as much of an attraction as the great films that have debuted and played there. It was designed as a fanciful version of a Chinese temple inside and out. Sid Grauman built the theater in 1927, and his name is noted in many of the early handprints and signatures in the concrete outside.

Ozzie and Harriet House. 1822 Camino Palmero Drive. A must-see for those of a certain age. This was the actual home of the Nelson family, and it was used as the model for the house occupied by the family in their TV series. The home is now a private residence and not open to visitors.

Glendale

Just above Hollywood in the shadow of the San Gabriels, this old settlement is best known for its proximity to a very quiet neighborhood: **Forest Lawn Memorial Park.** This 300-acre final resting place (they're positively ghoulish about their desire that it not be called a cemetery) resembles more a rolling green religious theme park. There are several famous church replicas, including the Wee Church o' the Heather and the Church of the Recessional. Displays include huge murals of Jesus and a mural of the signing of the Declaration of Independence accompanied by patriotic music.

Residents of the necropolis and the nearby Forest Lawn Hills Memorial Park include Clark Gable and Carole Lombard, Stan Laurel, Buster Keaton, and Liberace.

Forest Lawn is free to the public, and visitors can view some of the spectacular artwork including the *Paradise Doors*, made from a cast of Lorenzo Ghiberti's original Gothic masterpiece; *Bronco Buster*, an original bronze by Frederic Remington; a mosaic rendering of John Trumbull's *Signing of the Declaration of Independence*; a full-size re-creation of Michelangelo's *David*, and a large collection of coins mentioned in the Bible.

Culver City

Another of the "suburbs" of Hollywood, Culver City flourished as the site of no less than five Metro-Goldwyn-Mayer lots. MGM is all but gone, but operations by Columbia Pictures, Lorimar Telepictures, and Culver Studios continue.

Long gone is the famed Hal Roach Studios, home of classic silents from Harold Lloyd, as well as the films of Laurel and Hardy and the "Our Gang" series.

Another former giant of Culver City was Howard Hughes, who set up his Hughes Aircraft in the area, nearby to another of his interests, moviemaking.

Century City

Century City is mostly famous for what it once was—the formal sprawling back lot of 20th Century-Fox and, before that, the ranch of cowboy actor Tom Mix.

Just a small part of 20th Century-Fox remains, at 10201 Pico Boulevard. The studio is not open to the public, but you can drive by the formal gates to catch a glimpse of the huge New York set used in *Hello, Dolly!* and many other classic films.

The back lot was mostly sold off in 1961 and became an almost-instant city of office buildings, restaurants, shops, and condominiums mostly catering to the entertainment industry.

Pasadena

The end of the trail for numerous parties of settlers from Indiana in the 1880s, the city became a winter playground for the East Coast wealthy; many of their fabulous mansions can be still be seen along Orange Grove Avenue.

The name means "crown of the valley" in the language of the Chippewa Indians.

Today Pasadena has a population of more than 132,000 and includes some of the best museums in the West, including the Norton Simon Museum of Art and the California Institute of Technology, which includes the NASA Jet Propulsion Laboratory. Pasadena is most famous, of course, for the Rose Bowl football game and the Tournament of Roses Parade that precedes it each New Year's Day.

Altadena

With its back against the base of the San Gabriel Mountains north of Pasadena, Altadena is famous for its impressive—and out of place—Himalayan deodars that line Santa Rosa Lane. Deodar cedars—the name in Sanskrit means "timber of the gods"—were imported from India in 1885.

From mid-December through New Year's Eve, the imposing trees are festooned with thousands of colored lights in a spectacular Christmas salute.

Angeles National Forest

On top of Old Baldy (known on the maps as Mount San Antonio), the view from 10,064 feet is unsurpassed. The huge wilderness area also includes lowland deserts and verdant meadows.

If you're not up to using the hundreds of miles of hiking trails, campsites, ski trails, and downhill slopes, you can take a spectacular 64-mile drive from one side of the forest to another along Route 2 from La Canada off Interstate 210 near Pasadena. The road threads its way among many of the larger peaks, with views of Crystal Lake and Old Baldy; the road connects to Route 138 southbound to San Bernardino on the other side of the forest. Call (818) 574-5200 for information on facilities.

Anaheim

German immigrants took "ana" from the nearby Santa Ana River and "heim," meaning home, and named their remote village in 1857. They also brought cuttings from the Rhine and made Anaheim California's first important wine-making region and, before long, the leading wine area of the country. A blight caused by a plant virus some 30 years later wiped out the grape crops, and growers switched to oranges.

Industry and the discovery of oil changed the economy again. The opening of Disneyland in 1955 changed the nature of the area once more, and now tourism is one of the leading industries.

See the chapters on Disneyland and Knott's Berry Farm for details about those attractions.

Ontario

Graber Olive House. 315 East 4th Street, Ontario: (909) 983-1761. Free tours of one of California's leading olive processing companies. Open daily; closed major holidays.

Barstow

Calico Ghost Town. On Ghost Town Road, off I-15, 10 miles northeast of Barstow: (619) 254-2122.

Step back into California's mining past, in a restored boomtown of the 1880s. The Calico Mountains included some of the richest silver finds of the West, including the Maggie Mine which is part of today's ghost town. Most of the buildings in the park are real; there is also a museum with artifacts from the mining past.

The town was restored by Walter Knott, the founder of what has become Knott's Berry Farm in Buena Park. Knott had worked in the mining camp near the end of its use at the turn of the century. Today the ghost town is run by San Bernardino County as a park.

Special events include the Calico Hullabaloo over Palm Sunday weekend, featuring "horseshoe pitchin', stew cookin', and tobacco spittin'" competitions. Calico Days, held on the Columbus Day weekend, includes a Wild West parade, gunfights, games, and other events. A Western Fine Arts Show over the first weekend of November includes Old West and Indian art and sculpture.

Open daily from 9 A.M. to 5 P.M., except Christmas. Adults, $6.55; children, $5.55 on weekends, with weekday prices slightly less.

Victorville

Roy Rogers-Dale Evans Museum. Seneca Road and Civil Drive, Victorville: (619) 243-4547.

Sure, there are old guns, saddles, boots, and lots of pictures from the fabled movie and television career of Roy and Dale. But you really want to see the stuffed carcass of Trigger, right?

The museum, located off the Roy Rogers Drive exit of the Interstate Highway 15, underwent a major expansion and renovation in 1995 and 1996.

Open daily from 9 A.M. to 5 P.M. Adults, $5; children from 13 to 16, $4; children from 6 to 12, $3.

San Bernardino

Big Bear Lake. A year-round recreation area in the San Bernardino Mountains, about one hundred miles east of Los Angeles. Summer activities include swimming and boating (rentals available) in Meadow Park, hiking, and camping. In the winter, there are several downhill ski areas and numerous cross-country trails available. Contact the Big Bear Ranger Station at (909) 866-3437 for information.

Drivers can explore the Holcomb Valley—location of some of the sites of the 1860–75 Gold Rush—on a three-hour tour north of the lake. Maps and descriptions are available at the Ranger Station.

From Memorial Day through the end of October, visitors can take a 90-minute tour of Big Bear Lake aboard a trimaran that departs several times a day from Pine Knot Landing in Big Bear Lake: For tour information, call (909) 866-2628.

To get to Big Bear Lake, take I-10 to San Bernardino, to State Route 18 into the mountains.

Riverside

California Museum of Photography. 3500 Main Street, Riverside: (909) 784-3686. Photographs and equipment from the dawn of the art through modern day. Open Wednesdays through Sundays; closed major holidays.

Castle Amusement Park. 3500 Polk Street, Riverside: (909) 785-4141. An old-style park with a 1905 carrousel, miniature golf courses, log flume, and more. Open daily except Mondays in summer, weekends only rest of year.

March Field Museum. March Air Force Base, Van Buren Boulevard: (909) 655-3725. From antique flying machines to the U-2 spy plane and the modern F-14. Closed Mondays and holidays: Free.

Orange Empire Railway Museum. 2201 South A Street, Perris: (714) 657-2605.

A sprawling museum of old railroad, trolley, construction, and maintenance cars from in and around Southern California. On the weekends, several trains or trolleys (still decked out in their original colors and advertising placards) cruise about on the museum's tracks.

Open daily from 9 A.M. to 5 P.M.; trains and trolleys operate weekends and holidays from 11 A.M. to 5 P.M. Free admission to museum; all-day train pass $5 for adults and $3 for children from 6 to 11.

Santa's Village. Off Highway 18, Sky Forest, San Bernardino Mountains: (909) 337-2481. The merry old gent is on duty year round at a small amusement park and reindeer zoo up in the hills. Other attractions include a puppet theater and sleigh ride.

Open daily from 10 A.M. to 5 P.M. from mid-June to mid-September, and from mid-November through the end of the year. Open weekends and holidays from 10 A.M. to 5 P.M. the rest of the operating season. Closed March 1 through Memorial Day. Call to check on road conditions in wintertime. Tickets $8.50 for all visitors; children under 3 admitted free.

Palm Springs

Palm Springs Aerial Tramway. Tramway Road, Palm Springs, off Highway 111: (619) 325-1391.

A spectacular climb more than a mile up the side of Mount San Jacinto in an 80-passenger tram. The view from the cool top of the tram extends across the San Jacinto Valley; on a clear day you can see as far as the Salton Sea, nearly 50 miles away. A trail from the top of the tram leads six miles to the peak of Mount San Jacinto. During the winter, you can rent sleds and saucers for use on a snow hill.

The base station for the tram is at 2,463 feet, and the mountain station tops out at 8,516 feet. The tram travels about 12,800 feet in total over the 14 minute ride. There's a gift shop, cafeteria, and cocktail lounge at the top, too.

Open weekdays from 10 A.M. to 9:15 P.M.; weekends from 8 A.M. to 9:15 P.M. The tram usually closes for maintenance for about a week in August; call for details. Adults, $13.95; children 3 to 12, $8.95.

Joshua Tree National Monument. Off Highway 62, at Joshua Tree and Twenty-nine Palms (another entrance can be found at Cottonwood Springs, 25 miles east of Indio off I-10): (619) 367-7511.

The stark beauty of the Colorado Desert in the valleys and the high Mojave Desert is within an easy drive from Los Angeles or Orange County. The two deserts come together at the Joshua Tree National Monument, which draws its name from the many Joshua trees found there—they are actually giant desert lilies that can reach to 40 feet or more. They were given their names by Mormon emigrants who thought they resembled the biblical prophet Joshua with upraised arms.

You can take your car on an 18-mile exploration on the Geology Road, which goes to many of the park's more interesting areas. Hiking trails reach to Twenty-nine Palms Oasis and other destinations.

Chapter 19

Along the Coast to Long Beach, the *Queen Mary*, and Catalina Island

Long Beach

The long beach was a strip of sand used as a trading area between Indians of the mainland and those who came across from Catalina Island in canoes.

Outsiders built up the area after the turn of the 20th century when Henry Huntington's Pacific Railroad arrived. When oil was discovered at Signal Hill in 1921, the population nearly doubled to 100,000. Today's economy is built on shipping and tourism, including the ocean liner *Queen Mary* which is moored in the harbor. Fort MacArthur in San Pedro is an important military installation. The Long Beach Grand Prix is held in the city each spring.

Long Beach features two restored parks worth an afternoon stroll. Both are open Wednesday through Sunday afternoon and are free. A beach within the harbor is a popular spot for swimming, waterskiing, and other water sports.

Aerial Tours. Ace Aerial Tours. (800) 595-1544.

Archery. El Dorado Park archery range, site of the 1984 Olympic competition. (310) 421-9431, ext. 3415.

Farmer's Market. Fridays from 10 A.M. to 4 P.M. at Long Beach Promenade in downtown. (310) 436-4259.

Looff Carousel. Ride the historic carousel, circa 1906, at Shoreline Village. (310) 590-8427.

Long Beach Naval Station. Warships available for tours on certain weekends. (310) 547-6202.

Rancho Los Alamitos. 6400 East Bixby Hill Road: (213) 431-3541. This features an early 19th-century ranch house with period furnishing and half a dozen agricultural buildings, including a working blacksmith's shop.

Rancho Los Cerritos. 4600 Virginia Road: (310) 424-9423. Includes a Spanish-style adobe dating from the mid-19th century and surrounding gardens.

Whale Watching Tours. January through March. Catalina Cruises, (310) 253-9800; Queen's Wharf Sport Fishing, (310) 432-8993; Shoreline Village Cruises, (310) 495-5884; Spirit Cruises, (310) 831-1073.

The *Queen Mary*

The *Queen Mary* is a most unusual floating museum, a 62-year-old relic of the grand era of transatlantic ocean liners. Tours of the vessel take visitors from the keel to the upper decks, with stops at the engine room, luxury staterooms, spectacular dining rooms, and the bridge.

The self-guided tour gives you access to the many public rooms of the ship as well as the engine room and the upper deck including the bridge. The guided tour adds visits to the first-class salon and dining room, a luxury stateroom, the boiler rooms, and more; it is worth the extra charge.

The *Queen Mary* is an easy 20- to 30-minute drive from Anaheim. You will see the big ship as you drive alongside the harbor across from the City of Long Beach. *Discount coupon in this book.*

Self-Guided Tour:

Adults	$10
Seniors	$8
Children, 4 to 11	$6

Guided Captain's Tour:

Adults	$6 additional
Children, 4 to 11	$3 additional

Recorded audio tour	$4
Parking	Hourly rate
Valet parking	$8

At her height, the *Queen Mary* was the queen of the Atlantic, a floating palace of elegance, grace, and power. At the time of her creation, she was unlike anything ever seen on the sea, a combination of engineering, craftsmanship, and artistry.

The *Queen Mary* began life as the glamorous solution to a difficult prob-

The Queen Mary

lem facing Cunard, the leading steamship company of its time. Cunard had lost many of its best vessels during World War I and faced competition unlike anything it had seen before. The company decided to create two ships that would be bigger and faster than any ocean liner in existence, two ships that would do the work of three.

Designing the plans for the ships took two years, with revolutionary solutions in hull shape, propeller design, and powerplant. The four steam turbines each generated 40,000 horsepower, making the ship the fastest ever made.

If the *Queen Mary* was in service today, she would still be one of the fastest boats afloat, capable of a top speed of up to 36 knots, equivalent to about 40 miles per hour. The speed came at some expense, though; at full cruising speed, the *Queen Mary* got 13 feet per gallon of fuel.

When completed, the *Queen Mary* was a bit more than 1,019 feet in length, with the showcase Promenade Deck stretching 724 feet; there were 12 decks in all. The hull's draft was 39.5 feet, and the ship weighed 81,237 gross tons with hull plates from 8 to 30 feet in length and up to 1.25 inches thick. The hull was held together with more than 10 million rivets; there were more than two thousand portholes.

The ship's rudder weighed 140 tons. There were two 18-foot-tall anchors at the bow, each weighing 16 tons; the 900-foot anchor chain added 45 tons, with each two-foot-long link weighing 224 pounds itself.

The *Queen Mary* could hold 1,957 passengers, plus 1,174 officers and crew.

Air conditioning was a new art at the time the ship was constructed, and only three rooms on the *Queen Mary* were cooled: the first-class dining room, the ballroom, and the ship's kennel.

Finally, in 1934, Cunard was ready to launch the greatest, most luxurious ocean liner ever built. Queen Mary herself pressed the launch button that released her floating namesake into the River Clyde. It took two more years to outfit her as a passenger vessel.

In May 1936, with her three massive, one-ton steam whistles blasting, the *Queen Mary* embarked on her maiden voyage to New York with nearly 2,000 passengers and a crew of almost 1,200 aboard. She received a spectacular greeting as she steamed up the Hudson River, including an airborne drop of thousands of white carnations.

In 1939, a round-trip first-class ticket sold for about $2,000, which was a lot of money; third-class passage was a pricey $500.

Dining aboard the *Queen Mary* was an event. All eight hundred first-class passengers could be served at once in the largest room ever built within a ship. The wine cellar on board contained over 15,000 bottles, rivaling the finest restaurants in Europe.

The ship's engines were improved in 1938, allowing her to cross the Atlantic in just under four days, a world record which she held for 14 years. At her peak, the *Queen Mary* cruised at 28.5 knots (almost 33 miles per hour).

By the summer of 1939, the *Queen Mary* was an unqualified success. In September of that same year her first career was abruptly halted when Great Britain was drawn into war with Germany. The *Queen Mary* was conscripted into the war effort for use as a troop carrier.

Camouflaged with gray paint and capable of evading warships and even outmaneuvering torpedoes, the *Queen Mary* became known as the *Gray Ghost*. Berths were stacked up to six high, with troops sleeping in shifts during the five-day crossing. Sleeping accommodations were placed in drawing rooms, in lounges, and even in drained swimming pools. Five double-barreled cannons were installed, and 20-mm guns lined the upper decks; four sets of anti-aircraft rocket launchers were installed. The guns, though, were never fired in anger.

On one memorable voyage, some 16,000 troops and crew were shoehorned into every corner of the vessel. No ship before or since has carried so many.

Special assignments included transporting British Prime Minister Winston Churchill three times to conferences. Churchill approved the D-Day invasion plans aboard the ship. During the course of the war, Adolf Hitler put a $250,000 bounty on the ship and offered Germany's highest military honor to the captain who could sink her.

By the end of her war service, the *Queen Mary* had carried more than 800,000 troops, had traveled more than 600,000 miles, and had played a part in every major Allied campaign of World War II. She was also used to carry German and Italian prisoners of war to camps in North America.

At the end of the war, the *Queen Mary* was fitted out as a floating hospital with surgical and intensive care units to bring home the wounded. She later carried many returning troops and their war brides.

Regular passenger service resumed on July 31, 1947.

After completing 1,001 crossings of the Atlantic, the *Queen Mary* retired from regular passenger service on September 19, 1967; she made one "Last Great Cruise" from October 31 to December 9, 1967, pulling into port for the last time at Long Beach, California. The RMS Foundation, which took over operation of the *Queen Mary* in 1993, signed a new 20-year lease in 1996, and the ship was added to the National Register of Historic Places, so the queen may have found a very long-term home.

Among the interesting stops on the guided tour is the first-class lounge, an extraordinary room paneled with rare woods collected from around the world—some are from species no longer available.

On the wall of the first-class dining room is a huge mural showing the North Atlantic from England to the United States. Two tracks, occupied by small glass ships, mark the progress of the *Queen Mary* and its sister ship the *Queen Elizabeth*; at the peak of Cunard's history, the two ships crossed the Atlantic weekly on opposite schedules, passing in mid-ocean.

In 1997, restoration will begin on the first-class swimming pool, which will reopen to the public as an elegant spa.

Art of the *Queen Mary*

Among the sometimes overlooked treasures of the *Queen Mary* are her works of art. Many of the original art pieces, including the huge murals and decorations of the principal public rooms, many smaller works of art, and decorative items are located throughout the ship in areas where the public does not usually visit.

In 1995, the ship opened a permanent exhibition of some of the art pieces in her own gallery on the *Queen Mary*'s Promenade Deck, immediately forward of the Queen's Salon.

Featured in the gallery are Dame Laura Knight's *The Mills Circus* from one of the first-class private dining rooms; S. Nicholson Babb's *Jupiter and Europa*, and Gilbert Bayes' *The Sea King's Daughter*, both bronze figure groups borrowed from the corner niches of the Queen's Salon. Kenneth Shoesmith's *Madonna of the Atlantic*, originally the altarpiece for the Roman Catholic Chapel, and Walter and Donald Gilbert's bronze doors, which originally adorned side entrances of the first-class restaurant, are also included.

Restaurants at the *Queen Mary*

Sir Winston's. The *Queen Mary*'s most elegant restaurant offers a spectacular view of the coastline from the upper deck, with dinner served from 5:30 to 10 P.M. Specialties include Swordfish Filet Nicoise for $19.95 and Beef Phylo Sir Winston's for $28.

Chelsea. A seafood eatery with a view of the sea. Specialties include Lobster Pappardelle (rainbow pappardelle pasta with lobster tail and spinach in roasted bell pepper sauce) at market price, and Seafood Phylo for $15.95. Open Wednesdays through Sundays from 5:30 to 10 P.M.

Promenade. Open for breakfast, lunch, and dinner, from 6:30 A.M. to 10 P.M. Specialties include chicken linguine for $9.95 and blackened halibut for $10.75. Salads and pasta dishes are also available.

The Verandah Grill. The elegant first-class restaurant and nightclub on the Sun Deck at the stern of the ship had been converted into an uninspiring fast-food eatery when the *Queen Mary* came to Long Beach in 1967; in 1996 it will reopen in all its original finery for receptions, banquets, and special events.

Sunday Champagne Brunch in the Grand Salon. A buffet featuring food from around the globe with more than 50 entrees, including a special island for children. Served from 10:10 A.M. to 2:30 P.M.

Observation Bar. Evening entertainment, cocktails, and dancing in the original first-class bar, an art deco masterpiece. Open nightly, with complimentary hors d'oeuvres served Sundays through Fridays from 5 to 7 P.M.

The Hotel *Queen Mary*

The Hotel *Queen Mary* today offers 365 first-class cabins for rent at rates as low as $68 per night for a standard inside cabin without a porthole to $650 per night for a two-bedroom parlor suite.

One of the rooms not available for rent but visited on the escorted tour is the Duke of Edinburgh Room, a luxury suite which over the years was occupied by the Duke and Duchess of Windsor, Winston Churchill, and comic actors Laurel and Hardy, among others.

Other Attractions at the *Queen Mary*

The Dome at the *Queen Mary*. Originally constructed in 1983 to house Howard Hughes' gigantic *Spruce Goose* seaplane, it is the world's largest clear-span dome. The dome closed in 1992 when the plane was sold to become the planned centerpiece of the Evergreen AirVenture Museum in McMinnville, Oregon.

Plans are in development to use the dome as a family-oriented entertainment complex; in the meantime, the facility has been leased for use as a motion picture soundstage; it was home of the Batcave in *Batman Forever*.

MegaBungee. One of the tallest freestanding bungee towers in the world, at 210 feet (21 stories), stands alongside the *Queen Mary*. Jumpers wear New Zealand-style ankle restraints and plunge from the tower toward the waters of Long Beach Bay, which may or may not be safer than doing it over a concrete parking lot. Rebound height once the elastic bungee cords are fully extended exceeds 160 feet. Open Wednesdays through Sundays, the cost per jump is about $85. For information, call (310) 435-1880.

Newport Beach

Newport Harbor Art Museum. 850 San Clemente Drive, Newport Harbor: (714) 759-1122. Contemporary paintings, sculpture, and photography. Closed Mondays, major holidays, and between major exhibitions.

Newport Harbor Cruise. 400 Main Street, Newport Harbor: (714) 673-5245. Harbor cruises from the Balboa Pavilion. Daily except Christmas.

Newport Harbor Showboat Cruises. 700 East Edgewater Avenue, Newport Harbor: (714) 673-0240. Daily except Christmas.

Balboa Island

Balboa Island in Newport Harbor is an old-style amusement zone that includes the Balboa Pavilion, built in 1905 and restored to its former glory. Nearby is a Ferris wheel, bumper cars, arcade games, and fast-food stands.

A ferry—25 cents per pedestrian—runs from the end of Palm Street on the Balboa Peninsula, 24 hours a day in the summer and all day for the rest of the year.

From Balboa Island you can take harbor cruises, including one on board a replica of a Mississippi River riverboat, or a more traditional boat. For information on the tours, call (714) 673-5245 (riverboat) or 673-0240 (traditional boat).

Catalina Island

About 27 miles off the coast and a world away, Catalina Island was a pirate and smuggler's outpost after its discovery in 1542 by Juan Rodríguez Cabrillo.

The original occupants of the island were Gabrieleno Indians, who were wiped out by various later arrivals including Russian seal hunters. The island was bought and sold by several wealthy Californians until it came into the hands of the Wrigley (as in chewing gum) family. William Wrigley, Jr., built the famous circular casino in 1929, and the modern era of the island as a tourist destination began.

Current residents of the island include a herd of free-running buffalo. The original animals were brought over to the island for the filming of a

Hollywood movie called *The Vanishing American*; the beasts have flourished ever since.

You can travel to the island by ferry (about one to two hours) or by small plane (a 20-minute hop).

The 8-mile-wide, 21-mile-long island includes spectacular beaches, hiking and horseback riding trails, a golf course, campsites, and deep sea and pier fishing facilities. The principal settlement on the island is Avalon, which includes the famous casino; another port is located at Two Harbors. Nearly all of the island is owned by the Santa Catalina Island Conservancy and will be preserved as forever wild.

Cars may not be brought to the island, but bicycles and golf carts can be rented in Avalon.

Write to the Catalina Chamber of Commerce, Box 217, Avalon, CA 90704 for a copy of the Visitor's Guide, or call the Visitors Information Center at (310) 510-2500 or (800) 428-2566.

Attractions on Catalina Island

Lovely Santa Catalina Island lies 27 miles off the coast. Visitors come here to hike, ride horses, scuba dive, play golf, sportfish, or explore the Mediterranean charm of Avalon, home to numerous shops, hotels, restaurants, and cafes. The island's architectural landmark, the Casino, was built in 1929 by chewing gum magnate William Wrigley, Jr., who once owned the island.

Constructed at a cost of $2 million at a time when a dollar was worth, well, a dollar, it houses a charming ballroom still used for big-band concerts, an art gallery, and the Catalina Island Museum, where fossils, Native American artifacts, and natural history exhibits are on display. The museum is open daily, from 10:30 A.M. to 4 P.M.

Beyond Avalon, Catalina's 42,000-acre interior is a designated nature preserve with unique plants and animals, including a buffalo herd. Developed campsites, cabins, and primitive camping areas are available.

There are numerous services including tours and taxi (by land and sea) on the island. One new attraction is especially intriguing: the ***Starlight*** semi-submersible vessel. Not quite a submarine, it's a tour boat with a basement. Passengers sit in a cabin beneath the sea level with a panoramic view of the waters and marine life around Catalina Island. Adult tickets are about $18; seniors, $16.50; and children, $12. Tickets are available at Discovery Tours outlets on the island.

Boat Service to Catalina

Catalina Channel Express. (800) 995-4386 or (310) 519-1212. Fast passenger boats with airline-like seating, from Long Beach and San Pedro to Avalon and Two Harbors in about an hour.

Catalina Cruises. (800) 888-5939. Seven hundred–passenger boats from Long Beach.

Catalina Express Coastal Shuttle. (310) 519-1212. Tour of the coast of Catalina between Avalon and Two Harbors. Operates June through September.

Catalina Passenger Service. (714) 673-5245. Fast catamaran service on the 500-passenger *Catalina Flyer* from Balboa Pavilion in Newport Beach, about a 75-minute trip.

Island Navigation. (310) 510-0409. Water taxi and charter service to all points on Catalina.

Seajet Cruise Lines. (800) 875-0875 or (619) 722-2800. From San Diego, Oceanside, or Dana Point to Avalon and Two Harbors.

Airline Service

Island Express Helicopter Service. (310) 510-2525. Long Beach and San Pedro Ferry Terminals to Catalina.

Island Hopper Catalina Airlines. (619) 279-4595. San Diego to Avalon.

Sea Plane Safari. (619) 453-8833. San Diego or Los Angeles to Avalon and other locations on Catalina Island.

Hotels on Catalina

Hotels and standard accommodations on Catalina generally range from about $75 to $150 per night, with more expensive luxury rooms and condos also available. Because Catalina is an island, it is generally very important that you have a reservation.

Bed and Breakfast

Banning House Lodge at Two Harbors. (310) 510-2800. Hilltop views.

Catalina Island Seacrest Inn. (310) 510-0196. Double tubs or spas in all rooms.

Garden House Inn. (310) 510-0356. Near beach.

Gull House. (310) 510-2547. Pool.

Inn on Mt. Ada. (310) 510-2030. Classic 1921 home in hills.

Old Turner Inn. (310) 510-2236. Fireplaces in rooms.

Hotels

$	Budget (Room rates start under $75)
$$	Moderate (Room rates start under $130)
$$$	Expensive (Room rates start at $131 or higher)

Atwater Hotel. (800) 626-5440. **$**

Bayview Hotel. (310) 510-7070. **$**

Casa Mariquita. (800) 249-1197. **$$**

Catalina Beach House. (800) 974-6835. **$**

Catalina Canyon Resort. (800) 253-9361. **$$**

Catalina Cottages & Hermosa Hotel. Economy hotel in Avalon since 1892. (800) 666-3383 **$**

Catalina Island Inn. (800) 246-8134. **$$**

Catalina Island Seacrest Inn. (310) 510-0800. **$**

Catalina Lodge. (310) 510-1070. **$**
Catherine Hotel. (310) 510-0170. **$**
Cloud 7. (800) 422-6836. **$$**
Edgewater Hotel. (800) 894-6835. **$$**
El Rancho Hotel. (310) 510-0603. **$**
El Terado Terrace. (800) 540-0139. **$$**
Glenmore Plaza Hotel. Century-old Victorian. (800) 422-8254. **$$**
Hotel Catalina. (800) 540-0184. **$$**
Hotel MacRae. (800) 698-0266. **$$**
Hotel Metropole. (800) 300-8528 or (800) 541-8528. **$$**
Hotel Monterey. (310) 510-0264. **$$**
Hotel St. Lauren. (800) 645-2496. **$$**
Hotel Villa Portofino. (800) 346-2326. **$$**
Hotel Vincentes. (310) 510-1115. **$$**
Hotel Vista Del Mar. (310) 510-1452. **$$**
La Paloma and Las Flores. (800) 310-1505. **$**
Pavilion Lodge. (800) 626-5440. **$$**
Seaport Village Inn. (800) 228-2546. **$$**
Zane Grey Pueblo Hotel. 1926 "pueblo" home of author Zane Grey. (310) 510-0966. **$$**

Camping

For hiking and camping permits, call the **Catalina Island Camping Office** in Avalon at (310) 510-7265.

Hermit Gulch Campground. Avalon: (310) 510-8367. Nearby to Wrigley Memorial and Botanical Garden and hiking trails; about a mile and a half up Avalon Canyon. $7.50 per person. Tents available for $20 to $25.

Two Harbors Campground. Seaside camping. Tents and camping gear available. $7.50 to $8.50 per person, depending on location. Tents available from April through October. Call (310) 510-7265 for reservations.

Little Harbor is southeast of Two Harbors, in a protected cove with a sandy beach 17 miles from Avalon, and seven miles from Two Harbors; it is very popular with youth groups. Fees are $7.50 per person. Call (310) 510-2800.

Parsons Landing is a remote site on the northwest shore, accessible by a seven-mile trail from Two Harbors or by boat. Fee is $15 for the first person, and $5 for each additional person per site. Call (310) 510-2800 for reservations and further information.

Blackjack is in a grove of pine trees on 1,600-foot Blackjack Mountain in the center of the island, a 10-mile hike to Avalon or Two Harbors. Fee is $6.50 per person. Call (310) 510-2800 for reservations.

Ten undeveloped coves on coastline, accessible by boat only, include **Frog Rock Cove, Willow Cove, Italian Gardens, Goat Harbor, Gibraltar Point Beach, Lava Wall Beach, Paradise Cove, Rippers Cove, Starlight Beach,** and **East Starlight Beach.** Call (310) 510-1745 for information.

Mission San Juan Capistrano

The Mission at San Juan Capistrano is a place of quiet beauty, as old and history-laden as any place in California.

The mission was founded by Father Junipero Serra, a Spanish Franciscan priest, on November 1, 1776—four months after the Declaration of Independence of the original 13 colonies on the other side of the still-wild American continent. It was the seventh in a chain of 21 California missions.

Constructed of adobe (mud and straw), many of the early missions have fallen apart; San Juan Capistrano and several others were restored around 1900. Today the Mission San Juan Capistrano's chapel is the oldest building in California still in use. Fund raising for a $20 million restoration project is now under way.

The native Americans who were there to meet Father Serra were the Acagchemem, a peaceful tribe; the Spanish renamed them the Juaneno. Some descendants of the Juaneno work at the mission today.

In 1821, the newly independent Mexican government took over California and forced the Spanish padres to leave; the Mission was sold and the Indians evicted. After the Americans were victorious in the Mexican-American war in 1850, California came under dominion of the United States. In 1865, President Lincoln gave some of the California missions back to the church.

On the grounds of the mission is the remains of an old stone church which was destroyed by an earthquake in 1812, an event which killed 40 Indians who were in the church at the time. You'll be able to visit a number of rooms of the mission, restored as museums. There's also a display about Native Americans, an archaeological field office, and even an homage to the swallows.

Today, of course, the place may be best known for the celebration of the miraculous return of thousands of swallows to the mission each March 19, on St. Joseph's Day. (Of course, some also come on March 18 and March 20, but there's no party for them.) The locals have a parade and other events on March 19; by the way, the sparrows traditionally pack their bags and fly south on October 23.

Those square-tailed cliff swallows traditionally come to southern California in March to nest; they return to their homes in Argentina six thousand miles away in October. The oldest recordings of the migration of the swallows date to the late 1700s; however, there is evidence that the birds had been regular visitors well before then, nesting in the silt stone cliffs near the ocean.

To their credit, the modern-day keepers of the mission do not make the claim that the swallows magically reappear on exactly March 19. A few "scouts" often arrive ahead of time. The date of arrival of the main flock may vary from year to year because northward migration is affected by the weather's influence on available insect food as the birds travel. They move northward when the temperature warms up to about 48 degrees.

The mission is open daily from 8:30 A.M. to 5 P.M., except for Thanksgiving, Christmas, and Good Friday. For information, call (714) 248-2049.

Chapter 20

Western Beach Communities from Santa Barbara to Malibu and Santa Monica

Santa Barbara

Located 92 miles north of Los Angeles, Santa Barbara is one of the oldest settlements in California.

In 1542, explorer Juan Cabrillo entered the Channel and claimed the region for Spain. He was greeted by the true discoverers of the area, the Chumash Indians, who lived in small villages along the Santa Barbara coast and the Channel Islands.

Sixty years later, three Spanish frigates under the command of Sebastián Vizcaíno arrived in the Channel after surviving a fierce ocean storm. A Carmelite friar on board one of the ships named the area after that day's saint, Barbara. It wasn't until 1782, though—after the birth of the United States on the other side of the continent—that Spain established a permanent presence in the area, lead by Father Junipero Serra, Captain Jose Ortega, and Governor Felipe de Neve.

The Spanish governed the area until 1822, when California became a territory of Mexico; in 1846, Santa Barbara was taken for the United States by Colonel John Fremont.

Santa Barbara was one of the leading film capitals of the world when the American Film Company opened its Flying A Studio about 1910 in what is now downtown. The studio made more than 1,200 silent pictures, mostly Westerns, over a 10-year period before moviemaking's center moved south to Los Angeles.

Santa Barbara Airport, eight miles north of downtown, is served by American Eagle, Skywest, United Airlines, and USAir Express.

Arlington Theatre. 1317 State Street: (805) 963-4408. Now home to Santa Barbara's performing arts center, it was built in the 1930s as a grand motion picture palace. It includes a Spanish village in the lobby and a curved ceiling painted with stars.

Botanic Garden. 1212 Mission Canyon Road: (805) 563-2521. A public garden devoted to the display and study of California's native flora. Five miles of trails pass through re-creations of the deserts, the Sierra Nevadas, and the offshore islands. Open daily from 9 A.M. to sunset; guided tours are offered at least once a day. Admission is $3 for adults, $2 for seniors and children from 12 to 17, and $1 for children from 5 to 12.

Carriage Museum. 129 Castilo Street: (805) 962-2353. An unusual collection of horse-drawn carts and carriages used by pioneers and early settlers. The vehicles include stagecoaches, buggies, firefighting equipment, and an antique hearse. The museum is open daily from 9 A.M. to 3 P.M.; on Sundays, the exhibit is open from 2 to 4 P.M. Admission is free, but donations are accepted.

Some of the carriages take to the streets of Santa Barbara each August during the Old Spanish Days parade.

El Paseo. Within the area of State, De la Guerra, and Anacapa streets, a historic Spanish-style shopping arcade was built around a 1920s residence. The arcade includes specialty shops, art galleries, and restaurants. For information, call (805) 963-0608.

El Presidio de Santa Barbara State Historic Park. 123 East Canon Perdido Street: (805) 966-9719. Founded in 1782, the Presidio includes part of the original Presidio Real, the last Spanish military outpost in California. Among the restored buildings are the Presidio Chapel, the Padre's and Commandant's Quarters, and El Cuartel, the guard's house. El Cuartel, built in 1788, is the oldest building in Santa Barbara and the second oldest in California. The park is open every day from 10:30 A.M. to 4:30 P.M. Admission is free.

Mission Santa Barbara. 2201 Laguna Street: (805) 682-4713. Established in 1786 by Spanish Franciscans, it was the tenth of the California missions. The buildings were severely damaged in earthquakes in 1812 and again in 1925 but have been rebuilt. The mission continues as a Catholic parish church and is open to the public for self-guided tours including a museum, gardens, and chapel. Open daily from 9 A.M. to 5 P.M. Admission is $2 for adults and free to children under 16.

Santa Barbara County Courthouse. Anacapa Street, between Anapamu and Figueroa streets. A stunning Spanish-Moorish building completed in 1929, it is worth a visit for a peek at its ornate interior and to make a climb up the 80-foot clock tower for a panoramic view of the city. Guided tours are offered once a day on weekdays. Open weekdays from 8 A.M. to 5 P.M. and weekends from 9 A.M. to 5 P.M. Admission is free.

Santa Barbara Historical Museum. 136 East de la Guerra Street: (805) 966-1601. A broad collection of regional history including artifacts, books, maps, and photographs from the Spanish exploration, the Wild West, and the settlement of California. Nearby to the museum are two 19th-century adobes, including the Casa de Covarrubias at 715 Santa Barbara Street, built in 1817. Open Tuesdays through Saturdays from 10 A.M. to 5 P.M. and Sundays from noon to 5:30 P.M. Guided tours are offered on Wednesdays, Saturdays, and Sundays at 1:30 P.M.

Malibu

The Chumash Indians called this place by a word meaning "where the mountains meet the sea." Taken first by the Spanish, Malibu was then bought by a Frenchman named Leon Victor Prudhomme who sold off the land at ten cents per acre in 1857. Today, of course, the land is worth hundreds of thousands or even more per acre. The view of the beach is blocked in many areas by private homes. Malibu Surfrider State Beach is reserved for wave riders, but it's worth a peek for any visitors.

Santa Monica

Portuguese explorer Juan Rodríguez Cabrillo discovered the broad bay that today runs from about Malibu to Redondo Beach in 1542, as part of a journey that included the first European visits to the Santa Barbara Islands and San Diego.

First named the "Bay of Smokes" because of the rising smoke from Indian campfires, it was later renamed as Santa Monica in honor of the mother of fourth-century Saint Augustine.

The town became an important area in the 1870s with the arrival of a railroad line from Los Angeles; developers sold off small lots for beach cottages. With the growth of Hollywood, many movie stars built homes there.

The famous Santa Monica Pier (which includes the carrousel used in the movie *The Sting*) is worth a visit, as are the many shopping and dining areas.

Venice

Developer Abbott Kinney dreamed of a spectacular town in 1904 near the growing community of Santa Monica. It was to be an American re-creation of Venice. He built a system of canals, spectacular beach pavilions, a huge amusement park, and other facilities, and the resort enjoyed a brief success before economic problems and competition from other communities brought it into decline.

In the 1950s, Venice became one of the centers of the beatnik culture. Today a few of the original canals and some of the buildings remain, and it has become a fashionable area once again. It is well-known for its large artists' colony, and the boardwalk is one of the world capitals of weirdness.

Marina del Rey

A large man-made harbor usually jammed with thousands of pleasure boats. Tours of the harbor and rental boats are available. **Fisherman's Village** in Marina del Rey at 13755 Fiji Way is a replica of a New England town with shops and restaurants, open daily. For information, call (310) 823-5411.

Redondo Beach

Railroad magnate Henry Huntington added to his fortune by selling lots next to the new railroad system. California's first serious surfers discovered the beach about 1907, and their descendants still rise early to catch the best waves. Today the area has a spectacular marina at King Harbor.

Redondo Beach is a local center for whale (and porpoise and seal) watching in King Harbor from December to April. California gray whales migrate south each year from the Arctic Circle to the warm-water lagoons of Baja California, Mexico.

One cruise company is **Redondo Beach Sport Fishing** at (310) 372-2111 or (213) 772-2064.

Redondo Beach Pier is a favorite dining, shopping, and amusement spot and a popular sport fishing pier for visitors, located at the west end of Torrance Blvd. For information, call (310) 318-0648.

Seaside Lagoon, at Harbor Drive and Portofino Way has a heated saltwater swimming pool, a sand beach, and volleyball courts. Call (310) 318-0682 for information.

Chapter 21
Orange County Attractions

Movieland Wax Museum

The perfect stars: handsome, well-dressed, and completely amenable to any pose, role, or setting. They won't sign autographs, though: they're made of wax.

Movieland is the home of more than 400 wax likenesses that have been seen by millions over the past three decades. The museum is exclusively dedicated to the entertainment industry, surrounding the wax figures with re-creations of famous movie sets.

Some of the figures are dressed in actual costumes from the stars. Michael Jackson donated his outfit from his "Bad" video; Gary Cooper is dressed in the actual wardrobe from *High Noon*, and Dudley Moore's wax figure wears the real top hat from *Arthur*.

Details at the museum include a real pipe organ in the *Phantom of the Opera* set. The gold Rolls Royce in the *Beverly Hills Cop* scene is one of only five such ever made.

The newest stars include Leslie Nielsen (in a setting from *Naked Gun*), Whoopi Goldberg as a nun from *Sister Act*, Geena Davis in her uniform from *A League of Their Own*, and Robin Williams as *Mrs. Doubtfire*.

Special sections include the Gallery of the Silver Screen, featuring a collection of photos of movie and television stars, and the Chamber of Horrors, with 15 creepy movie sets and waxen appearances from Dracula and Frankenstein to Jason.

Laurel and Hardy were the first figures commissioned for Movieland in 1962.

Here are some of the things we saw on a recent visit:

• Elizabeth Taylor as the Queen of the Nile from *Cleopatra*. The wax figure was sculpted from a life mask of Taylor, and the gown is an exact copy from the movie.

• A scene from the remake of "Perry Mason," with Raymond Burr as the defense attorney and O. J. Simpson on the witness stand.

• Abbott and Costello in baseball uniforms performing their famous "Who's on First?" routine.

• John Wayne from the film *Hondo*, in which he costarred with Lassie! According to the legend, it took a makeup artist over an hour each day to make Lassie appear shaggy.

• A rather scary Chamber of Horrors section including scenes from *Psycho*, *The Exorcist*, and *Friday the 13th*.

Robert Redford and Paul Newman (from Butch Cassidy and the Sundance Kid)*, immortalized at Movieland Wax Museum.*

A full tour of the museum can take as long as two hours. The museum is located at 7711 Beach Boulevard in Buena Park, one block north of Knott's Berry Farm off the Santa Ana (I-5) and I-91 freeways. In 1996, adult tickets were $12.95; children from 4 to 11 were admitted for $6.95. Combination tickets are also available with Ripley's Believe It or Not! Museum, priced at $16.90 for adults and $9.75 for children. For information, call (714) 522-1152. Movieland is open every day of the year. *Discount coupon in this book.*

Ripley's Believe It or Not! Museum

Here are some of the things we saw on a recent visit:

• A dead bird in a glass container, killed by a golf ball in flight at the Coombe and Hill Golf Club in New York in 1920.

• A lifelike statue of the Lighthouse Man of Chungking, China, who once guided American military dignitaries through the streets by the light of a seven-inch candle inserted into a hole in the top of his head.

• Something to inspire every American homemaker: a large drawing made up entirely from lint, and a version of the *Last Supper* made from 280 slices of carefully toasted white bread.

• A man who smoked through his eyes, and a talented chap who could inflate a balloon through his ear.

Robert L. Ripley was born in 1893 in Santa Rosa, California. He began his newspaper career at the age of 16. On December 19, 1918, while working as a sports cartoonist at the New York Globe and at a loss for an idea, Ripley gathered together a few sports oddities that happened to be on his desk, made them into a cartoon, and captioned them "Believe It or Not."

The first book-length collection of Ripley's columns sold more than three million copies, and his career became completely dedicated to the column. As a reporter in search of the odd and unusual, Ripley visited more than two hundred countries.

In 1933, Chicago's Century of Progress Exposition first introduced the famous *Odditoriums*, where visitors were permitted to see some of the curiosities written about by Ripley. In the modern day, there are more than a dozen permanent museums in operation as commercial ventures.

Ripley was also a television pioneer, broadcasting 13 shows in 1949 in the early days of the medium. He died in 1949. A new and updated version of Ripley's column is published in 179 newspapers in 35 countries.

The museum is located at 7850 Beach Boulevard in Buena Park, one block north of Knott's Berry Farm and across the street from its sister museum, the Movieland Wax Museum. Admission in 1996 was $8.95 for adults and $5.25 for children ages 4 to 11. Combination tickets are also available with Movieland. For information, call (714) 522-1152.

Wild Bill's Wild West Dinner Extravaganza

7600 Beach Boulevard, Buena Park: (714) 522-6414.

Ropin', ridin', and rowdy indoor entertainment in a re-creation of a turn-of-the-century Wild West show. Family-style dinner is included, with shows nightly and weekend matinees. Admission is $32.95 for adults ($35.95 on Saturday evenings), and $21.95 for children ages 3 to 11. Reservations are suggested. *Discount coupon in this book.*

Medieval Times

7662 Beach Boulevard, Buena Park: (714) 521-4740 or (800) 899-6600 in California. Across from Movieland Wax Museum and up the road from Knott's Berry Farm.

Performances nightly, plus a Sunday matinee in summer. Admission was $32.95 for adults ($35.95 on Saturday evenings) and $22.95 for children 12 and under.

Crystal Cathedral

12141 Lewis Street, Garden Grove: (714) 971-4000. The all-glass Crystal Cathedral, with a 236-foot mirrored steeple and a 52-bell carillon, is home of the "Hour of Power" television ministry. The three thousand-seat cathedral and surrounding gardens are open to the public.

The Bowers Museum of Cultural Art

One of California's largest cultural arts institutions, with more than 74,000 objects exploring artworks of pre-Columbian, Meso-American, Native American, Oceanic, African, and East Asian cultures. Open Tuesdays through Sundays 10 A.M. to 4 P.M., and Thursday nights until 9 P.M.

The museum is located at 2002 Main St., Santa Ana, at the corner of 20th and Main streets. For information, call (714) 567-3600.

XI
Sea World of California

Chapter 22
Sea World

Four-fifths of the earth's surface is water, and yet we know so little about the world we live on. One of the guiding missions of Sea World—part of the Anheuser-Busch family of theme parks—is to teach. Sea World likes to quote the African Environmentalist Baba Dioum: "For in the end, we will conserve only what we love, we will love only what we understand, and we will understand only what we are taught."

Sea World of California is a 150-acre marine life and entertainment park on San Diego's Mission Bay, one hundred miles south of Anaheim, about a two-hour drive from the Disneyland area.

Ticket Prices

Prices were in effect in mid-1996. Admission includes all shows, exhibits, and attractions except Sea World's Skytower and Mission Bay Skyride. *Discount coupon in this book.*

Adults	$29.95
Children (3 to 11)	$21.95
Children (3 and younger)	Free
Parking	Cars $5, RVs $7
Skytower and Skyride:	
One ride	$2
Two rides	$3

Annual Pass (includes 20 percent discount on tickets purchased for guests accompanying annual passholder):

Adults	$59.95
Seniors (55 and older)	$44.95
Children (3 to 11)	$44.95
Parking	Free

Guided Tours. Four different guided, walking tours are available. Tickets are priced at $6 for adults and $5 for children.

Operating Hours. Opening and closing times vary by season. Hours are extended during holiday periods and summer nights from mid-June through Labor Day. Call (619) 226-3901 for current hours.

Directions. From north or south, exit Interstate 5 at Sea World Drive. From the east, exit Interstate 8, to Interstate 5 north to Sea World Drive west.

Shamu Backstage

The newest attraction at Sea World is **Shamu Backstage**, a 1.7-million-gallon habitat that allows guests to interact with killer whales. Visitors can experiment with hand and sound signals for the whales and watch training and feeding activities. A 70-foot-long acrylic wall allows guests to view the whales from beneath the surface of the water.

Shows

Killer Whale Show. Baby Shamu, Shamu, Namu, and Nakina star in Shamu: World Focus. Actress Jane Seymour serves as video host of the show, detailing the killer whale's remarkable adaptations and natural history. The show is presented in the 5-million gallon, 5,500-seat Shamu Stadium, among the largest marine mammal habitats ever constructed.

Bird Show. Birds from six continents perform in Wings of the World, the world's largest and most ambitious bird show. Bird Showplace seats 2,800.

Whale and Dolphin Show. Dolphins and pilot whales are featured in the dynamic multispecies show One World, presented in the 3,000-seat Dolphin Stadium.

Sea Lion, Otter, and Walrus Show. Sea lions, river otters, and a Pacific walrus are featured in Marooned! With Clyde and Seamore before an arena audience of 2,500. The popular sea lion team solves the riddle of the island's mysterious Mighty Surlaw. (Sounds like a word spelled backwards, doesn't it?)

Baywatch at Sea World. The thrills-and-bikinis television series bursts from the small screen to the big lagoon.

David Hasselhoff, who plays Lieutenant Mitch Buchannon on the TV show, narrates the show and sings the theme song. As guests enter the 3,500-seat stadium on Water Ski Lagoon, they encounter what seems to be a typical lazy stretch of beach, inhabited only by a few rollerblading kids and beachcombers. Within moments, the calm is broken as a reckless speed boater crashes into a buoy and is thrown into the water; a dramatic rescue effort follows.

Baywatch at Sea World bombards guests with an onslaught of jet-ski, water-ski, and aerial stunts, acrobatics, pyrotechnics, and musical numbers.

Sea World's ski show runs from Memorial Day weekend through Labor Day.

Featured Attractions

WOW **Mission: Bermuda Triangle.** Here's the safest way we know of to explore the mysteries of the Bermuda Triangle, the infamous graveyard of ships and planes. Climb on board Sea World's high-tech simulator for a voyage beneath the sea.

Aboard the scientific research submarine *Neptune*, passengers try to unravel the mystery of the Bermuda Triangle. You won't be able to answer with certainty what has happened to the more than 100 ships and planes that have vanished in the 500,000-square-mile triangle of ocean marked by Bermuda,

Puerto Rico, and Florida. But you can imagine what it would be like to join a fact-finding expedition in a submersible watercraft.

Aboard the *Neptune* you will investigate the Puerto Rico Trench—one of the Triangle's deepest places. The simulator cabin pitches, lunges, rocks, and tilts in sync with the view from the forward "window," which is really a large rear-projection screen. The sub shudders as it seems to plunge into the ocean and spiral deeper and deeper. Depth gauges spin wildly as the craft leaves daylight behind.

Among the "discoveries" you make on this ride is the U.S.S. *Cyclops,* a navy ship that vanished without a trace in 1918.

The experience is a lot like flying. You will feel surprisingly real sensations of acceleration and increased G forces. The preshow film is narrated by network personality Hugh Downs.

The Bermuda Triangle simulator has a fairly large capacity; each of the three cabins seats 80 people, so they swallow up large chunks of the line each time they are available. If the lines extend all the way to the outside of the covered area, the waiting time is probably no more than 20 minutes.

Rocky Point Preserve. Visitors will get a true appreciation of the beauty of bottle-nosed dolphins and Alaska sea otters in their natural environment in this two-part attraction. Alaska sea otters, survivors of the 1989 Prince William Sound oil spill, are displayed in the natural rocky habitat. The dolphin habitat also includes a sophisticated wave pool. Photographs, graphics, and models help guests learn more about these fascinating animals.

Shark Encounter. The world's largest display of these fascinating animals. A submerged viewing tube allows Sea World guests to enter the sharks' habitat, a 700,000-gallon tank.

Forbidden Reef. California moray eels and bat rays are displayed in one of Sea World's most popular displays. Visitors can touch and feed the graceful rays and enjoy underwater viewing of hundreds of moray eels.

Penguin Encounter. Sea World's penguins can be seen in the most exotic habitat ever constructed for these delightful birds. The majority of Sea World's nearly four hundred penguins live in the 25-degree indoor display. Featured nearby are auklets, puffins, and murres, the penguin's Northern Hemisphere cousins. An outdoor area houses Magellanic penguins, a temperate-zone species.

California Tide Pool. The California Tide Pool re-creates one of the ocean's richest environments, an intertidal zone. Guests are invited to roll up their sleeves and touch starfish and view sea urchins, sea cucumbers, California moray eels, spiny lobsters, and a variety of fishes.

Marine Aquarium. Displays feature hundreds of fishes and marine invertebrates from oceans throughout the world. Marine species as exotic as the lionfish and chambered nautilus live in re-creations of their natural habitats.

Freshwater Aquarium. Aquariums display fish from freshwater habitats in Africa, Asia, and the Amazon River Basin. The archerfish, capable of downing insects perched on branches overhead using bullets of water, is among the species on exhibit.

World of the Sea Aquarium. Four 55,000-gallon tanks exhibit kelp bed, coral reef, schooling, and large game fish. The aquarium features the first Pacific blacktip sharks born in a U.S. zoological institution.

Commerson's Dolphins. Sea World's underwater theater is a display that reveals the fascinating world of these seldom-seen black-and-white dolphins. A video presentation details their natural history and echolocation abilities.

Window to the Sea. An excellent introduction to the Sea World philosophy is presented in this eight hundred-seat auditorium. Board the Sea World research vessel *Oceanus* and slip below the surface of the world's oceans.

Seal and Sea Lion and Walrus Habitats. Guests may purchase fish and feed California sea lions, harbor seals, and Pacific walruses, including Dozer, a male walrus born in 1993.

Avian Exhibits. Thousands of birds populate Sea World's avian exhibits. Project Survival: Under Our Wing is used as a nursery where endangered bird species are hatched and reared. The habitat also serves as a clinic for treatment of injured birds.

Shamu's Happy Harbor. A two-acre dream world for children of all ages, but especially adventuresome youngsters. Happy Harbor is like any other playground, although much more so. There are more than 20 places to explore, crawl, slide, jump, bounce, climb, and get wet.

The heart of the harbor is the two-story Net Climb, which includes criss-crossing climbing nets, crow's-nest lookouts, a net room with tire swings, web tube crawls, suspended bridges, and exit slides.

Other elements include the **Wahoo Two**, a two-story fun ship that allows kids to climb aboard the landlocked square-rigger and try their hands at the ship's wheel as well as test their aim with on-board water cannons; **Pete's Waterworks**, a wet and wild water maze where gentle streams of water shower guests as they crawl though plastic bubbles and colorful net tubes; and a sand play area where guests can sculpt sand castles.

Coco Loco Arcade. The Shamu's Happy Harbor arcade features video games and dozens of different games of skill.

Clydesdale Hamlet/Anheuser-Busch Hospitality Center. Two teams of the magnificent Clydesdale horses, symbol of the brewery company that owns Sea World, are housed permanently at Sea World of California. A stable and grooming area is bordered by a two-acre paddock. The neighboring Anheuser-Busch Hospitality Center gives a history of the company and its many operating divisions.

Rides

Skytower. The 320-foot tower gives visitors a panoramic view of San Diego's Mission Bay, skyline, foothills, bays, beaches, and the Pacific Ocean. The Skytower, a San Diego landmark for more than 25 years, seats 57 guests.

Skyride. Enclosed gondola cars ascend to a height of one hundred feet on a half-mile, round-trip journey over Mission Bay.

Present this coupon at any Universal Studios Hollywood
admission window to receive your discount.
Discount valid for up to 4 people toward the purchase of a
one-day adult or child studio pass through December 31, 1997.

This coupon has no cash value. Not valid with any other specials or discounts.
Offer subject to change without notice. Parking fee not included.
Coupon must be presented at time of transaction.

0 01040 21921 6   0 01040 21922 3

Expires 12/31/97

Please present this coupon at check-in to receive discounts. This
offer is not valid in conjunction with any other discount. If guaranteed
reservation is made and subsequent neither used nor cancelled,
the traveler will be billed for one night's room charges plus tax.

Super 8 Motel Handling Instructions

Please send a copy of the coupons received to:

Super 8 Motels, Inc.

Marketing Department

1910 8th Ave. N.E.

Aberdeen, SD 57401

Paramount Studios Tour

10% Off with This Coupon

Paramount Studios, the only major classic studio still located in Hollywood, stands rich in history and tradition while continuing to set the standard for global entertainment. Your tour of Paramount is a guided, 2-hour historical and informational look behind the scenes of a major motion picture and television facility in its day-to-day operations. No two tours are exactly alike due to spontaneous nature of production activities. And don't be surprised if you suddenly encounter one of your favorite celebrities . . . after all, this is their workplace!

Paramount Visitor Center, 860 N. Gower St., Hollywood
For additional info call Paramount Guest Relations (213) 956-1777

Expires 12/31/97

CA97-07

ECONOGUIDE

Six Flags
Magic Mountain
Theme Park
A Time Warner Entertainment Company
Minutes north of Hollywood off I-5

Save $5

On Six Flags Magic Mountain General Use Tickets
Excitement You'll Flip Over!

Present this coupon at a Six Flags Magic Mountain ticket booth & save $5.00 on each full price general use ticket. Limit six (6) general use tickets per coupon.

Does not apply to special ticketed events or special price tickets for kids (under 48"), Senior Citizens (55+), or Six Flags Hurricane Harbor general admission.

Coupon cannot be sold or combined with any other discount or promotional offer. Cash value not to exceed $.001.

Expires Dec. 31, 1997

CA97-06

37734

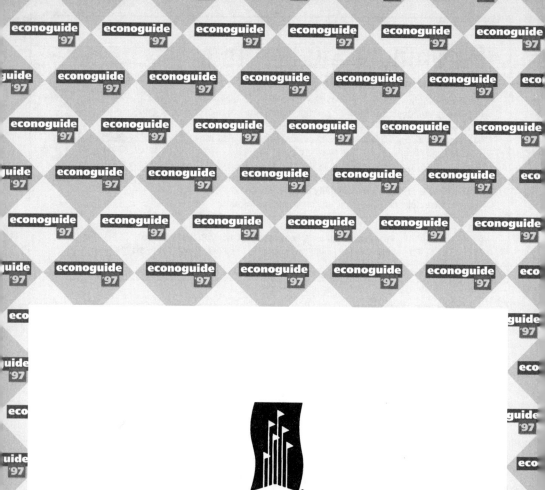

Come to Six Flags Magic Mountain and explore ten themed lands of fun, fantasy, and adventure. Discover the most exciting rides and action-packed shows on earth. Six Flags Magic Mountain is open weekends and holidays all year and daily April–October. Park opens at 10 a.m. Call for specific operating days and hours. Schedule subject to change.

26101 Magic Mountain Pky., Valencia, CA 91355, (805) 255-4129

20% Hotel Savings

Plan a legendary stay aboard the historic Hotel Queen Mary.
Select from 365 first class original staterooms
aboard the elegant liner.

May not be combined with any other offer.
Advance reservations required and based on availability.

Expires 12/31/97

CA97-08

HOTEL QUEEN MARY

1126 Queens Highway
Long Beach, CA 90802
(310) 435-3511

Save Up to $12 on Admission

Present at the Box Office and save $2 on each ticket. Limit 6 per coupon.

	REGULAR PRICE	YOU PAY
General Admission	$10	$8
Seniors 55-plus and Military with ID	$8	$6
Children 4-11	$6	$4

At the south end of the 710 Freeway
on the water in Long Beach
Attraction Hours 10 a.m. - 6 p.m.
Daily, Rain or Shine. May not be
combined with any other offers.
Prices subject to change without notice.
Offer expires 12/31/97.

CA97-08B

1126 Queens Highway
Long Beach, CA 90802
(310) 435-3511

10% Off Queen Mary Merchandise

Save 10% on Queen Mary Merchandise at participating shops.
Please verify prior to purchase - Discount only applies to
Queen Mary Merchandise. Minimum $5 purchase.

May not be combined with any other offer. Offer expires 12/31/97.

CA97-08C

1126 Queens Highway
Long Beach, CA 90802
(310) 435-3511

Chelsea & Promenade Cafe Discount

Save 20% on the second entree. Purchase one entree
at regular price, and save 20% on the second entree.
Fabulous dining with panoramic views
aboard the legendary Queen Mary.

At the south end of the 710 Freeway, on the water in Long Beach
Offer expires 12/30/97.

CAS97-08D

1126 Queens Highway
Long Beach, CA 90802
(310) 435-3511

$3 Off

General Admission

Open April to September.
Call for dates and hours for 1997 season.

Present coupon at main gate ticket booth and receive $3 off
each general admission ticket. Offer cannot be combined with
any other discount offer. Operating schedule subject to change
without notice. Limit 4 people.

111 Raging Waters Dr., San Dimas, CA 91773
(809) 592-6453
Expires 12/31/97

CA97-16

Present this Coupon at the Box Office and Receive

$2 Off

Each Adult or Child Admission

Limited to 6 people per coupon.
Not valid with other discounts.
Not for resale.

7850 Beach Boulevard, Buena Park, CA 90620, 714-522-7045
Across the street from Ripley's Believe It or Not!
Expires 12/31/97

CA97-19   **PLU ECONOGUIDE**

Ripley's Believe It or Not! MUSEUM

Present this Coupon at the Box
Office and Receive

$2 Off

Each Adult or Child Admission

Limited to 6 people per coupon.
Not valid with other discounts.
Not for resale.

7850 Beach Boulevard, Buena Park, CA 90620, 714-522-7045
Across the street from Movieland Wax Museum
Expires 12/31/97

CA97-20   **PLU ECONOGUIDE**